PENGUIN B

I SAW ETERNITY THE

'Monumental . . . The King's ch . . . . . .
the heart of Day's massive, impeccably researched book. Its scope,
however, is far wider . . . So the notion, still prevalent, that what
you hear today is a choral sound that represents a glorious unbroken
line back to the days of Tallis and Byrd, is piffle. The sound is a
20th-century British invention, which – because it coincided with
the rise of broadcasting and recording – went on to conquer
the world' Richard Morrison, *The Times*

'Timothy Day's *I Saw Eternity the Other Night* stands out
among the festive throng . . . scholarship in a jolly jumper.
The perfect Boxing Day gift for your serious uncle'
Ian Samson, *Guardian*, Books of the Year

'Magisterial but extremely readable . . . full of fascinating detail
and shrewd insights' Clare Stevens, *Choir & Organ*

'Day's meticulous history of a special choral sound . . . investigates
the creation of a style, and the evolution of a tradition, that now
feels as anciently English as the tentacular late-Gothic stonework
of King's chapel itself . . . One of the many revelations contained in
Day's erudite, original and surprisingly moving book is the discovery
that we owe this sound of angels to musicians plagued by the same,
wholly human, fears and doubts' Boyd Tonkin, *Arts Desk*

'Extensively researched and drily witty'
Ysenda Maxtone Graham, *Country Life*

'Day is an expert guide to the often closed world of cathedral
and college music-making. He wears his authority lightly, balancing
tremendous knowledge and obvious affection for its institutions
with just the occasional flicker of impatience towards their many
quirks and shibboleths – not all of which are entirely benign'
Alexandra Coghlan, *Spectator*

'This is Tim Day at his best. It's great research and it's
properly opinionated' Jeremy Summerly, BBC Radio 3

'A perfect Christmas present for anyone for whom the broadcast
Carols from King's is an essential part of Christmas' Morwenna Brett,
Stop Press, the Royal College of Organists blog

ABOUT THE AUTHOR

Timothy Day was for many years Curator of Western Art Music in the British Library's Sound Archive. He has written and lectured widely on the history of music in performance and on English cathedral music. He was a visiting senior research fellow at King's College, London 2006–11, and served on the Management Committee of the Research Centre for the History and Analysis of Recorded Music. For his work on this book, he was awarded a Leverhulme Research Fellowship. His previous books include *A Century of Recorded Music: Listening to Musical History* and *Hereford Choral Society: An Unfinished History*.

TIMOTHY DAY

I Saw Eternity the Other Night

King's College Choir, the Nine Lessons
and Carols, and an English Singing Style

PENGUIN BOOKS

PENGUIN BOOKS

UK | USA | Canada | Ireland | Australia
India | New Zealand | South Africa

Penguin Books is part of the Penguin Random House group of companies
whose addresses can be found at global.penguinrandomhouse.com.

First published in Great Britain by Allen Lane 2018
Published in Penguin Books 2019
001

Text copyright © Timothy Day, 2018

The moral right of the author has been asserted

Set in 9.35/12.5pt Sabon LT Std by Jouve (UK), Milton Keynes
Printed and bound in Great Britain by Clays Ltd, Elcograf S.p.A.

A CIP catalogue record for this book is available from the British Library

ISBN: 978–0–141–98859–7

In loving memory of my parents

I saw Eternity the other night,
Like a great ring of pure and endless light,
All calm, as it was bright;
And round beneath it, Time in hours, days, years,
Driv'n by the spheres
Like a vast shadow mov'd; in which the world
And all her train were hurl'd.

– Henry Vaughan, 'The World'

Contents

CONTENTS

List of Illustrations

29. A-side of Benjamin Britten, Missa Brevis in D, Op. 63, recording by the Choir of Westminster Cathedral, directed by George Malcolm. DECCA CEP 654 (7″ 45 rpm mono/stereo disc; recorded in 1959, released 1960). (© *Decca/Universal Music Group*)
30. George Guest. (*Clive Barda/ArenaPAL/TopFoto*)
31. Sacred music by Claudio Monteverdi, recording by the Choir of St John's College, Cambridge, directed by George Guest. ARGO RG 494/ZRG 5494 (12″ 33⅓ rpm mono/stereo disc; recorded in December 1965, released 1966). (© *Decca/Universal Music Group*)
32. Simon Preston conducting the Choir of Christ Church Cathedral, Oxford, during a recording session in 1972. (*The Archive of Recorded Church Music, Great Malvern*)
33. Simon Preston. (*Clive Barda/ArenaPAL/TopFoto*)
34. Edward Higginbottom, photograph by Tom Pilston. (© *The Times/News Licensing*)
35. Thomas Tallis, *The Glories of Tudor Church Music*, recording by the Clerkes of Oxenford, directed by David Wulstan. CLASSICS FOR PLEASURE CFP 40069 (12″ 33⅓ rpm mono/stereo disc; recorded and released in 1974). (© *EMI/Warner Classics*)
36. Henry Purcell, *Music for Queen Mary*, recording by the Monteverdi Choir, Monteverdi Orchestra and Equale Brass Ensemble, directed by John Eliot Gardiner. ERATO STU 70911 (12″ 33⅓ rpm mono/stereo disc; recorded and released 1977). (© *Éditions Costallat*)
37. *For Your Pleasure*, recording by the King's Singers. MUSIC FOR PLEASURE MFP 5585 (12″ 33⅓ rpm mono/stereo disc; released 1982).)
38. John Tavener, *Ikon of Light*, recording by the Tallis Scholars and Chilingirian String Quartet, directed by Peter Phillips. GIMELL 1585-05 (12″ 33⅓ rpm stereo disc; recorded and released 1984). (© *Gimell Records, Ltd.*)
39. Tenebrae. (© *Sim Canetty-Clarke/courtesy The Tenebrae Choir*)
40. Voces8. (© *Andy Staples/courtesy Edition Peters Artist Management*)

Every effort has been made to contact all copyright holders. The publishers will be pleased to make good in future editions any errors or omissions brought to their attention.

Preface

Of all the musical sounds we create it is perhaps our singing voices that reveal us best. The great Welsh baritone David Ffrangcon-Davies, a friend of Elgar, said, 'The whole spiritual system, spirit, mind, sense – *soul* ... will be in the wise man's singing, *and the whole man will be in the tone*.'[1]

This was as true for the performing styles of the blues in the Deep South in North America at the end of the nineteenth century, or of scat singing during the bop era or of Tibetan chants or Balkan folk music, as it was of the Shomyo chanting styles in Buddhist Japan, or of the singing of Byzantine chants of the Eastern Orthodox Church.

We perform music, we listen to music, we study music. But most important of all, we live music. We try and work out who we are through music, and what we stand for, what our values are. The sounds we listen to can be like the books we keep on our shelves and the pictures we hang on our walls; as Cathy says of her dreams in *Wuthering Heights*, they go through us like wine through water, and alter the colour of our minds.[2]

Why did this small band of men and boys in a famous fenland town in England sing in the way they did in the twentieth century? Who were the singers in English cathedral and college choirs? What was their social background and education and training? Why did they cultivate certain timbres and not others? Why did they enunciate in the way they did?

If you lived in England in the second half of the twentieth century and had any interest in churches or cathedrals or singing or early music of any kind, or indeed of 'Englishness', you thought you knew the sound of the singing of the Choir of King's College, Cambridge, very well, whether you liked it or hated it. But it was not just in England. The sounds seemed to attract the attention and the interest and sometimes the enthusiasm of men and women all over the world who knew nothing of Anglican cathedrals or choral evensong or the

xvii

antiphonal singing of the psalms for the day. In England itself some
music-lovers had heard the sounds so often and they seemed so un-
exceptional, for better or for worse, that they had given up listening to
them attentively at all. The sounds were so familiar that many listeners had forgotten that they were so remarkable, that they were so
odd. For recording in the twentieth century had given us a vast library
of singing styles. We knew that nowhere else did human beings make
sounds like these.

Why did they sing like that?

I

An Ancient English Tradition

KING'S COLLEGE, CAMBRIDGE, AND THE ENGLISH CHORAL TRADITION

Throughout the twentieth century music-lovers and historians and journalists and critics – as well as church musicians themselves – referred to a style of singing they described as the 'English cathedral tradition'. In 1917 *The Musical Times* hailed this 'cathedral tradition' of singing as one of the 'great glories of our national musical life'. The services held every day at the Anglican choral foundations were conducted 'with dignity and reverence' and the singing at nearly all of them provided 'a perfect model of refinement and good taste'. The writer liked to think of 'the long line of cathedral organists contributing, each in his generation, towards this achievement, in a succession almost unbroken since the days of the Tudors'.[1] In 1980 the tradition could still be described by a young English choral conductor as 'one of the most tenacious and characteristic aspects of English musical life'.[2] The style was immediately identifiable, many lovers of the singing style claimed, whatever the style of the music and from whichever historical period it came.

Whether writers admired the style or listened to it with distaste they generally agreed that, as an admirer put it in 1952, the 'essence' of this choral style was the boy's voice and the men were 'at their best when they blend with that clean white tone'.[3] This was the 'secret' of the English cathedral tradition, one cathedral choirmaster explained in 1987, having spent his life attempting to cultivate it.[4] Another musician, in 1962, considered that the term 'cathedral tone' was popularly used to refer just to the sound of English trebles, as a sound 'which for many years past has been cultivated in the "best" English church choirs . . . familiar to all, and instantly recognisable'.[5] The sound derived its particular character, a writer in 1912 was sure, from the 'fluty, hooty, aloof quality' of the boy's head voice being carried down and cultivated 'beyond its natural limit'. It allowed the production of 'a sweet and pure tone' that was 'almost entirely colourless and inexpressive'.[6] But many liked the sound a great deal. A critic in *The Gramophone* in 1934 considered that England had 'an enormous advantage' over other lands in 'the exquisite quality of its boys' voices. In no other country have they the same ethereal purity and pathos.'[7] In 1936 the Archbishop of Canterbury was sure that there was 'no such boy-singing in the world as we have here in England'.[8] In 1935 a group of music critics from Germany and Hungary went to Oxford and marvelled at the 'incomparable' singing at New College, at the sweetness and clarity of the voices.[9] In 1942 a BBC executive argued for a series of programmes with boys' voices alone for the Overseas Service. He remembered meeting another party of foreign musicians before the war who told him it wasn't the adult vocalists in England who had impressed them so much, nor the British orchestras; it was something completely new to them, the singing of English choirboys.[10]

By the end of the century the 'English cathedral tone' could be held by an expert in international singing styles to be distinctive by its 'straight, vibrato-less quality', which was 'thought to produce a tonal purity' and now to be used in solo song literature and in early music as well as in cathedral music itself. The singer employing such colour and timbre was aiming to direct conscious attention away from the emotional content of the music. 'The public revelation of an interior, private world would appear to the English singer as an unnecessary bit of personal exhibitionism. Voice recitals in England tend to be exercises in propriety.'[11]

From the beginning of the twentieth century, one of these choral foundations was held in particular esteem. In 1906 at a ceremony in the College Hall of King's College, Cambridge, a testimonial was presented to Dr Mann, the organist, to mark the thirtieth anniversary of his appointment as organist and choirmaster there. Scattered among the whole English-speaking race, the Provost reminded those gathered on that occasion, were men and women who had treasured memories of the beautiful services in the Chapel.[12] The services at

King's were better known than those at many of the other choral foundations partly because of the fame of the stupendous architecture of the Chapel and partly because of the generations of impressionable young students who passed through the University and carried their memories of the choir far and wide. In November 1929 during an obituary address in the Chapel the Provost remembered Arthur Henry Mann as 'the maker of the King's Choir as England knows it'.[13] By then England had known the choir by repute for several decades. But it was just beginning to know of the singing in a different way.

Evensong from King's was broadcast by the BBC for the first time in May 1926,[14] and on Christmas Eve in 1928, Dr Mann's last Christmas on earth, the College's Festival of Nine Lessons and Carols had been broadcast by the BBC. It was broadcast again in 1929 but then not in 1930. Instead listeners that year were taken to the Beaufort Cinema, Birmingham, where the organist Reginald New gave them his own *Tunes of Christmastide*, Percy Fletcher's *Demoiselle Chic* and Franz Schubert's *Ave Maria*. But in 1931 *The Radio Times* announced 'a welcome reappearance of the Christmas Eve Carol Service from King's College, which was broadcast in 1928 and 1929. It is one of the loveliest services to be heard anywhere . . . In spite of the unusual arrangement of the Chapel and of the tremendous echo, the first relay of the Carol Service in 1928 was hailed as one of the most successful Outside Broadcasts ever made.'[15] 'By the way,' *The Radio Times* continued, 'people who want a copy of the Order of Service from King's had better write early to the Dean, enclosing their shilling, so that they can be sure of getting it in time.' And soon the College annual report was telling old members that 'our carol service was again broadcast to all parts of the world'.[16] It informed its readers that the 1936 service was broadcast 'to every continent',[17] and in 1938 'to the whole Empire and the United States'.[18] *The Manchester Guardian* was already calling the service 'traditional' in 1932: 'In the afternoon . . . of Christmas Eve, just as it is getting dark, there comes the carol service from King's College, Cambridge. This is a tradition now on the wireless.'[19] *The Birmingham Daily Mail* surveyed Christmas broadcasts and thought that 'Of all broadcasts expressive of the Christmas message, none to my mind, was more impressive than the service from King's. The reading of the lessons, the quality of the singing in the carols, and, in fact, the whole atmosphere made the service one to remember.'[20] By 1938 *The Daily Telegraph* was referring to the 'much loved Festival of Nine Lessons and Carols'.[21] For *The Manchester Guardian's* radio reviewer that same year, the Festival of Nine Lessons and Carols, was, as it probably was to many listeners, he thought, 'the one broadcast of this day which must not be missed'.[22]

At the earliest Festivals you had been able to make out empty seats in the candlelit Chapel on Christmas Eve.[23] Very quickly technology changed all that. It was pressure for places on Christmas Eve in the early 1930s, as well as the call by members of the University for their own carol service during term time, that led to the creation of the Advent Carol Service in 1934, 'which made a deep impression on a crowded Chapel'.[24] By the late 1930s it seems to have been widely accepted that King's occupied a pre-eminent place among English choirs. In an article in 1936 at the time of the choir's first continental tour *The Times* explained that it represented a pinnacle of achievement to which all other choirs aspired, whether in cathedrals, college chapels or parish churches.[25] During the war, news reached Cambridge of secret listeners to the Christmas Eve service in Belgium, Holland and Czechoslovakia, and of services of lessons and carols arranged in German and Japanese prisoner-of-war camps. In one camp in Japan a curtain had risen on a man at a desk reading a script. 'This is the BBC Overseas Broadcasting Service,' he said, 'and we are taking you to a College Chapel somewhere in England.' And another curtain rose on two lines of prisoners, dressed in improvised white costumes made out of sheets, meant to look like surplices, and they sang carols to the accompaniment of camp-made instruments, and they prayed for peace and good will over all the earth.[26] In a ten-minute film about the Blitz made by the Ministry of Information in London for American audiences – 'today England stands unbeaten, unconquered, unafraid' – the commentator explained that on Christmas Eve 'England does what England has done for a thousand years, she worships the Prince of Peace' and the film cut to a King's treble singing 'Come and behold him, born the King of Angels'.[27]

The singing at King's had entered the consciousness of the English as no other choir had ever done. For long periods during the war weekly Evensong was broadcast either from New College, Oxford, or from King's, Cambridge – from 'a College Chapel' to prevent identification. But even with wartime wireless reception, some of the natives at least could be pretty sure about that astonishing acoustic. Organ recitals too began to be broadcast from King's more frequently.

And then after the war for weeks on end weekly Evensong continued to be broadcast from King's. A series of motets was recorded in 1946 to be used by the BBC to fill in spaces regularly on its new Third Programme.[28] In the 1950s several performances of Schütz's *Historia der Geburt Jesu Christi* (1664) were relayed by the BBC. 'There may be better singing than that at King's College Chapel,' wrote the editor of *Musical Opinion* in 1954; 'if so, we should certainly like to hear it.'[29] After Christmas in 1956, with 'the rapt strains from King's still haunting' his ears, a leader writer on *The Times* pronounced the service the 'flower and crown' of music at the universities, a 'supreme manifestation' of the singing heard day by day all over England 'in quires and places where they sing'.[30]

From the 1960s King's College Choir began to tour abroad regularly and to an English diplomat in Stuttgart in 1965 the 'pure, dispassionate quality' of the singing of English trebles seemed something 'peculiarly our own' and particularly refreshing 'after the sometimes exaggeratedly "musical" voices of young singers from other countries', as they seemed to him.[31] The recordings of the time at least demonstrate the distinctiveness of the English tradition whether a listener shared the diplomat's tastes or not. In their singing of Gibbons in the 1950s, one commentator found 'the English manner of performing music brought off to perfection',[32] and in 1960 a recording of motets by Bach provided a 'superb example' of English church singing.[33] King's could not have been mistaken for the singing of German choirs of the time nor for Italian ones either.[34]

Now, because of technology, because of magnetic tape and the long-playing disc, music-lovers could live with the sounds and cathedral musicians themselves could dissect them and analyse the minute details of a performance. Of all the choirs of the choral foundations it was King's who made by far the most records during the later 1950s and the 1960s. The first long-playing disc of the Christmas carol service was released in 1954, the second in 1959 and the third in 1965, though the technology of the time required that all these three were abbreviated versions.[35] There were discs of music by Orlando Gibbons in 1956 and 1959. There was a record of Evensong in 1957 and of 'An Easter Mattins' in 1958, of Bach's *Jesu, meine Freude* BWV 227 with seven sacred songs from G. C. Schemelli's *Musicalisches Gesangbuch* (all these works sung in English), discs of the Byrd masses in 1960 and in 1963, of the Advent Carol Service in 1961 and of Croft's Burial Service in 1962. The music recorded under David Willcocks, who directed the choir between 1958 and 1973, ranged from Taverner, Tye and Tallis to Elgar, Vaughan Williams and Britten. There was much music outside Anglican liturgies: there were Bach cantatas and motets and Handel's Chandos anthems and his *Dixit Dominus*. There was Bach's St John Passion. There was Haydn's 'Nelson' Mass and Marc-Antoine Charpentier's *Messe de minuit pour Noël*, Fauré's Requiem and Vaughan Williams' Mass in G minor. There was Evensong for Ash Wednesday, which included Allegri's *Miserere*, and 'Christmas to Candlemas', an anthology of sixteenth- and seventeenth-century motets. In the sixteen years that Willcocks was director of music there were five dozen twelve-inch long-playing discs released. In those years most cathedral choirs recorded very few twelve-inch discs, many none at all: the choirs at Westminster Abbey and New College and Magdalen at Oxford recorded fewer than half a dozen each. Canterbury recorded four LPs, Salisbury two.

When a choir was formed at the new Cathedral of Guildford in 1961 it was clear to choristers and lay clerks alike that for the Guildford choirmaster the choir at King's represented some kind of ideal at which they, like he himself, should be aiming.[36] The sound, the sonic image of King's, and the singing style under the direction of David Willcocks were utterly distinctive in the Chapel's extraordinary resonance[37] – sounds are prolonged by about six seconds in an empty chapel – and his recordings were enormously influential. Distinguished choir-trainers of the next generation like Edward Higginbottom of New College, Oxford, sometimes explained that they had moved away from 'the traditional English sound'; it was King's under Willcocks that had provided such musicians, maybe unconsciously, with this touchstone.[38]

The sound and the style also made an indelible impression on young women at Oxford who sang with the Clerkes of Oxenford in the 1960s. When they were asked to sing sixteenth-century polyphony 'like sixteenth-century choirboys', their models for imitation were the choristers at Magdalen College where they had attended Evensong and the recordings of King's which everybody was listening to. The Clerkes, made up of undergraduates and recent graduates, an amateur choir, spawned groups like The Sixteen and the Tallis Scholars who became professional bodies, recording energetically and touring worldwide and making exactly the kind of sound, according to a former chorister at Durham, 'that has leaked out of college chapels on foggy nights since time immemorial, even if there are now women's voices in the choir'.[39] To devotees of the choirs at the English choral foundations and the professional concert-giving choirs, sensitive to the most minute differences in each choir, this might be claiming too much. But few would dispute that all these choirs share a common ancestry.

Half a century on from the moment when those recorded performances by King's directed by David Willcocks were first heard by countless listeners all over the world, the choir could still be marketed as 'the pre-eminent representative of the great British church music tradition'.[40] A journalist who had lived in the shadow of the Chapel as an undergraduate at Clare College in the late 1960s suggested that if the building had a voice, 'it would a boy's treble ... Unfruity. Lofty yet unintimidating. Simple in its intricacy. Modest in its richness. Weightless. Luminous. Graceful.'[41]

What were the hallmark characteristics of this singing style? In 1959 King's released a recording of Byrd's famous Eucharistic Hymn for the Feast of Corpus Christi, *Ave verum corpus*. A contemporary critic considered it 'magnificently done: it has a mysticism that is not without humanity and warmth, and a dynamic architecture that Byrd must surely have intended even though he wrote no expression marks in his part-books. This freedom of line and distinction of phrasing is as natural as it is beautiful.'[42] How could the style be characterized? The voices blended seamlessly. The ensemble was perfectly disciplined: 't's and 'd's were synchronized with unerring precision. The timbre was unforced; even in *forte* there was no sense of strain, or indeed of drama, or at least not of any emotional outpouring. Expressive gestures were intense but subdued. Tempos were almost invariably steady. Vibrato was avoided. The tuning was immaculate. The sounds shone with an unearthly silvery glitter.

When the choir made its first foreign tour, to Scandinavia, Holland and Germany in 1936, it sang to capacity audiences. But they weren't really audiences. The listeners said they felt themselves part of a solemn rite. Everyone was startled by the irresistible beauty of the voices, and the concentration and the intensity of the singing. So now, in 1960, that critic listening to Byrd really felt himself in the antechapel, he said, 'with the flickering candles and the choir just visible through the screen'. It was the inwardness of the singing that was so striking, the 'spiritual refreshment' of the music-making.[43]

Sylvia Plath attended the Advent Carol Service in November 1955. She wrote home to her mother afterwards. 'It was evening, and the tall chapel, with its cobweb lace of fan-vaulting, was lit with myriads of flickering candles, which made fantastic shadows play on the walls, carved with crowns and roses. The King's choir boys processed down through the chapel singing in that clear bell-like way children have: utterly pure and crystal notes . . . Honestly, mother, I never have been so moved in my life.'[44]

HOW OLD WAS THE TRADITION?

But was the English cathedral tradition of singing of ancient lineage? Many were sure that it was. It became a journalistic commonplace that such sounds had been echoing down the aisles of English cathedrals for centuries. In the next half-century, as more and more choirs recorded more and more of the cathedral repertory, convictions about the tradition seemed to grow stronger. In 2003 a former organist of Gloucester Cathedral was sure that 'choirs of men and boys have been for many hundreds of years the glory of English church music and the envy of the world'.[45] In a novel published in 1988, the headmaster of a choir school at the fictional Aldminster Cathedral reminded the parents of the 'unbroken tradition' going back to Thomas à Becket, to St Augustine, of this particular sound of English choristers, 'a sound of unrivalled beauty and power'. 'For five hundred years, music has been composed to that top line of extraordinary sound, and it is in English cathedrals alone that it remains still uncorrupted, strong and free.'[46] In 1993 one of the most authoritative scholars of singing in early music repertories was sure that 'the voice of the choirboy has, since at least the later Middle Ages, imparted an angelical quality – a unique and inspiring blend of purity and innocence – to the music of divine worship'.[47] At the turn of the twentieth century a choir-trainer thought that 'the evanescent beauty of the boy's voice, a crystalline cry to a world outside and beyond us', had for 'centuries' provided 'poignant comfort and spiritual insight'.[48] In 2009 the organist at Leeds Parish Church claimed still more for the boy's voice as cultivated in England. It was a sound that would have fallen 'soft upon the ears of Christ Himself as He prayed in the Temple'.[49]

But is this true? Is this style, of which the singing of King's was recognized as the quintessence, one that had been cultivated for centuries? In 1934 Sydney Nicholson, the former organist of Manchester Cathedral and Westminster Abbey and founder of the School of English Church Music, took the 'cathedral tradition' to mean 'a long line of church music composition from Tallis and Byrd to [the] favourite composers of to-day sung by choirs of boys and men trained in the style appropriate to the Offices of the Church of England'.[50] But has there been an enduring 'style appropriate to the Offices of the Church of England'? One historian in 1938 agreed that the singing in English cathedrals maintained a tradition that was unequalled, but he suggested that the tradition was 'more recent than is often thought, or it was for a time much weakened'. He referred to the opinions of a church musician from Boston, Massachusetts, who came to Europe in 1852 with the express purpose of listening to choral singing and reported unfavourably on English cathedral choirs.[51]

What do we know of the singing styles that could be heard in English cathedrals in the nineteenth century? Dr Martin Routh was an Oxford scholar of the Church Fathers, 'very, very, very learned', as an admiring contemporary described him,[52] and President of Magdalen College, dying in office in 1854. This was just before Christmas and his remains were buried on 29 December in the chapel, which was hung with black cloth throughout. But the Christmas holly and evergreens were still in place and seemed to reinforce the solemnity and the poignancy of the occasion.

The Bishop of Oxford preached a eulogy on that occasion:

> He sleeps before the Altar, where the shade
> He loved will guard his slumbers night and day;
> And tuneful voices o'er him, like a dirge,
> Will float for everlasting.

Everyone had processed behind the coffin and walked around the cloisters and someone else present thought that the sound of the choir processing through the cloisters was of an 'exquisitely solemn but piercing character'.[53] But what does that word 'piercing' mean? There was a leader in *The Times* in 1993 that talked of the 'piercing beauty' of the singing of cathedral choirs 'that is entirely British'.[54] That surely meant poignantly beautiful, that the heart was pierced, not that the sound itself was piercing. What would we have thought in 1854? Someone else on that occasion in 1854 spoke admiringly of the 'solemn wailings of the choir'.[55] Obviously everyone was extremely moved. The President's faculties had seemed undimmed, and his research was continuing unabated even though he was in his hundredth year. It was such a shock. After all, he had been head of the College for sixty-three years.

A colleague of Dr Routh at Magdalen had described a treble voice admiringly a few years earlier as being 'clear and shrill'.[56] What are we to make of that 'shrill'? Was the writer referring simply to the voice being high-pitched? As in *Twelfth Night* when Orsino says to Viola, thinking her a boy, 'thy small pipe / Is as the maiden's organ, shrill and sound', without meaning to be pejorative.[57] In a novel published in 1861 the parish church of a Berkshire village in the 1840s had a little band of gallery musicians. Alongside the bass-viol, the fiddle and the clarinet were two or three young women who sang treble, 'shrill, ear-piercing treble . . . with a strong nasal Berkshire drawl in it'.[58] Would we recognize similarities between these women's voices and those of the boys at Magdalen?

Clearly, relying on a few descriptions is not altogether convincing. But it is certainly possible to come to some general conclusions about the singing styles of these mid-century English choirs.

That American choir-trainer from Boston, Lowell Mason, went to Evensong at Worcester Cathedral in January 1852. He was astonished.

Everything was characterized by 'rapidity of utterance'; the psalms were carelessly enunciated and the speed at which the words were gabbled prevented any attempt at expressiveness of any kind.[59] At St Paul's it was the same. The men and boys were like guests at some cheap, third-rate American hotel, he thought, where everyone thoughtlessly woofed down the food as fast as possible. It made you sympathize with the Puritans wanting to do away with singing in church altogether.[60] The Chapel Royal Lowell considered 'a poor choir', the choir at Westminster Abbey 'very indifferent'.[61] The services at York Minster, he was told, were the best sung of any in England; well, the rapid chanting was certainly no worse than the similar gabbling he'd heard at other English cathedrals. But the 'terrible roughness' of the boys' voices at York was enough 'to tear out one's soul'. How did English choirs, though, compare with those on the continent?[62]

His impression was that in most French cathedrals worship was a kind of 'grand pantomime', consisting of 'bowings, crossings, and kneelings, with grand processions' to loud and powerful organ accompaniments.[63] It was in Germany where he heard the best choirs in Europe. At St Thomas's in Leipzig he attended a concert given by the boys, trebles and lower voices, about fifty voices in all, to mark the opening of a newly decorated music hall in their school. They sang an ambitious programme entirely unaccompanied which included Bach's motet *Der Geist hilft unser Schwachheit auf* BWV 226. Lowell Mason was bowled over with the energy, alertness, confidence and intensity of these performances. He'd never heard such accuracy in rhythm and intonation.[64]

But then he went to Berlin and heard the choir of men and boys at the cathedral there. He could believe, as it was claimed in Germany, that this was the best choir of men and boys in the world, better even than the Sistine Choir in Rome. There were about fifty singers arranged in a double chorus with twenty or thirty boys aged between eight and ten who were candidates for membership and led the singing of the congregation. The choir sang in a gallery behind the altar, with a conductor using a baton standing in front of them the whole time and when they sang on their own they were always unaccompanied. All the boy singers were pupils at the same school, trebles and lower voices alike. They rehearsed daily and the education they received was intended to equip them for a professional musical life as executants, whether as vocalists or instrumentalists, or teachers or composers of music. The choir sang 'Palestrina, Lotti, Durante and others of the Italian school; Bach, Graun and others of the German school, together with the best modern authors', with nothing of Mozart or Haydn or frivolous modern sacred music with orchestral accompaniment, he was pleased to report. Needless to say, they were perfectly accomplished in all the technical aspects of singing, enunciation, tuning, beautiful tone. But they also sang with taste and expression and a kind of inner conviction and seriousness. The singing was easy and natural, the tone never coarse or crude or rough, but neither was there any affectation, no artificial elegance. Who could tell whether they themselves were indeed devout worshippers? But at least they created through their singing and their behaviour a perfect setting for the worshipping of others.[65]

Even though Lowell Mason was moved and inspired by the standards reached by the choir at Berlin Cathedral he still pointed out that, though the blend of boys and men was very good – the best he had ever heard by such a choir – really it was not possible to achieve with boys, with trebles, the kind of satisfactory blending of voices that is only possible with fully mature men and women. In England no attempt was ever made to match quality and character of sound from boys and men, and anyway these wretched English choirs were far too small. The choir at Berlin Cathedral provided an example of just what it was possible to achieve with boys, but, however good this was, inevitably their vocal and emotional immaturity could not be disguised. The singing of boys of twelve or fourteen with men could never match the results that could be obtained by choirs consisting only of adults. In support of his views Lowell Mason cited the choir at the Catholic Chapel of All Saints in Munich. Here in 1852 the choir consisted of about twenty-four singers, or six voices to a part. Here there was a fullness, richness and blending of choral sound that even the Berlin Cathedral Choir could not match. And the reason for this was that the voices were the best professional vocalists or opera singers available, with the soprano and alto parts taken by female voices.

Lowell Mason never expected to hear the unaccompanied singing of the Munich Choir surpassed.[66]

Not that England had no excellent amateur choruses. Perhaps the large German choruses he'd heard were a little firmer and more confident than the chorus at the Birmingham Festival in Mendelssohn's *Elijah* in 1852, though really the singing in Birmingham was excellent. There were between eighty and ninety voices on each part, the balance was good, the blending was superb; there was no hint of individual voices coming through the textures. In Haydn's *Creation* the chorus were superb and there was a glorious performance at the Festival that year of Handel's *Samson*. After that work Lowell Mason came to the conclusion that there could be no place on earth other than Birmingham where such a band and chorus could be assembled.[67] After Birmingham he went to Norwich in September. The Festival Chorus here, about 250 in all, was much inferior and the reason not hard to seek. At Birmingham the top line was taken almost entirely by 'the full-grown voices of females'. Here at Norwich there were forty-one female sopranos but singing along with them were thirty-four boys, enough of them to spoil almost any soprano line, he thought, and the effect was certainly harsh. At Birmingham there were male altos singing but the females were able to keep them 'in good subjection'; only once or twice during all the four days of music-making did the tone become hard. Now, at Norwich, there were five women and forty-seven 'men altos'. You shrank away whenever the men altos started up; it was as if a severe blow to the body had been inflicted. The men altos couldn't quite reach the top notes and not only were these notes out of tune but the singers made the kind of howling noise on them that organ-tuners talk about, the so-called 'wolf' notes on an ill-regulated instrument. A sudden entry by the men altos was like a saw going through wood and suddenly hitting a nail.[68]

Just before he left London to return home Lowell Mason ran into the Austrian composer Sigismund Neukomm and asked him about English trebles. 'Boys' voices,' that gentleman replied, 'are like cats' voices.' It was the shrillness and the screeching of English boys, Neukomm told him, that had so got on Mendelssohn's nerves on one occasion in Exeter Hall in 1837 as he sat listening to a rehearsal of his *St Paul* oratorio. And Mendelssohn had wondered why on earth the

English didn't follow the German example and employ women for both soprano and alto parts.[69]

A decade before the American from Boston had been so disappointed with the English cathedral tradition a young Anglican priest called John Jebb had taken a hard look at the choral foundations and had wrung his hands. The choral tradition, he thought, had been utterly degraded, the cathedrals brought into disrepute through 'the secularity, the neglect, the indevotion, the pretermission, or perfunctory performance' of its most holy duties. He found inadequate numbers of singing men – called lay clerks in most of the foundations – prayers said which should have been intoned, responses left to be sung by the boys alone, choir members sitting or slouching when they should be kneeling, and ambling into the stalls rather than processing.[70] He watched soloists in verse anthems leaving the stalls and ascending into the organ loft and sounding like opera singers, performing ridiculous adaptations of Marcello and Mozart, all of them characterized by 'an exaggerated expression of sentiment, foreign to our national character, and inconsistent with its manly strength'. There were even worse composers than Mozart. There were the 'gaudy phantasms' from Haydn's *Creation* that were sung as anthems.[71]

King's College, Cambridge, maintained the sixteen choristers on the foundation but had merely a handful of lay clerks, far too weak for the number of trebles or the building or the magnificent organ which accompanied them.[72] Winchester College had sixteen boys on the foundation but there were only four who actually sang and these boys did not receive their education at the College itself as they ought to have been doing under the statutes. Three ordained chaplains and three lay clerks ought to have been singing but the chaplains no longer sang as members of the choir at all and so the proper antiphonal performance of the services was impossible.[73]

There seemed to be some perverse rubric at the choral foundations that all reading had to be indistinct, monotonous and rapid.[74] And why were congregations allowed to join in inharmoniously during the choral service?[75] Why when the choirs sang the music of Tallis – which they certainly ought to do – must it be drawled or sung 'with an unfeeling rapidity'?[76]

To the inexcusable disgrace of our Chapters and Colleges, it has been forgotten that the members of our Choirs, whether lay or clerical, are living stones of the Temple, are Ministers of sacred things, and have an interest in every part of the Ritual, as members of Christ's body, and as the examples of his people.[77]

The cathedral service constituted a 'school for irreverence', one Fellow of Magdalen College, Oxford, observed in 1848. In some was found 'hardened impiety'. At some choral foundations choristers appeared at dinners and parties and concerts, which constituted a prostitution of their musical powers.[78] In 1849 S. S. Wesley, then organist at Leeds Parish Church – he had previously been organist at Hereford and Exeter cathedrals – considered the music at cathedrals to be a 'source of grief and shame to well disposed and well instructed persons'. It had long been 'shamefully neglected'. This music was designed to be performed by two choirs singing antiphonally. Which meant that on each side of the chancel there must be one voice to each part for solo passages in verse sections and at least one other voice for the two to constitute the chorus in full passages, six men on each side. He thought that there was not one cathedral in England with twelve men in daily attendance. Ask the audience in an opera house, or the members of choral societies, or the singers of the mill towns of Yorkshire and Lancashire, what they would think of a chorus with one to a part.[79] There were too few singers everywhere; the singers, nearly all of them, were untrained and uneducated. There were wrong notes, there were stylistic infelicities, everywhere disorder reigned.[80]

And there was 'manifest injustice' in the way choristers were abandoned when their voices changed, the Magdalen Fellow was sure. The authorities might protest that the boys were given a sum of money to gain an apprenticeship. But the poor quality of the education they had received did not equip them 'for even worldly purposes'. There were many examples of choristers leaving the choir for a life 'of gradual, but not slow decline, through various stages of inaction, embarrassment, and dissipation, to utter ruin both of soul and body'. Wesley urged deans and chapters to establish scholarships for their choristers at Oxford or Cambridge or Durham or at the new theological colleges to enable the best of them – 'The flower of the order in physical and intellectual qualifications' – to become ordained. They should ensure that others were enabled to become national schoolmasters, printers, booksellers or music-sellers, 'or members of other congenial trades'. Such was the demand now for more and more priests that bishops were having to accept for ordination 'national schoolmasters' and men of different classes – not gentlemen at all – whose principal qualification was their merely being 'literate persons'. But choristers had been 'ecclesiastical persons' for several years and the best of them should be secured for ordination. Other choristers might continue in the choir as lay clerks, provided deans and chapters ensured that the 'moral condition' of the body of adult singers in their choirs was improved.[81]

In 1852, the year in which the American choir-trainer spoke of his astonishment at discovering the English cathedral tradition to be a sham, the Ecclesiastical Commission began collecting evidence on the state and condition of the choral foundations. The commissioners asked organists and precentors whether it was desirable to give their choirs 'greater musical power' for the performance of Divine Service. The organist at Wells considered six men with eight trebles quite sufficient for his cathedral, 'the choir not being large, and the expression of sound being free and easy'.[82] But nearly everyone else considered their choirs far too small to do justice to the music or to operate effectively day by day.

In 1853 the choir at Oxford had eight boys and eight lay clerks. Of the men only five or six were really of any use at all. Only four of them were required to attend on weekdays, which demonstrated just how inadequately performed the services must be. The organist wished he had six men at the weekday services and nine or twelve on Sundays and at festival times.[83] The organist at Norwich agreed, there should be twelve men. As it was they had only eight, and, as the precentor explained, the voices of some of these had deteriorated or were altogether useless.[84] At York in the early 1850s there were ten choristers and fourteen lay clerks, though only six of these were present at every service, the supernumeraries singing only on special occasions, on Sundays morning and evening and at Evensong on Wednesdays.[85] At Ely there were twelve boys and eight men joined 'occasionally' by two young supernumeraries, who had usually been choristers and were preparing themselves for full-time posts as cathedral lay clerks. At Durham Cathedral – and at others too the precentor there was sure – there were no regular full practices and the lay clerks did not regard rehearsing as part of their statutory duties at all.[86]

Wesley told the commissioners that choristers were 'procured from a class of the community amongst which the delicacy of voice and utterance requisite is not easily found'.[87] The Master of the Cathedral School at Christ Church in Oxford told the commissioners that the choristers there were mostly 'the sons of professional gentleman', but this was most exceptional.[88] The precentor at Gloucester gave his opinion that the raising of standards in the education of the boys was the first requirement if the singing in cathedral choirs was to be improved. Only if this happened would 'the better class of tradesmen . . . be induced to send their sons'.[89]

The commissioners noted that, in general, cathedral choristers were provided with an education free of cost and that the boys usually received annual stipends, varying between £27 (c. £2,165 now) per annum at Durham, and £3. 6s. 8d. in the least wealthy cathedrals, with other small allowances. At many cathedrals most boys received an apprenticeship on quitting the choir, of £10, £20, or £30.[90]

In 1854 the headmaster at Bristol Cathedral Grammar School was sure that the boys' daily attendance at two services throughout the whole year was 'injurious to their health, education and morals'. He suggested that it would only work satisfactorily if there was a double choir, two choirs, in effect, working alternately.[91] The commissioners themselves identified the difficulty in integrating the choristers into the regular school timetable[92] when 'so large a portion of their time [was] devoted to musical instruction and practice'. At Canterbury there was an existing ancient grammar school attached to the cathedral with about one hundred boys attending at this time, open to day boys and boarders, fifty of them being King's scholars 'on the foundation'. But the choristers, all day boys, did not attend this school, being taught by one of the lay clerks.[93] It was widely perceived that choristers in the past had come from the poorest families. The Dean and Chapter at Ely Cathedral explained that they had to recognize that to allow poor boys to enter the school would be 'fatally to degrade the tone and character of the school', and the sons of middle-class parents would exclude themselves.[94]

The lay clerks drew attention to the inequalities in the incomes of cathedral staff in the 1850s. The Chester lay clerks requested that the commissioners consider their financial position in that cathedral. A canon at Chester received £500 for his three months' residence each year and then returned to his beneficed living, his full-time job, with its own generous salary. Generous at least in their terms, for the lay clerks, for their twice-daily attendance at Divine Service throughout the year, were given £50.[95] The lay clerks at Peterborough would be only too willing to give up their trades, 'harassing and precarious' as these were, they told the commissioners, and devote themselves exclusively to their sacred duties, if only they could be recompensed with an increase in the £40 annual income they currently received.[96]

The commissioners reported that the annual income of a lay clerk varied between £114 12s. at Durham and £30 at Christ Church and generally a lay clerk was not provided with a house.[97] The organist at Carlisle thought lay clerks 'very ill paid'.[98] John Jebb had thought their endowments 'often shamefully small'.[99] In order to survive and support their families it was always necessary to find some other work which could be fitted around their singing at the cathedral. Nearly everywhere the men as well as the boys in the choirs at the choral foundations were poorly educated. They had received or were being given a poor general education as well as meagre, unsystematic musical training.

There was one class of singers in cathedrals, though, who had received, by the standards of the time, a decent general education. The priest vicar, the clergyman who was also a singing man, was an anachronism, a throwback to the pre-Reformation vicars choral, the musical deputies that each canon was required to have to maintain the daily offices in his absence or because he had no singing voice. The precentor at Salisbury in 1853 looked back mournfully to the foundation of the cathedral in the thirteenth century when fifty-three canons were required, each with his own singing deputy, his vicar choral.[100] At one time the priest vicars constituted the choirmen, singing in everything the choir was required to perform. What did they sing now though, in the middle of the nineteenth century? At Exeter four priest vicars in the early 1850s were regarded as members of 'the choral staff', but they no longer sang with the choir at all; they now merely intoned the responses and prayers.[101] It was the same at Salisbury, where none of the minor canons, until recently known as vicars choral, took part in anthems or services, or at least, according to the precentor, didn't 'regularly'.[102] At Ely two of the four minor canons didn't even intone the prayers, since, as the Dean explained, they were appointed 'when reading was the custom'.[103] At Canterbury the precentor explained ambiguously that the choir consisted of twelve men and ten boys 'with such assistance as is given by the minor canons', which would seem to imply that the minor canons did indeed at least sometimes sing in service settings and anthems.[104] At Christ Church in Oxford there were eight resident college chaplains who were required 'to perform exercises according to their standing and degrees',[105] which exercises did not ever include singing with the eight lay clerks.

When the pious Bishop of Winchester, William of Waynflete, founded his College of St Mary Magdalen in the University of Oxford in 1458, he ordained that there should be eight lay clerks and sixteen choristers in daily attendance in the College Chapel in order that 'the Divine Offices might, by God's grace, be performed with the greatest devotion, honour, and perfection'.[106] The *University Calendars* for the middle decades of the nineteenth century were quite clear, the Founder's wishes were being followed to the letter, sixteen choristers were listed by name every year and eight singing men.

Unlike most of the choral foundations in the middle of the nineteenth century Magdalen maintained a boarding school for its choristers and most of them were not local boys but came from far away. In the 1840s there were boys from Kent, Lincolnshire, Hampshire, Norfolk, Wiltshire, as well as from Oxford. Nearly all of them were the sons of 'gentlemen', as the College's registers style them, or 'clerks', for 'clerks in holy orders', that is clergymen. The 'gentlemen' might be solicitors or schoolmasters. They might be doctors or army or naval officers. One boy was the son, another the nephew, of a baronet. Comparatively few of the boys were described as being the sons of, as the registers put it, Pleb, that is Plebeian, or for Latin *plebs*, the class into which the overwhelming majority of boys at the other choral foundations would have fallen.[107]

What sort of occupation did the College register mean by 'pleb.'? When the registers indicate 'gent.' they usually indicate too the actual occupation of the gentleman father, clergyman, schoolmaster, physician and so on. They rarely indicate the actual occupation with the designation 'pleb.'. But it meant a baker or a blacksmith, a cabinet-maker, a coach-maker, a plumber or glazier or shoemaker or domestic servant or, it could be, a college servant, the father actually working in Magdalen College itself. He might be an usher of some kind at university ceremonies. He might be a singing man in one of the college choirs. One chorister whose father was designated 'pleb.' was – the registers do record this detail – the organist of Salisbury Cathedral.

Why did this choir, unlike the other cathedral and college choirs, have boys with such different social backgrounds? The College had some ancient endowments and some more recent ones too, which made choristerships particularly attractive to parents. Payments were to be made to those elected to these scholarships for choristers until their days singing treble ended. But if they stayed on or came back to read for a degree then the payments would continue until they had graduated. One chorister looking back years later thought that the choir in 1850 was rather a good one, but he did have to admit that this was remarkable considering that so many of the boys were appointed 'without any respect to voice or musical ability . . . a considerable proportion of those appointed were unable to sing at all'. Of course there were others who sang very well, he says, and these made up for the silence of the unmusical.[108] The scholarships for the boys at Magdalen were in the gift of the College, and the President could exercise his privilege of patronage if he wished to. He was evidently pleased to exercise it on numerous occasions. He was keen to give scholarships to bright boys who showed promise academically, who might perform well as undergraduates, whatever their background, and whether they could sing or not. For example, if there was an Oxfordshire parson doing such important work as editing the plays of Publius Terentius Afer, the College should certainly be on the look-out for any sons of his who might be thinking of coming to Magdalen. And if one of them were found to have a defective ear at his first attempt for a choristership, the President would ensure the boy had a retrial. And if he were informed of a second failure the President would give the matter due consideration. On balance he would probably decide that a defective ear was not an insuperable handicap. And so the organist would be overruled. This was certainly not an isolated example.[109] So the choir consisted of singing choristers and non-singing boys.

Of the eight singing men at Magdalen listed in annual editions of the *University Calendar* in the 1850s, four of the men are listed as having matriculated at the University, and as having become members of the College. The others listed hadn't matriculated and some of these names crop up on the lists of other college choirs. They were not members of the University. They were clearly the (so-called) professional singing men.

But what of the four singing men who had matriculated, that is, who were undergraduate members of the University? With a royal commission now investigating the two ancient universities in quite unnecessarily minute detail – it had been established in 1850 – the College was having to explain practices the rationale and usefulness of which had long been obvious to the Governing Body. In 1856, in preparation for a submission to the Royal Commission about the choir at Magdalen, a committee secretary had put 'Bible clerk' on a draft report and then this had been scribbled over and the ambiguous term 'undergraduate clerk' had been substituted.[110] The four students sitting in the choir were in fact 'Bible clerks'. Most colleges had Bible clerks. They were men awarded a small scholarship to read the lessons. Some of them would be hoping to become ordained. Lewis Tuckwell remembered that when he was a chorister around 1850 the academical clerks were expected to do no more than read the lessons.[111] Some would have hardly had much vocal prowess as tenors or basses anyway; several of them matriculated at the University at the age of seventeen. Some were sixteen. William Sanders, in 1850, was fifteen.[112] Tuckwell himself became an academical clerk and in 1857 was given a financial reward for 'the great services rendered by him to the Choir'. The College minutes have an explanatory note: 'The President recorded that Mr Tuckwell was appointed [an academical clerk] under the Old System and was not necessarily obliged to sing.'[113]

The 'Old System' seems like a designation dreamt up retrospectively to make things crystal clear to the members of the government inspectors, but really to befuddle them. A college historian writing in 1857 described the practice of having non-singing academical clerks in the choir stalls as a 'strange abuse'.[114] But it was indeed an abuse. Magdalen should have had eight singing men in the choir, according to its statutes, and Bible clerks in addition. But it had placed four Bible clerks in the choir stalls, doubling as academical clerks, whether they could sing or not. For who was concerned about the standard of the music? It can only have been about 1856 that the practice ceased.

Perhaps some of the non-singing choristers developed a taste for music as they sat in the choir stalls for years on end. Perhaps some of them practised conjugating Latin verbs. But at any rate a considerable number of choristers became academical clerks. They simply moved from the front desk of the choir stalls to the back desk. And some remained, presumably, just as unmusical, though probably better at conjugating Latin verbs. But there were happy accidents. Lewis Tuckwell himself didn't fail a voice trial; he didn't even have one. His father was Surgeon to the Radcliffe Infirmary and restored the President to health after a very serious accident. When the President heard of his father's death – his mother had died a few years earlier – the little boy was summoned to the College and ushered into the presence of the President, who told him he was being offered a choristership: 'God bless the lad, be a good boy, and do what the Organist tells you.'[115] He developed a most beautiful treble voice and people came from far and wide to listen when he sang a solo.[116] He was a chorister from 1847 to 1857, an academical clerk between 1857 and 1863 and chaplain from 1866 until 1877, being styled precentor between 1869 and 1877 – the post in effect being created especially for him.[117]

What of the four lay clerks? An undergraduate recalled that one of the altos in the early 1850s 'had a real knowledge of music, but his voice was (to speak mildly) unpleasing'. There was a tenor who possessed a voice of good quality but his sense of rhythm was so uncertain that in a verse anthem the organist had to solo his part out in an attempt to hold the performance together. He was once chosen as the foreman of an Oxford jury but failed to grasp court procedure. When he was asked to give the jury's verdict he addressed the judge: 'My

Lord, we finds the prisoner guilty of manslaughter for taking them boots, and we sentence him to six months imprisonment.'[118]

In the middle of the nineteenth century, then, Magdalen had some boys who didn't sing at all. Four of the eight men were a succession of Bible clerks, most of whom probably didn't sing at all either. At least some of the four lay clerks had received an elementary education. Perhaps some of them had good voices; perhaps some of them had had good voices once.

The education of the boys was as unsatisfactory as at so many schools all over England before the reforms of Thomas Arnold at Rugby led to universal reform. We know that in the 1840s the choristers at Magdalen regularly had bloodthirsty fights with the 'blackguards', the town boys; the senior boys in the choir bullied the little ones out of money; the deputy headmaster was robbed of his clothes as well as money; one boy shot a barking dog, another descended from the top of Magdalen tower in a basket, another threatened to horsewhip a Fellow of the College, another filled a pudding destined for High Table with nails; one May Morning after they'd sung from the top of the Tower the boys pelted the spectators below with a hundred rotten eggs. When their musical duties were over for the day the boys sat around smoking their pipes and consuming rather too much alcohol even for the most senior of them, the fourteen-year-olds.[119]

ANGLO-SAXON ATTITUDES TO MUSIC

Even within the hierarchy of the Church of England itself few had ever considered liturgical music of much importance. At least this was how it had been for as long as anyone could remember. In 1844 an eminent residentiary canon of St Paul's told a friend that it was a matter of perfect indifference to him if the choir at Westminster Abbey bawled louder than the one at the cathedral. 'We are there to pray, and the singing is a very subordinate consideration.'[120]

John Jebb blamed the 'superior Clergy' for having allowed 'the art of sacred music to be degraded into a mere secular accomplishment'. But the poor quality of the singing, he recognized, was only a component part of the slovenly and irreverent performance of the daily services.[121] The singing in cathedrals was not likely to be good when the side chapels in cathedrals were crammed with junk.[122] It was not likely that proper attention would be given to the music when the choir wore filthy surplices and the singers did not process but scuttled into their places,[123] and when the lay clerks ignored the rubric to kneel and lolled or sat during prayers, which should have been chanted but were habitually read.[124]

Although in most cathedrals a weekly service sheet was drawn up, choristers would frequently be instructed by precentors during a service to take details of a change of service or anthem up to the organ loft, or there might even be signalling from choir stalls to loft.[125] Sometimes listed anthems were set aside because of the requests of visiting *amateurs de musique* in the congregation.[126] How could the duties of the lay clerks be properly fulfilled if they exchanged jokes during services and did not receive Communion during a Choral Eucharist or, if they did, did so in a 'perfunctory and indevout manner': it were better if they did not take Communion at all.[127] To those that protested, these were not small matters. All this slovenliness and disturbance destroyed the intensity and the focus that words and sounds and silence and setting could create. 'And thus young souls may be murdered,' said one precentor.[128]

The decent celebration of the daily services had not counted for much during the eighteenth century, but then music itself had not counted for much either. It was true that Roger Ascham, one of the great English pedagogues of the sixteenth century, advocated the study of music in the education of young men, just as he said Plato and Aristotle did. The kind of music, though, was of crucial importance; music of a 'nice, soft, and smooth sweetness' must be avoided since it would rather 'entice them to naughtiness than stir them to honesty'. They must be introduced to music with a 'manly, rough, and stout sound in it'. Too much sweetness would dull men's wits, making them 'so soft and smooth, so tender and quaisy, that they be less able to brook strong and tough study'.[129]

In the seventeenth century, music seems to have played an increasingly small part in boys' education. The attitude towards music that was to prevail throughout the eighteenth century was stated in a most influential book on education published in 1693. The author considered that, besides the learning acquired from study and books, it was indeed important for the boy to cultivate accomplishments such as fencing and horse riding. Dancing too should be studied, not to learn the 'jigging part' of dancing and all the steps of various dances, but to develop confidence and poise and, above all things, to develop that manliness that can be demonstrated in perfecting a 'graceful Carriage'. As for music, it was true that many people 'mightily valued ... a good Hand, upon some Instruments ... but it wastes so much of a young Man's time, to gain but a moderate Skill in it, and engages often in such odd Company, that many think it much better spared.'[130]

Educated and thoughtful English men, when they thought about music at all in the eighteenth century, recognized that it could be positively dangerous, that it had a tendency to 'effeminate the Mind', 'enervate the more Manly Faculties', and 'erase from the Soul all manner of Martial Ardour'.[131] An eighteenth-century man of the theatre considered singing and dancing as arts which nature had bestowed upon 'effeminate Nations' such as France and Italy. No doubt he deeply resented foreign competition in the London theatres. But his sentiments were doubtless shared by a great many professional men in England, that singing and dancing were beneath the dignity of Englishmen 'and the Majesty of the British Genius'.[132] English was a masculine language, with its hard consonants, he thought, and the consonants had to be decisively articulated, which meant you had to keep shutting your mouth, which was no good in operatic arias. There was always a danger with music, especially with 'soft and delicious' music, that it made a man 'too much in love with himself', and it 'emasculated' and 'dissolved' the mind, it drove out reason, and 'shook the very Foundation of Fortitude'.[133]

If your son had 'an Itch' for music, another eighteenth-century English writer advised, it might be best to give way and allow him to give himself entirely to its study. This was certainly necessary to obtain any skill in the art. He might be able to pay his way working in places such as Vauxhall Gardens in the summer and in the opera house and theatres in the winter and assisting at music clubs. But really, 'any other Mechanic Trade is much more useful to the Society than the whole Tribe of Singers and Scrapers; and I should think it much more reputable to bring my Son up a Blacksmith . . . than bind him Apprentice to the best Master of Music in England'.[134]

The same author was sure that, though socialites might well support the Italian opera in London, English men of education and sensibility and discernment could not but steer clear. Ancient Rome did indeed rule the world and the ancient texts suggested it was not at all unmusical. But in those days Italian music was full of discord, it was more noise than harmony, and – it was to be expected – the Italians had fought in far-off lands 'with Courage and Intrepidity'. Inevitably with refinement had come moral and physical degeneration until Italy had become what it was now, 'a Nation of Priests, something less than Women . . . a Race of mere effeminate Cowards'. You could see a similar transformation in the Irish, who were once a war-like people, and still had the makings of good soldiers outside Ireland. But at home their spirit was broken; there was a 'dead Languor' about Irish tunes. They had 'a mourning complaining Sound, and you must fancy you hear the Rattling of Chains in their most sprightly Compositions'.[135]

Opera singers earned vast sums. And it was true that the Italian opera in the eighteenth century in London was tremendously popular. An astute German, though, watched the English audiences and thought that hardly anyone understood a word of Italian and the audiences paid 'very dear' for being bored out of their minds. That could be tolerated, he was sure, because they were there to flaunt their wealth; it was that that gave them so much pleasure. They were also able to spend a lot of money at the celebrity concerts that the best-known musicians and singers gave in the Hanover Rooms or at the Little Theatre in the Haymarket. The best and the best-known musicians were foreigners; London had long been overloaded 'with such heaps' of these foreigners, according to Daniel Defoe in 1728, who were paid extravagantly and at the end of their careers could return home and live in luxury.[136]

The reason why London had to pay all these foreigners was that England had no teaching academies of music of its own. Defoe proposed establishing a musical academy in London to train and encourage composers, singers and instrumentalists. He suggested that the governors of Christ's Hospital create thirty places for boys (and perhaps two girls) with special musical aptitude. At the end of a decade the alumni would be able themselves to give concerts and perform operas and the money generated could be ploughed back into the academy.[137]

Defoe's proposal came to nothing. More than a century later, in the 1850s, an English lawyer and man of letters, in attempting to give useful advice to worried parents, acknowledged that the honourable title of 'profession' had been extended to include now 'artists, sculptors, and architects'. More recently civil engineers had been granted recognition, and then actuaries. Even more recently these men of science had been joined by a body of men, long looked down upon but now endeavouring to establish themselves as belonging to the professional classes, 'the professors of education'. 'By the followers of music, and the stage, the term has always been claimed, and has been by society accorded with a degree of reluctance, if not at first even with ridicule.'[138]

The difficulty of according musicians the status of professional gentlemen could be seen when the defining attributes of the word 'profession' were clearly stated. A calling was a profession when 'a man for a reward places at the public service his intellectual labour, and the fruits of intellectual knowledge, and experience'. Now what were the intellectual labours of a musician? Part of the trouble, he granted, was the vagueness of the term. A musician might be 'an itinerant fiddler', and so of the lowest position in society. He might move in 'the most exclusive circles' as a man of letters, like the famous Dr Charles Burney, an executant musician and a composer, certainly, but also a man of learning, a friend and companion of Johnson, Garrick, Reynolds and Burke.[139]

When did an Englishman encounter music in his everyday life besides the raucous disordered singing he heard in church? Sometimes, even at the most refined private supper parties in the 1790s, the German visitor noted, a gentleman or a lady would sing, which sometimes could be entertaining. Sometimes it just gave you earache. He realized that music was generally recognized as part of a girl's education, yet very few girls in England learnt to sing or play very well and the little they did learn most of them quickly forgot when it had served its purpose and they had acquired a husband. On the London streets it was impossible to avoid seeing a great many washed-out fellows and 'tattered sirens' singing their 'silly songs' and gathering crowds around them. It was doubtful whether the crowds were wholly entranced by the charms of the songs. It was as likely that the gentlemen at least were made dizzy by the roaming fingers of the female pickpockets.[140]

An English gentleman in the middle of the nineteenth century might belong to a musical club, a glee club, sometimes called a harmonic society. There were a number of these in London and you found them too in provincial centres such as Bath and Salisbury and Chichester. They would meet weekly during the winter to sing catches, glees, choruses and songs, and the evening might include a cold collation with port wine and sherry. The persons eligible would be 'noblemen, gentleman and professional men', but there would also be 'honorary professional members', that is professional musicians, and it was they, almost always of a lower rung in society than the other members, who would lead the music-making, and without whom, really, music-making would hardly be possible. There might be an octet of singers, including two men singing 'soprano', though there might also be a handful of boys on occasion. A member might play upon the piano-forte but more often than not it would be an 'Honorary Professional Member' who would assist on the pianoforte or the violin or the vio-loncello or the clarinet. Such clubs were essentially for the 'promotion of harmony', for 'innocent and refined enjoyments', to foster 'delicacy, moderation, and respectability', for networking, and, to that end, political discussion and indecent songs were banned.[141]

England hadn't wanted a musical academy in 1728. England still didn't have any national training school for musicians in 1818 when the *Quarterly Musical Magazine and Review* regretted that England had 'no conservatorio except the very very poor establishments con-nected with the celebration of devotion in the cathedrals of England, and which we believe we are warranted in saying are not generally very creditably supported'.[142]

So the neglect of music in England until late in the nineteenth cen-tury was the result of perfectly reasonable attitudes – about the time necessary to become an instrumentalist of even moderate ability, for example – but also a tangled web of conscious and subconscious notions about masculinity and sexuality, foreignness, Roman Cathol-icism, and social and intellectual status.

THE MYTH OF AN ANCIENT TRADITION

Why did the myth about the music in English cathedrals persist? Lowell Mason, that choir-trainer from Boston, Massachusetts, thought it quite extraordinary that 'good people from America, ministers and others, should write in such glowing terms of the cathedral music of England'.[143] Why did this idea of a singing tradition of great vitality persist when the reality was rather different?

In 1835 a historian claimed that England was 'entitled to boast that her cathedral music is superior to that of any other country, and that, while the music of the church in Italy, and even Germany, has degenerated, ours retains the solemn grandeur of the olden time'. It only becomes gradually apparent that the author was referring to the cathedral music repertory when he conceded that the English choral establishments were, at that time – it had to be admitted – 'inadequate to do justice to the grand and solemn music which they have to perform'.[144] But he was at pains to emphasize that there was indeed a tradition of composing 'grand and solemn music'. There was tangible and concrete evidence in several handsome volumes: there was John Barnard's *First Book of selected Church Musick, consisting of Services and Anthems, such as are now used in the Cathedrall and Collegiat Churches of this Kingdome*, which appeared in 1641. (The outbreak of the Civil War and the establishment of the Commonwealth prevented the publication of a second volume.) There were the three widely used volumes of William Boyce's *Cathedral Music*, which appeared respectively in 1760, 1768 and 1773, with new editions in 1788, 1841, 1848 and 1849.

There was the collection compiled by Samuel Arnold that appeared in 1790 of 'the most valuable & useful Compositions . . . by the Several English Masters of the last Two Hundred Years'.

Charles Burney in the eighteenth century noted that it wasn't that England's church music was bad, but that it was 'ill performed'. 'But till we have music schools under the Direction of men of Taste & Genius, like the Conservatorios of Italy, & better salaries are given to the performers, our singing men must be so barbarous as to ruin the best Compositions of our own or of any Country on the Globe.'[145]

But there has evidently been a tendency to talk of the 'tradition of cathedral music' and blur the distinction between the works and the performance of them. E. H. Fellowes was a minor canon at St George's Chapel, Windsor, where his singing of the priest's part was 'of exceptional dignity and beauty', according to Watkins Shaw.[146] He was to remain in that post for fifty years. Between the death of Sir Walter Parratt in 1924 and the appointment of Sir Walford Davies as organist of St George's in 1927, he acted as master of the choristers with responsibility for the full choir, and he was the first to make recordings with them. In 1941 he published a classic study of *English Cathedral Music*. He acknowledged that the standard of performance in cathedrals had been 'allowed to degenerate to a deplorable extent' in the eighteenth and nineteenth centuries. And yet at the same time he maintained that there had 'never been lacking a plentiful supply of men and boys well qualified for the skilled task of singing music which is often of an elaborate and difficult character'. Perhaps his own experience of training the choir at Windsor and his amazement at 'the quickness with which the boys learn their work', skewed his judgement and made him careless with generalizations.[147]

Listening to the singing of a succession of cathedral choirs in 1852, Lowell Mason from Boston could well understand, indeed had some sympathy with, those seventeenth-century Puritans who wished to do away completely with all this disagreeable noise. He did in fact admire much of the organ playing he had heard in England. There were outstanding musicians in cathedral establishments. Although the singing was very poor, the organ playing, at Westminster Abbey, at the Chapel Royal, at York, in fact almost everywhere, was very good. He particularly admired the Introduction and Fugue he heard at the end of Evensong at Worcester, which was noble, elevated, learned. And the organ accompaniment to the extracts from *Messiah* he heard at the Foundling Hospital, London, was bold, and clear, and demonstrated great skill.[148]

When he was appointed organist at Norwich Cathedral in 1819, Zechariah Buck visited most of the English cathedrals to listen and learn from their singing. But before the middle of the nineteenth century and the advent of railways it had obviously been difficult to form an opinion about the state of cathedral choirs generally. It was often difficult even in the cathedrals themselves to be sure what was going on. 'The illusive and fascinating effect of musical sound in a Cathedral unfortunately serves to blunt criticism, and cast a veil over defects otherwise unbearable', was the way that S. S. Wesley described it. 'No coat of varnish can do for a picture what the exquisitely reverberating qualities of a Cathedral do for music.'[149]

Choirs of men and boys had continued to exist in English cathedrals after all, which is more than could be said of France, for example, where they had been closed by state edict in 1791. In some it seemed that efforts were made from time to time to recruit singers, but English travellers in nineteenth-century France were usually unimpressed. In 1893 one denied that 'in the ordinary run of provincial Cathedrals in France' there was 'anything worthy of the name of music . . . to be heard'.[150]

THE ROMANTIC REFORMATION

Now, though, in the middle of the nineteenth century, the vast shift in human consciousness in western Europe that we call Romanticism was changing the very notion of musical experience. Music in the eighteenth century was regarded as an accomplishment, 'calculated to sooth the Mind, and unbend its most racking Cares and Anxiety'.[151] It also had great practical value for both men and women: 'it saves a great deal of Drinking and Debauchery in our Sex, and helps the Ladies off with many an idle Hour'.[152]

The nineteenth century made of music something much more tremendous. The attitudes of Romanticism towards music have so permeated the texture of our lives and everyday thoughts – on the rich ambiguities of music, on the mystery, the depth and profundity of musical expression, the impossibility of making a satisfactory verbal paraphrase of music, the inexhaustibility of music's meaning – that it is difficult for us to comprehend the startling effect that these attitudes had on nineteenth-century sensitivities. The phenomenon is summed up for us in the towering figure of Beethoven in his garret, the artist as prophet, priest and king. But the English cathedral close was not immune from the power of the new metaphors. The intensity of musical experience was conveyed by Gerard Manley Hopkins in his poem on the music of Henry Purcell written in April 1879 in which he found that 'meaning motion fans fresh our wits with wonder'. Hopkins saluted the genius of Purcell: 'whereas other musicians have given utterance to the moods of man's mind, he has, beyond that, uttered in notes the very make and species of man as created both in him and in all men generally'.[153]

One of the most powerful poems on music in English in the nineteenth century is Robert Browning's 'Abt Vogler'. The organist improvises and his creative energy bursts forth while seeming to obey mysterious laws, whether of a scientific or divine origin. And Browning alludes to the miraculous creation of triadic harmony, to the way in which, as George Herbert had put it two centuries earlier, 'musick is but three parts vied and multiplied':[154]

> But here is the finger of God, a flash of the will that can,
> Existent behind all laws, that made them and, lo, they are!
> And I know not if, save in this, such gift be allowed to man,
> That out of three sounds he frame, not a fourth sound, but a star.

And the musician, at least the composer or improviser, wields commanding power and authority among creative artists:

> But God has a few of us whom he whispers in the ear;
> The rest may reason and welcome; 'tis we musicians know.[155]

It was not an overnight revolution in taste. It may be that John Ruskin expressed still generally held views among middle-class Englishmen in an essay he wrote for his friend Charlotte Withers in 1838 when he was nineteen. Charlotte was very fond of music. In fact her enthusiasm for music shocked Ruskin. How could she be so superficial? He wrote her an essay, nine foolscap pages long, which he entitled 'The Comparative Advantages of the Studies of Music and Painting', with the object of demonstrating the superiority of art over music and the silliness of attempting to deny this. Love of music and the ability to recognize different kinds of music, Ruskin explained to Charlotte, was simply a 'naturally implanted faculty', like the ability to savour food and distinguish between sweet and sour tastes. Brute animals after all derived enjoyment from music; music did not require a cultivated mind or an elevated intellect. Didn't she know that mice are entranced by music? Horses are excited by trumpets, and may be taught to dance very rhythmically. You could actually kill the iguana, he told her – 'a kind of lizard' – by whistling at it, for, even if you were not a good whistler, delight in the sound would root it to the spot and then you could easily break its neck. Snakes and elephants both danced to music very elegantly. Music was just sensual gratification. But had she ever heard of an animal showing any kind of appreciation at all of the works of Correggio, say, or Raphael? Of course she hadn't.

Think of sacred music, he told her. Think of a hymn sung by a congregation to a simple up-and-down hew-haw sort of tune in a shabby little chapel with no echoes, and no fine architecture. This would produce no elevating effect at all. But the clear pure sounds of choristers and the thundering of a noble organ down the dim and misty aisles of some vast and shadowy cathedral, this could undoubtedly have an astonishing effect on the mind and might even lead a listener into a delusion, imagining that the sounds were addressing his intellect. But no, without the unending aisles, the sculptured columns, the tinted windows, the pale monuments, it would be nothing at all, nothing but ear-tickling emotionalism.[156]

Ruskin was very young, and he was to change his views, but his attitudes would not have been dismissed by many comparatively sophisticated men and women of his time interested in ideas and aesthetics.

And then most musicians earned so little. S. S. Wesley, who aspired to be first a composer and considered that all musicians directing music at a cathedral should have composition as their central preoccupation and principal activity, resented the vast difference in the earning power of artists and composers. The talent of painters was a source to them of fortune and honour. Landseer, it was said, spent eight days painting a picture of a horse and was rewarded by a thousand guineas. A church musician who composed a work of the highest merit in eight days would not be offered a thousand farthings by any Dean and Chapter, who would even refuse to defray the expenses of copying the music for performance.[157]

To what extent did these new ideas about music alter attitudes in English society? Wesley claimed that there was evidence of a new status for music in its 'universal adoption as a branch of education in the middle and upper circles'.[158] It is difficult to know on what evidence he was relying. He himself drew attention to the titter that ran round the House of Lords when a member of the Royal Commission remarked facetiously that they did not wish 'to tax the musical abilities of the Minor Canons'. You did not hear sniggering in the cathedral cities, he snapped back, whose inhabitants longed to hear the choral services decently performed.[159]

In 1856 one of the ten chaplains who sang in the choir at New College was encouraged that there were now probably more pianos in individual colleges at Oxford – at least in some of them – than in the whole University thirty years earlier. A Madrigal and Mottet Society had been recently formed and a Plain-Song Society and undergraduates would sing and play in their own associations and chamber groups. But what he longed for was the integration of music and the study of music within the universities, to see 'our Bachelors and Doctors of Music rising up within our own walls', with music degrees requiring proper residence requirements and not being awarded simply to candidates who came to the University only to sit examinations.

For musicians must benefit from 'the social intercourse of educated minds': 'A man that is all Music is no better than a mere sportsman, or any other enthusiast.' Music must be part of the everyday life of all the men at the universities, for it was 'the greatest of all humanizing agencies'. Only now was it being realized that all children were endowed with remarkable musical gifts and that making music and listening to music brought health to both body and mind. Science was being brought back into the curriculum of the universities, and music, which also formed part of the quadrivium of the medieval university, should be too.

But if the Chaplain thought he detected an increasing knowledge and love of music among the general population he was also sure that this was not reflected among academics and the clergy. The people might be becoming 'learned in song, and even in harmony' but their pastors continued 'utterly destitute of all knowledge' of music. 'A Musician, let him be ever so talented and exemplary in moral conduct, ranks scarcely above an ordinary artizan.'[160]

Why were voices being raised now about the feeble performance of the singing in cathedrals? John Jebb had referred to a 'Spiritual Reformation' that was taking place in recent years, in the late 1830s and the early 1840s.[161] The leaders of what became known as the Oxford Movement were intensely concerned with particular theological issues and doctrinal questions, and the changes in liturgical practices that they ushered in were intimately bound up with these. But, ultimately, it was a movement of the heart rather than the head. Above all this great spiritual reformation in the nineteenth century changed not the so-called High Church wing of the movement which gave birth to it, not just one wing of the Church, and not the forms of dogma and doctrine on which all the theological discussion centred. The Oxford Movement changed the spirituality of the English Church. It changed the spirituality of the English. It was an Anglican manifestation of the great upheaval of Romanticism.[162]

The writings and the lives of those who created the Oxford Movement led to the revival of ceremonial, to the Eucharist becoming central to Anglican worship, to vestments becoming commonly worn. These men introduced more colour and decoration into churches and cathedrals, and processions, and side altars, and the use of ancient hymns. By recreating the outward forms of the medieval Church, by building in the Gothic style, a medieval sense of piety would be rekindled: that was one hope of the Movement. There was renewed interest in old music, in plainsong, and ancient polyphony, in carols, in liturgies and medieval liturgical practices.

Nineteenth-century churchmen thought of the Puritans and of the Church during the Commonwealth in the seventeenth century when cathedral choirs were silenced. In his book on the choral service John Jebb quoted Bishop Jeremy Taylor, who had looked back during those dark grim days at the past glories of the Church's liturgies before the Civil War. He called to mind 'the pleasures of the temple, the order of her services, the beauty of her buildings, the sweetness of her songs ... these were the pleasures of our peace, and there is a remanent felicity in the very memory of those spiritual delights, which we there enjoyed, as antepasts of heaven, and consignations to an immortality of joys'.[163]

The signs of the spiritual reformation that men like John Jebb identified and the Tractarians did seem to herald were hard to detect at any of the choral foundations in the 1840s. The Tractarians themselves made no detailed pronouncements at all about music. But in 1839 a group of younger men, mainly clergymen or ordinands, had formed the Cambridge Camden Society, which became later the Ecclesiological Society. They were concerned first with church architecture, to create churches whose design in the tiniest detail would allow that 'the Rubricks and Canons of the Church of England may be consistently observed, and the Sacraments rubrickally and decently administered'.[164] They were concerned with the precise and particular liturgies of the Middle Ages; they were moved and energized with a typically nineteenth-century excitement for the Middle Ages.

PIETY, MUSICIANSHIP AND THEIR DANGERS

In 1846 restoration work had been begun on the chapel at Queens' College, Cambridge, and in 1848 daily chanting of the services was undertaken by a group of undergraduates, just tenors and basses. They sang Gregorian chant and a few Anglican single chants and one visitor considered their chanting conveyed 'a singular effect . . . very earnest and solemn'.[165] Not until 1854 did the College arrange for the introduction of choristers into the choir and in 1860 it elected a choral scholar. Further choral scholars were elected from time to time but the assumption must be that they were singing with lay clerks, singing men who would have considered themselves professional musicians, and singing not plainsong but psalms to Anglican chants and settings of canticles and anthems.

One of the most important of all the discoveries of the Ecclesiologists was the medieval hymn and the publication in 1851 of *Medieval Hymns and Sequences* and *The Hymnal Noted*. In 1854 some enthusiasts formed the Cambridge University Society for Promoting the Study and Practice of Church Music and, around the same time, the Oxford Society for the Study and Practice of the Plain Song of the Church. The Society in Cambridge quickly recruited more than a hundred members, undergraduates mostly but also Fellows of some of the colleges. They instituted twice-weekly practices, being taught the rudiments of musical notation as they learnt to sing. This was music for congregational singing and the aim of at least some of those taking part was to be able to encourage congregations to sing in the parishes to which they would be sent as young priests. In 1861 there existed a St John's College Choral Society; it was divided into elementary and advanced classes, each meeting weekly under the direction of the College organist. The advanced class sang with trebles from the College Chapel Choir and practised music in parts as well as plainsong. But the aspirations of nearly all those singing would have been not to develop knowledge of and expertise in cathedral music but to equip themselves for stimulating the participation of congregations. The membership of the Choral Society proposed that two of its altos, two tenors and two basses practise with the Chapel Choir and sit in seats reserved for them beside the choir. The organist and choir-master at St John's, Dr Garrett, explained that it would have been 'impracticable . . . for the present'. No further explanation seems to have been recorded in the College's records.[166]

There might have been several reasons for this and for the luke-warm interest taken at Queens' College in their pious undergraduates. The musicians at the choral foundations were acutely aware of their low status both socially and professionally and jealous in preserving their flimsy claims to musical expertise and vocal distinction. They would certainly have watched with jaundiced eyes as the young gentlemen struggled with singing and with notation. Many church musicians still believed in progress in art and music, in this still untouched by one of the central notions of Romanticism. S. S. Wesley referred to plainsong as 'the unisonous Chants of a period of absolute barbarism'. Would these enthusiasts with their 'amateur efforts' as musical performers look Michelangelo in the face and tell him that Stonehenge represented the perfection of architecture?[167] The scholar and composer Sir George Macfarren referred to plainsong as 'Pagan, Popish, barbaric, crude Gregorianism'.[168]

The associations of plainsong with Roman Catholicism and a whole host of interrelated theological and social characteristics made many Anglicans and Anglican institutions uneasy. Some members of the Church of England in the mid-nineteenth century were greatly alarmed, as was the Bishop of Oxford, by the rumours that some young curates were ' "unmanly", that their training bred effeminacy'. He wrote to a friend that 'Our men are too *peculiar* . . . I consider it a heavy affliction that they should wear neckcloths of peculiar construction, coats of peculiar cut, whiskers of peculiar dimensions – that they should walk with a peculiar step, carry their heads at a peculiar angle to the body, and read in a peculiar tone . . . it implies to me a want of vigour, virility'. He thoroughly disliked the habit of men kneeling in rapt prayer on the steps of the altar, not at service time but when others were walking about and talking: 'such prayers should be "in the closet" with the "door shut" '. This form of behaviour, the Bishop thought, 'really force[d] on visitors the feeling that they might be not in England at all but . . . in Belgium'.[169]

Or consider the letter that was written on Advent Sunday 1860 by the Warden of New College, Oxford, to one of the undergraduates, Mr Adams:

> I could not help observing this morning, as well as on a former occasion this term, the peculiarity of your attitude during the administration of the Holy Communion, and I wish to suggest to you to consider whether it would not be better in future to avoid a practice which has, at all events, an appearance of singularity about it.
>
> Remember that the attitude which the Church prescribes for us is 'kneeling', 'meekly' & 'humbly' kneeling, and it is questionable to my mind, whether an attitude which if not actually amounting to prostration, yet approaches very nearly to it, can fairly be considered as the sort of posture which the Church intended us to use. At any rate you will feel, I am sure, with me that at such a time, it is a duty not only to keep our own minds in the most quiet & collected state possible, but also take care that there be nothing in our own behaviour that may in any degree disturb the minds of others. And as the peculiarity can scarcely fail to attract observation, contrasting as it does with the usual attitude of other Communicants in the Chapel, may I hope that you will see the propriety of yielding to my suggestion.

On the letter there is a later annotation pencilled in: 'Mr Adams left the Church of England, & joined the Church of Rome in aet. 1862.'[170]

In Thomas Hughes' novel *Tom Brown at Oxford*, published in

book form in 1861, Tom went to a drinks party, sublimely ignorant of his hosts' proclivities. He began to feel uneasy as soon as he saw the muslin curtains and bottles of scents and of eau de cologne on the mantelpiece and a piano in one corner. He had fallen among a group of ecclesiological High Churchmen who went on and on laying down the law on fasting, and apostolic succession, and passive obedience. Tom goaded them by saying he thought England was well rid of monks and then he had to defend the architecture of St Paul's Cathedral, which they described as 'a disgrace to a Christian city'. He'd never met, he thought, such a group of 'waspish, dogmatical, over-bearing fellows'.[171]

It is not impossible to imagine numerous reasons why Queens' College took no steps to encourage the chanting undergraduates in its chapel and why Dr Garrett at St John's was uneasy at the thought of admitting the fervent members of the College Choral Society to the Chapel Choir. The very enthusiasm for music of certain undergraduates might well have stood in the way of improvements in chapel choirs.

AN EXPERIMENT AT NEW COLLEGE

In the choir at New College, Oxford, in the early 1850s the lower parts were taken by ten chaplains and three lay clerks. The chaplains were priests with parishes around Oxford, having very lowly status in the College, and in fact they attended services at the College only irregularly, because of their priestly duties elsewhere. Should the College replace the chaplains with lay clerks or should it try to recruit undergraduates as choral scholars? On the whole, the College thought, the recruitment of lay clerks exclusively would be likely to ensure better singing. Most obviously the choice would be much larger; the College was so small at that date. It hesitated. The idea of allowing men to earn their education through their singing was certainly an attractive one, at least to some of the Fellows. It was obviously excellent preparation for ordination. But was it likely that enough good voices would emerge from the schools? In the end, after much heart-searching and shaking of heads by some highly sceptical

Fellows, the College passed a statute in 1858 whereby there would be eight to ten choral scholars, whose 'special duty' it would be 'to take part in the Choral Services of the Chapel'.[172]

Gradually the chaplains began to be phased out: by 1862 there were seven chaplains and four choral scholars, and in 1863 six chaplains and six choral scholars, and this number again in 1864, though the College had hoped for eight choral scholars that year. And then in the official *University Calendar* for 1865 all mention of the new 1858 statute is dropped and in addition to five choral scholars there now appear four lay clerks. In 1866 there are four choral scholars listed and five lay clerks. And then in 1867 one choral scholar, seven lay clerks and three chaplains, and again the same numbers in 1868.[173]

It had quickly become apparent, as one of the Fellows reported, that the plan would not work, 'except at the cost of having a choir far below its proper level'. The voices of the choral scholars were immature. Some of the better ones were appointed from men in their second year from other colleges, but these older choral scholars seemed to disappear almost as soon as they had arrived. The undergraduates required far more training than lay clerks to learn new repertory – for some of them everything was new – and to develop and master basic vocal techniques. And because voices were hard to find among schoolboys seeking admission – at some of the voice trials no single candidate reached an acceptable standard – there was a tendency to accept candidates whose academic limitations might otherwise have ruled them out. But then such candidates were likely to struggle with work for their degrees, and the need to devote several hours a week to musical duties meant they had less time and less energy to unravel the complexities of Euclid's parallel postulate, or to learn how to generate the second aorist passive stem for Greek irregular verbs. 'Nec cantare pares, nec respondere parati,' sighed one irritated tutor.[174] 'Can't sing, can't answer exam questions either.' This was not quite fair but not wholly a distortion either.

Such difficulties can have done little for the morale of either the undergraduate singers not quite equipped for the task or the chaplains whose services were gradually being reduced. All the twelve choral scholars who were appointed during the experiment became priests.[175]

By 1869 there were three chaplains and eight lay clerks, the arrangement settled upon by a new statute of 1864. For in that year New College had decided that the experiment had failed.[176]

DESPERATE REMEDIES

When the Cathedral Commissioners published their reports in 1854 and 1855 and laid bare the sorry state of cathedral music, what recommendations could they make to remedy or at least improve the situation? One of the problems facing the commissioners was the decision taken by Parliament at their own prompting twelve years earlier. The cathedrals possessed the huge wealth of the Church of England. But what were they for? Some thought they were perceived only as providing retirement homes for superannuated clergymen, or comfortable libraries for scholars, the value of whose scholarship was not always immediately obvious. They provided choirs of men and boys but in most the daily liturgy was celebrated in so slovenly a manner that secular musicians would have considered it a disgrace to be attached to such foundations.[177] 'Better far to shut the doors, sell the organs for old metal and fire wood, and turn the surplices into some more useful apparel, than thus to disgrace the science and bring its professors into utter contempt.'[178] What the cathedrals clearly required was money to reward expert and properly qualified musicians. When the clerical staff at cathedrals were threatened with reduction through the suppression of canonries in what became the Dean and Chapter Act of 1840, some urged the Ecclesiastical Commission to allow the cathedrals to retain the savings and require them to be spent on their choral establishments.[179] And yet the burgeoning inner cities required human and material resources – the conurbation of Manchester and Salford, for example, had room for under 24,000 in their existing churches and a population of 182,000.[180] The necessity for some kind of reform was denied by almost no one. And the cathedrals' canonries were duly suppressed. Seeing the financial dilemma they faced with their choirs the commissioners had asked the cathedrals whether they considered it possible that 'laymen of approved piety and zeal' might be recruited as honorary lay clerks, particularly for the Sunday services.[181] In his recent pamphlet, after all, S. S. Wesley had reported that it had been possible at Leeds Parish Church to find such men who attended 'with regularity and with good effect'.[182]

Now he was less sure. Such additions, he told the commissioners, should be made 'with great watchfulness' or they would do more harm than good.[183] Others were even less sanguine. Durham was not aware of any such persons in that city. Nor was Norwich. Canterbury thought that such an experiment 'would tend rather to endanger the general harmony than to promote efficiency'.[184] Wells thought that such an idea would not have 'the remotest possibility' of success there. After they had listened to the opinions from the cathedrals the commissioners accepted that the introduction of volunteers was not a realistic solution.[185] Lay volunteers could not improve the situation.

The commissioners' judgement was that the vicars choral or minor canons, the singing priests, should be young men who could combine their musical work, the intoning of the responses and prayers, with pastoral duties in the neighbourhood of the cathedral. If the voices of some remained 'good and strong' and they did not wish to be given a living – to become a parish priest – it seemed sensible to keep them principally as singers while allocating them additional diocesan work assisting one of the canons. The acceptance of such work would in time no doubt justify an increase in stipend and it would also allow the payment of a pension when a voice failed. Such an arrangement also preserved the distinction – this required no underlining – and might be used as a justification for the difference in income, between priest vicar and lay clerk. So much for the intoning of prayers. As for the men who actually sang in the choir, after due deliberation the commissioners recommended that 'suitable stipends' be paid to lay clerks, and that, 'if possible . . . a fund be established for retiring pensions'.[186]

But most cathedrals did not have the financial resources to increase salaries and to create appropriate pension schemes. As for the boys, the commissioners suggested that 'there should be connected with every cathedral a school in which the choristers should receive a sound, religious, liberal and useful education, in addition to their musical training'. They recommended that choristers receive an 'apprenticeship fee' on quitting the choir unless they hoped to attempt an exhibition to the University. They recommended that the cathedrals give preference at the voice trials to boys who would be likely to gain admission to a university.[187] Such views had been widely articulated long before the commissioners began their work. And as the cathedrals had already made abundantly clear, they had no money to raise lay clerks' stipends. About the lack of financial resources the commissioners were silent in their report.

The commissioners' responses must have been judged unhelpful by most cathedral musicians and most of the chapters too. And they were couched in terms that many cathedral musicians must have regarded as patronizing: the commissioners 'had reason to believe' that the daily choral services were being conducted 'with increasing solemnity'. The commissioners said that they entirely agreed with a suggestion made by 'several Chapters' that the choral services in cathedrals should be maintained 'in full efficiency'. They thought that 'a love for sacred music is on the increase in our larger communities'.[188]

Most disturbing of all to cathedral musicians, they were convinced that 'the music of the choral service is often too elaborate and intricate for an ordinary congregation', which complexities had tended to diminish congregations, though they give no evidence for this assertion. While services and anthems might require special skills, the singing of metrical psalms in which the congregation can join did not – this they encouraged – and they exhorted choirmasters to ensure that chants for psalms and canticles were of a simpler character to encourage members of the congregation to join in.[189]

Even in the responses, John Jebb thought, the choir represented the congregation. There was no need for the congregation even here to join in with an 'inharmonious crash'.[190] No doubt many of the cathedral musicians who read the words of the commissioners agreed with S. S. Wesley, that the cathedral service, 'like other sublime things, would necessarily render the auditor speechless'.[191]

It was not as if there were no helpful ideas or practical suggestions in the air. The organist at Exeter, in his submission, had reminded the commissioners that the reduction of ecclesiastical revenues at the Reformation, which coincided with the reduction of duties required of the singing men, had led to the permitting of these men to follow 'small trades or other secular occupations'. He considered this necessity amounted to an evil that must be rooted out. The lay clerk should be trained by the cathedral, within the cathedral precincts, exclusively for ecclesiastical employments, and have a very strong attachment to the cathedral and all its work. As it was, men were elected primarily for their musical attainments and vocal powers and, on appointment, little was known of a man's moral character 'beyond the uncertain testimony of strangers', which led to 'not infrequent scandals'. In the face of continuing demands for more and better education in England the organist suggested that the choral and educational activities of a cathedral might be blended. Could not special training be given to some of the trainee teachers who were also prospective lay clerks in the recently established diocesan training colleges? Or institutions could be established exclusively for the training of 'lay vicars, parish clerks, or other minor ecclesiastical and scholastic offices'. Not only would this be likely to result in higher musical standards in the singing men but likely too to foster a greater loyalty to the cathedral and create better relations between members of the Chapter and the musicians.[192]

In 1855 a musical clergyman developed a similar idea and suggested that in cities like Chichester students at both the training college for teachers and the theological college for ordinands could be recruited into the cathedral choir and receive vocal training from the singing men, five students having lessons with one lay clerk. With such improvements in the choir and the local improvements in boys' education that training colleges could create, a rise in candidates for choristers might safely be predicted. The Cathedral Choir at Chichester currently numbered sixteen boys and men. With the two colleges and the additional boys it would soon number sixty. And then the Cathedral Chapter could appeal to members of the congregation, enthused not just by the new choir but by the life being breathed into cathedrals everywhere. There was to be more frequent preaching and more frequent classes for confirmation and more celebrations of the Eucharist. Inspired by what had already been achieved, members of the congregation would surely come forward and further swell the numbers. In nearly every market town choral societies were springing up. In these, 'mechanics and tradesmen, and indeed most of the more intelligent of the middle classes' were joining together for the first time, making 'vast strides . . . in choral harmony'. Maybe the cathedral organists were too conscious of the need to safeguard their professional status. But he was convinced that recruitment of volunteers at this point stood a chance of success. Indeed, the transformed cathedral choir might meet weekly to rehearse secular music. The cathedral choirs lack 'vigour, power, mass'. By means of the approach outlined they might create a grandeur of sound to match the grandeur of the buildings. Through their music they could draw around them 'a vast bulwark of devoted followers'.[193]

A future Regius Professor of Modern History at Oxford, Edward Freeman, had ideas in the 1850s about the choral foundation at Wells Cathedral. The College of Vicars there, the creation of a fourteenth-century endowment, contained singers of various ages, some of them clergymen – who merely intoned prayers and responses – some of them lay clerks with secular occupations in addition to their singing duties. Freeman considered that the work of singers in a cathedral was the work of young men. He thought it as incongruous to see grey-haired old lay clerks or minor canons croaking away as it was to see grey-haired old ensigns and lieutenants in armies of old. The office of the singing man was certainly an honourable one even if a subordinate one, and the subordination to the older canons could be 'natural and graceful' if the singers were young men. Let the newly created theological college take over the College of Vicars. Let there be young men who were candidates for ordination, theological students, who were also musicians, and these would sing in the choir as choral scholars. The priest vicars, slightly older, might act as teachers in the College. Both categories would continue in the College until marriage or preferment. The important point was that all the members of this college, whether they were already graduates or not, should be 'men of some measure of liberal education and of a manner of life becoming holders of an ecclesiastical office'.[194]

Yet the Church did not attempt to create a training school for lay clerks. It did not attempt to create choral scholarships at the new theological colleges and the teacher-training establishments in cathedral cities. The local conditions in which choristers were being taught varied so greatly that special arrangements would have to be worked out in each cathedral city. There were individual initiatives. In the middle decades of the nineteenth century the King's School at Worcester was nominally educating the choristers, but their absences resulted in their being regarded by teachers as ' "casuals" on whom no particular trouble need be expended'. And so in 1881 the precentor proposed the establishment of 'a preparatory school for the sons of gentlemen and professional men' and promised to carry it through until it became self-supporting. It did so and after twenty years could point to many distinctions achieved by past pupils: seventeen entrance scholarships to senior schools, four choral scholarships to Cambridge, a scholarship to the Royal Academy of Music, a D.Mus. at Oxford. Five of its pupils had been ordained. Another gain to the cathedral, according to the precentor, had been the 'care and reverence with which, since the establishment of the choir school, the daily services are rendered'.[195] There were always potential problems with such arrangements since schools for the choristers alone would generally not be big enough to offer a sufficiently wide range of subjects or facilities such as proper sports grounds and laboratories.[196]

In the absence of any kind of general improvement in standards, seventeen cathedral organists met in the Chapter House at St Paul's on 6 February 1880 and reiterated a number of resolutions which they sent to the Ecclesiastical Commissioners. They considered it desirable that a cathedral choir consisted of no fewer than twenty boys and twelve men: four altos, four tenors and four basses. They were sure that the choristers should be boarded, lodged and educated free of expense, in their own school, which would give them 'a classical education'. They urged that the cathedral organist should not need to give private lessons to supplement a meagre salary. His cathedral duties were such – if he were to obtain appropriately high standards – that they alone required his full attention. A cathedral organist should receive an annual salary of not less than £400 and a lay clerk not less than £120 for his daily duties, and there should be a pension scheme for both organists and singers.[197] But in 1880 the Church of England still seemed reluctant to show any collective will to improve the lot of its musicians or the standard of its music.

Charles Ellicott was Bishop of Gloucester from 1863 until 1905. His wife was very musical and their daughter, Rosalind, studied at the Royal Academy of Music. She appeared as a soprano soloist and her chamber music and songs were widely performed. Her oratorio *Elysium* was a success at a Three Choirs Festival performance in Gloucester in 1889 and then heard in London and Chicago and

Dresden. Some readers of the *Gloucester Citizen*, the correspondent thought, might be pursing their lips. He continued reassuringly: 'Miss Ellicott has not allowed her personal work to interfere with her home duties; she does a good deal of secretarial work for her father, and helps her mother most devotedly in the many tasks which fall naturally to a bishop's wife and daughter.'[198]

One day Miss Ellicott was singing a duet with her mother at home in the Bishop's Palace when her father came into the room and found the fire nearly out. He gave it a good rattling with the poker. That had little effect and he continued rattling away. The singers had to stop.

'My dear, my dear,' said his wife in a reproachful voice.

'No, no, don't stop,' responded the Bishop. 'No, really, don't stop. You're not disturbing me in the least.'[199]

THE DIFFICULTIES OF REFORM: HEREFORD CATHEDRAL

The problems facing the reformers of cathedral music in the middle of the nineteenth century seemed intractable: additional resources seemed non-existent; there was no satisfactory existing organization for the training of choir-trainers and lay clerks; nearly all middle-class Englishmen knew little or nothing of music; the social gulf that lay between musicians and the members of cathedral chapters seemed unbridgeable. Moreover, the idiosyncratic history of each cathedral and its organizational structure meant that it was difficult to see how any kind of model could be formulated that would serve for choral foundations as a whole.

Consider the problems facing the Dean and Chapter and the musicians at Hereford Cathedral. Hereford was one of those few cathedrals in the 1840s where there were vicars choral in the choir and not lay clerks. All the singing men at Hereford were ordained clergymen. This was because of a charter of 1395 granted by Richard II that had never been abolished. It had established a college and endowments for twenty-seven expert singing men chanting the offices and celebrating the Masses daily at altars all round the cathedral, deputizing for the more senior canons and prebendaries. In the 1830s there had

been twelve surviving posts in the College but the Cathedrals Act of
1840 had decreed that these should become six by natural wastage,
attempting not particularly to impoverish the music but to claw back
revenues and divert them into supporting the Church in the burgeoning cities of the north of England which were crying out for more
resources.

Several of the vicars in recent times had been choristers at Hereford
and then, their musical and academic gifts being apparent, they had
been carefully taught – some of them had had extra coaching in the
College of the Vicars Choral – and they proceeded to Oxford University. They had then returned and spent their lives as vicars choral.
Their musical duties being not so heavy – just daily Matins and
Evensong – and much more straightforward than those of their medieval predecessors, they were given the care of a local parish in
addition. Their salaries, which derived partly from ancient endowments, might have been adequate for single men living in the College
but were insufficient for married men with families, constantly traips-
ing along muddy roads from their parishes to the cathedral. Their
music-making was inefficient, partly because the other work led to
frequent absences from the choir stalls, partly because their musical
training had been inadequate. No doubt there were some good voices
among them, but even those with good voices had not all been given
the appropriate tuition, neither musical nor vocal. They certainly
loved music, and were much more musical and knowledgeable and
educated than most lay clerks of the time, though not such musical
experts as they thought they were.[200]

In June 1848 the Dean had looked at his body of singing men, these
MAs and gentlemen. There were eight of them left, aged seventy-eight,
sixty-seven, sixty-five, sixty-two, fifty-five, fifty-three, fifty and forty-
nine. One was 'asthmatic', one 'in bad health', another 'in very bad
health'. One had a parish six miles outside the city, another's was seven
miles away.[201]

Not only was their music-making not as good as it should have
been, but the vicars choral were brittle characters. In an age when
musicians were held in such low regard by English men and women
they were acutely aware of their low status within the cathedral. They
were hardly ever given promotion by the Chapter, hardly ever offered

larger and more valuable benefices. As John Jebb conceded in 1843 –
he was to become a future residentiary canon at Hereford – the vicars
choral were looked upon as 'the drudges of the Chapter, as an order
of men inferior in caste'.[202]

In 1850 the organist saw the advantages of retaining the 'peculiar
constitution' of the choir at Hereford with its educated ordained
priests. This was on condition they were relieved of their parish duties
so that they could devote all their energies to their musical work.

In 1848 the Dean had thought it would be best if the singing of the
lower parts were undertaken by lay clerks. His views were no doubt
affected by his years of attempting to devise a workable system with
querulous vicars choral jealous of their vested interests. But the Dean's
views were not at all incoherent. He thought the college buildings at
Hereford ideal for the foundation of a college for 'the promotion of
sound instruction and training in Church Music', preference being
given to those who had been trained as cathedral choristers, so that
'the whole country might be supplied with soundly educated performers, whether they were required for choral or parochial purposes, and
a deficiency supplied which is universally felt and acknowledged'. But
the Dean died prematurely in 1850, and in 1851 the Chapter swept the
vicars choral aside and appointed a body of lay clerks. With them came
the disadvantages that the organist had foreseen, lay clerks inadequately paid who were compelled to find other paid work and 'hurried
from secular employment at the Call of the Bell – a Surplice thrown
over Mechanics' Clothes – anxious to get through the Choral Service
because it interferes with their other labors, frequently soliciting leave of
absence suffering from illness caused by incessant occupation'.[203]

The College of the Vicars Choral at Hereford now did no more than
intone the services. But they paid the singers. They still counted themselves the musical experts and continued to point out failings, ignoring
the fact that the music had been bad when they had total responsibility
for it. It all continued unsatisfactorily, and the College went on repeat-
ing that 'it was never contemplated by the Cathedral Statutes to throw
the principal part of the Choral Duty upon Laymen'. In the 1860s the
College persuaded the Chapter to employ a handful of 'assistant vicars
choral', ordained men who had recently taken degrees at Oxford or
Cambridge or Trinity College, Dublin, to sing alongside the lay clerks.[204]

They were very good but most of them did not stay long; perhaps they did not care to live daily lives in College and Close with perpetually strained relations between vicars and lay clerks and members of the Chapter. It was not until 1907 that the Chapter was able to assume proper control of the choir; the succentor, who had been a member of the College, died in that year, and the Chapter immediately announced that they were to appoint the organist to this post, the holder of which bore responsibility for choosing the choir's music and for directing full practices. 'We are credibly informed,' the College told the Chapter, 'that there is a conspiracy afoot among cathedral organists to bring about a total exclusion of the clergy from any authority or influence whatever in the regulations of the musical services.'[205]

There was no conspiracy among the organists. By 1907, though, the cathedral organist's role and status had been transformed. How had this happened?

2
Reform

A NEW FOUNDATION: ST MICHAEL'S COLLEGE, TENBURY

The ancient and important office of precentor at Hereford Cathedral was abolished under the Cathedrals Act of 1840. The office should have lapsed when the postholder at that time died in 1855. Bishop Hampden though was determined that the title should be preserved in his cathedral and given to a man who could speak with authority on musical matters even if he could not be appointed a canon residentiary nor rewarded with the endowment of £500 p.a. enjoyed by his predecessor. The man he appointed was twenty-nine – he'd been ordained six years earlier – and he was shortly to be appointed Professor of Music at Oxford, Sir Frederick Ouseley.

Ever since he was a boy Ouseley had made a special point of visiting English cathedrals and listening critically to their choirs. He knew as much as anyone about them. In 1851 he had travelled on the continent and listened to church choirs there. He had never heard anything equalling or even approaching the excellence of the singing of the boys in both the Lutheran and Catholic churches of Dresden. In the Kreuzkirche in Dresden and in the Thomaskirche in Leipzig he found boys and young men whose intonation was 'so true, and the style so tasteful and refined, and the quality so rich and full and round, that it leaves nothing to be desired'. Ouseley thought every precentor and choirmaster in England should go and hear what was possible in the churches of Dresden, both Catholic and Lutheran. He suspected that these boys were chosen from 'a somewhat higher class of Society' than choristers in England usually were and that this was the underlying reason for 'their more refined style'.[1]

After two years as precentor at Hereford, Ouseley could bear it no longer. He steeled himself. He wrote to the Chapter 'in all humility', he told them, hoping that he would not be misunderstood, that what he wrote would not be considered 'an arrogant assumption of superiority over those who are my senior in age and position'. The precentor told the Chapter that he considered their choir the worst cathedral choir he had ever heard in England. In his letter he left aside entirely the vexed question of the lay clerks and vicars choral. He wrote only about the Hereford boys, whom he considered 'notoriously and disgracefully inefficient as vocalists and musicians, vulgar and provincial in their address, and irreverent in their behaviour'. The situation was getting worse each year, and the chances of finding a cure seemed to be receding. The Cathedral Grammar School would no longer take the choristers, and, without the advantage of a decent education, respectable parents would no longer consider putting their sons forward as choristers. The homes from which the present choristers came exercised a 'vulgarizing' and 'demoralizing' effect over the boys. Their irreverent behaviour was now so common it ceased to attract notice any more and went on unchecked, while the attendances at Divine Service became ever more meagre.[2]

Ouseley acknowledged that his position at Hereford was merely advisory. Nevertheless he said that he found it galling that while he was responsible for the condition of the choir – theoretically at least – he was yet 'practically unable to benefit it in any way whatever'. He hoped that his report was deemed worthy of consideration by the Chapter and that it might be a contribution towards 'the great object for which I am labouring – the improvement and restoration of the Choral Services in the Cathedral Church of Hereford'. He could not have held out any great hopes. He had already begun to make other plans for the improvement of choral services in the cathedrals.

For, unlike most cathedral precentors, Sir Frederick Gore Ouseley had inherited both a considerable fortune and a baronetcy. He was the son of the Ambassador Extraordinary and Minister Plenipotentiary to the Persian Court, born in 1825 and the godson of the Duke of York and the Duke of Wellington, rich, privileged and convinced of the power of music and the necessity of it as a handmaid to religion. He was said to have played duets as a child not only with Mendelssohn but also with Queen Victoria.[3] Besides being a fine writer, a competent linguist and a fluent composer, he was an excellent organist, a fair player on the cello, and he was 'a capital player' on the guitar, on which instrument he would accompany himself singing Italian or Spanish folk songs. But it was as an improviser on the piano at home to a friend or two that he demonstrated his astonishing qualities, at least that's what his closest friends thought. He was quite able to extemporize a four-movement sonata lasting half an hour, 'each movement in perfect form, full of invention, rich in melody, and novel harmonic combinations'.[4] But though he was a prodigiously gifted musical child he received little in the way of systematic musical education. He was educated privately at home and then at Christ Church, Oxford, where he read for a degree in mathematics and classics, in neither of which did he distinguish himself particularly. A contemporary observed that he had 'wonderful abilities as a linguist and as a mathematician, but his passion for music prevented the full development of the sterner pursuits'.[5] His academic studies were also affected, his teachers thought, by the duties required of him in attending to the family estate, for in 1844 while he was an undergraduate he had inherited the baronetcy.

When he explained to the Dean of Christ Church that, having taken his bachelor of arts degree, he now intended to sit for the bachelor of music exams, he was told that it was 'utterly derogatory for a man in his social position to entertain such an idea'.[6] He took the degree anyway and then a musical doctorate, for which he composed an oratorio called *The Martyrdom of St Polycarp*, 'a happy blending of Handelian dignity with Mendelssohnian grace and refinement, and here and there a trace of Mozart and of Spohr', as a contemporary critic characterized it. The work might not have been totally original but a march from the oratorio – a 'bright and tuneful' march – became, at least for a time, 'one of the most popular organ pieces in existence'.[7]

So Ouseley spoke with considerable authority both within the Church of England and in the musical world at large. He must have felt duty bound to say something to the Chapter at Hereford even though he could not propose any practical steps to effect improvement. If he could do nothing to persuade deans and chapters, though, he could, with his inherited wealth, go his own way. He had no idea where he might establish a choir school. He thought of Shropshire – his family had ancient links with the county. Might it be possible in Ludlow? Might it possible to rebuild the Cistercian Abbey at Buildwas by the Severn? Bishop Wilberforce in Oxford was planning the establishment of a theological college near the Bishop's Palace at Cuddesdon; perhaps he might be sympathetic to Ouseley's ideas. But the Bishop was nervous of Ouseley's supposed High Church leanings. Then Ouseley discovered that money had been left to build a church at Tenbury Wells, a little market town on the borders of Herefordshire, Worcestershire and Shropshire.[8] He decided to build a school adjacent to the parish church in which the boys would sing cathedral services every day with their masters and a handful of professional singing men. In 1856 he founded the College of St Michael and All Angels.

Boys served two years as probationers, during which time fees of £30 had to be paid. When they became full choristers there were no fees. The education they received 'was such as gentlemen might well desire to give their sons'; that was how the *Worcester Journal* expressed it.[9] The College advertised that the boys would be taught classics and mathematics, 'and all other parts of a Public School Education, with French, Drawing, and Vocal and Instrumental Music in addition'.[10] Those who were not the sons of clergymen in the earlier years included sons of a civil engineer, of the organist of Chesterfield Parish Church, of the Governor of the House of Detention in Clerkenwell, of the President of St John's College, Oxford. They came from all over the British Isles, from Henley, Towcester, Dublin, Bristol, Salisbury, Cirencester, County Antrim; most of them went on to public schools, to Clifton, Malvern, Bradfield, University College School in London, Bromsgrove, Magdalen College School, Oxford. One of them went straight to Magdalen College as an undergraduate. Many became priests, one a vicar choral at York Minster, one the precentor at Truro, another the precentor at Canterbury, one the missionary Bishop with Spiritual Superintendence of the Kingdom of Korea and the Province of Sing King in the Empire of China. Some became musicians, one the organist at Christ Church Cathedral, Montreal. Some became surgeons, some physicians. A few became soldiers, one serving in India and Afghanistan and in the Boer Wars in South

Africa, who took part in the Siege of Ladysmith and was mentioned in despatches. A few became scholars, one an authority on the Venerable Bede and the author of *The Life and Times of Alfred the Great*.[11] This was entirely new, boys from middle-class homes becoming choristers of whom high standards both musical and devotional were expected, a steady stream of choristers from a single choir all being given the basics of what was then termed a classical education, with the expectation that they would move to a public school, then take a degree, and then wish to join one of the professions.

What impression did the singing of the men and boys of St Michael's make? At the fifth anniversary of the founding of the College, at Michaelmas 1861, they sang Benjamin Rogers' setting of the Te Deum and Jubilate in D, a local reporter claimed, 'with a vigour and precision that is seldom heard or obtained elsewhere'.[12] In 1872 *The Morning Post* considered the progress that had been made at St Michael's after sixteen years and concluded that 'the performance of the daily service breathes a spirit of such refinement and devotion that our many cathedrals may take as an example, and perhaps imitate successfully, although the present nature of their several constitutions makes it doubtful to believe that they will ever surpass . . . so noble a pattern.'[13] One vicar choral at Hereford Cathedral – he had been a chorister at New College, Oxford, and later a Bible clerk there[14] – had never heard anything before like the singing of the choristers at St Michael's, he said, 'so sweet and refined are their voices'. Their behaviour was admirable and they were very carefully trained.[15]

Commentators mostly considered that St Michael's did indeed provide a most valuable model for the choral foundations to follow and imitate. The repertory it drew on avoided 'a secular and ultra-florid style on the one hand and all crudities of a Gregorian or like character on the other'. It was 'purely Anglican and devotional'. The services were 'neither ultra-High Church, so-called, nor ritualistic, but thoroughly and conscientiously in accordance with the rubrics of the Prayer-book'. In their reverent behaviour, the boys were encouraged by the excellent example set by the singing men,[16] who usually included the Warden and the headmaster and the second master – all university men – as well as the lay clerks, a constitution quite unlike any cathedral choir of the time. Everyone agreed that the College was set in a most beautiful location, the rolling countryside and woods and orchards of Worcestershire, a 'healthful and salubrious neighbour-hood' too for the boys.[17] Ouseley's position in society and his family connections meant that the College inevitably attracted a good deal of attention within the Church of England. Because of Ouseley's standing in the musical world famous musicians visited Tenbury too. Sir George Grove, Jenny Lind and her husband Otto Goldschmidt (the founder of the Bach Choir), Charles Gounod and Sir Joseph Barnby, all might be found walking over the fields around the College; and distinguished bishops and theologians came to preach, men like Henry Liddon, later Canon and Chancellor of St Paul's Cathedral, and Bishop Samuel Wilberforce from Oxford.

But was anyone listening except on special occasions, as at the annual dedication festival at Michaelmas when excursion trains were specially run from Hereford and Shrewsbury, and carriages rattled down the country lanes, and the church was crowded 'even to excess by a fashionable élite of the three adjoining counties'?[18] If a chorister grumbled about the absence of any congregation at a weekday service he was roundly rebuked: the singing was to the honour and praise of God Almighty and in the invisible presence of His Holy Angels, he was reminded.[19]

'Bustle, even on a market day, does not seem to be a special char-acteristic of Tenbury', a visitor noticed in 1900.[20] Friends had urged Ouseley to build his college near London, or at least with easier access to one of the great centres of population in England.[21] Its isolation undoubtedly led to difficulties in recruiting the few lay clerks who sang with the College's teachers in the choir. Singing in the 1920s were Barrie Maund, who sang bass at St Michael's for forty years, and Arthur Cox, who sang tenor and acted as the College factotum for forty-four years.[22] The reputation of the College was enhanced by its music library, a collection created by Ouseley himself together with a few items he inherited from his father, which ranked among the most important music libraries in England, though its true value was only revealed after the First World War when it was properly shelved and catalogued.[23] The ethos of the College and the recruit-ment of trebles from educated families did foster disciplined singing of a kind that was completely new. It had to be admitted, though, that not very many ever actually heard the singing at St Michael's.

The organist when St Michael's, Tenbury, opened in 1856 was the Rev. J. C. Hanbury, but he left within a year to become a chaplain at Wadham College, Oxford. At the time Ouseley was considering whom to appoint as his successor, he called in at St Paul's Cathedral. Maybe he was even visiting the cathedral specifically to confer with the organists there about the vacancy. He climbed up into the organ loft and found that both organists were away and that a seventeen-year-old ex-chorister called John Stainer was there sitting at the console. Ouseley watched him closely while he played for Evensong and later that day sent him a letter inviting him to become his organist at St Michael's. Maybe Ouseley was already thinking of Stainer that afternoon he climbed up into the organ loft. He had heard about him. Indeed he had actually met him a few years earlier at St Paul's when, as a gifted young chorister, Stainer had played to him from memory a prelude and fugue from Bach's *Das wohltemperierte Clavier*.[24]

John Stainer's father was a cabinetmaker, a vestry clerk and a registrar of births and deaths at a parish church in Southwark and, for a time, a parish schoolmaster there. He was self-educated, curious about many things, a bibliophile and a keen amateur musician, a flautist and a violinist. He was not much of a keyboard player, his performances of hymns on piano or organ being of 'the slow and sure kind', according to one of his daughters.[25] But at one time there were five pianos in the house, one with a pedal-board, and he built an organ for his eldest daughter, who was to become organist of the Magdalen Hospital Chapel in Streatham for fifty years. Six children survived infancy and the family members were devoted to one another. Going to tea at the Stainers, a childhood friend of John's remembered, was always like going on holiday.[26]

John Stainer was educated as a chorister at St Paul's. He had an exceptionally beautiful voice as a boy and was frequently asked to join adult choruses round London singing works such as Handel's *Israel in Egypt*, *Judas Maccabaeus* and *Messiah*, Mendelssohn's *Elijah* and *St Paul* and Spohr's *Last Judgement*. He was selected by a

London composer called Charles Steggall to sing as a soloist at the required performance of his D.Mus. exercise at Cambridge. He was also invited to take part in the first performance of Bach's St Matthew Passion in England, in 1854, given by the Bach Society and directed by William Sterndale Bennett.[27] As a treble he could easily have ruined his digestion, a contemporary observed, if the money he was given by admirers in the St Paul's congregation after his frequent solos, 'half-crowns, crowns and even half sovereigns', had been spent on sweets and iced buns.[28] Even as a treble he stood out as much for his engaging personality as for his voice. All his life he seemed to win over everyone, small boys in awe of him, or suspicious and recalcitrant lay clerks, or eminent scholars and theologians, or politicians and statesmen. He was short, not a particularly impressive figure, but animated and energetic, and as a young man he had a striking shock of thick black hair which exploded jauntily from the back of his head. It made him look as if he were about to run onstage and perform a music-hall turn.[29]

He took organ lessons from an assistant at St Paul's and organist at the Chapel Royal, George Cooper. Even while he was still a chorister Stainer played at a City church, St Benet's, Paul's Wharf. At Tenbury, Stainer played for two services every day, rehearsed the choir and taught the boys the piano. His duties gave him ample time to practise the organ and to study for an Oxford music degree. He enjoyed the inestimable advantage of having Ouseley as a teacher and mentor with whom he could explore the riches of his music library.

And then at the age of nineteen, after two years at Tenbury, Stainer applied for the post of Organist and Informator Choristarum at Magdalen. Ouseley was the Oxford Professor of Music and his testimonial for him must have counted for much. The College had hoped that Edward Vine Hall would accept the post; he was only twenty-three but had been a chorister and academical clerk at Magdalen. Vine Hall was an expert musician but also a university man, the son of the Printer to the University. He was the kind of man the devout Tractarian Fellows of the College must have dearly wished to appoint. It seems that New College and Exeter had also wished to make him their organist.[30] He was later ordained and became Precentor of Worcester Cathedral.

They had also hoped much of Stainer's predecessor, Benjamin Blyth, who had been an academical clerk and taken a degree Disciplinis Mathematicis et Physicis. He had had to resign under such painful circumstances, the College historian recorded, that he had not had the heart to set them down in the records of the College.[31] A chorister remembered once how Vine Hall, as a chorister, had left his seat in the Choir during a service to play for the anthem when Blyth had become 'incapacitated'.[32]

Among the other candidates for the post in 1860 were George Garrett, a former chorister at New College and currently organist at St John's College, Cambridge, and another, a pupil of S. S. Wesley. Four of the applicants were invited to come to Magdalen and play for services. The President, Frederick Bulley, considered Stainer the man for the job but, given his age and inexperience – he was younger than a typical modern organ scholar – it was perhaps not so surprising that he was given not a full contract but a three months' trial, which was then extended for a further three months. After that the President was fully satisfied.[33] One condition in the contract Stainer had to sign stipulated his attendance in Chapel on Fridays when the services were traditionally unaccompanied. He was there not simply to play the organ but to have complete command of chapel music, choir and organ.[34] The organist and choir-trainer's jobs were by no means always held by one man at the choral foundations of the time. He was to stay at Magdalen for twelve years.

JOHN STAINER AT OXFORD

Magdalen College Chapel was regulated by a small governing body several of whom were devout Tractarians. There was James Elwin Millard, headmaster of the School and later Dean of Divinity, who had himself been a chorister, and one of whose brothers was headmaster of St Michael's, Tenbury. Millard wrote a novella for boys called *The Island Choir* and another book called *Historical Notices of the Office of Choristers*. There was the historian of the College, John Rouse Bloxam, who had been J. H. Newman's curate at Littlemore. Both were aware of the 'wretched state' of the choir in recent times[35] and longed to see the services at Magdalen celebrated ' "with the greatest devotion, honour, and perfection" . . . according to the pious intentions of our Founder'.[36]

Stainer arrived at Magdalen six years after the death of President Routh. There were now no more boys standing in the stalls who could not sing. President Bulley took a lively interest in the choir and though he may often have been present at choristers' voice trials he was certainly prepared to defer to the opinions of the organist on all matters musical. Now, if ever he was approached by parents, he would insist that they should make no preparations for sending their son to Magdalen until after the voice trial by the organist.

Stainer now took not only the Oxford D.Mus. but a BA arts degree. This was most unusual for musicians. And since the fees at Magdalen would have been too expensive for a young musician and the President at Magdalen wished to discourage contact between boys and undergraduates – which would have been almost impossible if Stainer had himself been an undergraduate at Magdalen – Stainer matriculated at St Edmund Hall, where the vice-principal was Henry Liddon. That Stainer held a BA degree at once singled him out from most musicians of his day. It invested him with much greater authority, academically and socially, than his music degrees alone would have done.

The boys were now being provided with a sounder education. In the middle of the century Magdalen College School had been reduced to a school catering for the choristers only. Partly as a result of agitation from the citizens of Oxford – in 1845 a lawsuit was brought against the College by the Town Clerk acting on behalf of certain citizens, persons unnamed – the school began to admit non-choristers, and day boys as well as borders.[37] Between 1846 and 1864 the School's numbers increased from eighteen to more than eighty.[38] In 1866 there were sixty-three boarders and twenty-eight day boys. Its close connection with the College and its presence in a university town brought it the kind of success in these years that its actual record in recent decades would have hardly predicted. The long-standing tradition at the school of accepting boys from all kinds of family backgrounds continued. The fathers of the ten oldest day boys in the school in 1866 included two solicitors, a land agent, the President of St John's College, a sea captain, a college butler, a widow and an Alderman of Oxford.

The fathers of the ten youngest included a college servant, a university professor, two tradesman, two clergymen and a veterinary surgeon. Of the choristers many had fathers who were Anglican clergymen. The aim was now to create a school modelled on the 'Public School type that was beginning to be established throughout the country'.[39]

The fortunes of the school waxed and waned in the second half of the nineteenth century, partly as a result of new independent schools opening in Oxford during these years, including the preparatory schools Summer Fields in 1864 and The Dragon School in 1877 and the public school St Edward's in 1863, schools that had been opened particularly to give the sons of the newly able-to-be-married university dons an excellent education. Perhaps that explains why Magdalen, eyeing its rivals, began to employ university teachers as part-time masters and managed to give older boys access to university lectures. Mysteriously some of them in the 1860s and 1870s actually matriculated at Oxford colleges while still at school.[40]

What of the academical clerks? In 1850 a Royal Commission was set up to investigate the two ancient universities. In a draft of a memo in 1856 for the government commissioners planning a report on university reform the College stated its intention of doing away with academical clerkships, making all the singing men lay clerks with their stipends slightly increased to obviate the need for them to sing at Christ Church or St John's in order to make a living.[41] But this never happened.

The category of academical clerk was retained but now strictly for undergraduates who could sing. In the later decades of the nineteenth century these academical clerks came from public schools all over the country: Sherborne; St Edward's School, Oxford; Malvern; King's School, Gloucester; Exeter Cathedral School; Reading School; Radley; Lancing; Magdalen College School; St Saviour's Grammar School, Southwark. A few had been choristers at Magdalen, a few at St Michael's College, Tenbury, one had been at Salisbury Cathedral, one at St Paul's. As well as being given a singing trial they were expected to sit a Matriculation Examination in classics and mathematics or to have already passed Responsions, the university entrance examination.[42]

A considerable number of them migrated from other colleges. They came at different times, one in his sixth term as an undergraduate, one in his eighth term. They came from a great number of colleges: St Edmund Hall, Keble, The Queen's College, Exeter, Merton. In December 1892, Harry Köblich, a married man aged twenty-six, was elected to an academical clerkship. There was a reasonable hope when he appeared for a voice trial that he could pass Responsions within six months. He had sung in the Chapel Royal and at Chichester Cathedral and the organist considered him the best alto he had ever heard. He did indeed pass all his exams and was ordained and became the Vicar of St Michael at Thorn in Norwich.[43]

It is impossible to deduce much about the general standard of the applicants. There were often about eight or nine of them. On one occasion there were twenty for two places.[44] Once there were only two for a tenor academical clerkship and one of those turned out to have 'a low Baritone voice'.[45] Like the choral scholars at New College, many of Magdalen's academical clerks had difficulty with their studies; the description 'academical' was a relative one. The Presidents' notes from tutorial board meetings record a succession of melancholy examination failures for academical clerks. In 1872 Mr Bramley undertook to write to Mr Luard's father to the effect that he should either resign his clerkship or obtain private tuition during the vacation.[46] Mr Luard did obtain private tuition but failed Responsions again.[47] In 1877 the Bursar was instructed to remove Mr Platt's name from the College books after he had failed Responsions a second time.[48] In June 1888 Mr Carrington was not allowed to return into residence until he had passed Responsions.[49] In October Mr Carrington had to resign his academical clerkship, having failed to pass Responsions a second time.[50] (John Carrington then won a place in the choir at King's College, Cambridge, where he was remembered by the organist as among the very finest choral scholars he had ever had. He had 'a glorious Bass Voice'.[51] But he left King's without taking a degree there either.) At any rate, whether because of the musical inadequacies of candidates or because of their sudden departure when they failed university exams, the organist in the 1870s increased the number of lay clerks to six and reduced the undergraduate members of the choir to two.[52]

This was the arrangement that continued more or less until the 1950s, six or seven lay clerks with one or two undergraduate members of the College singing. There were certainly some exceptionally good singers and musicians among the academical clerks. There was Lewis Tuckwell. There was Harry Köblich. There was Basil Johnson, who came from Malvern College in 1879 and read Literae Humaniores and afterwards studied the organ with Walter Parratt at the Royal College of Music, and then became director of music at Rugby, followed by Eton.[53] In 1883 there were five candidates for an alto academical clerkship.[54] In October 1880 there were twenty candidates for two academical clerkships,[55] and in 1881 'about ten' for one.[56] Occasionally an academical clerk was able to stay on for a year while he trained for the priesthood at St Stephen's House, for instance.[57]

The high standard of at least some of the academical clerks at Magdalen is suggested from the history of the Magdalen Vagabonds. In 1862 a group of singers, 'a Society composed of members of the University of Oxford', as one of them described it, 'belonging for the most part to the Magdalen College, Oxford, who meet together, from time to time, for the purpose of giving Concerts in various places, for various Charitable objects'. Most of the singers were past or present academical clerks at Magdalen. There were generally about a dozen of them in each concert, typically three altos, four tenors, and five baritones and basses, and they usually took along an accompanist with them, quite often the current organist at Magdalen.

In almost forty years – they gave their last concert in December 1899 – about thirty singers sang with the Vagabonds and they raised £5,000 for the work of parish churches. Their first concert was in 1862 in St Peter's Church at Titchfield in Hampshire and the following year the group sang at the Magdalen College Ball. They sang before Her Majesty Queen Victoria in Eton College Hall in 1867 and in 1888 gave a concert in Princes' Hall, Piccadilly, to raise money for a new organ in the twelfth-century church of St Edburga at Leigh in Worcestershire. There they were 'honoured by the presence of her Royal Highness the Princess Christian, and attended by a numerous and fashionable company'. But though their audiences were invariably genteel, the locations of their concerts were not usually quite so grand. They sang in town halls and shire halls, and churches and royal assembly rooms all over the country. They sang madrigals, ancient and modern, and glees and part-songs. Very often one of the

Vagabonds would step forward and sing some solos, songs such as Meyerbeer's 'Ah! lovely lovely Maiden', or Hatton's 'The Ocean' or Sterndale Bennett's 'May Dew'.

In the 1890s B. P. Lascelles, the 'Magdalen Giant' – he was 6ft 10½in tall – entertained with recitations: 'Beware the Jabberwock, my son! / The jaws that bite, the claws that catch! / Beware the Jubjub bird, and shun / The frumious Bandersnatch!' His rendering of the memorable lines by Mr Dodgson of Christ Church was especially admired. The Vagabonds seem not to have used boys' voices very often but at two Christmas concerts they gave in Leamington Spa in December 1865 four or five trebles 'gave a very sweet character to the music', the local newspaper reported. Indeed the last item of the first half, Pearsall's arrangement of *In dulci jubilo*, which 'by particular request' had to be repeated, haunted the memory of the writer. One of the Vagabonds – he sang with them during the four decades of their existence – remembered that 'The choruses were sung with immense spirit & used to make a tremendous impression upon our audiences.' Local papers were invariably enthusiastic: the performances were 'next to perfection', such 'finished singing'; 'the chief alto' possessed 'a superb falsetto voice'. A local reporter in Leamington in 1865 was sure that 'if ever these gentlemen revisit Leamington we believe that their presence will be greeted most heartily by all those who have listened with so much pleasure to the beautiful ancient and modern music which they have rendered with so much taste, feeling, and intelligence'. And even the London critics thought they were very good: 'The manner in which the glees and part-songs were given on this occasion was extremely good. Floreat Magdalena!'

'This amateur society', the reviewers called them. 'A Concert by Oxford Amateurs', the advertisements would announce, or 'GRAND AMATEUR VOCAL PERFORMANCES'. And *The Musical Times* explained that 'although the members counted in the lists many who afterwards became eminent as professors' – for had not the organists of Magdalen College appeared as accompanists? – 'yet with this Society they worked *en amateur*'. 'The Singers were all gentlemen,' one of them remarked, not entirely facetiously. Most of them were clergymen and though the singing gave them – and clearly their audiences – a great deal of pleasure, it was undertaken in a serious and devout spirit. One of them could not conceive, he said, 'of any occupation in the Vacation more appropriate for Magdalen men than this – the work of going from Parish to Parish, and from County to County, and helping in the work of restoring Churches, building up Schools, & strengthening the hands of hard-working Parish Priests'.[58]

At Christ Church earlier in the century the singing men were appointed, by the Dean of the Cathedral himself, mainly from the ranks of old, infirm or exhausted college servants and bedmakers. The four lay clerks at Magdalen in the 1850s were poor; the standard certainly improved in the later decades of the century. In 1858 Henry Trenham came from Winchester Cathedral. James Ling, who had been a chorister at Ely Cathedral, came to Magdalen in 1860 from Chester Cathedral Choir. In the 1870s two lay clerks came from Lincoln Cathedral. In 1868 John Large came from St Andrew's, Wells Street, London. Increasingly Magdalen was able to attract the best singers. In the 1870s there were four candidates for one vacancy, nine for another.[59] In 1899 there were nearly fifty candidates for a tenor lay-clerk vacancy and the same number for a bass.[60] In part this must have been because pension arrangements of some kind were being offered to Magdalen lay clerks at least from the 1860s.[61] There was a national Choir Benevolent Fund established in 1851 to which lay clerks could subscribe, but the pension arrangements at the choral foundations as a whole were not generous.[62]

Certainly at least a few of the lay clerks at Magdalen were outstanding. There was William Barrett, who was born in Hackney in London and was a chorister at St Paul's – he was an older contemporary of John Stainer – and when his voice broke he proceeded to an apprenticeship with a wood-engraver. But his evident gifts as a singer and his energy and enterprise enabled him to obtain the post of choirmaster at St Andrew's, Wells Street, a famous church with a choir school. Barrett took the fellowship diploma of the College of Organists, became a lay clerk at Magdalen in 1859, and then returned to St Paul's as an assistant vicar choral. But he also took an Oxford music degree and while singing in the choir at Magdalen he began work as a journalist: in 1867 he became music critic on the staff of *The Morning Post*, for which he wrote until his death in 1891, and he edited *The Musical Times* for several years. Barrett also wrote books:

one was *The Chorister's Guide*, another was on English composers, another was on the life and works of the composer Michael Balfe. With Stainer he wrote a *Dictionary of Musical Terms*. He edited books of songs and of folk songs and himself composed songs and glees and madrigals.[63]

James Phillips, a bass at Magdalen, with his name appropriately dignified for soloist's status, frequently advertised his services in *The Musical Times*: 'MR. ADOLPHUS PHILLIPS (Bass) begs to announce that he is at liberty for Oratorios, Miscellaneous Concerts, &c.'[64] Before coming to Oxford he had been a lay clerk in Lincoln Cathedral and while he was there he would often appear in local concerts;[65] he sang as a soloist when the Wesley Chapel Choir in Lincoln performed Sterndale Bennett's *Woman of Samaria*.[66] When his fellow lay clerk at Lincoln, Mr Hemsley, formed a choral society at Market Rasen, Phillips and Mr Dunkerton, another lay clerk, helped it out by singing solos at its first concert, in the Corn Exchange.[67] In January 1881 he made appearances as a soloist in Banbury, Northampton, Rochester, Canterbury and London and also with the Brigg Choral Society in Lincolnshire.[68] Phillips spent his summer holidays in 1880 singing all over the place, with engagements on the pier at Folkstone, Rye and Dover.[69]

Over certain matters lay and academical clerks at Magdalen were now treated alike. Both had to ensure, for example, that they had arranged for an adequate deputy if they had first applied for and obtained leave of absence for one service.[70] Since there was no mention of choir practices in the ancient statutes of Durham Cathedral, for example, the lay clerks at this time considered attendance at any such practices as 'an encroachment upon their privileges'. The precentor knew that the Chapter would not contest this as they feared any edict being ignored by the lay clerks, as it most undoubtedly would have been.[71] At Magdalen in the 1860s the edict from the President of the College was that 'the singing men be required to attend the practisings of the Quire' when required by the organist, and that was the end of it.[72] It may have helped discipline that academical clerks – who were *in statu pupillari* – were unlikely to display the kind of truculence towards the college authorities that lay clerks had shown over the centuries and continued to show towards deans and chapters.

Most of all, Magdalen was fortunate in appointing John Stainer organist and Informator Choristarum in 1860. He was a brilliant organist – he was invited to play organ solos at the famous Crystal Palace concerts from 1868 – and a wonderfully imaginative accompanist and improviser.[73] The choristers were devoted to him and the senior members of the College admired his musicianship, appreciated his transformation of the singing in their Chapel and liked him very much indeed.[74] An undergraduate remembered the '"fragrance" and "magic" . . . of that wonderful music' at Magdalen.[75] Informed contemporary opinion held that, while at Magdalen, Stainer had 'raised the choir to a higher standard than had hitherto been known in the Anglican Church'.[76]

STAINER AT ST PAUL'S

'Do not imagine that you can make any changes or improvements,' Robert Gregory was told on his appointment as a canon at St Paul's in 1868; 'this is an Augean Stable that nobody on earth can sweep.'[77] Robert Church, who was appointed as Dean of St Paul's in 1871, thought that his chapter expected him to awaken St Paul's from its long slumber, 'to set [it] in order, as the great English Cathedral'. Church realized immediately that this would be a 'very tough practical business' and concluded that among the most daunting tasks he faced was 'to fight and reduce to order a refractory difficult staff of singing men, etc., strong in their charters and inherited abuses'.[78] The gentlemen of the choir behaved 'like spoilt children', his predecessor, Dean Mansel, had once remarked.[79] In 1872 Dean Church invited Stainer to become organist at St Paul's and to reform the music there. One of the canons, Henry Liddon, had known Stainer when he had matriculated at St Edmund Hall in Oxford in 1861. But everyone knew of his achievements at Magdalen. If Stainer accepted the appointment, the organist's salary would be raised from £250 to £400 on condition that he undertook 'the whole musical instruction and superintendence of the cathedral choir' and make himself available 'whenever his services were needed at the cathedral, and that he accept[ed] no other appointment'.[80] Stainer did not accept the offer until he had attended a Chapter meeting to discuss his anticipated work. This was immediately an entirely different kind of relationship between organist and Chapter than was characteristic in recent times. He obtained agreement that he could in fact accept other work provided it did not clash with the new extended duties at the cathedral. He also obtained assurances from the Chapter – whom he described as the 'best in England' – that they would back him up 'to any extent'. He was told that 'funds are being squeezed out of the Eccles: Commissioners for a very large Choir – probably 3 times as numerous as now'.[81] A condition was attached that Stainer should appoint a deputy, and he accepted the Chapter's suggestion that he appoint George Cooper, who had been acting as a kind of unofficial deputy since 1838. When Cooper died in 1876, Stainer replaced him with his pupil George Martin, who had been appointed 'Master of Song' at the choir school in 1874. Whether Martin's deputizing duties were initially restricted to taking singing lessons at the school or included taking choir practices is not entirely clear. Neither is it clear how they shared boys' practices in later years. But the choir-trainer's instruction manual that Martin was to publish eighteen years later provides evidence of their common approach to the work.[82]

When a writer on *The Musical Standard* attended Evensong at St Paul's in January 1871 – a year before Stainer's appointment – he found ten men's voices and thirteen 'boys' and babies' voices'. One or two of the men's voices were very good; some might have been good once but now were feeble or rough. The trebles with perhaps two exceptions he considered '[not] good enough for the meanest church in London, or indeed anywhere else', producing little more than 'an irregular confused hum'. In the anthem towards the end of the final chorus the boys 'stopped singing altogether, and stood staring at each other till it was finished'. The singing on this occasion he considered 'disgraceful'.[83]

The Chapter had decided in 1871 that a boarding school for the choristers should be established, but a foundation stone was not laid until St Paul's Day 1874. Early in 1875 the boys moved into a new building with excellent facilities, a large dining room and kitchens, properly equipped dormitories and washing arrangements, and studies. Contemporary visitors considered these spacious and 'very bright and comfortable'.[84] On the roof of the building was a playground, surrounded by wire mesh to prevent footballs and cricket balls from hitting pedestrians below on the head.[85] There was a rehearsal room, which in time was to contain a duplicate set of all the copies used in cathedral services so that bundles of leaflets did not constantly need to be carried back and forth to the cathedral.[86] The site and the building of the school cost £20,000, an enormous sum that continued for several years to 'cripple' the Chapter, according to Liddon.[87] The school provided facilities, both musical and domestic, that most cathedrals could only dream of in the 1870s. The headmaster was to be a minor canon and assistant masters would be provided to teach a full preparatory-school curriculum.

By 1880 there were forty boys boarding from all over the country.[88] In the early 1870s all or nearly all the boys had lived with their parents or lodged with friends in the suburbs. They came to St Paul's for the ten o'clock service and remained until after Evensong at four. They were nearly all sons of tradesmen, and the families, being poor, welcomed the considerable sums that music halls were prepared to pay them for singing. The choristers that were lodging with families were among the first boarders. As quickly as they could the Chapter replaced these boys with 'the sons of gentlemen, chiefly of poor clergymen'. Even if new boys had families in London, they had to become boarders. The exclusion of boys from uneducated families was deliberate, though at least some of the Chapter regretted it 'as partly cutting off the Cathedral from the sympathies of the people'.[89] They adopted the policy not just because it meant that no time had to be devoted to eradicating cockney pronunciation. They had a very clearly imagined idea of the establishment they wished to create, of the accents, mannerisms, physical gestures – or absence of them – to be found in the teachers and boys in the schoolrooms. The Chapter were even prepared to forfeit a good voice if a boy's family background were considered unsuitable in their efforts to convince educated families that it would be a privilege for a son to attend such an establishment. They might have pointed to the new legislation providing universal primary education as being a better solution to the problems of educating boys from poor families than they could offer. But evidently they seem to have made social exclusions with pangs of conscience.[90] Between 1873 and 1885 the boys had a month's leave in August and September and short breaks after Easter and Christmas, half at a time, the remainder continuing to sing without the usual daily practices, it seems, as well as they could.

John Goss was the organist at St Paul's between 1838 and 1872, and just that. He neither trained the choir – the boys were trained by one of the lay clerks – nor chose the music – the responsibility of the succentor. John Stainer took all full practices himself – from the start – though the training of the boys remained in the hands of one of the lay clerks, a professor at the Royal Academy of Music, until the appointment of George Martin in 1874.[91]

Of the ten men singing in the choir at St Paul's on Stainer's appointment five were vicars choral, while five 'supernumeraries' were available for Sunday duty; six men should have been provided from these for all the weekday services but a faulty rota was resulting in only five appearing on Wednesday and Friday mornings. And of the five on Friday mornings, three were tenors.[92]

Originally both the six vicars choral, as they were called at St Paul's (the lay clerks), and the twelve minor canons (men in holy orders who were also singers) were all members of the choral foundation. Now, in the nineteenth century, the only musical duty of the minor canons was the intoning of services. Their number remained at twelve until it was reduced to six by the St Paul's Minor Canonries Act of 1875. The problems facing the Chapter were similar to the ones facing the Chapter at Hereford. Both vicars choral and minor canons were members of their own medieval corporations, whose purpose and function had long since dissolved. But under their medieval statutes the vicars choral still held the freehold of their posts and controlled the finances that derived from the gifts of land and money they had received centuries before in return for prayers and Masses said on behalf of their patrons. They had the right to retain their position in the choir and neither sickness nor the deterioration of their voices was ground for dismissal. They had to provide deputies in their absence, but the quality of these seems never to have been monitored. Perhaps under the ancient statutes the Chapter had no authority to give judgement on vocal quality or musical skill. Stainer attempted to introduce regular practices but as rehearsing was an entirely new concept, unknown to many generations of cathedral singers and not in the medieval statutes of the men at St Paul's, the vicars choral considered they had no obligation to attend them.

Stainer thought that the Chapter should allow the vicars choral to die off one by one and not be replaced or else that their corporation should be abolished by Act of Parliament. The Chapter did not follow either course. Perhaps they wished to avoid direct confrontation or the long wait for the demise of the corporation member by member. Instead they created a new post, that of assistant vicar choral, whose holders would not belong to the corporation and therefore could have new and more stringent terms of employment imposed. The regulations under which the vicars choral sent deputies were also made stricter – designated deputies would have to be approved in advance by the Chapter. Fines for absence and lateness were also to be imposed rigorously. A member of the Chapter promised one vicar choral who was minded to contest a conviction that if he fell down dead on the steps of St Paul's on his way to a service his wife would be fined for his absence.[93] As the Chapter began to recruit these new assistant vicars choral, younger and more conscientious in discharging their duties, regular in attending the weekly practices newly instituted, and no doubt making their more senior colleagues uneasy, the Chapter tactfully and astutely encouraged the few remaining vicars choral to mend their own ways by raising their salaries.

In 1873 the number of men was increased so that there would now usually be twelve men in the stalls on weekdays and eighteen on Sundays. By-laws passed in January 1879 codified the new regulations that had been introduced relating to the 'satisfactory testimonials from a beneficed clergyman as to his high moral character', which had to be submitted on application for the post of a singing man at St Paul's, and to the assurances that had to be given that a candidate was a communicant member of the Church of England. Detailed regulations as to attendance were laid down together with salary scales and pension schemes and disciplinary procedures.[94] And then in another supplementary statute, in 1883, it was quietly noted that 'The present Assistant Vicars-Choral shall become Vicars-Choral'. The object of the Chapter had been achieved.[95] A new kind of lay clerk had been created and substituted for the old one. That this had happened to the choir at St Paul's also owed much to the cathedral being in London and so able to rely on attracting a large number of candidates whenever a vacancy occurred.

It had been achieved because Dean Church was himself wise and patient and he was also blessed with the 'most distinguished and harmonious chapter in the Church of England'.[96] All of them were public figures of immense authority: Joseph Lightfoot a Professor of Divinity at Cambridge, Henry Liddon the most powerful preacher of his day and Robert Gregory a future Dean of St Paul's. The improvements in the singing and the more reverent behaviour of the singers were part of the transformation of worship in the cathedral in the 1870s. Vestry prayers were introduced before and after services in 1872. Cassocks began to be worn beneath surplices by choristers in 1872 and by the vicars choral the following year. Holy Communion began to be celebrated every day from 1877.[97]

But the transformation of the music at St Paul's also owed much to Stainer's musicianship and to his personal magnetism. His attitudes and methodical manner in teaching boys can certainly be perceived in the advice that George Martin, his pupil and successor at St Paul's, gave to choir-trainers. The choirmaster who would maintain good discipline must first know what was necessary to secure it. He should exercise discretion in giving commands, and should insist upon exact obedience: if a rule had been made, it must be obeyed. The choirmaster's manner should be dignified and decided, but not obtrusive. He should not be noisy. He should not speak more than was necessary. He should not give too many commands. He should not threaten punishment. He should behave as though he did not expect disobedience of any kind. Prompt and exact obedience was a habit and must be nurtured.[98]

Stainer had an immense effect on music in primary state education as well as in cathedrals as Inspector of Music in schools and in training colleges for teachers. In 1895 he explained that great strides had been made in the teaching of music to the children, 'particularly in singing sweetly, for unless the children sing sweetly they [state elementary schools] receive no money grant'. Teachers had been trained to stop singing 'through the nose, and all cockney and provincial twangs'.[99] He accepted this post – and retained it until he died – because of his social conscience, because of his belief in state education and his belief that music should occupy an important place in any school curriculum, and that music required knowledgeable and skilful and inspiring teachers.

Throughout his busy life as an organist and choirmaster he continued to compose. He wrote songs and part-songs and madrigals, he made a great many arrangements of traditional and folk songs and carols, and composed a considerable body of church music. He pointed psalters and compiled chant books. His oratorios *The Crucifixion*, *The Daughter of Jairus* and *St Mary Magdalen* were among the works most often performed by choral societies during Stainer's own lifetime. He wrote educational primers – on harmony, the organ, musical composition, and a set of exercises for choral societies. By the time he died, these primers had sold nearly 320,000 copies. He collaborated on a *Handbook to St Paul's* and the *Dictionary of Musical Terms*. He wrote *A Theory of Harmony* and a book on *The Music of the Bible*. With others he produced editions of early music, including *Dufay and his Contemporaries*, which demonstrated his awareness of all the latest continental scholarship. Hubert Parry described Stainer's work on Dufay as a 'revelation'.[100] He lectured on aesthetics in papers on 'The Principles of Musical Criticism' and 'Music in its Relation to the Intellect and the Emotions', in the course of which he showed his acquaintance and understanding of the philosophical writings of such men as Kant, Hegel, Eduard Hanslick, Avary Holmes-Forbes, Herbert Spencer and Eugène Véron.[101] He examined for London University's music degree and for the Cambridge Doctor of Music degree.[102]

In other words Stainer gave the musical profession, and especially church musicians, a new authority. From 1889 he was for a decade Professor of Music at Oxford; Durham University gave him an honorary doctorate; he was President of the College of Organists; he played an important role in the foundation of a learned society for musicians that became the Musical Association in 1874, and, from 1944, the Royal Musical Association, and he served as its President. In 1888, the year he resigned from St Paul's, he was knighted; he attended Buckingham Palace Garden parties; he was elected to the Athenaeum; he was consulted by the Archbishop of Canterbury about

Lambeth doctorates; and by the Prime Minister on church bells, on which he was also an authority. All his four sons he sent to private schools and they all went on to Oxford. His two daughters finished their education in Germany.[103] At the end of his life he was selected as the Liberal candidate for the City of Oxford for an election he never lived to see.[104] With all Stainer's great achievements and worldly successes his friends remembered him for his amiability, his sense of fun, his kindness, his modesty. He was, in Sir Arthur Sullivan's words, 'a man of blameless honour'.[105]

WALTER PARRATT AT WINDSOR

There was another choir too which had demonstrated that reform was possible. Looking back decades later when he was Archbishop of Canterbury, Randall Davidson had wondered whether it was not St George's, Chapel, Windsor, in the 1880s when he had been Dean, which had been the cradle of a transformation in singing that had been effected in styles and standards at the choral foundations. He remembered that at the time he had detected 'a new spirit in Church music' and those attending services in St George's 'a revelation of new things in prayer and praise'.[106] And he had certainly recognized the influence that the organist of the time at Windsor was wielding among younger musicians.

This was Walter Parratt, who had been Stainer's successor at Magdalen in 1872. When he was appointed organist at St George's a decade later Parratt wrote to his wife that 'to get this service refined will ... have to be the work for the rest of my days and not an unworthy one'.[107] And there he remained until he died in office in 1924.

Walter Parratt came from a musical family in Huddersfield. His father and his brother served successively as organist of Huddersfield Parish Church for a total of ninety-one years.[108] Between 1861 and 1868 he was the private organist to the Earl of Dudley at Witley Court in Worcestershire. It allowed him to make the acquaintance of Sir Frederick Ouseley at St Michael's College, Tenbury, and his magnificent library there. Parratt would often walk the twelve miles from Witley to Tenbury before breakfast.[109]

Perhaps those years at Witley Court crystallized his views on education and character. Parratt was to demand the highest technical standards in music-making, precision and unstinting attention to detail, but powerful and moving performances could only be given by rounded human personalities, he was sure. He admired Sir Hubert Parry as the country gentleman managing his estates with minute care, a country magistrate 'with an attractive tinge of Socialism', 'who fined the offender five shillings and then rushed round and paid the fine himself', an enthusiastic motorist, a fearless yachtsman, a musical historian, a composer, the Professor of Music at Oxford and the Director of the Royal College of Music.[110]

A friend of Parratt's remembered endless conversations with him on English literature; it might have been on Wordsworth, it might have been on Walt Whitman, it might have been on Robert Browning. He knew inside out *Progress and Poverty*, Henry George's famous treatise on social inequality and the cyclical nature of industrial economies. But he also knew the latest cricket scores, the billiards records, what was a good time for the quarter mile, and the weak points of the Evans Gambit in chess.[111] Parratt had a fabulous memory in many spheres. It was said that he could play Bach's Forty-Eight complete from memory at the age of ten.[112] He could certainly play chess blindfold and at the end of a long contest could recall every move; he could even play chess while playing the piano. He once played chess with the Prime Minister Bonar Law and, according to King George V, 'beat his head off'.[113]

Parratt demanded precision and accuracy at a time when standards in organ playing and singing were in most places slovenly, with resonant acoustics and distance lending if not enchantment then at least a not disagreeable muddle. Rhythms had to be articulated decisively. His choristers would practise maintaining the tone and preserving the shape of short vowels while enunciating consonants very clearly. They would often be asked to sing on one note the words 'clap the glad hand'. Nothing at all could be accomplished, Parratt maintained, without unwavering accuracy of pitch,[114] and inexactitude in singing or in playing was an impertinence. A wrong note would cause an eyebrow to be raised in incredulity and pain. Any musical utterance had to be phrased, a short melody repeated in a choristers' practice, a pedal passage played by itself in an organ lesson, even they had to be articulated, had to be given meaning. He would say that 'the only phrasing that is completely wrong is when there isn't any'.[115] Many loved him; some could not quite. Such an uncompromising personality with remorselessly high standards could be misunderstood and a few pupils did not grasp his idiosyncrasies at all. Some were rather frightened of him. A smug and self-satisfied young organist might be addressed peremptorily. One new pupil who had played fluently but inaccurately and flashily was asked: 'Sir, do you wish to play the organ, or to play at playing it?'[116]

A friend described his personality as 'radioactive'. And it was true, the friend explained, that to please Parratt by a fair performance 'was as good as winning the Victoria Cross, and required much the same qualities'.[117] His judgement was unfailingly shrewd, his humour playful with a satiric twist. He was companionable. If he detected trouble or sorrow – and he remained marvellously alert and sensitive to the end of his days – then he could draw on vast reserves of kindness and generosity.[118]

He received a knighthood in 1892; he was appointed a Member of the Royal Victorian Order in 1901, a Commander of the Order in 1917 and a Knight Commander in 1921; he was Master of the Queen's or the King's Musick between 1893 and 1924. He was awarded honorary doctorates from Oxford, Cambridge and Durham. And yet those who talked of his genuine modesty were not mistaken.[119]

When he talked to you he listened carefully and treated you as an equal, and this was encouraging and could be liberating if you were a young and inexperienced pupil. His name never appeared on the music lists at St George's when his own music was sung; neither was it given against his chants in the Chapel Chant Book.[120] Performances of which he approved were spoken of as 'classical'. He deplored histrionic exhibitions of any kind. He very rarely descended from the organ loft to direct the choir himself from the stalls. He considered this generally unnecessary and unsightly.[121] The increased precision in ensemble, he thought, would not be offset by the loss of spontaneity. Although he valued discipline in performance very highly he still wanted to hear flesh-and-blood men and boys singing; he did not want the performance to sound too good to be true. A chorister who had been at Windsor with Parratt's predecessor was turning the pages for him playing a Bach fugue as a voluntary and anticipated the addition of the full swell and a crunching reed for the final pedal entry. He became more and more frustrated as Parratt continued to the very end using only a stopped diapason. Later on the chorister realized the exhilaration that the clarity could generate – the revelation of the intricacy and the energy of the part-writing – and that this could be far more exciting than the sensational roar of a mighty instrument in a resonant acoustic.[122] At the same time Parratt was not at all doctrinaire or formulaic. He himself would rarely play the same work with the same registration. And he encouraged enterprise and initiative in all aspects of his pupils' work and in their lives too.[123]

Walter Parratt's pupils included Ralph Vaughan Williams (an organ student unfortunately without much natural talent), W. H. Harris at New College, Oxford, and St George's, Windsor, Madeley Richardson at Southwark Cathedral – the author of an important book on training choirs – H. C. Stewart at Magdalen College, Oxford, Cyril Rootham at St John's, Cambridge, and Henry Ley and Thomas Armstrong at Christ Church, Oxford. And he also taught two musical men of King's College, Cambridge, Edward Dent, the Professor of Music, and the organist Boris Ord.

THE REINVENTION OF BOYHOOD

S. S. Wesley, the greatest cathedral musician in the middle decades of the nineteenth century, was by no means alone in ascribing no particular value to boys' voices at all; he simply regretted that he had to use what he considered in 1849 a 'poor substitute for the vastly superior quality and power of those of women'.[124]

For much of the twentieth century though – certainly the first six decades – almost everyone accepted that the boy's voice was the defining feature of the cathedral and college choir. Leaving aside the injunction of St Paul in Corinthians that women must be silent in church,[125] which many cathedral chapters and cathedral musicians would have considered the end of the matter, there was the question of the appropriate tone colour. In 1940 the editor of the journal *English Church Music* gave the orthodox view: 'Many ladies, of course, sing very beautifully, but they are not the kind of singers for whom our great church music was written; it can never produce its proper effect unless sung by boys.'[126] And in the same issue of the magazine an anonymous writer of a letter to the editor described the use of the mixed-voice BBC Singers in church services as 'a dangerous object of imitation ... daily put before our clergy and church musicians'. If such a choir had to be used for the duration it had to be firmly established that 'the employment of Ladies' was only 'a *pis aller* and that when conditions return to normal it must be the duty of everyone to see that the old tradition of wholly male choirs is restored'.[127] Neither women nor girls, then, could produce the appropriate tone colour. The organist of Westminster Abbey in the 1920s knew – it was almost self-evident – that 'the boy's voice, properly developed, is a characteristic and beautiful musical instrument, while that of the young girl, however pretty and attractive it may be, is at best unformed and only distinguished from the adult woman's voice in its lack of maturity. Taking children's voices as a whole, and assuming equal skill in training, it will be found that boys' voices are superior to those of girls of similar age in power, compass, and resonance, while in expressive instinct and true musical feeling the boy is at least the equal of the girl.'[128] This pronouncement did not take into account that no girl had ever had the intensive training that boys had had in cathedrals. Nonetheless it was certainly the accepted wisdom throughout the earlier decades of the twentieth century among cathedral musicians. St Paul's edict might be ignored in some parish churches but it could not be in cathedrals.

How was it that the boy's voice was regarded with distaste or at least with little enthusiasm in the middle of the nineteenth century and yet almost with reverence at the end of it? This shift in attitude owed something to the Romantics' reinvention of childhood. We see this most famously in Wordsworth, to whom John Keble dedicated his Oxford Lectures as Professor of Poetry in 1844. Wordsworth transformed ideas about childhood, about boyhood, most famously of all in his poem 'Intimations of Immortality':

> Not in entire forgetfulness,
> And not in utter nakedness,
> But trailing clouds of glory do we come
> From God, who is our home:
> Heaven lies about us in our infancy!

It was as if this little child had moved so recently out of God's presence that the Divine Light still shone forth and irradiated older, sadder people with whom he had contact. And so childhood was uniquely valuable, and the utterances of a little child, the sounds, the tone of voice, were to be hearkened to, to be listened to with rapt attention. These sounds were to be listened to indeed with the very wonder and curiosity of the child himself, with the same unselfconscious intensity. Wordsworth again, from *The Excursion*:

> I have seen
> A curious child, who dwelt upon a tract
> Of inland ground, applying to his ear
> The convolutions of a smooth-lipped shell;
> To which, in silence hushed, his very soul
> Listened intensely; and his countenance soon
> Brightened with joy; for from within were heard
> Murmurings, whereby the monitor expressed
> Mysterious union with its native sea.
> Even such a shell the universe itself
> Is to the ear of Faith; and there are times,
> I doubt not, when to you it doth impart
> Authentic tidings of invisible things;
> Of ebb and flow, and ever-during power;
> And central peace, subsisting at the heart
> Of endless agitation.

The 'bawling' of the choristers may have been a matter of no consequence at all to that canon residentiary at St Paul's in the 1840s. Twenty years later the quality of the boys' singing did indeed matter to a great many churchmen. A Fellow of Magdalen wrote a manual for choirboys in 1848 called *The Devout Chorister*. In it he says that 'the vocation of a Chorister, although of course inferior to that of a Priest in ministerial power, is yet higher than that of a Priest, so far as the odour of sanctity peculiar to childhood imparts a glory to the office which appertains to none other'.[129]

The change in attitude made it possible for musicians of the highest distinction to take the training of boys seriously. Still in the 1870s at St George's Chapel, Windsor, boys' practices were usually taken by ex-choristers who were apprenticed to the organist, Dr Elvey.[130] At Carlisle in the 1860s, the head boy took the first three-quarters of an hour of the early morning practice.[131] And S. S. Wesley had considered that the director of music in a cathedral should have a deputy for the training of boys.[132] Men like Frederick Bridge though, the organist of Westminster Abbey from 1882 until 1918, did not consider the training of boys beneath them. Indeed they considered it a vital part of their work.

How was the appropriate singing style to be developed?

'THE BEST EXAMPLES IN THE WORLD'

There were precious few, if any, books on the subject to be recommended, George Martin at St Paul's complained. It was not enough for these young men to be skilful organists. It was not enough for them to be the possessors of fine voices. They must also have particular skill in training voices to sing in this very particular style. In his discussion of the recruitment of boys Martin pointed out that the choir schools to be found in university towns and cathedral cities were not as well known as they ought to be 'to parents of the middle and higher classes'.[133]

It was the 'clear and unemotional' quality of English boys' voices that was considered particularly fitting in imparting a 'devotional element' to the singing.[134] Without succeeding in teaching the appropriate tone quality all other training would be futile. The sound of a boy in a village church would have a brassy edge to it.[135] The sound of a cathedral chorister should have a soft, flute-like quality.

Boys could sometimes demonstrate obvious vocal talent as early as six years of age but it was at about the age of eight that most of the choirs at the choral foundations selected them. Such were the imitative gifts of children that, even at eight, a boy could have developed bad vocal habits through imitating the voice and mannerisms of a bad teacher. These choirmasters emphasized that the first essential was to teach boys to cultivate what they called the 'head voice' and to sing quietly whenever they used what they designated the 'chest voice' or 'chest register', which some musicians rightly called the 'shouting' notes. This 'chest' register contained the notes lowest in pitch, and these 'should never be forced, but always sung softly'. These were the precepts of the organist at Magdalen College, Oxford, at the turn of the century, J. Varley Roberts, who had succeeded Parratt in 1882.[136] These terms were misleading, as he acknowledged. Human sounds were all produced not in the head or in the chest but in the vocal folds of the larynx, which consisted of a complicated system of muscles and ligaments and connective tissue.

The choirmasters explained that the boy's voice consisted of two registers. The lower one, usually called the modal voice register, employed the whole of the vocal folds. As the chorister sang up the scale tension in the folds increased and their edges became thinner. The higher sounds – from A, B or C above middle C – were produced by the use of the outer edges of the vocal folds alone. Every individual voice had a distinct point – an actual pitch – at which the mechanism for producing sound had to be changed, and this was called the 'break' or the 'passagio'. It was possible for most voices to go above this 'break' and continue to apply the mechanism using the whole extent of the vocal folds. A great deal of force was required to do this and the resulting sounds would be harsh and raucous. The employment of the full vocal cords resulted in sensations being felt by the singer in the chest; the use of the outer folds was felt just in the head. Hence the terminology, the 'head voice' and the 'chest voice', so often referred to.

The 'head voice' had an obvious disadvantage: it was not a powerful voice. But it had a very great asset, according to these choirmasters, namely its purity. The distinctive sound of a boy's head voice was pure as the sound of a tuning fork is pure. And the lower notes sung with the chest voice, even if they were not strong – as they would inevitably be if they were unforced – could still have the startling penetrating quality of the open G string of the violin.[137]

George Martin urged the choirmaster to watch like a hawk in the early stages of training when the treble was singing notes in the middle of the range, A above middle C to E a fifth higher. These notes could easily be sung either with the chest voice or the head voice. The choristers must learn to sing them habitually with the head voice. In order to acquire the right sensation with these notes the boys should sing on the vowel 'oo' – as in 'spoon' – since it was impossible to sing that sound with the chest voice.[138] Great care though must be shown in using the vowel 'oo', another choirmaster pointed out: the sound can quickly permeate every other vowel sound with results 'that verge on the ludicrous'.[139] Varley Roberts recommended practising descending scales; the chorister would begin by having to use the head voice and be encouraged to continue using it as far as possible with the lower notes.[140] When the notes from both registers had been developed and enriched by frequent practice a chorister would be able to sing as much as four hours a day without any fatigue or sign of hoarseness.[141]

So the basic approach was to encourage boys 'to sing softly and with a pleasant tone, and never to force the chest register of the voice'.[142] The boy could become accustomed to the sensation of all the 'head' notes, Varley Roberts explained, 'by humming the sounds with closed lips'.[143] Normally a whole phrase should be sung with one or the other voice, he recommended. Occasionally, though, a phrase would span the break. In singing Handel's 'I know that my Redeemer liveth' he would teach the treble to sing the first two notes – 'I know' – quietly with the head voice, and then, after a quick breath, the rest of the phrase sung *forte* with the 'chest' voice.[144] The tone quality habitually cultivated should be 'pure and free from harshness', never nasal or 'throaty', never 'tonsillitic', as Martin described it.[145] This style of restrained singing could only be obtained if the boys were encouraged to sing easily. Jaws must not be stiffened; the throat must be loose.[146] There must be a steady breath pressure behind each note but no more breath should be used than is absolutely necessary.[147]

The organ tone that was so effective in accompanying boys' voices was that of a *gedackt*, a stopped flute stop, the old-fashioned type of stopped diapason or *lieblich gedackt*, but not the overblown *wald* flutes or *hohl* flutes found on the great manual of some modern organs. Soft silvery English mixtures, where these exist, might also be used to enhance the glittering quality of the sounds of English trebles.[148]

Unforced tone was a crucial element of the style. So was unwaveringly accurate tuning. Forcing the tone might be a cause of poor intonation. So might illness, or tiredness or idleness. The teeth must never be closed nor the tongue curled up but lying naturally on the bottom of the mouth, the tip against the front teeth. Some choirmasters recommended that a shilling be held edgeways between the teeth, which would indicate to the chorister the feel of a wide-open mouth. No! said George Martin. This was much too wide. Let the boy place his thumb in his mouth edgewise as far as the first joint. That is better. And the head should be held still and erect. Any tendency to poke forward the chin must be checked immediately.[149] A provincial rustic 'burr' must be eliminated. So must the Londoners' 'foice' or 'fece' for 'face'. The tendency to slur spoken words together must be eliminated, where 'my stony rock, and my defence' becomes 'my stonyrockon myde fence', and 'As it was in the beginning, is now' becomes 'As it was sin the beginnin' nis now'.[150] Games and physical exercise were to be encouraged with choristers, but prolonged shouting that strained voices and made them hoarse must be avoided. Nuts must never be consumed by choristers at any time.[151]

What was the choirmaster looking for at the trial of an eight-year-old boy? The voice should be full of 'ring' – with resonance and clarity and brightness – and free from 'huskiness' or nasal tone. A good compass at audition would be from middle C to A, an octave and a sixth above it, and an excellent one from B flat below middle C to the B flat two octaves above it. The quality of the 'head' voice was paramount. If at audition the boy had a ringing head voice but poor lower voice, take him, Martin advised. The lower notes could usually be strengthened. Reject, though, eight-year-olds with husky voices, or with a very pronounced break between 'head' and 'chest' registers.[152]

Martin distinguished four kinds of boy's voice. Some might have a 'large, horn-like' tone quality. Others possessed more agile and flexible voices with a flute-like quality, some voices having a 'reedy, penetrating quality of tone'. Others still had a fair compass but the voice was 'devoid of ring' and rather inexpressive, the timbre lustreless.[153] At the age of ten, after about a year or eighteen months of training, Martin thought that the boy's range upwards was greater than it was ever likely to be again. The physical changes that a boy went through would be reflected in rapid and unpredictable changes in the quality of tone, and the choirmaster must watch and listen to each boy individually in order to take immediate advantage of these vocal developments.[154]

Most practices would be held in a rehearsal room, not in church. The vocal exercises, essential to the development of tone and flexibility, were secular in character and inappropriate in a sacred building.

Moreover the choirmaster would be unduly restrained in church in attempting to make the lessons as effective and interesting as possible.[155] Although it might be necessary to put the finishing touches to a performance with organ accompaniment, the organ should not be used habitually in rehearsal, both Varley Roberts and Martin were adamant. The choirmaster must be observing and constantly guiding the choristers in minute particulars. And so an upright piano was no good; it must be a grand or square piano with horizontal strings to allow eye contact between master and boys and immediate reaction to a raised eyebrow. A harmonium was not advisable and if one had to be used it must be employed very sparingly and not used to accompany the voices at all; the choristers might very soon begin to imitate the tone quality they were hearing and 'acquire a nasal production of tone and a drawling style of vocalisation', both of which were entirely undesirable.[156] The piano allowed the choirmaster to indicate minute inflections and suggest expressive details such as no other instrument was able to convey to the singers. The choirmaster should always exercise the greatest care when demonstrating with his own singing voice since his own idiosyncrasies and mannerisms would be reproduced by choristers and exaggerated. When the full choir were rehearsing together most of the singing would be without accompaniment.[157]

The choir was a team, its members constantly changing. In a choir of sixteen boys, therefore, the model would be to have four boys aged from nine to ten, four from ten to eleven, four from eleven to twelve and four from twelve to thirteen. Because voices could change with little or no warning it was always important to have probationers in waiting, preferably at least four. And it was important too never to retain boys whose voices were changing. To sing with a changing or recently changed voice, Martin was sure, was very likely to mar or destroy the tone quality of the voice for ever. No boy with a changed or breaking voice should be allowed to sing; it was as if you forced a boy with a fractured leg to keep on walking. An occasional exception was the very light or thin voice which appeared not to 'break' at all, but eased itself down to the alto range. Each voice changed in its own particular way: boys' voices generally changed between the ages of thirteen and sixteen. But some voices had collapsed at twelve, and some had retained their treble quality until the age of twenty-four. Sometimes the change

happened very quickly, in only a few days; sometimes the change could
come about over a year or even two years. Sometimes the singing voice
was retained with a reduced compass of perhaps only an octave,
between middle C and the C above, say, when the speaking voice had
clearly broken, or at least was very gruff. But the general rule must be
that the chorister stopped singing when the first signs of the change
appeared and did not resume while the voice was 'in a transitional
state'. There were some 'scientific defenders' of the practice of retaining
boys in choirs after their voices had begun to change. Do not listen to
them, Martin warned. In this way had many voices been overstrained
and lost for ever. Neither pay attention to physiologists who would tell
you about the precise changes that actually occur in the vocal organs
themselves during puberty. It was a very interesting subject but unfortunately no two physiologists ever agreed with each other.[158]

Like all other boys, choristers were unpunctual, lazy, untidy,
insubordinate, careless, sullen. But they behaved as individuals. The
choirmaster was not training the top line of a four-part texture, nor
two teams of boys, decani and cantoris, standing there facing each
other from opposite sides of the choir-stalls. He was teaching a collection of individuals and must know each one. He must know the
vocal and musical capabilities as well as the temper and temperament
of each boy. If two of them sang too loudly too often, and so risked
injuring their voices as well as destroying the blend, he must be able
to distinguish between one who was excitable and one who simply
loved singing or one who worked too hard out of a sense of duty.

The choirmaster must know the strength of this particular chloris-
ter's B flat below middle C. He must know the changes that have
occurred in the quality of his notes above top G over the past month;
he must know of this boy's carelessness in pronouncing consonants;
he must know of this one's steadiness on solemn public occasions
when the cathedral is full; he must know just how much this one likes
Wesley's *Blessed be the God and Father* and how dull he finds the
lines he has to sing of William Byrd. He must be kind and humane.
He must talk to a chorister who had misbehaved and discover what
the boy himself thought of his own behaviour.[159]

Choristers should be given a musical education which was 'thorough and complete' and not just taught to sing.[160] Boys were often

taught to sing parrot-fashion. This was of no value. The choirs at the English choral foundations had a large repertory and time was always severely limited in the ceaseless round of daily worship. They must learn music theory and be able to give a decent account at sight of an anthem in an idiom to which they were accustomed. It was as hard to learn to sing properly as it was to learn Latin and Greek, Madeley Richardson, the organist at Southwark, told the clergy.[161]

Each boy had to become self-reliant and should be prepared to sing alone when called upon, Richardson insisted.[162] But each man and each boy would constitute a weakness unless each possessed the virtue of self-effacement.[163] ' "Solo-boys" who sing like prima-donnas', agreed Charles Moody, the organist at Ripon Cathedral, 'are out of place in church choirs, and for this reason a group of boys, singing in semi-chorus, is preferable to the emotional youth whose wavering production brings tears to the eyes of over-wrought spinsters.'[164] The individual timbre of a solo voice was inappropriate in this music articulating the voice of the community. And there was also the danger of giving 'solo-boys' swollen heads. For which reason some choirmasters – a later one included Conrad Eden at Durham – nearly always used two boys on a solo line.[165] There must be no slackening when the tone is diminished or hurrying with a *crescendo*. There must be no violent changes in dynamic. Even in hymn-singing any 'over-expressiveness' must be eliminated. Even when a choir is singing of life, or death, or angels, or principalities, or powers, there must be nothing theatrical in the expression, nothing at all extravagant: that is what these choir-trainers insisted upon. A 'reverent, intense, subdued expression is perhaps the final goal of our work,' wrote the trainer of the boys at All Saints', Margaret Street.[166]

There were a number of manuals on training choristers published in the decades around 1900 but these were not matched with books about training lay clerks. Even if no choirmaster at any choral foundation in 1900 spent quite so long each day with his choristers as Zechariah Buck had done earlier in the century, nonetheless musicians of the calibre of Sir George Martin and Sir Walter Parratt wielded enormous influence in cultivating the singing styles of the children in their charge. It was not quite the same with the lay clerks.

The intentions of the choirmasters and the performing style they sought to cultivate with their lay clerks were clear from the books on training choristers. At a few of the best choirs they felt that they had succeeded. After he had retired from St Paul's, Sir John Stainer remembered sitting at the organ console and listening to the choir and realizing that the vicars choral 'entirely subordinated their own wills to the general effect and beauty of the music' and that at the close of a anthem or canticle he 'more often felt inclined to say "Thank God" than to say "Thank you, gentlemen of the choir." And I am sure we all feel that that is what should be the case.'[167]

But at most of the choral foundations the organists in 1900 were all too aware of the failings of the lay clerks and yet felt powerless to do anything about it. When Edward Bairstow went to York Minster in 1913 he was told by his predecessor Tertius Noble that most of the men in the choir were 'old and worn-out' and that there was no pension scheme for them.[168] When Bairstow had heard them he pronounced them 'a mixed lot'. There were two good altos and another, a 'dear old man', who had been singing in the choir for nearly fifty years, who did not make mistakes but 'had very little rhythm'. One tenor was good and had perfect pitch but his voice was thin. The other two were 'very little good'. There was a bass, the senior songman, who had 'in his prime been an ideal lay clerk' and set an excellent example and followed prayers in his prayer book and as Librarian ensured that every direction given out by the choirmaster was inserted into every copy. He was also an educated musician. At almost the first full practice Weldon's anthem *Hear my crying* came up. The smart-aleck young choirmaster, appearing to wish to show the singers up, remarked that this work was 'supposed to contain the first known example of the use of a certain chord'. And he airily wondered whether anyone knew what that was. 'Yes,' said the senior songman, 'the last inversion of the augmented sixth on the last page.' The other two basses had weak and ineffectual voices, what were called at Leeds Parish Church, where Bairstow was previously organist, 'lamb basses'.[169]

A visitor remembered being in the organ loft at New College, Oxford, early in the century when Hugh Allen was organist. As a solo approached, the organist murmured as he played, 'Now, Mr Tenor, don't be vulgar!' And then the visitor told of Allen's quiet exasperation when the singer did sing with a theatrical swagger.[170] It was not just that most lay clerks did not possess the necessary musical and vocal skills. Most of them did not quite aspire to create a performance of the same style and character as the reforming organists.

A successor of Walter Parratt at St George's Chapel, Windsor, W. H. Harris, acknowledged that Parratt's approach, some thought, resulted in 'undue coldness of expression'. According to Harris, Parratt insisted that a short anthem such as the anonymous sixteenth-century setting of the words 'Lord, for thy tender mercies' sake' be sung 'without any nuance or variation of tone colour whatever in a perfectly level impersonal style', however much his lay clerks might protest.[171] It was a tradition that Harris himself maintained – at least that was the opinion of one of his own lay clerks – and it required singing that the lay clerk himself considered 'inhibited', in which 'any form of individuality was anathema'.[172]

The same lay clerk considered that the last quarter of the nineteenth century had represented a high point of 'choral activity' in England. He denied that 'fine solo voices' could not be disciplined 'into a perfectly satisfactory blend' and lamented the disappearance of the 'cathedral voice' of the nineteenth century, a voice that was rarely found in twentieth-century cathedral choirs, 'a particularly fine voluminous sound, suited to vast spaces, and effective equally in solo or ensemble'.[173] One characteristic of cathedral choirs throughout much of the twentieth century, repeatedly commented upon – that this lay clerk omitted to mention – was the continued presence in nearly all of them of older singers whose voices had deteriorated. Such singers did indeed make their presence constantly felt, so that the kind of blend and balance to which choirmasters aspired became impossible to achieve.

In 1895, more than four decades after Lowell Mason, the American choirmaster from Boston, had declared the famous English cathedral tradition to be a sham, some more American visitors came to England and attended services at cathedrals and college chapels. They were particularly struck by the singing at Magdalen. In that moderately sized chapel there was no need for the sixteen trebles and eleven men to force the tone at all. That was the first characteristic that caught their attention, the beautiful tone of the choir, the great 'refinement' and restraint of the singing without 'the slightest trace of harshness'. They discovered that the boys were 'the sons of gentlemen', all scholarship boys given excellent schooling and board. For each chorister vacancy, they were told, there were thirty or forty applicants. Then it was the discipline of the singing that impressed them, the training that was so thorough that everything, including the psalms and the responses, was sung 'as with one voice', with perfect 'precision of attack'.

The American visitors contrasted the singing of Magdalen with that of Chester, which they regarded as the best cathedral choir they heard. Comparison of the two choirs was made easier because they heard both sing the same anthem by Stainer, *Lead, kindly light*. The Chester performance was full of 'snap', incisive and brilliant at the climaxes, the tone not so smooth or beautiful as at Magdalen. The Chester Choir would probably have sounded 'rough' and 'coarse' in Magdalen Chapel, though it was certainly imposing in Chester Cathedral. The Americans noted that cards were posted in the ante-chapel at Magdalen, which enjoined visitors to join in the services silently, and that hymns were rarely sung, 'the music being primarily of the impressive order'.[174]

Some of the Magdalen lay clerks made a few recordings in the 1900s, singing as the Magdalen Glee Singers of Oxford University, 'this world renowned quartette' as they were described in characteristically inflated record-company advertising, 'acknowledged to be the best quartette of trained voices in England, if not in the world'.[175] A. H. Brown (1830–1926) was an Essex church organist, and his setting of a fifteenth-century carol, *When Christ was born of Mary free*, which they recorded in 1907, was included in the second of three sets of *Christmas Carols, New and Old*, edited by Stainer when he was at Magdalen with a Fellow of the College, the Rev. Henry Bramley. These three books, seventy carols in all, were enormously influential, a key component of the modern revival of carol singing. The singing of the Magdalen lay clerks strikes a twenty-first-century listener as artless in its lack of phrasing. But it is accurate, the intonation is secure and there is little hint of vibrato. They do sing together very well, particularly considering the appalling conditions in which they were recording; the singers would have had their heads rammed down possibly two recording horns, it would have been hot and extremely uncomfortable, and they would not have had any eye contact. The mellowing effect of the rich acoustic in Magdalen Chapel is entirely absent.[176]

The bass in the recording was one of the best-known lay clerks in England in 1900, John Lomas, who was elected a supernumerary at Magdalen College, Oxford, in 1890 – he had come from Bristol Cathedral – and a full lay clerk in 1893.[177] He was a much-valued member of the choir, 'far and away the finest voice' was the opinion of one of the boys: 'his range was immense, control perfect, and his tone resounding and effortless'.[178] The chorister listened to him 'in a kind of rapture', he wrote, remembering it all in old age.[179] In 1915, having served twenty-five years, he was entitled to retire on a pension, but was allowed to remain in post until 1918. The organist kept on putting his retirement off.[180] He was still singing energetically at choir reunions in the 1940s.[181] John Lomas also appeared as an occasional soloist in Oxford concerts. He offered vocal interludes with Miss Gwendolen Hayes during a recital by the organist of St Peter-le-Bailey Church in 1897.[182] In a packed Town Hall on Easter Sunday in 1910 he made a great impression with his rendering of the bass arias from Handel's *Messiah* in a performance of selections from the work by the Free Church Choir Union.[183] He made occasional appearances around the country too, at a Festival of Parish Choirs in Tewkesbury Abbey,[184] in Calne Town Hall in Mendelssohn's *42nd Psalm*,[185] in *Judas Maccabaeus* with the Sidmouth Choral and Orchestral Societies.[186] Had John Lomas been as trained a musician as he was a superb vocalist, it was generally considered, he could have had a reputation far beyond the walls of Magdalen.[187] But though a 'professional' lay clerk, he remained essentially an amateur, spending most of the week working behind the counter of his tobacconist's shop.[188]

The singing of the Magdalen Glee Singers was very similar stylistically to the singing of another group of the time, the Meister Glee Singers, of whom Sir Henry Wood said that, 'Up to this time [1899] no vocal quartet had achieved anything approaching their success, probably because they rehearsed for a whole year before making an appearance in public . . . It was not that their voices were so good, but that their diction and ensemble were perfect.'[189] Two of the regular members of the group were vicars choral at Westminster Abbey. They were hailed as 'genuine artists' and the finish and delicacy of their singing was much admired, the 'purity of intonation', the 'beauty of tone', the 'distinctness of enunciation', the 'perfection of balance and blend' that were commented upon everywhere. They charmed the Queen and the Prince of Roumania and Prince and Princess Henry of Battenberg when they appeared by royal command in the Drawing Room at Windsor Castle – the Duke of Edinburgh had heard them in Plymouth and knew the Queen would like them. Their performances, it was said, 'gratified skilled musicians as well as the amateur public'. Even if the patience of men such as Martin and Parratt would no doubt have been tested a little by the succession of musical jests and humorous glees, by pieces like 'The Old Folks at Home' and 'Down in a Flowery Vale' and 'An Italian Salad' and 'Old Daddy Long-Legs', nevertheless they would certainly have admired the vocal discipline these men achieved.[190]

Then in 1899 came another visitor from North America, Miles Farrow, the organist of Old St Paul's Church, Baltimore. He visited seventeen English cathedrals and heard sixty choral services. 'Really satisfactory and finished renditions' he found in comparatively few of the choirs. Like countless visitors before him he immediately noticed that in a number of choirs there were men who had 'grown old in the service, and their voices are no longer either pleasant to listen to or useful, and yet they are retained in the choir. Consequently the music suffers.'[191]

Madeley Richardson considered cathedral music at the turn of the century to be in a state of chaos. But this he welcomed. Change was afoot, the old days of lethargy and stagnation were past.[192] The organist from Baltimore found passionately held views on all kinds of systems of training 'head' voices and 'chest' voices but not the consensus he had expected to find in this 'home of the boy choir'. The tone quality and the standard of singing varied enormously. He considered the weekday services at Westminster Abbey 'very carelessly and dismally sung', the three men on each side quite inadequate for achieving a proper blend, and he disproved of the 'inordinate rapidity' with which the Creed and the Lord's Prayer were gabbled, though he did admire the singing of the twenty boys at the Abbey.[193]

The assistant organist there was a man called Walter Alcock, who was also in charge of the music at Holy Trinity, Sloane Square. There, the American tells us, he had a 'large and excellent choir of 40 boys' who, like the boys at St Paul's and Magdalen and King's, sang with 'head' tones entirely.[194] Three choirs Miles Farrow considered out-standing. Finest of all he thought was the choir at Magdalen College, Oxford, and of a similar standard and quality were the choirs at St Paul's Cathedral, London, and at King's College, Cambridge. He thought these three afforded 'the best examples in the world of the possibilities, the beauty, the perfection of vested choirs of men and boys'.

How had the singing at King's been transformed?

3

A New Choir at King's

At King's in 1850 there were sixteen choristers as required in the original statutes. There were also sixteen choristers at Magdalen and New College in Oxford at this time but not so many in any cathedral; there were ten at Canterbury, ten with four probationers at Durham, eight at Christ Church and Wells.[1] The boys at King's not only sang but, until 1871, were required to wait at table on the undergraduates and Fellows every day at five o'clock.[2] Some members of the College no doubt considered their serving at table to be their most important function. Most of the College officials must have seen them as they waited in hall and sang in Chapel but they paid them no attention at all.

They were given a very rudimentary education at the back of the dining hall, and had singing practice between two and three o'clock each afternoon before Evensong at half past three, the only service they sang daily. Most cathedral choirs at this time sang Matins as well as Evensong and had two practices each day. After Evensong the twelve seniors made ready for their duties in hall and the rest traipsed off home in their little gowns and high silk hats to prepare lessons for the next morning.[3]

The boys were all local boys from the town and all the sons of poor families, some of them college servants. It was very unusual for any chorister at King's to go on and take a degree. They were not, one of them recalled, 'the best specimens' of the species.[4] One who did go on and take a degree was called Tom Hewitt and he sang in the choir between 1842 and 1850. He was the son of a currier, a leather worker, and his mother was a laundress, and he was the most untidy boy any-one could remember. But a clergyman took him in hand and in the end he entered Emmanuel College, obtained a first-class degree in math-ematics, and became rector of Preston St Mary in Suffolk.[5] Another boy, called Thomas Moore, who entered the choir in June 1847, later attended St Mark's College, Chelsea, and obtained a teaching certifi-cate.[6] In the 1860s there were at least three boys who did take Cambridge degrees; a few of the boys of that decade became schoolmasters, several became parish church organists; one became an ironmonger, one a clerk on the Great Eastern Railway, one a basket-maker, one a book-seller, one a bank clerk.[7] Looking back at these years in 1929, the Provost confessed that the College could hardly take much pride in the way it had maintained its choir and educated its choristers.[8]

Singing at all the services with the sixteen choristers in 1850 were eight lay clerks. Five years earlier two additional lay clerks had been added to the existing six.[9] In order to supplement their stipends as singing men the lay clerks at King's worked as artisans or tradesmen, some of them as college servants. One or two seem to have been pri-vate music teachers. In 1799 we know that one was a weaver, one a pianoforte tuner, one a shoemaker, one a tailor, one a cook at Pem-broke College, one a music engraver.[10] On mid-century census records some of them put 'lay clerk' alone as their occupation, which they evidently considered their principal occupation, or their vocation, though they must have had other remuneration.[11] One had a music shop. At least one undertook other work for the College. Mr Piper, singing tenor in the choir in the 1840s – the only lay clerk with a beautiful voice, one chorister thought – was waiter to the Senior Fellows' table in hall and also helped out in the College Library.[12]

In 1809 the lay clerks had submitted a memorial to the Governing Body. They could not afford to employ a scrivener. The version they submitted was scrawled in inelegant copperplate. 'Suffer us once more to lay before you our very distress'd situations and with the utmost humility to entreat that you will have the goodness to grant us an Augmentation to our Salaries; which at the present Moment are utterly inadequate to our Necessities.' Since the last pay rise, rents, the poor rate and taxes had all increased. So had the price of prov-isions. Surely the Governing Body wished to see their lay clerks 'in decent apparel'. There was no need to inform the Fellows how the cost of clothes had risen. Other choirs had seen their salaries revised in the last five years – some had seen them doubled. 'We alone seem Stationary.' And yet Cambridge was perhaps 'the dearest place to live in, of any in England'. This rather pitiful document is signed 'The Singing Mens' with the 's' crossed out.[13]

Half a century later the singing men requested another pay rise. They were experiencing 'much difficulty in maintaining that position of respectability to which we feel we are entitled as Lay Clerks of your College' and 'earnestly and most devoutly and respectfully' solicited the favourable consideration of the matter. They pointed out that they had received no pay rise from the College for fifty years. They also pointed out that their stipends from Trinity College had been recently 'greatly improved' but that, as they no longer sang at St John's, their total salaries had been reduced.[14]

On 26 March 1858 the Governing Body at King's agreed to a quarterly addition of £2 10s to the salary of each of the six full-time singing men,[15] who duly begged most respectfully to express their thanks for the announcement of the Provost and Fellows' kind intentions to augment their stipends. The annual salary of a lay clerk would now amount to £55.[16]

A chorister of the 1830s remembered the services at King's being gabbled through, and he thought any kind of reverence was shown only by one or two lay clerks and perhaps three or four boys. He could never understand why, at the announcement of the anthem, the four corner boys – the choristers standing at the end of each row on each side of the Choir – had to distribute the books containing the texts of all the anthems sung in Chapel open at the page with the words about to be sung. Two boys delivered the books to the seats to the west of the stalls, starting with the Provost and Vice-Provost, and two to the stalls to the east between the Choir and the altar, during which time an organ prelude to the anthem would be improvised. Why weren't the books left in the stalls for the members of the congregation to find the place for themselves? the chorister wondered. He remembered conversations being carried on during the intoning of the Creed. He remembered the lay clerks' noisy whispering on the Fifteenth Evening, with the seventy-three verses of Psalm 78, ordering the boys not to drag.[17] He remembered the opportunities for larking about and being rowdy that oil lamps gave, and the flint and steel tinder boxes and the rushlights – with pieces of rush soaked in fat or grease – and the possibilities for mischief offered by sedan chairs.[18] When he lost his own treble voice the chorister became apprenticed as a carpenter and joiner to a lay clerk who sang in the choirs at St John's and Trinity Colleges, and he also had singing lessons from Mr Piper.[19]

It is difficult to imagine the particular tone quality of the King's Choir at this time. Looking back many years later a loyal Fellow concluded that the musical services of the 1850s and 1860s 'were not destitute of a certain solid grandeur'. But he acknowledged that there was not much refinement.[20] What evidence there is would seem to corroborate this assessment. In March 1836 fourteen or fifteen candidates for admission as choristers aged about eight were given voice trials. They also had to sit a written examination, not unduly taxing: they had to write their names, both Christian name and surname, their age and their address. Four were then selected for a further voice trial. Before this, one of them remembered, he had been coached by one of the senior boys in the choir. The parents of both boys were servants at Caius College. The senior boy played notes on the piano for the candidate to sing. He had also taken him out on to the Backs for 'a shouting stroll', strengthening the voice by shouting as loud as possible at lengthening distances. The second trial was a great ordeal for the little boy but he was one of the two successful candidates. Perhaps it was the glass of sherry with a raw egg yolk in it that his mother had given him just beforehand that did the trick.[21]

The services at King's in the 1840s then, in their slovenliness, in the 'inefficiency' of the singing, as it would have been characterized at the time, were similar to the services at the other choral foundations. No doubt the acoustic of the Chapel resulted in a sound that could be distinguished from other choirs. But the singing was probably no better.

In 1852 the Governing Body dispensed with the two additional men singing at all the services who had been appointed in 1845, and instead, with the six full-time lay clerks, employed four supernumeraries, who sang only on Sundays, saints' days and Saturday evenings.[22] Otherwise little change to the choir seems to have been effected at all throughout the 1850s and 1860s.

The Provost from 1850 was Richard Okes. Okes was born in 1797. He had been educated at Eton, then at King's, and then he returned to Eton where he was a master for twenty-seven years. He had come back to King's in 1848, and he held the post of Provost for thirty-eight years until he died at the age of ninety. In many spheres of college life, though he did now seem 'an old-world clerical gentleman, genial and courtly', Okes presided over far-reaching reforms.[23] The 1850 Royal Commission on the universities resulted in the promulgation of new statutes for Cambridge in the Cambridge University Act of 1856. Okes himself always gave every assistance to the members of the Royal Commission. Even if he himself considered proposed changes misguided he usually gave wholehearted support to the vote of the majority. At King's in 1865 the first two non-Etonians came into the College. In 1873 the first non-Etonian Fellow was elected. The Universities Tests Act of 1871 meant that, in future, non-Anglicans could be educated at Cambridge, and at King's there began a flow of Nonconformists, notably Quakers and Methodists. Numbers increased. There were fifteen undergraduates at King's in 1860, twenty-two in 1870, seventy-one in 1880 and ninety-four in 1888, the year of Okes' death.[24]

King's examined its own statutes, and also those practices which on closer scrutiny were revealed to be simply ancient customs with no statutory authority whatsoever. In 1862 the College drew up a revised set of statutes. New proposals were enshrined there about the Chapel and its music. Under these there were to be two chaplains, an organist, twelve lay clerks, sixteen choristers and a schoolmaster given the title Master over the Choristers. The choristers were to be 'boarded and lodged under proper supervision'. Any chorister who 'had a talent for music' was to have 'instruction in instrumental music under the Organist'. Any chorister who displayed 'a special aptitude for academical studies' might receive financial support in entering the University. And there were to be services 'daily throughout the year, unless for some cause to be approved by the Provost and Fellows'. In the recent past there had been services only during term time and during part of the long vacation. The members of the subcommittee recommended that there should be at least two full practices a week and that one service each week should be sung without organ accompaniment.

That same year, 1862, the College considered that the services in the Chapel were 'not in a satisfactory state or in one which corresponds with the outlay upon it'. The Governing Body's opinion was to be conveyed to the precentor and organist, who were to be exhorted to use 'their best endeavours to ensure the immediate improvement of the same'.[25] The men in the choir at King's were also singing in the choir at Trinity College at this time and this was felt to be a disadvantage.[26]

Even with the formal revision of the statutes, though, nothing was implemented. Nothing had been done by 1869 when a committee was appointed 'to consider what changes are necessary to ensure a satisfactory Choral Service in Chapel'. It reported that the lay clerks were 'singers of unequal proficiency, and such as have served their time in the Choir and whose voices are failing, should be able to retire on pensions, and so make room for competent successors'.[27] The College Congregation requested in February 1871 that this recommendation be carried out 'without further delay'.[28] Later that year Trinity College decided to end the sharing arrangement of lay clerks with King's. So action of some kind had to be taken. Still King's chose not fully to implement the new statutes of 1862, continuing to employ just ten lay clerks of its own, not the twelve as stated there, with only six at weekday services.[29] The College, though, did now implement one provision of the 1862 statutes, resolving in 1871 to hold an afternoon choral service daily throughout the year except during September when the Chapel was normally closed for cleaning.[30]

The revised college statutes of 1862 had provided that the choristers 'be boarded and lodged under proper supervision', but nothing had been done about that either. In 1871 Austen Leigh, now the Vice-Provost, registered his disappointment when a new Master over the Choristers was appointed in 1871 without its being explained to him that moves were being considered to try to obtain a 'higher class of choristers' through the founding of a boarding school. If this were to happen the College might wish to offer a higher stipend to 'a superior Master'.[31]

How can this inertia over the music be explained?[32]

Music in Anglican worship had been so poor everywhere for so long. Men like Okes knew nothing of music and wished to know nothing. They knew nothing of musicians either and regarded them with suspicion and distaste. John Eastes was one of the lay clerks at King's in the middle of the century. The organist once objected to the way he sang the solo part in Clarke-Whitfield's anthem *Wherewithal shall a young man cleanse his way*, and, not having the right to criticize the singers himself, he reported his views – as he was bound to do – to the Provost, who was in absolute command of all aspects of college life, the choir included. Okes summoned the singer and said to him: 'Mr Easts, or Mr Easties, or whatever you call yourself, the organist has complained to me that you do not render this anthem properly. Please reform upon it.' And the lowly lay clerk replied to the high and mighty Provost: 'Well, Dr Oaks, or Dr Oakies, or whatever you call yourself, I beg to say that my rendering of the anthem is superior to that suggested by the organist, and I shall stick to it.'[33]

The truculence of the musician's attitude is uncannily similar to that displayed by a lay clerk at Trinity College exactly two centuries earlier. This is reported in an autobiography published in 1676 by one of the singing men there called Thomas Mace. The Dean of Chapel at Trinity College admonished one of the lay clerks, Mace thought quite correctly and appropriately. He had had a solo in the anthem and had got out of time – 'Notoriously and Ridiculously Out', Mace says – and this had caused the undergraduates to laugh, 'to the Great Blemish of the Church-Service, and the Dishonour of God'. When the Dean had rebuked him 'This Bold-Confident-Dunce-Clark', as Mace calls him, put on 'a most stern Angry Countenance', and in 'a vehement Rattling Voice, even so as he made the Church Ring withall', told the Dean that he sang according to his rate of pay and 'except ye Mend my Wages, I am resolv'd Never to Sing Better whilst I live'. The 'Cholerick Dean was so fully and sufficiently Answer'd, that turning immediately away from him, without one word more, He Hasted out of the Church, but Never after found the least Fault with This Jolly Brave Clark; who was Hugg'd more then sufficiently by all the Rest of the Puny-Poor-Fellow-Clarks, for This his heroick Vindication and Wit.'[34]

Perhaps these two anecdotes do not reproduce exactly the events they purport to describe. John Eastes was very unusual indeed in having obtained a Cambridge BA degree that he had taken at Sidney Sussex College. He had also published a little book, *The Rudiments of Music*, which was advertised in 1856 as being used in the training of the choristers at King's, St John's and Trinity. He composed too. His *Musical Sketches of Many Lands*, ten songs with piano accompaniment, were advertised in *The Musical Times* in 1860. It was probably John Eastes who was the lay clerk described by a Fellow of King's as 'an adventurer, who had clambered into a degree'.[35] But these two exchanges do encapsulate the deep and abiding mutual suspicion and the simmering resentment that often existed between lay clerks and clergy – between highly educated men and men mostly with little formal education or training – and would continue to exist in many cathedrals into the twentieth century. Neither was ever unaware of the social gulf that lay between them.

REFORM AT KING'S: CHORISTERS

In the earlier years of the 1870s the fathers of the choristers worked as a builder, a trader at Newmarket, a coal merchant's clerk, a watch-maker, a tailor, a coach painter, the College Chapel Clerk and the College shoe-black, a butcher, a general labourer, a domestic servant, a millwright, a tailor. At the end of the 1870s the boys included the sons of clergymen – including the Vicar of St Andrew's, Norwich, and the Rector of St John's, Manchester – and of a surgeon of Piccadilly, and one in Newport in Essex, a GP, an inspector of schools.[36]

For in November 1875 the College agreed that, after Lady Day 1876, vacancies for choristerships be open to all candidates and those not living in Cambridge should be lodged at the College's expense.[37] The first voice trial of boys to whom boarding facilities would be offered was on 2 November 1876 when twenty-four boys were examined and three taken.[38] In the end a school was built for sixteen choristers and a Master and his family and was ready for occupation late in the autumn of 1878.[39] In the meantime a house at 5, Pemberton Terrace – beyond Trumpington Street and near The Leys School – was occupied by the few boarders, six eventually, until the school was ready. There were eleven boarders and five day boys when the new building opened in December 1878, and by 1880 all sixteen choristers were boarding.[40]

In the words of the man who became Provost in 1889, 'the conviction had gradually forced itself on the College, that the old system of

recruiting the boys from Cambridge boys of the lower classes produced
a result which was not satisfactory either musically or morally ... The
boys are drawn from a higher class than formerly, and come from all
parts of England, and they receive a classical education, at very small
cost to their parents, till their voices break, or till they are of an age to
go to a public school. Besides the musical gain to the College, something
is thus done towards restoring the advantages of a liberal education to a
class which the Founder meant to benefit, but which is apt to be left
behind in an age of unreconstructed competition.[41] The Provost meant
poor middle-class boys from educated homes. As at St Paul's, the very
poor boys from homes without any educational advantages at all were
in effect being cast aside, though the College, like St Paul's, would
probably have argued that universal free elementary state education –
through the Elementary Education Acts of 1870 and 1891 – would
assist those boys more effectively.

In 1879 the College authorized the School to accept the sons of
Cambridge graduates as day boys and in 1881 the College allowed
the School to take non-chorister boarders.[42] By the end of the century
there were about forty boys in the school; in 1898 there were sixteen
choristers, four non-chorister boarders and nineteen day boys.[43] In
1883 the College recommended that assistant masters be undergraduates of the College with a salary and remission of certain college fees
and in 1905 the teaching was being undertaken by the Master over
the Choristers and four undergraduate part-time staff, the Chaplain
and the Master's sister.[44] Undergraduates taught in the school until
1950, after which date all the staff were fully qualified graduates,
though undergraduates continued for some years after 1950 to assist
in games and the supervision of out-of-school activities.[45] One reason
for the original decision to appoint undergraduates was that they
could be more easily dismissed if they were unsatisfactory than professional teachers. But prospective ordinands – which some of them
were – would also be likely to be conscientious and might be excellent
teachers and to have a real sympathy with the aims of the school. In
1920 there were fifty-five pupils;[46] in the 1930s there were between
eighty and ninety.[47] In 1922 two probationers were introduced, who
would attend practices but not sing in the choir unless a chorister
were ill. Previously, and sometimes even under the new arrangement

when the full complement of probationers could not be maintained, a new boy would serve no probationary period at all and go straight into the choir stalls on arrival.[48] In the 1960s the number of probationers went up from four to eight.[49]

REFORM AT KING'S: CHORAL SCHOLARS

In 1872 those Fellows who had most wanted improvements in the singing of the lay clerks apparently proposed a reduction in their number from ten – six full lay clerks and the four supernumeraries who attended only on what were called 'Surplice Days', Sundays and saints' days and special occasions – to only six at all times.[50] But they had not given up. In 1873 an item appeared on the agenda for a college meeting proposing 'To permit undergraduates to sing in the Choir under Rules to be drawn up by the Provost and Officers'. The minutes record simply that the motion was lost, 'Ayes, 6, Noes 8 – and the Provost'.[51] That is to say, the Provost himself was against this suggestion.

A few days before this meeting the Provost had sat in the United Universities Club, Pall Mall, and thought hard about this particular item on the agenda. He scribbled two pages of notes, pressing his pen hard into the paper. He summarized the present position and drew attention to the abolition of the supernumeraries. Which curious experiment had failed, he agreed, and he continued: 'the choruses are found to be without sufficient body and volume of sound, and it is sought to supplement the Choir by the musical talent said to exist in certain Undergraduates of the College – who they are and how many is not mentioned. The Provost has been given to understand that the Senior Chaplain is responsible for the suggestion and supports it by his recommendations.'

The Senior Chaplain would not be present at the meeting and there is no evidence that it was he alone who was indeed responsible for the suggestion. The Provost apparently cited him so that his own robust views would seem not to be aimed directly at some of those sitting around the table who, everyone knew, were wholeheartedly for the proposal. His notes continued:

It is said that the volunteers, whoever they be, are ready to attend the practices of the Choir and that there would be no difficulty in teaching them. It is not to be expected that the Senior Chaplain should know what must be the objections to such a proposal as the above; nor, if he does, that he can have considered them, nor, if considering them, that he can properly estimate them. The opinion of the Senior Chaplain may be safely put out of court, as having no proper place in a matter which comprised educational considerations beyond his province and thought. The question before the Govg. Body involves a care for the young men as Students of the College, sent with a specified object to the University and admitted into the College for distinct purposes and into a defined position in the Society.[52]

If there were further pages of scribble they have been lost. At any rate, the tenor of the Provost's remarks at the meeting was clear. The 'defined position in the Society' to which the Provost referred was not one occupied by those who mended chairs or prepared food for the Society. That was the Provost's argument.

Who were the Fellows who were pushing for change? Oscar Browning had taught at Eton and had attempted to develop the artistic and musical taste of his pupils. He leant them pictures to hang in their rooms. He knew a great many professional musicians and every other Saturday organized concerts at which they came and played chamber music to the boys. This practice though, he realized, 'was disliked by some of my colleagues, and especially by the Head Master, who thought it effeminate and demoralizing'.[53] But the two Fellows of the College who did most to bring about the introduction of students in the choir were two brothers, the Austen Leighs, one of whom, Augustus, was to become Provost.

The Austen Leighs were great-nephews of Jane Austen. Here at the end of the nineteenth century was a struggle for middle-class English university men to sing in public. They would not sing as professionals, not as lay clerks. It might be expected that a certain number of those who would sing as choral scholars at King's would be hoping to be ordained and, as Mr Collins put it in *Pride and Prejudice*, it was possible for music to be considered 'as a very innocent diversion, and perfectly compatible with the profession of a clergyman'.[54] It was just about possible as an 'innocent diversion'. Men in Jane Austen's novels do not play musical instruments; they might occasionally sing, though they keep quiet about that. Their musical function is not to make music but to admire the musical talents of the young ladies singing and playing in private. In the later decades of the nineteenth century that was just beginning to change. The King's College Annual Report for 1938 recorded the death of Walter Ford, who had come up as a student in 1880: he was 'probably the first professional singer in this country . . . who came from the well-bred and well-educated classes'.[55] His brother became headmaster of Harrow and Dean of York.

Seven years after that initial failure the Governing Body again discussed choral scholarships and this time the two Austen Leighs found a way of overruling the Provost (now in his mid-eighties) and the clique still horrified by the prospect of the young gentlemen 'assisting' in the choir. The answer lay in what they referred to as 'private liberality'.[56] The Austen Leighs themselves offered to donate money to establish scholarships – exhibitions, as one Fellow insisted they be designated, very minor scholarships.[57] The Austen Leigh family was still making regular donations to the Choral Scholarship Fund after the First World War.[58] Even before the funding had quite been settled the scholarship was widely advertised, in local and national newspapers, in *The Musical Times* and *The Musical Standard*, and circulars were sent to other universities and theological colleges:[59]

A CHORAL SCHOLARSHIP at King's College, Cambridge, value £90 a year, for three years, will be offered for competition on March 8, 1881. Candidates must be not more than 25 years of age, and have either a BASS or TENOR voice. Besides proficiency in music, a knowledge of elementary classics and mathematics will be required.[60]

And Mr P. A. Thomas, a bass, was duly elected. Mr Thomas came from the King's School, Gloucester, and Denstone. He read Mathematics, was placed in the Third Class in both parts of the Tripos, and spent his life as a schoolmaster.[61]

In 1883 the examiners for two choral scholarships reported to the College's Educational Council that in their judgement there was no candidate of sufficient merit for election.[62] It was hardly surprising that boys were not queuing up to sing. After all, the choral scholarship scheme at New College, Oxford, in 1858 had had to be abandoned after five years because of the lack of suitably qualified candidates. In 1889 the editor of *The Musical Times* conceded that musicians may as well acknowledge the strong prejudices against music and musicians, that many sensible men and women were sure that 'devotion to the study of music is inevitably attended by a weakening of moral and physical fibre' and so 'they avoid all personal contact or association with ... these nerveless and effeminate natures', men 'destitute of any manly vigour or grit', who had never played cricket or been on a horse in their lives.[63] Such prejudices were embedded deep within English society.

In *Tom Brown's School Days*, which pictures life at an English public school in the 1830s, Tom watches a group of boys surround George Arthur, a new arrival at the school, and pummel him with questions: 'What's your name? Where do you come from? How old are you?' He thinks it best not to interfere and to let the new boy try to stand on his own feet. Until they ask him, 'Can you sing?' At which point he interrupts: 'You be hanged, Tadpole.' And Tom explains to Arthur later: 'you must answer straight up when the fellows speak to you, and don't be afraid. If you're afraid, you'll get bullied. And don't you say you can sing; and don't you ever talk about home, or your mother and sisters.'[64] Clearly, admitting you could sing was among the very worst confessions a boy could make.

By the end of the century, though, there were regularly three choral scholars in the choir at King's. From 1906 until the First World War there were four; in the 1920s – after wartime reductions – the number crept up, to four again in 1921, five in 1923, seven in 1924, eight in 1925, ten in 1927, eleven in 1929 and finally twelve in 1930. And, except during the Second War, twelve more or less it has remained ever since, supplemented with a few, normally two, volunteers.[65]

REFORM AT KING'S:
A. H. MANN, 1876–1929

Arthur Henry Mann was the youngest of five children and his father, Henry, who was born in Norwich in 1809, had been apprenticed as a woosted weaver. His forebears had all been weavers or shoemakers.

But then, just before he married in 1843, Henry set up as a music teacher. Two of his sons became choristers in the cathedral choir at Norwich under the most famous trainer of boys' voices of the day, Zechariah Buck. Arthur, who was born in 1850, became a probationer in the late 1850s and a full chorister in April 1860, soon after his father died. Buck had promised his father that he would equip his son with a musical training that would enable him to earn his living at music and he was as good as his word. Arthur became an apprentice to Buck when his voice changed. Not only did Buck make an allowance to Arthur's mother in her widowhood but he paid back in full her son's fees at the end of his apprenticeship.[66]

Buck was born in 1798 and had been taken into the cathedral choir in 1808 when the cathedral organist heard him singing in the street. He was organist from 1819 to 1877 and he died in 1879.[67] He was renowned for creating an unending succession of extraordinary solo boys, and, long after he had gone, old lay clerks would remember the grace notes, cadenzas and shakes with which the boys would embellish solo lines.[68] He trained the boys twice a day; he treated them very carefully, all like prima donnas. He remonstrated with the school headmaster against their receiving corporal punishment; he hated them to be birched. Didn't the headmaster understand? The screaming of the boys when they were beaten was no good at all for their voices. If they were hoarse he would give them cloves or gum-arabic. And if there was a specially demanding solo, the boy was equipped with a phial of port to be taken surreptitiously during the service a few minutes beforehand.[69]

In January 1864, when Master A. Mann was thirteen, he appeared as a soloist with the Bury St Edmund's (sic) Athenaeum Choral Society in a performance of *Judas Maccabaeus* and his 'delightful and judicious singing surprised the audience – especially those who were unacquainted with the precocious powers of the choristers in our cathedrals'.[70] The same month he was a soloist in a performance of *Messiah* in the Corn Hall in Fakenham and the correspondent of *The Norwich Mercury* observed that 'although applause is very unusual, and generally forbidden, at the performance of an oratorio, on this occasion the feelings of the audience frequently found vent in loud and prolonged applause. Master Mann was particularly successful, and received renewed tokens of admiration.'[71]

Buck himself was not an exceptional organist and in his last twenty years at Norwich rheumatism in his hands prevented him from playing the organ very much at all. And yet even then he did like playing the 'Dead March' from *Saul* whenever the opportunity arose and putting down his left arm across the lower keys to cause fear and trembling.[72]

This was the world in which A. H. Mann grew up. The daily regime at Norwich when he was a chorister is said to have followed this plan: 8.30 until 9.45 a.m. scales and exercises; 10.00 to 11.00 Matins; 11.00 to 12.30 schoolwork; 2.00 to 3.45 p.m. rehearsal; 4.00 to 5.00 Evensong; 5.00 to 7.00 schoolwork. In Buck's earlier years at Norwich the hour and a half after Matins had been allocated to further boys' practice.[73] In all the thirteen years another young musician spent as chorister and apprentice to Buck at Norwich, he remembered, he had had in total four weeks' holiday.[74] Buck provided Mann with the basic training in all the essential musical activities in which he was to spend his life. Mann was devoted to his teacher, and his friends noticed that even his handwriting resembled his master's.[75]

One day when Mann was still quite a junior chorister a train delayed the apprentice who had been expected to play for Evensong for the arthritic Buck. Mann volunteered: 'I think I can do it,' he told his choirmaster.[76] That was a very characteristic reaction. He possessed great resolve and determination and a strong constitution almost to the end of his life. When he was on his own in his seventies after his wife died, he went to New York to see a friend during the summer vacation.[77]

After his days at Norwich, Mann was organist at two churches in Wolverhampton and at Beverley Minster before being appointed organist at King's in 1876. Mann became a Fellow of the College of Organists in 1871. He took the B.Mus. at Oxford in 1874 and the D.Mus. at Oxford in 1882, while he was at King's. Oxford and Cambridge music degrees, including doctorates, required residence only during the few days of the exams. So a candidate would register as a member of a college on the day before the exams began – Arthur Mann matriculated at New College – and would receive accommodation there during the exams themselves. Even if the successful candidate for a doctorate in music attended the degree ceremony in person he

would not be seated with those being similarly honoured in other subjects; the doctorate in music was not in any way considered of equal
standing to other doctorates.

The statutes of 1882 at King's allowed that the position of organist –
as well as Chaplain and Master over the Choristers – could be tenable
with a fellowship. 'One day,' one of the Fellows thought, 'we may gain
a valuable resident by this provision.'[78] It was not until 1921 that
Mann was in fact made a Fellow, when he had been organist for forty-
five years.

Perhaps the Fellow was thinking of Stainer at St Paul's, or perhaps
the work of Parratt at Magdalen had come to his attention. They
were to become Fellows of Magdalen and both knights of the realm.
In fact King's had delayed making an appointment after considering
six applications and then hearing Mann and another play at King's
with Joseph Barnby, the organist at Eton, as the expert assessor. They
had summoned Langdon Colborne, who had been organist at St
Michael's, Tenbury, between 1860 and 1874, and then briefly organist at Beverley Minster and Wigan and Dorking parishes churches.[79]
The Tenbury connection must have augured well. But having met him
and heard him play they offered the post to Mann. Perhaps, even
though Colborne was almost forty, they concluded that he did not
have the authority they thought would be required to discipline the lay
clerks, nor the personal distinction that would make him a 'valuable resident'. They might have been right. Two years later he became organist
at Hereford Cathedral, where he proved himself perfectly competent
but without powers of leadership. His conducting 'lacked grip and
spirit', *The Gloucester Citizen* told its readers after a Three Choirs
Festival performance,[80] and an obiturist concluded sadly that he was
not really one of those 'who were born to wield the baton'.[81]

When Mann arrived at King's in 1876 the lay clerks were still only
one to a part on each side of the stalls at ordinary weekday services,
and they were incompetent. In the recent past one of the college chaplains had taken practices with the choir and Mann's predecessor had
simply played the organ. The men were not prepared to be told how
to do things by this twenty-six-year-old upstart. One Sunday morning in the Easter Term of 1877 Mann asked the choir, both choristers
and lay clerks, to stay behind after morning service for a practice in

the stalls. When the lay clerks discovered that they were being asked to stay not to rehearse the anthem for Evensong that afternoon but to work at parts of the morning service they had just sung, they all objected and declined to proceed.[82] The Fellows treated Mann as a menial: he couldn't walk in the Fellows' Garden, he couldn't go into the Combination Room – the senior common room – he couldn't dine in College. After an exhausting first year he asked whether he could have a summer holiday. He explained to the Governing Body that he had trained his deputy, Mr Bowman, who knew all the music to be performed in his absence. No, he was told by the Provost: 'An absence would be inconvenient.'[83] Mann was allowed to use the College Combination Room and walk in the Fellows' Garden in 1882 when he was also given dining rights for a certain number of days each term. In granting dining rights it was customary to allow the holder to entertain friends. When Mann was granted them two of the Fellows attempted to restrict these privileges to him alone.[84] It was only in 1889 that he was allowed to have a set of keys to the Chapel, this between Lady Day and Michaelmas, so that he could enter the building when it was closed to the public, though he was forbidden the use of candles or lamps by which to play the organ.[85]

When Mann arrived at King's there would have been four dozen undergraduates in residence, half of them from Eton, the rest almost all from public schools, and only a handful of Fellows in permanent residence. Among Cambridge men the College had the reputation for friendliness and informality. Until very recently, after all, the young gentlemen had shared boyhood memories of Eton. It continued to strive to create a family atmosphere, though the Provost was not at all sure that the recent admission of young men from schools other than Eton was not irretrievably damaging the character of the community.[86]

It may have seemed like a family to Fellows and undergraduates; to outsiders it must have appeared a forbidding fortress. To a young musician from Norwich, whose training had precluded him from acquiring more than a smattering of the liberal education so highly prized by that little community,[87] and perhaps not even a smattering of the social ease and grace of Etonians that nearly everyone so admired, it must emphatically have seemed like a family to which he

did not belong. Even to one who had grown up witnessing the idiosyncrasies of a nineteenth-century cathedral close, it must have
seemed dauntingly artificial, resolutely hierarchical, excessively intellectual, obsessively inward-looking, and highly self-conscious.

He was never quite accepted by all the Fellows of the College. One
former chorister returned to King's as a choral scholar in 1913 and
was astonished to find that the man of whom he had been in awe as
a chorister was regarded by some within the College, him 'and all his
works . . . with ridicule and disgust'.[88] He was too unsophisticated,
too lacking in guile, too amiable. He invariably walked through the
College with a sprightly step and displayed unfailingly good spirits.
He could not be mistaken for a don, though his stocky figure did
indeed embody a kind of authority.

Who first gave him his nickname no one could remember. But soon
after he arrived at King's, everyone, from Provost to junior chorister,
was calling him 'Daddy' Mann. He may have clipped boys round the
ear but no individual boy lived in fear and dread of him. The choristers and choral scholars and lay clerks alike would recall the intensity
and drama of the practices in the Chapel. Occasionally illness meant
singers from outside the College had to be drafted in for odd services.
They usually left the practice in a state of shock, their eyes pricking
at the ferociousness of the choirmaster's denunciations. On the back
of a chapel music list at King's for February 1921 a choral scholar
scribbled a pencil note, 'Full practice tomorrow afternoon (Thursday)
at 3.45 BY ORDER', five times underlined. 'The Chapel will not be
heated to make it comfy', underlined.[89] It was never quite comfortable at rehearsals. The boys would also remember his gesticulating
and pointing at his watch before a morning practice, with them in
turn directing his attention to the school clock, invariably several
minutes slow. Or they would remember Christmas morning with sixteen cards on the piano top, which he only noticed one by one as the
practice proceeded and opened with pantomimic surprise and glee
and genuine gratitude.[90] Some would recall as senior boys going to
his house and a little group of them trying out the solos for the week,
and at the end of the session Mrs Mann appearing – 'Precious', Dr
Mann called her – and handing out sweets.[91]

'Squattez-vous,' he would say, patting the organ bench, as a chorister arrived in the organ loft to turn the pages of a voluntary. 'Now then, you young dodger.' He would hold up a finger as they listened to the final chord of the voluntary re-echoing round the Chapel. 'Well, my boy, they may say what they like: but there's nothing like music after all.'[92]

Edward Dent thought that Mann's position in College, at least for many years, must have been like Mozart's father in Salzburg or Haydn's at the court of Prince Esterházy.[93] At times Mann himself must have wondered. He considered applying for the organist's job at St George's Chapel, Windsor, in 1882. It was not that he was dissatisfied with King's; the College had been 'wonderfully kind' to him.[94] There were simply too few opportunities in Cambridge for supplementing his income. Additionally he was organist of Jesus College in 1880–81, and between 1894 and 1922 he was on the staff of The Leys School.[95]

What effect did his lowly position have on the singing in the Chapel in his early years? In 1885 one of the chaplains, Mr Biscoe, kept going flat as he intoned prayers and collects. The Vice-Provost knew how much Dr Mann disliked voicing criticism of members of the College but he insisted that the organist include a brief comment on the difficulty this poor intonation was causing in one of his bi-annual reports to the Governing Body. When Mann had done this, though, and his report was read to the Governing Body, the Provost took great exception to it. The Provost explained the position in a letter to the Vice-Provost. The Chaplain was not in any way 'under the juris' of the organist. The organist should have communicated the problem to the Dean of Chapel and that was the end of his responsibility. The Dean might have then communicated the organist's view of this 'defect of voice' to the Chaplain, though, in the Provost's own view, this would have been inadvisable. The Provost himself (who would have readily admitted he had no ear for music at all) had failed to notice any worsening at all in the Chaplain's singing. And the Chaplain had been selected after all by the appointed members of the College who were aware of the character of his voice and, it was important to note, of the great knowledge of music he evinced at his interview. The sounding of a note or a chord before the choir entered with each of the responses might be possible remedies but only as a temporary measure, in the Provost's opinion. But if the Dean did indeed wish to raise the matter with the Chaplain and considered he ought to have the authority of the College Council before taking this step, the Provost would be willing to call a Special Meeting.[96]

Such was the rigmarole required in attempting to have an intoning priest sing in tune.

And yet Mann stayed. One of the choral scholars remembered standing outside the Gibbs' Building in the Michaelmas Term of 1921. It was on the steps of Dr Mann's staircase and he overheard Professor Richmond, the Latinist, telling the organist forty-five years after he had arrived that the College had elected him to a fellowship. There were tears in both men's eyes.[97]

There was probably little exaggeration in the Provost's assertion in his memorial address that 'no man had fewer enemies or more affectionate friends'.[98] Mann was kindly and good-natured and funny and inspired enormous affection; indeed among the boys, at least later in his career, he was beyond criticism. He was incapable of malice, one of his choristers and choral scholars was sure.

He knocked to the ground a chorister who, in turning the page during an organ voluntary, stood on the pedals without realizing it. But afterwards he apologized and put his arm round the boy and explained what had happened.[99] He may have delivered withering criticisms to his young singers, but it was clear that he regarded all those in his charge with affection. No one held anything against him.[100]

Mann was once shown a collection of photographs of his past singers at King's and he scribbled comments in the margins: 'a magnificent voice', 'a glorious singer', 'a splendid choral scholar, a splendid fellow'.[101] He was courageous and stubborn and sensible enough to remain himself. He was an extrovert but he possessed the humility and the sensitivity not always found in larger-than-life characters.[102]

The organist of St John's during Mann's later years referred to his 'radiant youthfulness'.[103] When Mann moved into College, in his seventies, he became 'the youngest and merriest of the society'. He died young, one of his obituarists said, 'as they do whom the gods love'.[104]

He was certainly an excellent musician. His attention to detail was unsleeping, to wrong notes, to poor tuning, to imprecise ensemble. In spite of the difficulties and frustrations in the earlier years he evidently made some kind of impact quite quickly. In 1883 the College's Annual Report was already noting that the improved music was drawing larger congregations into Chapel.[105] No one could ever remember him playing a wrong note.[106] A future Provost of King's never forgot the startling and inspiring impression made on him as a freshman in 1883 by the first Evensong he heard there.[107]

A considerable number of the choral scholars of 'Daddy' Mann's day had been cathedral choristers. Some of them had been choristers at King's, the first of them returning in 1887. Many were the sons of clergymen. A great many of them became clergymen themselves; one became Precentor of Norwich Cathedral, one of Durham, another of Lincoln, another of Ripon, another of Coventry. One became Dean of Gloucester, one Bishop of Zanzibar. Many became schoolmasters. Some became priests and schoolmasters. A small number became cathedral lay clerks and schoolmasters. One became organist of St Asaph Cathedral. A few became doctors or surgeons, a few businessmen. One, who had been a chorister and was elected to a choral scholarship in his third year, became a solicitor and Chapter Clerk and Receiver-General of Westminster Abbey. One became a sheep farmer in Australia and a broadcaster. One became a BBC music producer. Charles Barkla, the possessor of a most beautiful baritone voice, sang as a volunteer in 1901. He was a Methodist from Widnes in Lancashire. He had been at Liverpool University and was a graduate at Trinity College when he migrated to King's. He became Professor of Physics at King's College, London, and Professor of Natural Philosophy at Edinburgh University. He became a Fellow of the Royal Society and in 1917 won the Nobel Prize in Physics for his work on X-rays.

The only choral scholar in Mann's time who became well known as a soloist was the tenor Steuart Wilson, who went to King's in 1909 and sang for a short time in the choir but found 'Daddy' Mann's tastes too old-fashioned for him – both repertory and performing style doubtless – and gave up his scholarship.[108]

There were no forcing grounds for the choral scholars of Mann's day, not even a small number of schools producing a regular stream of singers. Most were from independent schools, but not mostly the best known.[109] During Mann's time at King's there were two choral scholars from Merchant Taylors', and two from St Paul's, though one of these withdrew after his second year. There was one each from Eton

and Shrewsbury. There was one volunteer who had been at Harrow.
There were none from Charterhouse or Winchester or Westminster.

Tom Brown's School Days was based on Rugby in the 1830s,
though it aimed to reflect prevailing conditions and attitudes still in
evidence when it was published in 1857. On the last six Saturdays of
the autumn term as described there the members of School House
would sing around a vast fire while beer was drunk and all seventy
voices joined in 'The British Grenadiers' and 'The Siege of Seringa-
patam', and sea songs and songs marking bloody battles in the
Napoleonic Wars, 'not mindful of harmony, but bent on noise'.[110]
And in *Tom Brown at Oxford*, published in 1861, the songs roared
out at a bump supper at Tom's college, St Ambrose, caused the Dean
to 'amble about in a state of nervous bewilderment'.[111]

In 1894 at a meeting of the Musical Association a music-master
looked back at nearly twenty years of teaching music in a public
school. He concluded that of the hundreds of boys who had passed
through his school not twenty of them had when they arrived any
conception of music as an art form. A cherubic-faced youngster who
had been 'brought up in a refined home and would knock down any
other boy who said he was no gentleman' would know nothing of
music except 'barrel-organ jingles'. He might be the possessor of an
angelic voice but all he could do was 'howl the latest London music
hall vulgarity in a sort of bucolic imitation of the London performer'.
It was not the music-master's duty to care for the needs of the very
few boys gifted in music but for all the boys, even the most stupid. Is
the School Musical Society only for those boys 'who have beautiful
voices, together with some knowledge of sight-reading, or is it to
embrace everybody who wants to join it?' He had no doubt at all: it
was for anyone who chooses to come, 'whether he sings like an angel
or squeals like a pig . . . We are not aiming at perfect performances'.[112]
This attitude may have been very sensible in the circumstances but
such an approach did mean that boys who were musically gifted and
did have good voices were not given the kind of early training that
would allow many of them to participate in performances of a very
high standard while they were still students.

At the end of the talk, Sedley Taylor, a writer of books on science
and music, explained that it had been his job to test the qualifications

of candidates for admission to the town and gown Cambridge University Musical Society in the 1880s and 1890s. He said that only a very small proportion of boys from famous independent schools ever sought membership of the chorus, not more than three or four per cent of the boys from those schools who came to the University. Even of those that did, very few had learned to read music; very few could begin to sight-sing. And even those who had sung in a school choir had mostly had their part drummed into them by ear. In the discussion that followed it was reported that in the 1890s the government was spending £170,000 annually on providing musical education in the elementary schools set up under the Education Act of 1870, Britain's first state-run schools. This had resulted in dozens of children in these schools being able to sing very well and sight-read easily. A teacher observed that a child in an elementary school could simply look at a song by himself, and go through it, and say, 'I like it, let's sing that one.' One educationalist thought that, in singing, these twelve- or thirteen-year-olds, about to leave school and go out into the world, humiliatingly outstripped the expensively educated eighteen-year-old boys going to university.[113]

As late as 1922 a music-master in a boys' independent school – he had been organist of Wells Cathedral and Bristol Cathedral – told teachers that their first job was to identify those boys said to be gifted at music and then to stop all that nonsense. 'When the normal healthy English boy proves to be musically gifted the smallest overdose of the food he is longing for will turn him into a monstrosity which is neither normal, nor healthy, nor English.'[114] A grandson of Felix Mendelssohn's grew up in England and was educated at Haileybury in the 1870s, a school to which a number of boys from the Choir School moved in Mann's day. Since his boyhood he thought schoolmasters had concluded that they had failed to give music its due in the past and so more recently had unfortunately paid too much attention and respect to boys with 'a very moderate capacity for music'. He thought this disastrous for the musical boy, 'who had never been harmed by being regarded as a fool by his contemporaries'. It tended to make a musical boy a nuisance in the same way as one who was ostentatiously pious.[115]

The introduction of choral scholars and a considerable number of

volunteers from among the undergraduates had certainly strengthened the singing at King's. That was the verdict at the end of the
century of the Provost Austen Leigh, who had watched the progress
since the introduction of the first choral scholar in 1881. The young
singers had succeeded in giving the services 'a more devotional and
less professional character'.[116] Unsurprisingly, given the attitudes
towards music and musicians that prevailed in English schools, there
were in total very few choral scholarships offered at the universities
at the turn of the century. At St John's College, Cambridge, there
were five choral scholars singing with four lay clerks.[117] The first election of choral scholars at St John's had been made in 1889, when four
were elected. Besides these four singing it became common early on
for supernumerary choral scholars to be appointed, receiving half the
normal stipend, and a precedent was established whereby choral students who remained in residence to continue with further courses of
study could be appointed honorary choral scholars, sometimes with
an emolument, sometimes without.[118]

At the end of the century Magdalen College, Oxford, had two or
three academical clerks singing with six or seven lay clerks. There
were no choral scholars at New College and none at Christ
Church.[119]

We know that Miles Farrow, the American choir-trainer who visited
King's in 1900, was very impressed by the boys there who were
trained 'to sing absolutely in the "head" register'. Dr Mann did not
allow 'a single "chest" tone. The refinement of tone is marvellous, the
attack, shading and articulation perfect.'[120]

Was Dr Mann taught to develop the head register in such a thor-
oughgoing manner as a chorister at Norwich under the famous
trainer of boys' voices Zechariah Buck? The general impression conveyed by Buck's choristers cannot have been of restraint. One of his
choristers remembered how Buck had wanted him to inject true
emotional feeling into a passage of recitative: 'The host of Midian
prevailed, and Israel cried unto the Lord to deliver them; and the
angel said unto Gideon, Go! in thy might and save Israel; for this day
though shalt smite the Midianites as one man.' 'Now,' said Dr Buck,
'you must commence *mezzo-forte* and linger on the word "cried", as

if you were imploring aid, and when you get to the word "Go!" (on the top G), sing it as if it were marked sforzando, breathe into the note, and give it your full power.' Imagine, he told the choristers, that you were standing on the top of St James' Hill looking out over the whole of Norwich, 'and you wanted an army assembled around to hear the commanding word. Give due emphasis to "in thy might", and when you come to "smite", sing it staccato, just as if you were going to strike off a head at one blow, and [on] "as one man" give [the words] marked force.'[121]

Buck was not always successful in stimulating a chorister's imagination. In order that a boy might sing the word 'darkness' with genuine feeling – 'Thou hast laid me in the lowest pit: in a place of darkness and in the deep' – he put him in a cupboard and locked him up. 'Now,' he shouted, 'do you know what darkness is?' 'No sir,' the little boy shouted back. 'There's a great crack in the door and I can see quite well.'[122]

But the drama and emotion Buck sought to underline in performance was quite clear. So it was too with Mann. In June 1906 he directed a performance of Elgar's *Apostles* in the Chapel, conducting 'with great emotion', as one listener reported it to the composer. He described the experience as 'extraordinary . . . incredible'. One of the singers told the composer that after this performance the singers retired to bed with the music on their lips, they dreamed of it, then awoke singing it in the morning.[123] Clearly performers and listeners expected to and did share a turbulent emotional experience.

If 'Daddy' Mann directed at a service he would stand at the end of one of the choristers' stalls. At rehearsals though the Chapel would be closed and at these Mann would stand on a conductor's platform set up with its desk between the choir stalls, clad in a voluminous silk gown. He would bellow out criticisms, of tone quality, of tuning, of inaccurate rhythms. Dickensian 'gesticulations and looks of unspeakable anguish' warned the choir to sing yet softer. He would utter loud cries, and, in moments of 'extreme provocation', bang on the desk as he urged the singers on to 'rare peaks of *fortissimo*'. Copies were certainly annotated with expression marks all over the place. There was a 'King's' way of doing everything, the choral scholar admitted. Sometimes it could be 'regrettably sentimental', like the quartet at the end of the Magnificat in Walmisley's setting in D minor, sung *pppp*, or in the solo quartet in Wesley's *Wilderness*. But sometimes it could be 'dramatic to the point of tears'.[124] It was probably a style not unlike that of the choir at Magdalen under Varley Roberts; a chaplain there, doubtless of sophisticated tastes, thought that both Mann and Varley Roberts' music-making had appealed 'especially to the devout, uncritical multitude'.[125]

Some recordings were made in 1927, which were not released, and some more in 1929, which were issued after Mann died. To twenty-first-century listeners these come as a shock. The boys do indeed sing with the head voice. But otherwise the performances have little to do with the tradition of King's singing familiar through the post-war recordings under the direction of Boris Ord and David Willcocks. They seem to belong to a lost world of Victorian melodrama, redolent perhaps of the gestures to be observed in silent movies.

Some characteristics of these few recorded performances by Mann stem from the limitations of the technology of the time. Individual voices were caught by the microphone, especially individual tenor and bass voices, but little of the famous acoustic. Because lower voices were captured better than higher ones the balance is nearly always bottom heavy, not at all as it would have been perceived in the Chapel. But other characteristics cannot be put down to any technological shortcomings. The lumbering tenors and basses – as most will judge them now – hardly begin to resemble the light, lithe, flexible voices of the choral scholars of the 1950s. Although there were only two or three lay clerks left singing earlier in the 1920s, they were the experienced singers in the choir, and it would perhaps have been surprising if the choral scholars of the time had not continued to imitate at least some aspects of their singing and maybe some of their individual mannerisms, and surprising too if these had not survived for a short time after the last lay clerk.

Such Victorian emotionalism was not listened to with equanimity even in the 1890s by an undergraduate called Edward Dent who, as a schoolboy at Eton, had been guided and inspired by the organist at Windsor, Walter Parratt. At Evensong on a Sunday in March 1897 the anthem was Mendelssohn's *Hear my prayer* in which the treble soloist 'carried out Mann's hysterical & operatic interpretations with a marvellous fidelity. Everyone thought it extraordinarily beautiful,' Dent wrote in his diary, 'which it would have been if it had not been so studiedly theatrical.'[126]

'Hysterical' too was the adjective Dent used to describe Mann's playing of Bach's F major Toccata BWV 540.[127] He once listened to him playing Mendelssohn's Organ Sonata in F Minor with much wayward rubato, 'with the usual variations from the strict tempo'.[128] It was always a little more dignified, Dent thought, if Mann had no page-turner up with him in the organ loft and so no extra pair of hands for additional manipulation of the stops for 'expressive' effect.[129] He once wrote in his diary of Mann playing Bach's D minor Toccata BWV 565 'with the mordent fantastically distorted – O Walter Parratt!'[130] Dent feared Mann's playing of Mendelssohn and Bach would lead to the composers rising from their graves to strangle him. Dent himself very nearly did this on one occasion.[131] It was Dent who made about Elgar's music the notorious and inapposite remark – the comment appeared in an authoritative German dictionary article in 1924 – that it was 'over-emotional and not entirely free from vulgarity'.[132] Which remark nevertheless, given the performing style documented on Elgar's own recordings of his music, does illuminate Dent's attitude towards performances generally considered 'old-fashioned' during Mann's later decades.

To a chorister during Mann's last years everything seemed exaggerated, everything too loud or too quiet, the rallentandos too extended.[133] Mann had a habit of hanging on to the last pedal note of a piece after he had lifted his hand from the manuals. And then that pedal note hung in the air. It was like a stage gesture held still, awaiting the trembling sobs or the tumultuous applause of an ecstatic audience.[134] A journalist spoke of Mann's 'poetic spirit and art-infused temperament'.[135] His accompaniments to the psalms 'were inclined to be luscious, with passing notes and descants', *The Times* obituary recorded, and his improvisations before the service 'were wonderful pieces of colour and modulation, without any very precise development of form'.[136]

And yet it is not a just assessment to remember him simply as a Victorian reactionary. He recovered the original instrumental parts of *Messiah* at the Foundling Hospital and consulted the Buckingham

Palace score and the score used by Handel in Dublin for the first performance and then in the Library at St Michael's College, Tenbury, and he made his own edition for a performance he directed in the Chapel in June 1894. There may have been sixty-three members in the orchestra and two hundred in the chorus and Dr Charles Wood sitting there at the grand pianoforte but, as one critic observed, the interest this performance generated was not 'merely archeological'.[137]

In the 1920s Mann knew that everyone in the University was enthusing over sixteenth-century polyphony – he knew what an enthusiast the Dean was – but he belonged to Elgar's generation. For many decades the sounds of 'early music' carried for most sensible music-lovers evocations of eccentricity, and self-consciousness, and quaintness, and daintiness. It was all a little suspicious. There was that Frenchman, Mr Dolmetsch, with his squeaky recorders and those lutes and clavichords that nobody could hear, dressed up in his velvet suit playing all this abstruse music in the concert room illuminated just by wax candles.[138] Elgar himself had always been deeply suspicious. There was a certain preciousness about an interest in early music. In fact early music always reminded Elgar of Cambridge, towards which he felt a characteristic mixture of awe and resentment, and disdain too for its textbook composers and frigid scholars. When Elgar went to Cambridge he became 'all Gibbonsy', he said, 'all Croftish, Byrdlich & foolish all over'.[139] And yet Mann had been extremely curious about Thomas Tallis's forty-part motet *Spem in alium* and in 1888 had produced his own edition of the work.

Mann did not warm to the English Hymnal, nor to plainsong.[140] But he did his best and the Dean, Eric Milner-White, was clearly so proud of the music in his chapel. How could he be gainsaid? The College's Annual Review of 1921 explained that King's was 'the first of the great English churches' to sing Byrd's *This day Christ was born* on its republication.[141] This was the first report of the music in the Chapel ever to appear in the Annual Report, and it was almost certainly at Milner-White's suggestion.

Byrd's Short Service was sung in Mann's time – as Byrd 'in D minor' – and the Second Service too. Surrounded as he was by musical young men eagerly searching out the latest music, it is perhaps not so surprising that he introduced *There is no rose of such virtue* by Arnold Bax and Gustav Holst's *Lullay my liking*, and Vaughan Williams' 'Let all the world in every corner sing' from the *Five Mystical Songs* and his setting of the Evening Canticles in C written in 1925. Herbert Howells' *A spotless rose* was published in 1919 and sung for the first time in the Chapel at Candlemas in 1920. Milner-White told the composer that the shifting time signatures had puzzled Dr Mann and he suspected that not every bar had come out quite as intended, but nevertheless the music had sounded 'exquisite'.[142] For a musician in his seventies who didn't much like modes at all, neither their use in ancient music nor in new-fangled modern works, that does show a heart-warming curiosity or at least an admirable willingness to suspend judgement.

In his paper to the Council of 1918 Milner-White had told the College that he had long considered the Chapel's Holy Week bill 'distinctly unsatisfactory'.[143] He assembled texts which Charles Wood set as a *Passion according to St Mark*, and this was given its first performance, under Dr Mann's direction, on Good Friday in 1921.[144]

So even if the style of singing at King's in the 1920s was old-fashioned, there were at least a considerable number of significant new works introduced into the repertory. Equally important liturgical innovation was not neglected either.

THE VISION OF MILNER-WHITE

There had been a 'mouldy day bug' in the Choir School at King's before the Great War – for so the boarders called the day boys – who had gone on to Marlborough College and began to write poetry. For a few months when he was fifteen and sixteen he had become a devout believer and he had written a poem called 'Expectans Expectavi':

> This sanctuary of my soul
> Unwitting I keep white and whole,
> Unlatched and lit, if Thou should'st care
> To enter or to tarry there.

> With parted lips and outstretched hands
> And listening ears Thy servant stands,
> Call Thou early, call Thou late,
> To Thy great service dedicate.

But then his religious feelings had melted away. He won a scholarship to Oxford. There was no time to take it up, though, and he became a soldier – a very good soldier. He was made a captain at the age of twenty. Within four months Charles Hamilton Sorley was dead, killed at the Battle of Loos on 13 October 1915.[145] They never found his body in the mud but they did find his kitbag. It contained several new poems. As a boy at the choristers' school with compulsory attendance at both the choral services in the chapel at King's each Sunday, singing seems to have haunted him to the end. But the singing in his ears later on was not consoling or reassuring:

> From the hills and valleys earth
> Shouts back the sound of mirth,
> Tramp of feet and lilt of song
> Ringing all the road along.
> All the music of their going,
> Ringing swinging glad song-throwing,
> Earth will echo still, when foot
> Lies numb and voice mute.
> On, marching men, on
> To the gates of death with song.
> Sow your gladness for earth's reaping,
> So you may be glad, though sleeping.
> Strew your gladness on earth's bed,
> So be merry, so be dead.

What was to be done with the pain and disillusion and indignation of the men who had returned from the war? What had the Church to offer them? This was a question that preoccupied the Dean of Chapel in 1918. Eric Milner-White had come to King's in 1903 and obtained a Double First in History; he went to Cuddesdon in 1907, and in 1912 returned to King's as chaplain. Of his own distinguished war service Milner-White never spoke. It seems that he had led stretcher-bearers over the top again and again to bring back the wounded from no-man's-land. And he had apparently taken charge of his unit at the men's request when all the officers had been killed or wounded, becoming a combatant officer – which a chaplain should never do – for which it seems he was disciplined. He was nevertheless awarded the DSO. He was elected to a fellowship at King's in March 1918 and invited to be Dean of Chapel in July at the age of thirty-four.[146] If compulsory chapel was to be retained after the war, the Dean thought – and on the whole he thought it should be – it should be administered with a light touch. After he had been appointed Dean of Chapel he was asked formally 'to consider what modifications, if any . . . are desirable for the improvement of Chapel Services'.[147] Milner-White presented the Governing Body with a ten-page document consisting not just of comments about the services but encapsulating a vision of what worship in King's might be. In the 1870s Dean Church and John Stainer at St Paul's had 'revolutionized the public worship of England', he reminded the Governing Body. More recently, he said, Westminster Cathedral had revolutionized Catholic worship. He was referring in part at least to the introduction there of swathes of sixteenth-century polyphony, including pre-Reformation English works rescued from oblivion by the Cathedral's choirmaster, R. R. Terry, a former choral scholar at King's, a Catholic convert. King's was a college chapel and religious provision for the society must never be jeopardized, all would agree with this. But the architecture of the Chapel and its musical resources and the unending stream of young men passing through the College gave it the potential to be much more. Being a private chapel, and so 'free from the ecclesiastical authority which governs even the most "live" cathedrals', it could take a lead in liturgical reform and make experiments. 'At the present moment of utter chaos, and of superb hope in Church, as in State, we have a chance which, boldly taken, might make King's one of the most important churches in the land.' Milner-White did not doubt that the College would forgive him if what he envisaged sounded to them 'nothing but a dream'.[148] Some of his proposals did indeed come to nothing. His proposal to abolish Choral Matins on Sunday morning and substitute a sequence of an abbreviated Matins service, Litany and abbreviated Holy Communion was not taken up on a regular basis. But he also made suggestions about 'occasional services' that were taken up at once: an annual memorial service for the fallen in the war – men of the College, not the University – with a setting of three sonnets by a Kingsman, Rupert Brooke, and a short service of admission for a new chorister. He also wished for a 'richer provision for the Church Seasons'. Milner-White wanted more 'colour, warmth and delight' in the services at King's. He need not burden the members of the Governing Body with all the details he had in mind. Perhaps they would allow him to use his discretion. And they did and before the year was out he had devised A Festival of Nine Lessons and Carols upon Christmas Eve. This would be outside term, of course, so there would be very few students about. But this was part of his wider plan. The carol service was to be a gift to the City of Cambridge. As he explained in the preface to the order of service, it was intended 'to symbolise and express the loving bond between the two Foundations of King Henry VI here and at Eton, the goodwill between University and Town, and peace within the whole Church of the Lord Jesus, as well as the joy and worship of us all at the coming of Christ'.

He took as his model the service that had been devised by the first Bishop of Truro, E. W. Benson. It was first used on Christmas Eve in 1880 in the wooden shed that was being used while the cathedral at Truro was being built. The service consisted of a sequence of nine lessons – as was the custom at the greatest feasts in the Middle Ages – which were read by officers of the Church from the most junior, a chorister, to the most senior, the Bishop at Truro, at King's the Provost. Between the readings were sung carols by the choir and congregational hymns. Milner-White invited a member of the Free Churches in Cambridge to read one of the lessons and the chaplain to the Mayor of Cambridge another at that first Festival of Nine Lessons and Carols in 1918. Money from the collection at the service was not to be retained just for the work of the College and the Chapel but to be shared with the Church of England Waifs and Strays Society and the Cambridge Children's Convalescent Home.[149]

The first Festival began with the carol *Up, good Christian folk and listen* sung by a quartet of voices from the organ loft, which was followed by the processional hymn 'Once in royal David's city' starting out from the west end of the antechapel, and the service climaxed in the Magnificat. Fundamental changes were made after that first service, which included the removal of the first carol and the Magnificat. The changes since then have been slight, though every change in this famous service, however slight, was seen by some as momentous. Only in 1925 were there no changes whatever from the service of the previous year.[150] The first hymn and last two congregational hymns were unchanged between 1919 and 2016.

In the 1918 service there was nothing said after the Lord's Prayer, which followed the Bidding Prayer, a composition of Milner-White's. Then in 1919 the Lord's Prayer was followed by a phrase from an ancient benediction that must have caught some in the Chapel by the throat the first time it was uttered, some of the young men who had returned from the trenches: 'God, the Son of God, vouchsafe to bless and aid us; and unto the fellowship of the citizens above may the King of Angels bring us all.' And so it was until 1928, the year of the first broadcast. But for the second broadcast a year later, Milner-White fashioned for that concluding phrase an incomparable setting. It was as if his imagination had been seized at the thought of his proclamation being given out not just into the sublime spaces of his Cambridge chapel but now, through technology, out to every corner of England and soon – as his vision years ago seems to have imagined it – to every corner of the Empire and the United States of America. And as the susurrations of the Lord's Prayer faded away into the dim candlelight, the Dean's dignified voice returned with perfectly controlled intensity: 'The Almighty God bless us with His grace: Christ give us the joys of everlasting life: and unto the fellowship of the citizens above may the King of Angels bring us all.'[151]

It was the Twenty-Fifth Sunday after Trinity, 17 November that year, 1929, the feast day of St Hugh of Lincoln. The canticles at Evensong had been sung to the setting in F minor by Alan Gray, the organist at Trinity College, and the anthem was *Vox dicentis* by E. W. Naylor, the organist at Emmanuel College. After Evensong the organist gave his usual Sunday tea party for the choral scholars even though he wasn't feeling very well. The next morning he felt much worse and by the time they were singing Evensong that evening – 'In the multitude of the sorrows that I had in my heart: thy comforts have refreshed my soul' (for it was the Eighteenth Evening of the month) – Dr Mann lay dying in the Evelyn Nursing Home. He passed away on Tuesday morning and instead of Balfour Gardiner's *Evening Hymn* at Evensong that day they substituted the Russian Kontakion for the Departed. On the following Saturday, instead of the anthem down for that day, Purcell's *Rejoice in the Lord alway*, they sang for him the Bach chorale 'O sacred head, sore wounded'. He had put this down for Evensong the previous day, but that was the day of his funeral, and choral evensong had been abandoned.

At his funeral the choir sang William Croft's Burial Sentences with Henry Purcell's setting of the words 'Thou knowest, Lord, the secrets of our hearts', written for Queen Mary's funeral in 1695 and then sung at the composer's own funeral later the same year. There was heard on the organ the 'Dead March' from Handel's *Saul*, which Dr Mann's master, Zechariah Buck, had so loved to play. And the choir sang Richard Baxter's words to the tune called Darwall's 148th:

> Ye holy angels bright,
> Who wait at God's right hand,
> Or through the realms of light
> Fly at your Lord's command,
> Assist our song,
> For else the theme too high doth seem
> For mortal tongue.[152]

Boris Ord's appointment as organist was approved by vote of the College Council on 30 November. The boys immediately noticed some changes. 'That loony Ord has been messing the Psalms about,' one chorister noted in his weekly letter home.[153] It seems likely that Mann was still having the psalms chanted in essentially a nineteenth-century way. His successor, Boris Ord, required more flexible and fluid chanting in speech rhythm demanding constant alertness. He certainly demanded changes in the pointing of the psalter.

Otherwise the services seemed to continue much as they had done during the previous half-century: Patrick in G minor, Parry in D, Travers in F, Harwood in A flat, Wood and Stanford and Lloyd and Walford Davies, and Byrd's *Bow thine ear*, Walmisley's *Not unto us*,

1. The sixteen choristers dressed in their Eton suits and top hats walking from school to Chapel in the 1960s in a crocodile, two senior boys at the back keeping order. 'It's more odd when you go down town in old clothes, jeans and things, and nobody looks at you.'

2–4. The College of St Michael's, Tenbury, was established in 1856 with funds provided by Sir Frederick Ouseley (*right*). One of the very few senior clergymen who wished the Church of England itself to assume responsibility for training its musicians was the imperious Dean of Hereford, John Merewether (*left*). He died in 1850, aged 53, before he could realize any of his plans.

5–6. Sir John Stainer (*left*) at St Paul's and Sir Walter Parratt (*right*) at St George's Chapel, Windsor, raised musical standards and enhanced the solemnity of everyday worship. In so doing they also raised the status of the organist and choirmaster and became public figures.

7. Parratt's choir at St George's Chapel, Windsor, in 1899.

8. Augustus Austen Leigh entered King's in 1859 and was Provost from 1889 until his death in 1905. His family's 'private liberality' funded the choral scholarships for several decades.

9. A. H. Mann, the director of the choir at King's for over half a century, in the 1920s. He died in office in 1929.

A CHORAL SCHOLARSHIP at King's College, Cambridge, value £90 a-year, for three years, will be offered for competition on March 8, 1881. Candidates must be not more than 25 years of age, and have either a BASS or TENOR voice. Besides proficiency in music, a knowledge of elementary classics and mathematics will be required. Further information will be given by the Senior Dean, to whom testimonials as to character and musical ability should be sent not later than February 26.

10. Advertisement for the first choral scholarship on the front page of the February 1881 issue of *The Musical Times*.

11. The choir at King's in 1884, the earliest known photograph. Fifth from the left on the back row is the first choral scholar, P. A. Thomas. Two away on his left the second, Kenneth Marshall, then his brother Walter, also a choral scholar. Next to him is an undergraduate volunteer in the choir, William Boyle, 'a splendid fellow', in Mann's description. With Mann he compiled the chant book that remained in use into Willcocks's day. The other choral scholar is A. A. Hall, in a mortar board in the middle row.

12. The much-loved 'Daddy' Mann with his choristers, probably taken in 1914.

13. Four choral scholars in 1911. *Left to right*, A. J. W. Willinck, A. R. O. Swaffield, V. H. W. Thomas and H. G. Hiller. Thomas, who played rugby for Cambridge and Wales, was killed in action in September 1916.

A Festival of Nine Lessons and Carols in King's College Chapel upon Christmas Eve 1918

ORDER OF SERVICE

❡. *This service was drawn up from sources ancient and modern by Archbishop Benson for Cathedral use, the Lessons, which tell the whole story of our Redemption, being read in order by the Cathedral ministers from chorister to Bishop. In this Chape* ...
symbolise and express the loving ...
Foundations of King Henry VI ...
goodwill between University and T ...
the whole Church of the Lord Jesu ...
worship of us all at the coming of o ...

❡. *The congregation should stand fo* ...
Carols, and also for the Sixth Lesso ...
join heartily in the singing of t ...
specially marked for that purpose.

❡. *A Collection will be made during* ...
Carols out of which grants will be ...
England Waifs and Strays Society, ...
Children's Convalescent Home at F ...

[3]

INVITATORY CAROL.

Up ! Good Christian Folk, and listen.   16th Century

Ding-dong, ding: Ding-a-dong-a-ding:
   Ding-dong, ding-dong: Ding-a-dong-ding.
    Up! good Christen
    Folk, and listen
How the merry Church bells ring,
    And from steeple
    Bid good people
Come adore the new-born King:
    Tell the story
    How from glory
God came down at Christmastide,
    Bringing gladness,
    Chasing sadness,
Show'ring blessings far and wide,
    Born of mother,
    Blest o'er other,
Ex Maria Virgine,
    In a stable
    ('Tis no fable),
Christus natus hodie.

PROCESSIONAL HYMN.

Once in Royal David's City.   19th Century

❡. *The congregation should join in for the fifth and sixth verses.*

1 ONCE in royal David's city
   Stood a lowly cattle shed,
Where a Mother laid her Baby
   In a manger for his bed:
Mary was that Mother mild,
Jesus Christ her little Child.

2 He came down to earth from heaven,
   Who is God and Lord of all,
And his shelter was a stable,
   And his cradle was a stall;
With the poor, and mean, and lowly,
Lived on earth our Saviour holy.

3 And through all his wondrous childhood
   He would honour and obey,
Love, and watch the lowly Maiden,
   In whose gentle arms he lay;
Christian children all must be
Mild, obedient, good as he.

[4]

14. The Dean of King's, Eric Milner-White, who devised the Christmas Eve service, began the first in 1918 with the singing by a solo quartet in the organ loft of the Invitatory Carol, *Up! Good Christian Folk*. 'Once in royal David's city' has begun the service since 1919, though the singing of the first verse by a solo treble has been the rule only since the Second World War.

15. A group of choral scholars in 1930 with, seated on chairs, *left to right*: E. H. Fellowes, Percy Buck, Eric Milner-White, Sylvia Townsend Warner, Boris Ord. Fellowes, Buck and Townsend Warner worked together for a decade editing Tudor church music. It was Ord's performances using their performing editions that revealed new beauties in Byrd and Gibbons and Tomkins.

16. Milner-White, happy and relaxed in the company of the choristers at the Christmas party he gave for them in 1932.

17–18. The English Singers, 1920, *left to right*: Cuthbert Kelly, Flora Mann, Clive Carey, Lillian Berger, Winifred Whelen, Steuart Wilson and a programme from one of the group's US tours. It was from listening to and watching the English Singers that Boris Ord understood how to perform Tudor church music.

STEERS & COMAN
Present

The English Singers

FLORA MANN   NORMAN STONE
NELLIE CARSON   NORMAN NOTLEY
LILLIAN BERGER   CUTHBERT KELLY
Management: METROPOLITAN MUSICAL BUREAU

Municipal Auditorium, Friday Evening, March 2, 1928

PROGRAMME

(The Numbers correspond to those in the accompanying word-book)

		No. in word-book
MOTETS		
Praise Our Lord..............*William Byrd (1543-1623)*		1
Ave verum..............*William Byrd (1543-1623)*		2
Hosanna to the Son of David...*Thomas Weelkes (1575-1623)*		3
MADRIGALS AND A BALLET		
Sing We and Chant It..........*Thomas Morley (1558-1603)*		MS
O Softly Singing Lute..........*Francis Pilkington (1562-1638)*		11
Though Amaryllis Dance......*William Byrd (1543-1623)*		12
FOLK-SONGS		
The Dark-Eyed Sailor.........*Arr. by R. Vaughan Williams (1872)*		44
The Turtle Dove................*Arr. by R. Vaughan Williams (1872)*		45
Wassail-Song ....*Arr. by R. Vaughan Williams (1872)*		46

SHORT INTERVAL

		No. in word-book
ITALIAN STREET CRIES		
Chimney Sweeps..............*Jacques du Pont (c. 1600)*		55a
Rag and Bone..................*Adriano Banchieri (c. 1568-1634)*		55b
Hot Chestnuts.................*Jacques du Pont (c. 1600)*		55c
DUETS AND TRIO		
I Spy Celia......................*Henry Purcell (1658-1695)*		56a
John, Come Kiss Me now		
(16th Century)................*Arr. by E. W. Naylor (1867)*		56b
The Three Fairies.............*Henry Purcell (1658-1695)*		56c
MADRIGALS, A CANZONET AND A BALLET		
My Bonny Lass She Smileth....*Thomas Morley (1558-1603)*		42
The Silver Swan..............*Orlando Gibbons (1583-1625)*		19
I Go Before, My Darling.......*Thomas Morley (1558-1603)*		20
My Phyllis Bids Me Pack Away..*Thomas Weelkes (1575-1623)*		21

(The Edition of the Madrigal music is by Dr. E. H. Fellowes.)
Publishers: Stainer & Bell, Ltd., c/o Ricordi, New York

For numbers on this programme inquire Music Room, Public Library

COMING

SIGRID ONEGIN, Contralto	HAROLD BAUER, Pianist
"Onegin came, was heard, and conquered." —Henry T. Finck, N. Y. Evening Post.	"Harold Bauer is a master of masters."— Chicago Herald and Examiner.
AUDITORIUM, MARCH 19	AUDITORIUM, MARCH 26
Prices, including Tax:	Prices, including Tax:
Floor $2.20 $1.65	Floor $2.20 $1.65
Dress Circle $2.20 $1.65	Dress Circle $2.20 $1.65
Balcony $1.65 $1.10 50c	Balcony $1.65 $1.10 50c

MAIL ORDERS NOW
Send check and self-addressed, stamped envelope to STEERS & COMAN, 1405 Public Service
Building (from Columbia Building), Portland, Oregon
Telephone Atwater 5814
☞ PLEASE NOTE CHANGE OF ADDRESS ☜

OVER

19. Boris Ord (*right*) and a choral scholar, Noel Kemp-Welch, in 1933. Kemp-Welch had been a boy at St Michael's, Tenbury, and after acting as Chaplain at King's he returned as Warden (or headmaster) at his old choir school.

O Lord, and Morley's *Nolo mortem peccatoris*, and Sterndale Bennett's *God is a spirit*, and Gibbons' *Hosanna to the Son of David*.

And each day the long practice in the stalls before Evensong and a hurried tea for the choir, and then robing and the short procession from the vestries in the antechapel.

And 'I will arise and go to my Father and will say unto him, Father, I have sinned against heaven and before thee, and am no more worthy to be called thy son.'

The Festival of Nine Lessons and Carols was broadcast for the second time on Christmas Eve. No director of music's name had been given in 1928 in *The Radio Times* billing and none was printed in the 1929 issue.

4

Ord and Willcocks at King's, 1929–1973

'REALLY QUITE AMAZED'

In the summer of 1933 the International Society for Musical Research held its Second Triennial Congress in Cambridge, where Edward Dent, the Society's President, was now Professor of Music and a Fellow of King's. In early manhood Dent had become an unbeliever and ferociously anti-clerical and he studiously avoided chapel. During this 1933 congress he had been obliged to listen to his college's choir on several occasions in one week. He was taken aback. The choir had consisted just of choral scholars now for five years and had been under Boris Ord's direction for not quite four. As one who never rushed to bestow unnecessary praise on his compatriots, Dent was, he had to admit, 'really quite amazed'; never in all his life had he heard 'such technical excellence of playing and singing in Cambridge before'. The performances heard during the Congress would have 'a wonderful reverberation on the Continent and in America', he was sure.[1] A delegate from *Musical Opinion* marvelled at the sureness of the intonation and the subtleties of the tonal gradations, and he used the word 'perfection' about the singing of the King's choir.[2] The conference also included a serene summer evening of madrigals on the river sung by undergraduates, men and women. One journalist heard in the balance and restraint of the madrigal singing – 'the voices never enforced, the tempi always sensible and natural' – a tradition that had remained latent 'in certain classes of English men and women since the days of Byrd and Morley'.[3]

But, as we have seen, the characteristics of the singing of these twentieth-century men and women, which seemed to speak of English 'nobility', were not the result of ancient blood lines but were new,

anti-Romantic, of a piece with a post-war distrust of high-flown rhet-
oric. They were also of a piece with the ethos of particular strands
of nineteenth- and twentieth-century English education, a distrust of
emotion and of any nuance that might carry associations of effeminacy. It was an education that encouraged clipped and incisive
articulation in singing as well as in speech.

A delegate from France attempted to analyse the phenomenon. The
University of Cambridge, Paul-Marie Masson explained to his French
readers, not only provided tuition in musical scholarship but also
encouraged compositional and executive skills that with the French
belonged exclusively in *conservatoires*. 'One is startled at the number
of people capable of reading music fluently and of holding their part
in a choir or an orchestra.' There was nothing comparable in France
to this fostering of musical talent among the young. 'Qu'il nous suf-
fise de rappeler que ce sont presque uniquement des étudiants ou des
amateurs . . .' – 'It is enough to remind ourselves that these men and
women are almost entirely students or amateurs, directed it is true by
consummate professionals, who executed ('avec quelle distinction!')
all the works performed in the course of the festival.' This festival, he
said, concerned exclusively with works of the past, revealed not just
the grandeur of the English musical heritage but the intense musical
activity of the present in England.[4]

Nearly everyone was amazed, hardly able to find the right words to
describe this new experience. Not quite everyone though. The music
critic of *The Observer* was also there. 'The singing? Just the King's
College Choir as it happens to stand at the moment, with no great
voices, and deficient in bass, but a delicate, responsive instrument
admittedly, judging strength without forcing tone, using the resonance of the building without abusing it, under Bernhard Ord's
guidance.'[5]

This critic so determined not to be impressed was A. H. Fox
Strangways. He had been born in 1859, the son of an army officer
and educated at Wellington, Oxford and then Berlin, where he spent
two years studying music at the Hochschule. He became organist and
choirmaster at the school where he was a pupil, where he also taught
German and played the oboe. At fifty he retired from schoolmaster-
ing to go to India where he wrote a book on *The Music of Hindostan*.

He then became a journalist, founding the scholarly journal *Music & Letters* in 1920. In 1933 he was in his mid-seventies, gruff, masculine, learned, open-minded,[6] and very English and, like Dent, he did not heap praise on people, especially his fellow countrymen. Besides, he knew this setting; he had taught men like these for decades. And his estimate was in one sense just: these choral scholars were not members of a rare species. There were numerous boys like this in each generation, they came and went and more came to take their places. But he was evidently not alive to the sea change that had occurred in the singing of English church music here at King's. A new style of performance was emerging, and Fox Strangways didn't really sense the significance of it all. Intelligence, quick-wittedness and a kind of devotion to the task in hand, such qualities had been required of the boys now for several decades. Choral scholars had been singing alongside lay clerks for decades too. But now there were no lay clerks at all and the choral scholars were being directed by a man with the same cast of mind, moulded by the same cultural forces.

From 1925 electrical recording, converting sound waves into electrical impulses with microphones and electronic amplification, enabled the recording of sounds from sources ranged over a wide area. It made it possible to record a cathedral choir in a cathedral. Previously recordings of a 'cathedral choir', undertaken in a dead recording studio with acoustic horns, would have been made with a handful of boys and single voices on each of the lower parts. HMV held some recording sessions at King's in 1927 but the results were never issued commercially. They recorded the choir again in July 1929, just four months before 'Daddy' Mann died, singing two of the songs by J. S. Bach in *Schemellis Gesangbuch* and these were issued in 1931. Boris Ord made no recordings in the 1930s. The recording technology of the time clearly gave only a limited impression of the singing in the Chapel. If you wished to hear the singing of the Choir of King's College, Cambridge, Ord and others in the College too thought, you should come and listen in the Chapel. The recordings of *God liveth still* with Mann directing in 1929 and with Ord in 1956 clearly belong to different worlds and provide some explanation of the shock experienced by Dent in the early 1930s. The grand ritardando at the final line of the last verse with Mann illuminates particularly Dent's comments on the Victorian swagger in his performances with the choir or as a solo organist.[7]

In 1936 King's made its first tour abroad, to Sweden, Denmark, Holland and Germany. The choir sang to capacity audiences – except that they weren't really audiences, but participants in a solemn rite, or so they felt. Everyone was startled by the irresistible beauty of the voices, the concentration, the inwardness, the intensity that seemed to increase during a concert. Local journalists commented on the clarity and transparency and purity of the sound. They admired the extraordinary delicacy of the singing and at the same time the assurance, confidence and dependability of the performers, the matchless accuracy in intonation. To talk simply in terms of accuracy, though, might be misleading, one listener thought: these performances smacked nothing of pedantry or antiquarianism, however meticulously the text might be followed; this was a living dynamic harmony. A Swedish composer, marvelling at the phenomenal precision of the performances, noticed that Boris Ord led his choir with tiny movements of his left hand – with his right he held a copy of the music. But even this the Choir seemed not to need: when the choirmaster walked away to play an organ piece, the control and unanimity of attack never faltered.[8]

Mann had been the journeyman musician, quite clearly at the beginning of his time at King's a fairly lowly member of the College, far lower than even the junior chaplain, Mr Biscoe, who could not sing in tune. Boris Ord, aged thirty-two when he was made organist, the son of a member of the College, had been elected to a research fellowship in 1923. His musical interests were wide: in 1928 he conducted a performance of Stravinsky's *The Soldier's Tale* in Cambridge and he had spent the whole of 1927 working at the Cologne Opera House. It was his enthusiasm for Mussorgsky's *Boris Godunov* that led to the nickname Boris – his baptismal name was 'Bernhard' – which eventually supplanted his Christian name.[9] Some at King's imagined that Ord had been marked out as Mann's successor when he was appointed a Fellow in 1923. Others thought that it would have been Frank Shepherdson, an organ scholar at Clare College from 1913 until 1916, who had acted as an assistant organist to Mann and had been a volunteer in the choir for a decade. He had made King's his true home, as the writer of his obituary in the College Annual Report expressed it, announcing his sudden death in 1925 at the age of thirty-eight. It was said that his loss was 'the greatest that Cambridge has suffered since the war'.[10]

Mann was a High Victorian and an extrovert. Ord was a man of the deflationary anti-rhetorical 1920s with anti-Romantic aesthetic ideals and aspirations. Ord had been a pupil of Walter Parratt, the choirmaster at Windsor who had cultivated an impersonal tone without Mann's *espressivo* phrasing and tenutos, without the sudden *crescendi* and the whispered *pianissimi*. Ord had been an organ scholar at Corpus Christi College, Cambridge, but had not been a chorister and had never directed a choir of men and boys regularly until he was appointed at King's. In 1920, though, he had established the Cambridge University Opera Society as a result of the enthusiasm kindled that year by a performance of Purcell's *Fairy Queen* in Cambridge. The members performed largely for their own amusement and the name was changed in 1924 to the Cambridge University Madrigal Society. That year the Society gave its first public performance, of Byrd's Great Service in Little St Mary's Church, and from 1928 sang annually in May Week on the river.[11] These sixteenth- and seventeenth-century works were the first he directed and he had learnt about their idiomatic performance as a student in London.

THE ENGLISH SINGERS

When Ord had returned from the First World War to resume his studies at the Royal College of Music he had played the organ at the Grosvenor Chapel in Mayfair and at St Martin-in-the-Fields, and it was there, at St Martin's, that he had met a quartet of singers who were giving Saturday afternoon concerts of early music.[12] It was not just the repertory that the English Singers sang; it was the way that they sang it that was a revelation to Boris Ord. The soprano and the contralto of the quartet had been students at the Royal Academy as violinists as well as singers, the bass had been a chorister at Lincoln's Inn Chapel and the tenor was Steuart Wilson, who had sung in the choir at King's before leaving after a few months because of Mann's old-fashioned tastes. In 1919 two more singers were added, a soprano, and a baritone called Clive Carey, who had been a chorister at King's in the 1890s and an organ scholar at Clare College before studying composition and singing at the Royal College and then with Jean de Reszke in Paris and Nice.[13] The group themselves promoted a concert in the Aeolian Hall in February 1920, a concert of madrigals, canzonets and music by Henry Purcell, as a result of which they were invited to give more concerts, including one in the National Gallery to mark the opening of an Italian Room. It was for this concert that they coined the name The English Singers.[14]

As a result of Carey meeting E. H. Fellowes in 1920 the group began singing Fellowes' editions of madrigals and church music. It was Fellowes who was the minor canon at St George's Chapel, Windsor, for half a century. He was not only a scholar and a singer. He was also a gifted violinist – at the age of seven he had played to the Hungarian virtuoso Joseph Joachim, who had offered to take him as a private pupil (instead he was sent to prep school and Winchester) – and he remained all his life an excellent chamber-music player. In other words, he was an accomplished practical musician. His editions included thirty-six volumes of madrigals, thirty-two volumes of lute songs and twenty volumes of William Byrd's music. He was on the editorial panel of the ten scholarly volumes of *Tudor Church Music* published by Oxford University Press. But he was also responsible for countless octavo leaflets in a 'Popular Edition', as Oxford University Press advertised them, 'provided with expression marks and rendered practicable for performance'.

In 1921 Fellowes proposed to the Gramophone Company that records of the madrigals he had been editing be made. The Company wished to use their own house singers, musicians used to the difficult and disconcerting conditions in a recording studio of the time. But Fellowes proposed the English Singers, still comparatively little known, and a deal was struck whereby no fee would be paid unless the Company were satisfied with the results. They were indeed satisfied, and so were the critics. 'Discus' in *The Musical Times* thought the ensemble was 'about as near perfection as is possible', and paid tribute to the women particularly and the 'purity of their tone and the ease with which they attack and sustain high notes'.[15] Fellowes himself thought that their record of Byrd's Magnificat from his Short Service was 'a revelation as to its beauty when rightly performed' and was sure that it had 'widespread influence in church-music circles'.[16]

Much of what Ord learnt from the English Singers must have been by observation and then through experiment directing his own madrigal groups. But it was from Fellowes that the English Singers grasped the principles of singing Tudor church music and many of these are enshrined in the scrupulous performing editions he published. Fellowes devised marks to indicate to the singers the rhythmic subtleties above all of this music – the energetic independence of each part – using irregular barring or accent marks and dots not with their conventional significance but to show the phrasing of each line.[17] If the edition of Gibbons' *Hosanna to the Son of David* that Mann used is compared with Fellowes' edition with which Ord replaced it, the whiff of revolution may still be caught.[18]

The English Singers were invited to visit Prague in January 1922, where the thirty-two-year-old Adrian Boult was conducting the Prague Symphony Orchestra in Elgar's Second Symphony, and then Vienna that same month where he was conducting a work by Arthur Bliss. Later that year they visited Czechoslovakia and Austria and Berlin. In 1923 three of the singers had to be replaced but the replacements were 'worked in' to the ensemble whose identity and style had become established. In 1925 they travelled in America for the first time and made their debut at the Library of Congress. By 1931 they had given nearly four hundred concerts in North America and Canada. They sang mainly madrigals, ballets and folk songs, doing much to popularize Fellowes' *English Madrigal School*, but they also included works like Byrd's *Praise our Lord*, *Ave verum corpus* and *Exsurge Domine*, Tomkins' *When David heard that Absalom was slain* and Thomas Weelkes' *Hosanna to the Son of David*. In June 1926 they gave a concert in the Chapel at King's with Boris Ord's Cambridge University Madrigal Society. Together they sang Palestrina's *Stabat Mater* and Vaughan Williams' Mass in G minor, and by themselves the English Singers sang Byrd's *Praise our Lord* and *Ave verum corpus* and Weelkes' *Hosanna to the Son of David*.[19]

Both the repertoire and the performing style were new. The American critics talked of 'the miracle of the English Singers', 'the triumphant skill, the unfaltering taste, the insight, the delicate imaginative justice of the Singers', and the Germans thought that the English Singers' repertoire represented the 'most exquisite national culture', with one critic considering their singing style 'perfection such as I have never before experienced':

> What they [the English Singers] do is done so perfectly that it looks and sounds easy. No conductor brandishes an admonitory baton before their eyes. A lifted finger, a raised eyebrow or a nod from Cuthbert Kelly – who is the basso of the sextette as well as its leader – are all the signals they have to rely upon. But in precision of attack, in exactness of rhythm, in rightness and delicacy of phrasing, in subtle control of light and shade, this group of six singers is a revelation. Their diction is so crystal clear that even in an elaborate contrapuntal passage, with possibly three sets of words being sung simultaneously, one hears, not the unintelligible muddle that proceeds from the average chorus under such circumstances, but three clear strands of poetry, separate and perfectly understandable. They are to choral music what the Flonzaley and London String Quartets are to instrumental music, for their work possesses the same fluidity and transparence, the same satisfying homogeneity that is born of the perfected blending of several congenial personalities. Hear the English Singers when you can, for until you have heard them, you have not heard part-singing.[20]

Some commentators found their success difficult to explain. They thought it odd that so many people 'fancied the archaic'. It was agreeable, they admitted, this 'ancient music prettily interpreted'. Certainly the voices of the singers were not 'sufficiently exceptional to account for their present vogue'; there were no 'phenomenal voices here'. At the Salle de la Réformation in Geneva at a concert by four of the English Singers in 1934 one critic agreed that the ensemble was 'admirablement réglé et nuancé . . . et d'une remarquable homogénéité'. The precision and disciplined ensemble might be noteworthy but he considered that there was only one voice, the bass, of any distinction: 'quel dommage qu'un seul des chanteurs ait vraiment une belle voix!' The other voices were distinctly lacklustre, dull, without any richness in the tone quality.[21] But even those who conceded that the tonal quality of the individual voices was not remarkable allowed that the singers were outstanding in the precision of ensemble, the accuracy in intonation, the clarity in diction and the blend of the voices with virtually no vibrato.

Those who seemed to enjoy their concerts most did not evaluate them according to current norms but recognized in the music-making something new and unexpected. In the London Coliseum during a concert by the English Singers in 1927 a cockney girl in the gallery turned to her neighbour: 'It ain't music,' she said, 'and it ain't singin', but ain't it 'eavenly.'[22]

THE LAST OF THE LAY CLERKS

In a report to the College Council in 1926, Eric Milner-White explained that the inexperience and immature voices of most first-year choral scholars precluded their holding a voice part by themselves on one side; it had always been necessary to pair them with a second- or third-year undergraduate or a lay clerk. There had long been an abundant supply of candidates for bass scholarships. Even though many were really baritones, not basses, they had served well enough in the choir. It had been more difficult with tenors and altos. Milner-White naturally consulted the Research Fellow in Music and reported that Mr Ord did not think it would be possible to dispense with alto and tenor lay clerks, considering the few satisfactory scholarship candidates presenting themselves with those voices. The situation was finely balanced: good lay clerks were dependable and usually stayed for a number of years, but they found it more and more difficult to secure suitable additional employment in Cambridge. If they were older their voices would probably begin to decay. The voices of choral scholars were immature and they made more mistakes than lay clerks, but their voices were fresh and they were 'as a rule ... desperately keen'. However Milner-White acknowledged that music in public schools was improving and that music-masters had 'at last awoken to the opportunities and the honour of choral scholarships', and that King's reputation at that time guaranteed that the best candidates would apply there.[23]

What was to be done? In a report on Chapel expenditure that year Milner-White had told the College that the choir at Westminster Abbey cost £8,500 to run, more than twice as much as the total cost of the maintenance of the King's Chapel Choir and the Choir School. And the choir at King's, he added, was 'both more satisfactory and more famous'.[24] When the last lay clerk died in 1928, the white-haired Mr Collins, he was replaced by one choral scholar. 'Daddy' Mann had wished for two and Milner-White reported to the Governing Body that, with the current statutory number of ten choral scholars and without any maturer voices, 'the efficiency of the choir was gravely imperilled'.[25] Dr Mann, who had long wished for undergraduate choral scholars by themselves, without any lay clerks, made a plea in the College Congregation that the official number be raised not to twelve but to fourteen choral scholars – the only time he spoke at a college meeting in the years he was a Fellow. But though in 1931 the number of choral scholars was finally fixed at a statutory maximum of twelve,[26] the importance of the two volunteers was recognized and in 1938 the two volunteers were given the same privileges regarding free board and lodging as the choral scholars.[27]

From 1929, then, Boris Ord was in command of a choir that usually consisted of sixteen boys and fourteen young men. Mann had full rehearsals with the choir twice a week. Soon after Ord was appointed, it seems, full practices were inaugurated before each weekday Evensong.[28] Evensong in the 1930s was generally sung every day during term time, with Matins additionally on Sundays. On two Sundays each term Sung Eucharist replaced Matins and there were also choral celebrations at major festivals, on Christmas Day, on All Saints' Day, on Ascension Day. Under Mann one Evensong each week had generally been unaccompanied, the canticles often being sung to chants, with a hymn used instead of an anthem. Ord preserved the practice of an unaccompanied Evensong each week but very soon habitually sang canticle settings and an anthem at this service too. He continued to use the chant book that Mann had compiled in 1884 with the help of a graduate volunteer in the choir, a collection which would continue to form the basis of the chants used at King's until 1968.[29] Choral services usually began with the commencement of Full Term in October and they continued after Michaelmas Term

ended until Christmas Day, or, if the 26 December was a Sunday,
until Matins and Evensong on Boxing Day. On Advent Sundays from
1934 there was, in addition to the usual two Sunday services, the
Advent Carol Service at 8.30 in the evening. And the choir now sang
during the Long Vacation Term in the summer: the choir would have
a holiday after the university Easter Term ended in June and then
have about two weeks off before returning to the choir stalls for
about a month, ending early in August.[30]

Numerous Georgian and Victorian composers quickly disappeared
from the chapel bills when Ord took over: the services of men like
Clarke-Whitfield and Langdon Colborne and Turle and Smart and
Stainer disappeared, though Goss in E was retained to begin with
and the five settings of the evening canticles by Alan Gray, who was
organist of Trinity College from 1893 until 1930.[31] Ord also retained
a great many settings of the evening canticles by Charles Wood, a
recent Professor of Music at Cambridge; in the academic year 1931-2
eight of them were sung. Mann had had to be encouraged by Milner-
White to include Tudor music on the chapel bills, but Ord was keen
to introduce as much sixteenth-century polyphony as possible: in his
first few months new works by Palestrina, Victoria, Peter Philips,
Adrian Batten and Robert Johnson were introduced.[32] Many new
works also soon appeared by Byrd, including *O quam gloriosum est
regnum*, *Sacerdotes Domini*, *Rorate coeli*, *Senex puerum portabat* –
both four-voice and five-voice settings – *Haec dies* a 6, *Ave verum
corpus*, *Tu es Petrus*, and *Psallite Domino*. Ord introduced the
Third Service and the Nunc Dimittis of the Great Service into
the choir's repertoire in the 1930s. The new canticle settings at the
weekly unaccompanied Evensong on Fridays were often 'faux-
bourdon' arrangements derived from Tallis, Byrd, Tomkins and
Gibbons, some of which at least were already in the repertoire. Ord
introduced the evening canticles of Thomas Caustun. Mann had used
Gibbons' Short Service, but Ord seems to have used the Second Service
for the first time at King's. Weelkes' Evening Service for Two Trebles
was first done at King's in 1933 from E. H. Fellowes' edition published in 1931, and from his correspondence about this performance
it is clear that at that date Fellowes had never heard a performance
of his edition.[33] Under Mann the choir had sung Weelkes' anthem

Hosanna to the Son of David; Ord added his *Alleluia, I heard a voice* to the choir's repertory.

Many of the works Ord introduced were unaccompanied and the independence of the unaccompanied parts meant that they were difficult to sing idiomatically, requiring vocal expertise and musical intelligence not previously much cultivated by cathedral choirs in the 1930s.

Only a little contemporary music found its way into the repertory. Ord seems to have introduced 'Rise, heart' from Vaughan Williams' *Five Mystical Songs,* and *O clap your hands,* written in 1920, and the Te Deum in G written for the enthronement of the Archbishop of Canterbury in 1928. He introduced anthems by Rachmaninov and Kalinnikov,[34] and a setting of 'A Prayer of King Henry VI' which Henry Ley, the Precentor at Eton, wrote for the Founder's Day ceremonies at both foundations. Ord continued to perform Charles Wood's *Passion according to St Mark* on Good Friday.

He introduced Tallis's *Lamentations* during Lent in 1931 and on Good Friday that year a *St Luke Passion,* the manuscript of which is at least partly in Bach's hand – though the authorship is unknown and the work is certainly not by Bach.[35] In the Lent Term in 1930 the choir sang Schütz's *Seven Words from the Cross* (1645) and on Good Friday in 1937 his *Passion according to St John* (1665), both of which the College thought had never before been sung in England.[36]

When The English Singers visited Germany in 1923, Edward Dent had written, as music critic of *The Nation and The Athenaeum,* that 'Fellowes and the English Singers have shown Germany, if they have not yet convinced England, that such beauty as this comes not from inspiration, but from scholarship. When the English Singers gave a concert in Berlin a year ago the German critics imagined that their finished and individual style of interpreting English madrigals was the fruit of centuries of carefully preserved tradition . . . Their style is the fruit not of tradition, but of scholarship, of historical erudition, supplied, as every one knows, by Dr. Fellowes, and of common sense supplied by themselves.'[37]

The singing style of King's in the 1930s, which, through Ord, owed not a little to the performances of the English Singers, was clearly not the result of a centuries-old tradition either; the style would have astonished the singers in the choir even eighty years earlier. The singers in choirs at most of the other choral foundations in the 1930s would have been surprised too. The choristers and choral scholars certainly depended on the scholarship of E. H. Fellowes when they sang music by Byrd or Weelkes. But what was the 'common sense' of these choristers and choral scholars and their director? What were the origins of the shared assumptions and understandings that moulded their singing style? Why were they so disciplined? Why did the voices blend so that passages sung in unison by men or boys sounded like one voice with all personal nuance dissolved?

EDUCATION WITH RESERVE

At least until the Second World War there would nearly always be a considerable number of choristers at any moment at King's who were the sons of clergymen, as were the choristers in that period at St Michael's, Tenbury, Magdalen, St Paul's and St George's Chapel, Windsor, too. So also with the choral scholars, some of whom would later become clergymen themselves. Some of them had been choristers, and a handful in the 1930s had been choristers at King's. Of the four scholars who came up at Michaelmas in 1929, the term that Mann died and Ord took over the choir, one had been a chorister at St Michael's, Tenbury, and one at York Minster. Three of these choral scholars became clergymen who were also schoolmasters, the fourth – the son of a clergyman – was a schoolmaster for many years at King's School, Ely.[38]

The ethos of the school at King's was not at all dissimilar from countless other Anglican boarding schools then being established, both preparatory and secondary, schools of the Woodard Foundation, Wellington College, Bradfield, St John's School, Leatherhead, Malvern, and many other schools long in existence, all affected by the reforms originating at Dr Arnold's Rugby. The pedagogical and moral temper of such schools was captured in a book published in 1857 by a young lawyer called H. Byerley Thomson, *The Choice of a Profession: A Concise Account and Comparative Review of the English Professions*. He considered that there was much to be said for education by a private tutor at home and much too for education at a public school. On the whole, though, he concluded that lasting benefits were more likely to be obtained at a boarding school than with a tutor at home. What was the purpose of an education of an English gentleman? he asked. Learning to construct a Latin verse in dactylic hexameters or to drive a ball in cricket were not ends in themselves. The aim of education was to build a man's character through training his mind and his body and giving him a moral compass. All such training was likely to be more successful through a boy living in a community at a school, he thought, and not privately with a personal tutor. Team games were only possible at a school. Learning in class provided opportunities for healthy competition. Constantly turning to a parent or a tutor for guidance prevented the development of initiative and self-reliance. Living in a community of boys of a similar age was vital preparation for entry into the world and into a profession. Public education was calculated to produce the kind of worldliness that enabled a man to read character better and to learn how to thrive in patient coexistence with others. The idiosyncrasies of family life were seen and understood in a larger context. It was vital for success in their professional lives that boys learnt how to conform. The 'compulsory uniformity and regularity of the system' characteristic of the education that public schools were providing was of inestimable value, he thought, in preparing boys for the world, or at least the world in which most of them were to spend their lives.[39]

All this was reflected in the choir school at King's. A chorister there lived a life of even greater strictness and disciplined routine than boys at most other preparatory schools. In addition to lessons and games, there was a practice for the boys after breakfast, in Mann's time another after lunch. After games the head chorister would assemble them outside the school buildings and supervise them as they walked the quarter of a mile in crocodile formation from school to chapel. Before daily Evensong in the 1890s there would be chapel practices for the full choir on Mondays and Fridays and on Thursdays for the trebles only. From the 1930s there were full practices before each weekday Evensong. On Sunday there was Matins at 10.30 a.m. and Evensong at 3.30 p.m. There were occasional services at Great St Mary's on Sunday afternoons.

Every day of a chorister's life, almost every moment, was strictly organized. To depart from the rules was to risk immediate correction. Corporal punishment was not abolished until 1959. Canings by the masters of the choristers throughout Ord's years were not infrequent. The headmaster of the school between 1912 and 1927, Charles Jelf, wished his charges to understand the importance of honesty, hard work and single-mindedness, and to grasp the moral concept of justice and to see it working in practice. Under his rule justice was rarely tempered with mercy. Discipline was severe; it was by no means uncommon for eight strokes of the cane to be given. He had no interest in or time for any of his pupils as individuals and would have been horrified at the thought that any pupil might actually like him. Bullying he seemed to regard as nothing of very great importance – it would be useful in toughening up the boy for life in the professional community he would later inhabit. It was certainly not unknown during his headship.[40] In the 1950s the headmaster, D. G. Butters, would still punish a boy leaving a morsel of food on his plate.[41]

In the 1930s there were about eighty boys in the school, half of them boarders.[42] In 1922 two probationers had come into the school in addition to the sixteen choristers.[43] Even if the boys themselves regarded the choristers as a race apart there was certainly no inclination for the masters to treat them as exceptionally tender plants or accord them special status. None of the headmasters was musical until David Briggs, himself a former chorister and choral scholar, who became headmaster in 1959.[44] Both headmasters in Ord's time had been undergraduates at King's. C. M. Fiddian in the 1930s and '40s was a classicist, who rowed for the College, captained the University ice-hockey team, boxed and canoed.[45] Butters in the 1950s was a mathematician, the first headmaster not to be a classicist.[46] Fiddian was no scholar but both his predecessors were,[47] one of whom, T. C. Weatherhead, wrote classics textbooks and had also played soccer for the Corinthians,[48] a team of university men, amateurs – though they contained a number of men who represented their country – who would deliberately miss penalties, knowing that no gentleman would commit a foul on purpose.

The men who taught the choristers at King's were teachers by vocation. They believed in the discipline of the schooling, in the order and stability of the community they led. Intellectual, physical and spiritual elements all had to be blended – the masters wished to create 'rounded' or 'balanced' individuals, they would say – and it was also important for the boys to learn patience and perseverance and steadfastness, to learn how to endure the humdrum and the dreary and the routine, to learn if possible how to invest the everyday with significance. Such qualities were certainly emphasized by Anglican clergymen and teachers. In *The Making of a Man: Letters from an Old Parson to his Sons*, published in 1934, A. V. Baillie, the Dean of St George's Chapel, Windsor, explained that 'Whatever we do matters. Moses began to teach that lesson to the Israelites by declaring that there was glory in the perfectness of the service which a man gave even in the fixing of a tent peg in relation to the Tabernacle.'[49] Or, he might have said, in the timing of said Amens, or co-ordinating the precise pauses in mid-sentence in the psalms or those final consonants. The choir after all did sing of 'The task thy wisdom hath assign'd / O let me cheerfully fulfil',[50] and of he 'Who sweeps a room as for Thy laws, / Makes that and th' action fine', of making 'drudgery divine'.[51]

Singing required strength and stamina and also a steady nerve, particularly when undertaking a difficult solo. There was certainly a characteristic emphasis on developing a modicum of physical courage, chiefly in playing games. The headmaster in the 1930s also liked to take the boys ice skating when the Fens froze over. He wished all boys to become self-reliant, to be able to swim and mend their own bicycles, and he arranged extracurricular woodwork and metalwork lessons, assisting boys to construct canoes and then take them onto the river.[52] In choir practices self-reliance meant that a singer would raise his hand when he knew he had made a mistake to indicate that he understood the error, which he would correct next time.

A large number of the choral scholars played games. Few were particularly gifted sportsmen, though some of them were. H. W. Thomas, who went up in 1909, was a good cricketer but exceptional at rugby, and he played not only for the University but as an international for Wales.[53] Marcus Dods went to King's in 1936 and won a blue for rugby in 1938 and played against Oxford again in 1940.[54] But though the boys were encouraged to play games 'with vigour and enthusiasm', as an inspectors' report put it, it was clear that they were discouraged 'from making games a fetish'.[55] One of the best rugby players in Cambridge in the 1930s – he was to become a clergyman and the most distinguished church historian of his day – explained that he liked to play hooker because there in the scrum 'you can do your good anonymously, with no sense of display'; he did not wish to tear about on the field where people could watch him 'doing noble things and all that'.[56]

If not many of the choristers nor many of the choral scholars were outstanding athletes, they all valued the conformity, precision and teamwork that were encouraged and fostered in this society. 'Athleticism' in the choir was team spirit that emphasized the importance of watching the choral scholar beater on the other side of the stalls and timing the consonants and paying unstinting attention to tuning and immaculate blending. The musicians at King's were receiving or had received an education that was tough, austere, spartan. But at least in the 1930s, during Ord's first decade, the choristers' confidence was continually enhanced and their spirits invigorated by the presence in their lives of the Dean.

Eric Milner-White was rarely at ease in adult company. Some attributed his shy, nervous insecurity to the death of his mother when he was six years old and then the deaths in childhood of his two younger brothers from diphtheria.[57] Yet with children Milner-White was completely himself and it was his smiles and his encouragements that the boys remembered. His own kind deeds and charitable acts seemed to suggest that consideration for others was liberating and life-enhancing, that Christianity – at least the kind of Christianity that he practised – was 'no mere control of conduct', as the Dean of Windsor of the time told his sons, 'but a romantic quest after virtue'.[58] Milner-White was particularly good with boys who felt they were misunderstood or who behaved badly according to the lights of this driven, regimented, conformist society. Besides seeing the boys in divinity lessons he would visit the school on Sunday evenings and take them for walks or play cricket or just talk.

During every August between 1921 and 1939 he organized camps at Batcombe in Somerset for all confirmed choristers, ex-choristers, choral scholars and undergraduates at King's intending to be ordained.

The beautiful camping site was owned by a family that had provided King's with two choristers. There were morning and evening prayers, hymn-singing round the camp fire in the evenings and expeditions to Bath and Wells and to churches in the area and to the coast and to Longleat House. For some of the choristers this was a highlight of the year and the community spirit fostered at the summer camp seemed to pervade life back at school in the autumn term.[59] One boy who had been at the school for just a few months before the war went on to become Archbishop of Canterbury; he had a photograph of Milner-White on his wall when he died.[60]

What personal qualities were singled out in the King's College annual reports in their obituaries for these generations of students, many of them dying in the two world wars? Simplicity, straight-forwardness, fearlessness, modesty, reliability are words that keep cropping up: 'direct, resolute, and unassuming'.[61] The life of a soldier 'proved thoroughly congenial to him'.[62] 'In his reserve there was no hauteur and in his silences there was no censoriousness.'[63] Of one who had a very brilliant career both as athlete and academically, he 'appeared wholly unconscious of being in any way a celebrity'.[64]

Even if these boys and young men were marked out by their confidence and assurance, it was reticence above all that characterized their behaviour and their singing style. Milner-White prayed that God should:

> weaken, humble, and annihilate in me
> self-will, self-righteousness, self-satisfaction,
> self-sufficiency, self-assertion, vainglory.[65]

And he prayed that he should be delivered:

> from all imposition of my own fads and interests
>   upon my acquaintance;
> from burdening and boring others with
>   my own anxieties and ailments;
> from self-justification, self-excusing, and complacency . . .[66]

The Archbishop of York explained in the Preface to *The English Psalter* published in 1925 that the language found in the psalms – 'Let them be confounded and put to shame that seek after my soul', 'My soul is athirst for God, yea, even for the living God' – 'is pitched in too heroic a key for individual use, except at certain rare moments of crisis'. But such language could be used in church because it articulated the voice of the community, not of individuals. 'We desire that the main, broad meaning of each Psalm shall roll itself out in smooth rhythmic flow, as the voice of an abiding Community, rehearsing over and over again in unflagging patience, in uninterrupted persistence, the story of an experience that everlastingly and enduringly repeats its tireless refrain.'[67]

Hubert Parry wrote that, 'Culture and progress alike deprecate aggressive individual prominence',[68] and Charles Graves, his first biographer, tells us that it was his 'self-imposed reticence' that distinguished his life and character. His influence on several generations of musicians was profound, especially during his years as director of the Royal College of Music, where his students included Boris Ord. Graves speaks of his 'eminently sane outlook, his English distaste for all that was extravagant, flamboyant or exotic'.[69] He was not himself an orthodox Christian – though he was once called by such a believer 'a man after God's own heart'[70] – but he recognized that the ideal of 'the religious-minded' was the effacement of self and this was an ideal which he himself cherished.[71]

Such sensibilities derived from the heart of the Oxford Movement. John Keble thought that the Roman Catholic Church taught that you must be '"inebriated" with the love of God' whereas the chief characteristic of the English Church was 'sobriety'.[72] In his famous lectures, he explained that it was 'the function of Poetry to facilitate, yet without prejudice to modest reserve, the expression of glowing emotion'.[73] Religion and poetry were akin, he said, because each is marked by a pure reserve, a kind of modesty or reverence. 'Beauty is shy, is not like a man rushing out in front of a crowd.'[74]

One of the Tracts for the Times was entitled 'On Reserve in Communicating Religious Knowledge' and it referred to 'that reserve, or retiring delicacy, which exists naturally in a good man'.[75] Of course, it wasn't quite natural, even for the sons of English clergymen of the time. As Madeley Richardson at Southwark said, the 'one idea [of the average boy] is to make as much noise as possible, and in this, unfortunately, he is as a rule only too successful.'[76] But reticence could be learnt. It could be cultivated.

When Herbert Howells was asked whether he was conscious when composing for the Church that he was writing 'in a certain tradition of reserve', he responded that he 'almost rejoiced' in being unable to banish his awareness of this tradition.[77] In the work of a quintessentially English poet (and Howells' favourite), Walter de la Mare – who was himself a choirboy under the reforming John Stainer at St Paul's in the 1880s – W. H. Auden perceived at its heart a sense of wonder, awe and reverence, which represented 'the most favourable soil in which goodness can grow'. From this sense of wonder, according to Auden, could be learnt:

> a style of behaviour and speech which is no less precious in art than in life; for want of a better word we call it good manners or breeding, though it has little to do with ancestry, school or income. To be well-bred means to have respect for the solitude of others, whether they be mere acquaintances, or, and this is much more difficult, persons we love; to be ill-bred is to importune attention and intimacy, to come too close, to ask indiscreet questions and make indiscreet revelations, to lecture, to bore.[78]

This suppression of individuality accorded with the formality of manner, of tone of voice and of physical gesture that these singers had grown up with, reticence that acted as a kind of filter allowing emotion to be communicated purged of any taint of sentimentality or exhibitionism.

And there they stood, all quite still as they sang, half hidden by the choir stalls, each line sure and steady with not a trace of vibrato.

'OMINOUS AUTHORITY'

In the 1930s Ord would usually play for the psalms and for accompanied anthems, though by 1939 at least he would usually leave the voluntary to the organ scholar. He would direct the choir with very small movements of the hand (as that Swedish composer noted in 1936), sometimes with just the index finger of his right hand, standing at a desk at the end of the choristers' stall on decani. There was never any sense of showmanship in his reserved and economical directions.

And yet he was a formidable presence. In procession, one undergraduate remembered from the early 1950s, 'he moved with ominous authority', and in unaccompanied services he 'exhaled a chain-smoker's bass, pumping with his left hand to control the tempo and glowering horribly in the candlelight'.[79] George Guest remembered 'the magnetism of his eyes',[80] but David Willcocks recalled that he would often keep his head down, eyes fixed on the music in a manner never recommended by orthodox choir-trainers.[81] The threat of a stare was enough to fix the concentration on that index finger.[82] He had 'a gravelly, rasping voice'[83] and would pluck a tuning fork only to hum a note of indeterminate pitch to an anxious treble about to begin 'Once in royal David's city'.

He was not easy to deal with either: 'We have been having considerable difficulty in procuring timings for the above programme from Boris Ord . . .', reads an internal BBC memo from 1939, 'and I feel that the programme is now too long to be broadcast in full.'[84] In 1950 after Ord had repeatedly failed to sign ten contracts and return them to the BBC, one of them dating back three years, a BBC official was assigned to travel to Cambridge and call on him personally at King's and extract the required signatures.[85] In May 1953 a bursar at King's wrote to the BBC: 'I am afraid that it is quite useless to rely on Boris Ord to pass anything on to me as he is extremely busy and such things get often forgotten.'[86]

Ord could be notoriously unpunctual and chronically disorganized. He claimed to have learnt everything for the acoustics paper in the Mus.B. examination the night before the exam.[87] But his work with the choir was very carefully planned and practice schedules were meticulously drawn up so that not a minute was wasted. He would invariably be standing there in the Chapel ready to begin a 4.15 p.m. practice at 4.14 p.m. No choral scholar could ever contemplate being a second late for a practice.[88]

His authority seems to have been questioned only very occasionally, in the late 1940s, when some of the choral scholars were older, in their mid or late twenties, having served in the forces during the war. In 1946 a choral scholar who was twenty-six and a Fellow of the Royal College of Organists (FRCO), goaded by repeated criticisms, slammed his music down on Boris Ord's desk and stormed out of a practice. A party organized to effect a reconciliation ended up with them throwing hymn books at each other.[89] But such behaviour was not at all characteristic. Generally Ord was obeyed without demur.

He could be aggressive and sarcastic to boys and men alike, and rude too to the women in the Cambridge University Madrigal Society and the Cambridge University Musical Society chorus: 'Contraltos, you have about as much vitality as a slug in the bottom of the Cam.'[90] After a stormy practice in chapel and then a tense service the choral scholars would be leaving silently and rather sheepishly only for their director to catch them up and immediately begin asking whether it should be red or white wine after Wood in E flat and usher them into his rooms for a convivial gathering.[91] In chapel he would treat every-one as a professional musician, outside he would treat the choral scholars as his friends. He was in fact both tyrant and a friend to his choral scholars and there was evident affection on both sides. Behind his back, even those in awe of him would sometimes imitate the frog-like noises he made when he sang.[92] He was certainly famous for his parties, whether thrown for other Fellows of the College or for junior members. A colleague on high table remembered him for his 'abun-dant geniality' and his 'quick sense of humour'. And if he inspired fear among members of the choir as well as affection, it was 'whole-some fear', in the interests of the highest musical standards, the Fellow was certain.[93]

The boys, though, hardly ever saw this gentle, avuncular side. Chor-isters who joined the choir during the war were taught first by Harold Darke, who was deputizing for Ord while he was away in the RAF. Dickie Darke, they called him, 'a marvellous old man . . . *incredibly old*', one of them remembered – he was in his mid-fifties – 'very kind and very considerate . . . everybody loved him'. And then Boris Ord came back. This same chorister found Ord cruel and unkind. The fear he inspired was not altogether 'wholesome'. He took 'a sadistic delight in choristers making mistakes'. This boy could not think that any of the choristers of that time liked him.[94] He would show disappointment when things went badly but no enthusiasm or gratitude when they went well, as he expected they always should. David Willcocks himself was frightened of Ord before the war, though their relationship had altered when he returned, in his mid-twenties, a decorated soldier, when he was treated as a colleague and addressed by his Christian name. Willcocks himself could never understand why a man with such natural authority had to be so strict with the boys. Did it owe something to his German ancestry? he wondered.

When Willcocks won his organ scholarship, Ernest Bullock, his old choirmaster at Westminster Abbey, hoped that it was all right him going to King's. He admonished him to be careful. 'You've got to watch out, you know.' Willcocks assured him that he would indeed, not at all knowing what he was supposed to be watching out for. Only later did he learn of Ord's homosexuality, about which the whole of the musical profession seemed to know, he soon realized.[95] Rumours of Ord's homosexuality and scandals that attached to it were certainly still gossiped about in the College in the 1970s.[96] Willcocks was told that Ord had appeared in court two or three years before he went up on a charge of importuning a teenager in Bristol. He had been cleared of the charge and though some at King's considered he should leave the College the Provost insisted he stay.[97]

Boris Ord seems to have had no deep emotional attachment of any kind. Perhaps he suffered from what the novelist E. M. Forster, who had been made an Honorary Fellow at King's and lived in college at King's from January 1946, called the 'undeveloped heart'. This was the affliction from which many of those suffered, he thought, who had experienced an English public-school education and had been taught to control or stifle their emotions. They went forth from their public schools 'with well-developed bodies, fairly developed minds, and undeveloped hearts . . . An undeveloped heart – not a cold one. The difference is important.'[98]

Ord and Forster lived at a time when the tensions of living as a homosexual in England, as an outlaw, could be unbearable. In 1931, not two years after Ord was appointed organist, a brilliant mathematician entered the College, and four years later, at the age of twenty-two, he was appointed a Fellow. He completed a doctorate at Princeton University, but then returned to Cambridge. This was Alan Turing, a codebreaker at Bletchley Park during the war and essentially the inventor of the digital computer. Turing was convicted of 'gross indecency' in 1952 – for private homosexual relations – and then chemically castrated. He killed himself in 1954.[99]

There was no hint of any impropriety by Ord with any member of the choir. But perhaps his harsh treatment of the fair choristers of King's – and no indication of any wish to ingratiate himself with them – was indicative of a struggle to deny his deepest inclinations. The meticulously high standards he insisted upon certainly inspired some of the choir-trainers of the next generation. His cold and aggressive manner may also have been adopted by some of them, perhaps sometimes unconsciously, and may have contributed to the fierceness of the training that continued in some of the choral foundations for many years afterwards.

AN UNATTAINABLE IDEAL

It was broadcasting during Ord's years that really made the music of King's famous. The Festival of Nine Lessons and Carols became an institution. For the *Telegraph*, by 1938, it was the 'much loved Festival of Nine Lessons and Carols'. *The Manchester Guardian*'s radio reviewer had come 'to await its recurring beauty so eagerly that to miss it would be a positive loss, which can be said of few broadcasts indeed'.[100] It had quickly become potent and so beautiful and mysterious that myths could easily be woven around it. In 1939 the service, now in its twenty-first year, was relayed to France and Italy. The BBC provided French radio with an announcement: 'On a toujours célébré ce festival depuis la fondation, il y a cinq cents ans, de la Chapelle . . .'[101] 'This Festival of Nine Lessons and Carols has been celebrated ever since the foundation of the Chapel five hundred years ago . . .'

During the war more broadcasts were made from King's; a shortened form of Evensong lasting half an hour was regularly broadcast each week for several weeks at a time. For security reasons the transmission was from 'a College Chapel', yet cathedral musicians could work it out and it became an open secret among the natives. This happened on Tuesdays throughout the Michaelmas Term of 1941, for example, from 14 October until 16 December, and during that November and December there were also six broadcast organ recitals, each lasting thirty-five minutes.[102] It happened in the Easter Term of 1942 when again a shortened form of Evensong was transmitted on Tuesdays from 5 May until 9 June.[103] It happened in the Lent Term of 1945 on Tuesdays from 16 January to 13 March.[104] In 1946 King's also allowed the BBC to record a number of 'antiphons', anthems, for use 'on appropriate occasions' in the new Third Programme of the BBC. These were to be used as 'interludes' or 'fillers' in unexpected spaces between programmes.[105]

In 1946, as well as the carol service on Christmas Eve, Evensong was broadcast on Christmas Day. In March 1947 the choristers of King's sang in a broadcast with the Cambridge University Madrigal Society. During May, June and July, Evensong came from King's over eight consecutive weeks. In August the choir took part in a relay from the Cambridge Festival of Seventeenth-Century Music and Drama. In July, November and December, King's broadcast programmes in a series on English cathedral music.[106]

At the same time, broadcasting had found many cathedral choirs out. In 1937 the Head of Religious Broadcasting wrote in an internal memo:

> Cathedral singing is, admittedly, at a low ebb, and many experts hold that, so long as a choir is compelled to sing two full choral services on every day of the week, little improvement is to be expected. The present standard may be tolerable when worshippers have the atmosphere and the aesthetic help of a beautiful building, but the microphone mercilessly shows up its defects.

Cathedral musicians were fully aware that the microphone had begun to 'overhear' every mistake, as Walford Davies at Windsor put it in 1932, and not just every mistake, but 'the very thoughts behind the mistake', the innermost attitudes of the musicians towards the mistakes. It was 'a relentless truth-teller'. He was sure that this was a good thing, because a choir could only stand up to the microphone after 'untiring team-practice and the most devoted self-effacement'. Was music in churches and cathedrals less important than chamber music, or concerts of orchestral music? Had church musicians nothing momentous to say? Why should performances by choirs be presented with less accuracy and clarity and vitality? He spoke, he said, as one 'more continuously dissatisfied with his own efforts' than 'with any others'.[107]

At York Minster, where the celebrated Sir Edward Bairstow had been in charge of the music since 1913, there had been mutterings of dissatisfaction over the standards of singing in the mid-1930s. York broadcast Evensong weekly at this time, every Tuesday to the North Region. The North Regional staff formally requested an assessment and the BBC's Director of Music and three members of the BBC's Central Music Advisory Panel listened to one of the broadcasts. They were horrified by what they considered the atrocious standard of performance, referring particularly to the mutilation of a Te Deum by Charles Wood – it 'would have been a disgrace to a small village choir. I cannot think that Sir Edward Bairstow realizes how bad [it] is.'[108] Sir Walford Davies, the BBC's consultant on church music, was also asked to listen, and agreed in general terms with the criticisms.

The Dean of York requested that Dr Fellowes pay a visit and then give his considered opinion. Bairstow 'expressed himself warmly in favour of a visit from Dr Fellowes, declaring himself quite unwilling [sic] to accept any criticism Dr Fellowes might make'. Dr Fellowes accordingly went, as invited, and, 'while not agreeing with the previous rather wholesale condemnation, was not, speaking in confidence, entirely happy with what he heard'.[109]

Cathedral singing was not in fact at a low ebb: the tide had been far out for as long as anyone could remember. But there was a new choir singing cathedral music in a new way and everyone could hear it. In 1938 *The Times* could state that the services of the King's College Choir represented 'the aim, if not always the achievement, of cathedrals and collegiate churches, to say nothing of many parish churches, throughout the length and breadth of this country'.[110] The article was printed without attribution and it might indeed be Eric Milner-White who wrote it. Nevertheless it was not a controversial statement.

David Willcocks seems to have been in the habit of mercilessly reminding his singers at Worcester during his years there that 'Worcester's best day is equal to Cambridge's worst'. By 'Cambridge' he certainly meant King's.[111] And he was surely referring to the total effect of the

Worcester choir disfigured by the ragged ensemble and poor blend of the lay clerks – for even one lay clerk could mar blend and ensemble – rather than the trebles, whom competent critics remember as being outstandingly good under Willcocks and quite the equal of his later boys at King's.[112] At King's, Willcocks would sometimes admonish a choral scholar at a rehearsal: 'Mr X, you are making a noise like a lay clerk.'[113]

The Dean at Gloucester in the 1950s remembered how he had been disciplined at King's as a chorister and choral scholar to watch across unstintingly and time consonants precisely with the other side; he shuddered to see cathedral lay clerks with their eyes glued to their books or squatting with their heads in their hands, and he detested the ragged and indecisive singing that was the inevitable result.[114]

In another BBC internal memo, from November 1955, one of the music staff had informed the Home Service Music Organiser that, in his opinion, there were only a handful of cathedrals in the country that were worth broadcasting and not a single cathedral or 'minster' choir in Scotland or the North of England. And he repeated the refrain: he was sure that performing standards in most of the 'greater churches' were 'very mediocre indeed – a low ebb in the history of choral training and a most lamentable state of affairs'.[115] It was simply that in recent times the music-making had been subjected to the closer scrutiny of the microphone.

The explanation for the distinction and distinctiveness of King's was not far to seek. The sixteen boys and fourteen men were there at all the services, weekdays and weekends. Most of the cathedral choirs had now increased the number of boys since the middle of the previous century. In 1837, Worcester, Ely, York and Gloucester all had eight choristers. In 1913 each of them had twenty. Durham, which had had ten in 1837, also had twenty in 1913. Winchester had had eight in 1837; three-quarters of a century later there were eighteen choristers and four probationers.[116] But by no means all cathedrals had boarding schools for their choristers in the 1930s. The national reputation of the choir at King's meant that boys applied from all over England. There were always a few boys from Cambridge. In the 1930s and 1940s they came from Trumpington and Girton and from Storey's Way, not half a mile away on the western outskirts of the city. One came from the Master's Lodge at Corpus Christi College, one minute away from the Chapel. But boys also came from Chichester, from Swanage in Dorset, Swanton Morley in Norfolk, Billericay in Essex, Crediton in Devon, Sevenoaks in Kent, Cromwell Road in London SW7, Llanelly in Monmouthshire. There were boys' families also living in Zomba in Nyasaland – now Malawi – in Jerusalem and Cairo and Khartoum.[117]

If most of the cathedral choirs had increased the number of the boys, very few had fourteen lay clerks or even the twelve men stipulated as the absolute minimum by S. S. Wesley in 1849 and by the cathedral organists' resolution in the 1884–5 report of the Cathedral Commissioners. In 1934 Gloucester had only six lay clerks and not the nine they should have had, and of the six, four were aged between sixty and seventy – there was no retiring age at Gloucester nor any pension scheme – and it would have been impossible to perform, say, a Byrd Mass with these singers, the precentor was sure.[118] Salisbury in the 1930s still had six lay clerks,[119] Lichfield had nine lay clerks,[120] Hereford had nine, and this was reduced to six in 1945 in order to increase the salaries of the remaining singers.[121]

There remained an enduring notion that men who sang in church and cathedral choirs in England in the twentieth century were all old. In an arithmetic textbook for primary schools published in 1938 there was a section on averages; one question the children had to work on ran as follows: 'In a church choir are some men, aged 73 yrs. 6 mths., 72 yrs. 9 mths., 81 yrs. 3 mths., 78 yrs. 4 mths., and 79 yrs. 2 mths. What is the average age of these men?'[122] This was not realistic. Not all the men in church or cathedral choirs in the earlier decades of the twentieth century were old; it was not uncommon for advertisements for lay clerks to stipulate that applicants should be under thirty. But there was an element of truth behind it. There was Fred Naylor, after all, who sang at Peterborough Cathedral and then went to St George's Chapel, Windsor, where he remained in the choir singing alto until he retired in 1957 at the age of eighty-four.[123] At Worcester in the 1950s the senior bass lay clerk had lost his top notes and another, younger, bass in the choir would take over in mid-phrase during a solo, just for the top notes. The senior lay clerk handed over part of his salary for these top notes.[124]

Very few lay clerks in cathedrals had had a university education. Many had not had much general education at all; many had not had any kind of higher musical education. In the 1920s at Salisbury the lay clerks had additional employment as a watchmaker, a cabinet-maker, the owner of a garage, a traveller for a mineral-water firm and an employee of the Inland Revenue.[125]

At Magdalen between the world wars, applicants for lay clerkships were otherwise elementary school teachers or private music teachers. One applicant was a mechanical engineer, several were office clerks, one worked in the music trade, one in a printer's office, one in an engineering factory, one was a part-time clerk in a gas company. Some had attended training colleges but a number had received very little secondary education.[126]

At Canterbury in the 1950s the senior lay clerk was a part-time telephone operator; of the two teachers, one with a sympathetic head-master had a staff appointment, the other filled in when he could and was paid by the hour; another worked in the chapter office; another was an insurance agent; one was studying for a science degree. At another unnamed cathedral one who had sung in the choir as man and boy for thirty-eight years worked as an upholsterer; one had deputized for a music teacher on active service during the war but had then qualified as an accountant; one had done a variety of jobs, as an assistant in a hospital canteen, then an ironmonger's assistant, and later he helped in the cathedral choir school. One worked as a partner in a printing business, one as a cost clerk in a firm manufac-turing machinery. One taught music privately and also in two schools; another was a physical-training instructor at the cathedral school.[127] In the 1950s at Durham a few of the lay clerks worked for the Chap-ter, one as a painter and glazier, one in the Cathedral Library, one in the finance section of the chapter office. One worked as a hairdresser, one as a handyman at Hatfield College, one had no other employ-ment (but had once been a blacksmith, it was said), two were teachers at the choristers' school, one qualified, one unqualified, one ran an upholstery business.[128]

King's sang fewer services than some of the other choirs in the 1930s. At St Paul's in the 1930s they were singing both Matins and Evensong six times a week, and so were Lichfield and Wells, twelve services in all.[129] In the 1930s King's were singing eight services a week, Evensong every day and Matins on Sunday, although in the 1930s the choir did not start singing in the autumn until Full Term began in the second week of October.[130] And yet King's had much more rehearsal time than any cathedral. At most cathedrals between the wars there was one full rehearsal each week and at some two. In the 1920s at Salisbury there was one which the Gentlemen of the Choir attended 'with great reluctance' and they failed to attend at all if a deputy and not Dr Alcock was taking the practice.[131] At Southwell there were no extended full practices, and when rehearsals were introduced in 1946 some of the lay clerks left.[132]

A leader in *The Times*, in March 1956, commenting on a dispute between the lay clerks of Canterbury Cathedral and the Dean and Chapter, was supportive of the lay clerks' role, if not their financial claims. The writer seemed to see them as quaint components of an eccentric and amusing English tradition: 'the fruity, unique race of altos; the steadfast tenors; the almost legendary basses on whom the resounding title "Thunderguts" is bestowed *ex officio* in every English choir that ever was, and who as they chant antiphonally seem to be living embodiments of what the psalmist meant when he sang "One deep calleth another." It is a noble race . . .'[133] It was as if nothing had changed since the 1870s in Lincoln and there was hearty, bewhiskered Barraclough, the senior choirman, with his stationer's shop near the Exchequer Gate, and his 'harsh and over-emphatic' singing, and the anthem being announced not by a minor canon but by one of the lay clerks, in a manner which suggested that 'a little surprise had been arranged for the congregation'.[134] In August 1954 the Precentor at Westminster Abbey had written to *The Daily Telegraph* suggesting that students at the theological colleges in Durham, Ely, Lincoln, Salisbury and Wells could be given choral scholarships to sing in the cathedral choirs. He pointed out that the choir at King's College, Cambridge, 'one of the finest we possess', had 'for some years' relied on undergraduates for the lower parts.[135]

The principal difficulties facing the cathedral choirs were not new ones, but the same entrenched old difficulties and derived in almost all instances from the quality of the lay clerks. A very few singers in cathedral choirs were the possessors of beautiful voices and exceptionally sensitive musicians. Nearly all were loyal and conscientious and loved music and deeply respected cathedral traditions, yet had little musical training and mediocre voices. In all the provincial cathedrals the lay clerks remained essentially amateur musicians. They were directed mostly by very gifted and distinguished musicians who spent their lives coaxing the best they could from very slender resources.

The reforms of the nineteenth century had given professional recognition to organists – or at least a few of them – but the social position of the musicians who sang in choirs had hardly changed. Milner-White was extremely shy and reserved and socially ill at ease except within the narrow confines of such a community as the senior common room at King's. While he was able to relax with the choristers it was only with some difficulty that he managed to form easy friendships with the choral scholars at King's. But with the lay clerks at York, the songmen of the Minster, he did not speak, and appeared to turn away from them if they tried to talk to him.[136] Perhaps this was in part his overpowering shyness. But it also seemed to highlight the social gulf that had long prevented the dignitaries of the Church of England from engaging more closely with its music and musicians.

THE BOY SOPRANO

If it was recognized that the boy's voice was the essence of the English cathedral style, all cathedral musicians in the middle of the century also agreed, more or less, on the kind of treble voice they aimed to cultivate. There are no commercial recordings of solo boys at King's from the 1930s and 1940s, but there are glimpses in amateur recordings made off-air of a treble called Richard Podger, whom Boris Ord himself described in a letter to the BBC as 'one of the best soloists I have ever had at King's'.[137] This chorister and the boys with the first verse in 'Once in royal David's city' on the commercial recordings made in 1949 and 1954 all sing with the straight and steady tone held to be idiomatic by English cathedral choirmasters of the time.[138]

There was one quite uncharacteristic treble who emerged at King's in the 1950s, however, with an individual timbre and a distinctive vibrato. This was Richard White, who was a chorister from January 1953 until July 1957.[139] White's solo voice can be heard on a commercial disc of Evensong in Stanford's Magnificat in G. The way in which his voice suffused the treble line can be heard in the anthem, Patrick Hadley's *My beloved spake*, and this is especially clear in the antiphonal singing of the psalms.[140] White himself had had no special training and he had thought during his earlier years at King's that he was accurately imitating the senior boys. He knew of Ernest Lough, the treble who made some famous recordings in the later 1920s, but couldn't recollect having listened to them. The tenor Robert Tear, who was a choral scholar at King's during Boris Ord's last months, did remember that Lough's voice 'was being played on the radio all the time' in the earlier 1950s.[141]

Why did Boris Ord allow Richard White to develop this individual tone? It was certainly very beautiful and the boy clearly very musical. White's time in the choir coincided with the years during which Boris Ord was beginning to suffer from a degenerative disease of some kind. Perhaps it was the illness, perhaps age, perhaps a hint of sentimentality that had earlier never been seen, that led to him encouraging this boy more than he usually did – not that White himself was aware of much encouragement from Ord. He thought, on occasion, when he had sung Mendelssohn's *Hear my prayer* or 'Ye now are sorrowful' from Brahms' *German Requiem*, that Ord was visibly moved. But he was never sure. Certainly no fuss was ever made of his singing – although he did receive the 'odd anonymous letter' complaining that his voice 'was spoiling the traditional sound of the King's choir'.[142]

Ernest Lough, whose recordings Richard White might have heard, sang in the Choir of the Temple Church in London. He became the only English chorister who for decades was known by name all over the world, and yet he sang with a distinct vibrato, against the conventional wisdom of English cathedral musicians of the time. His most famous recording, of the solo passages in Mendelssohn's *Hear my prayer*, was made in March 1927 by the Gramophone Company when Lough was fifteen and a half. During the first six months sales exceeded 300,000 copies, and eventually the original masters were so badly worn that early in 1928 the Company decided to re-record the work. Within three years the two versions of the second section,

'O for the wings of a dove', had sold more than 700,000 copies. In January 1963 Ernest Lough and the Temple organist and choir director Thalben-Ball were awarded a gold disc; this was the first 'classsical single' in the history of the Company to sell more than a million copies. It has never been out of the catalogue of available recordings and it has continued to reappear on various CD compilations. In 2005 its sales were estimated at 'well over six million'.[143] The editor of *The Gramophone* magazine, the novelist Compton Mackenzie, was sure that he had never heard as beautiful a boy's voice as this. Here was 'an authentic piece of England'; this was a classic recording, and with it Ernest Lough joined the company of immortals, along with Caruso. 'The glory of a boy's voice is so brief,' the editor reminded his readers, 'hardly less fugacious, indeed, than spring flowers.'[144] Another critic in the same issue of the magazine could only report that much had already been said about this boy at the Temple Church, inform prospective purchasers that the piece had had to be cut to fit onto the record and that 'Master Lough's solo work evidently aims at being (to say the least) highly emotional.'[145]

The organist of Chichester Cathedral in 1928 didn't much like another record on which Lough and another boy sang with two of the men at the Temple Church: it was too 'precious'.[146] The ease and accuracy with which Lough took high notes made most women sopranos sound clumsy, but he threatened to join them in 'that curse of modern singing, the perpetual wobble'.[147] Sir Sydney Nicholson remarked in 1944 that he himself did not care to hear a treble sing Mendelssohn's *Hear my prayer* at all. It was intended for a woman to sing and was likely to sound affected sung by a boy. 'No healthy choirboy really longs for "the wings of a dove"; he much prefers the wings of an aeroplane!' Boys should never sing dramatic or highly emotional or sentimental music.[148] A talented treble may be able to imitate one style as easily as another, though, and not necessarily be aware of emotional or sentimental nuances or connotations that the sounds hold for adults.

Certainly Lough's records created an audience and a market for more recordings of boy sopranos, as the advertisements described them. Leslie Day was plucked out of the comparative obscurity of

St Barnabas, Hackney, and was introduced to London Pavilion audiences, who clamoured nightly for encores. He began to have 'great success in the music halls', it was reported, and he broadcast and became quite well known. One music critic thought that he seemed to have 'a very good voice and a strong sense of style', but that he had acquired 'a slight tendency to force his voice in modern fashion' and that there were 'some hints of certain bad tricks', without being more explicit.[149] 'Quite apart from the choice and appropriateness of songs', another critic thought – he meant the inappropriateness of 'I hear you calling me' or 'Love's old sweet song' – this was not singing: it was 'a perversion' of it.[150] Cathedral organists would be likely to purse their lips at the term 'boy soprano'.

Thalben-Ball himself had not been a chorister. He had been a prodigiously gifted pianist and organist and he had learnt about teaching boys to sing at the Temple Church from Walford Davies, to whom he had acted as assistant from 1919 until 1923, when he succeeded him. Walford Davies was Welsh and the son of Nonconformists, and his own choristers were not the most restrained of Anglican trebles. This was one reason why they recorded as well as they did on 1930s technology when he was at St George's Chapel, Windsor.

The likeliest explanation for Lough's singing style, or part explanation, was that he heard a broadcast or a gramophone record and imitated what he took to be the most appropriate style. His recording of Schubert's 'Hark, hark, the lark' ('Horch! Horch! Die Lerch', D889) is not at all dissimilar in style to one made by Elsie Suddaby, a well-known soprano of the day, one who was taught by Edward Bairstow, the organist at York, who, unlike most cathedral organists of his day, considered there to be no difference between the singing of boys and of women.[151]

The forcefulness and the vibrato that were cultivated by the choristers at York are apparent in recordings of the choir in 1927.[152] Why was blend not quite so important with Bairstow as with other cathedral choirmasters? In 1940 he complained that in the past four years he had not had a single first-class solo boy. He thought that a 'solo boy must be absolutely without fear, and self-reliant'. He blamed the parents, who were treating boys 'with too much care and solicitude'.

'Boys treated like this don't get very far in this world.' They needed
to develop courage to sing solos. 'I don't like quiet boys ... I like
them to be noisy boys.'[153] In March 1945 he told his pupil Francis
Jackson, a former chorister himself, that the boys were 'a disappoint-
ing and stupid lot at present. Yesterday at speech day I had a good
whack at the parents.'[154] Bairstow certainly liked to play up to his
blunt-talking no-nonsense reputation; 'the rudest man in Yorkshire'
was a phrase bandied about.[155] He was the son not of Anglicans but,
in his words, of 'ardently Wesleyan Methodists', who became for a
time members of the Salvation Army. He admired their 'intense sin-
cerity' and half admired his father's intolerance.[156] Musically most
English cathedral organists saw themselves as far removed as it
was possible to be from the kind of expressivity cultivated by Nonconformists. Bairstow received an old-fashioned apprenticeship as an
organist and was not educated at a university as the new men of his
generation were. He failed in an attempt to become organist at New
College, Oxford. When he was shortlisted for the organist's post at
Ely Cathedral the Dean asked him whether he knew anyone at Cambridge, Cambridge being so close. Bairstow immediately said that if a
man was a good Christian and efficient in his job it didn't matter
whether he knew people at Cambridge or whether he didn't.[157] He
was not appointed. He could clearly be prickly and suspicious, in
musical expressivity direct and forceful, and he wouldn't naturally
identify with any refinements in performing style that seemed to
emanate from Cambridge or Oxford. He certainly encouraged the
emergence of 'solo boys' until he died, in office, in 1946. He was succeeded by Francis Jackson and for a time York continued to have a
succession of 'solo boys', one of whom was Beverley Jones, singing
solos in 1954.[158]

Bairstow had died eight years earlier, so Jones can never have been
taught by him at all. But then all choirmasters agree that choristers
learn chiefly by a kind of osmosis. At York, trebles cultivating
vibrato with individual timbres seem to have continued for several
years after Bairstow had gone. In a recording of his *Blessed Virgin's
cradle song* made in 1959 there is still one distinctive dominating
voice, not quite blending with the others.[159] But then they seem to
have fallen away. Bairstow's successor, Francis Jackson, regretted

that such soloists had simply died out, but he could not explain it. The chief reason perhaps was that he was not at all forceful and bullying like his predecessor but a most gentle encourager of the choristers.

Although post-war singers have testified to the enduring influence of Ernest Lough's recordings,[160] most trebles of the later decades would not have wanted to adopt the characteristic qualities of his singing, and particularly not the vibrato. Fifty-five years after he had first recorded 'O for the wings of a dove' with Ernest Lough, Thalben-Ball, still directing the choir at the Temple Church, made another recording. The treble in 1982, Michael Ginn, seemed to owe more to choristers at King's – but not Richard White – than to his illustrious predecessor at the Temple.[161]

'THE WHITE RADIANCE OF ETERNITY'[162]

David Willcocks was born in Cornwall in 1919, the youngest of the three sons of a bank manager. His musical talents were first spotted by a visiting piano tuner who discovered that he had perfect pitch. The piano in the Willcockses' home was more an indication of conventional respectability than a sign of musical aspiration or accomplishment. Neither of Willcocks' parents was particularly musical and though his father sang in the church choir he could not read music, nor could either of his elder brothers.

The only musician his mother could think of for a consultation was Sir Walford Davies, later Master of the King's Music, whose weekly talks she heard on the wireless. So the six-year-old little boy was taken up to London for an audition. He was given some ear tests, and played a piece by Bach (he thought) and asked if he enjoyed it. Sir Walford then played over a short phrase and asked him if could hear God speaking to him. Though he could not, he said he thought he could, to please his mother. Walford Davies told her that he should audition for a place in the choir at Westminster Abbey in two years' time and that he would write to Ernest Bullock, the organist there, to tell him about her son. In the meantime he should continue with piano lessons and start a stringed instrument.[163] Three years later at the age of nine, having passed his audition with Dr Bullock, Willcocks was put on a train and sent from Cornwall to sing in Westminster Abbey. Lying in bed during that first night away at school he listened to Big Ben strike every quarter of an hour through his tears. But after that, it seems, most of the time he was exceptionally happy.[164]

Before he left home he had been educated by his mother, a strong-willed and dominant personality.[165] She was the daughter of a country parson and strict and severe with children. She had not been given a thorough formal education herself but had absorbed much from her father and her large family; she was one of seven sisters and two brothers. She taught David to read and write and to do arithmetic and if the letters he was required to write contained grammatical errors or were untidy he was required to rewrite the whole exercise. She herself was tidy and organized; her grandchildren remembered how the sweets she gave them were wrapped up with cellophane on the outside and then silver paper with a greaseproof paper backing. Children were required to put the cellophane paper in the bin; they must unpeel the greaseproof paper and then place the silver paper – which she was collecting – in a special container. This was a procedure very characteristic of David Willcocks, one of his children thought. His mother ensured that any traces of the Cornish accent her three sons might be acquiring from their father were obliterated.[166] David's received pronunciation seemed to have been tinged with the parsonical voices that surrounded him at the Abbey or perhaps from his grandfather too and all those aunts.

But if he was a malleable and generally obedient little boy he was not without spirit. He was nearly thrown out of the Abbey choir when he was caught smoking. Summoned before the Dean of the Abbey all he could say for himself was that he thought it not just that Matron had found his cigarettes because she had been going through his pockets without his permission. The headmaster tended to agree with this and he escaped expulsion on condition of assurances of good behaviour.[167]

The story displays an abiding characteristic: that Willcocks could keep his nerve and think clearly under pressure. He claimed not to have had a very good voice as a treble but he was clearly outstandingly musical and a natural leader; he remembered eagerly conducting a little group of boys in the dormitory.[168] When his voice changed early and he had a year at school without chorister's duties, Dr Bullock assured him that this time could be well spent on his piano and organ studies. He watched the services from the organ loft and was allowed to play the chord for an unaccompanied anthem, and later a hymn at Matins when there was no congregation present; on at least one occasion he played the voluntary at the end of a service.[169]

After Westminster Abbey, Willcocks won a music scholarship to Clifton College in Bristol (which Ord had also attended), at that time one of the few public schools offering such scholarships. Here he was taught music by Douglas Fox, who had himself attended Clifton and had been a prodigiously gifted organist and pianist. Fox had won a scholarship to the Royal College of Music and then in 1912 he went to Keble College, Oxford, as organ scholar. But in 1917 on active service Fox was badly wounded and his right arm below the elbow had had to be amputated. He was a notoriously exacting teacher and his pupils could be frightened of him but also, because of the importance and intensity he invested in music-making, mortified at their own failure to attain the high standards they knew he expected. He could never be bamboozled about the amount of practice a particular pupil had given a piece since the previous lesson. In a score-reading or sight-reading exercise he would never let the slightest error pass, insisting on an exact note value or the precise notated layout of a particular chord even if a performance had seemed fluent and plausible enough. Under his guidance Willcocks passed the fellowship exam of the Royal College of Organists and he played Beethoven's Fourth Piano Concerto with a local scratch orchestra and won a cup for his performance of Ravel's *Jeux d'eau*.[170]

But Willcocks did engage in other activities as a schoolboy: he represented the school as a cross-country runner and as a scout he went exploring caves in the Mendips.[171] In old age he could still recite the Scout's Law:

> Trusty, loyal, helpful,
> Brotherly, courteous, kind,
> Obedient, smiling, thrifty,
> Pure as the rustling wind.[172]

After school he spent a year at the School of English Church Music where he passed the ARCM exam in piano performance and the newly devised Archbishop of Canterbury's Diploma in Church Music, which included papers on the Book of Common Prayer, hymnody, plainsong and its accompaniment, and on the history of church and organ music.[173] A university entrant could hardly have been more comprehensively qualified in church music than Willcocks was.

In December 1938 he became the third holder of the Organ Studentship at King's, established in memory of A. H. Mann, which he held from 1939 to 1940 and 1945 to 1947. At his organ scholarship tests in Cambridge he was required to take a short practice with the choir in the Chapel. He had never heard Tallis's *If ye love me* sung so beautifully and as it drew to a close he realized that he had no idea what he could say to the singers. So he complimented them on a good performance. Could anyone suggest how they might improve their singing? he asked them. Immediately several boys' hands went up, and one or two choral scholars also ventured some thoughts. Nearly all these were points requiring attention, Willcocks agreed. Try again, he directed, watching out for these. And the choir gave a second expert performance, just as good as the first. 'Did you notice an improvement?' Willcocks asked. Rather to his surprise, they had noticed one. Still having no comments to make himself he told them that now, for the final performance, they were going to sing it transposed up a semitone into F sharp major to try to make the tuning even more secure. For he knew that singing in keys with a multitude of sharps or flats mysteriously does help choirs sing in tune. Afterwards he was congratulated by the Provost, who was observing the applicants being put through their paces: 'You seemed to involve the whole choir in the practice.'

When he was asked at the scholarship exam which work by Bach he wished to play he gave the names of half a dozen large-scale preludes and fugues and, the examiners having chosen, he played that one from memory.[174] When still a student he conducted the Cambridge Philharmonic Society, the town chorus and orchestra, in the St Matthew Passion, and he did that too from memory.[175] His cool head never seemed to fail him. Boris Ord once said that even very good musicians had a tendency to hurry just a little when things got very difficult, when the page got very black. But listen to David play, he said. When all gets really horribly tricky, he 'just slightly steadies himself'.[176] Willcocks was a supremely competent organ scholar; he took the three-year course for the Mus.B. in one year and got Firsts in both sets of exams.[177]

In 1940 he was called up and became an excellent soldier who was awarded the Military Cross for his bravery during a battle near the village of Fontaine Étoupefour in Normandy in July 1944. After the war he returned to fulfil Cambridge residence requirements, taking a joint history and economics degree, in which he also got a First. The College then gave him a four-year research fellowship, a singular honour for a performing musician and evidence of the confidence they had in his intellectual abilities in addition to his skill as a college organist. He spent one day in the library thinking about the life and times and compositions of the seventeenth-century composer John Blow. But then came a letter from the Precentor of Salisbury Cathedral inviting him to be organist there. Willcocks himself imagined that the precentor, who had been a canon at York, had consulted Eric Milner-White, now Dean there, as well as Boris Ord. After three years at Salisbury Willcocks was invited to become organist at Worcester, where he was in charge of the music between 1950 and 1957. And then he was invited back to King's, as he was also invited to become Director of the Royal College of Music seventeen years later. He never applied for a post in his life.

What qualities inspired such confidence? Willcocks was certainly ambitious. His older brothers noticed how competitive he was in everything as a small boy, in running races on the beach, in spelling games in the family. He remained able to give his undivided attention to the task in hand throughout his life, whether playing a Bach fugue or directing fellow choristers in the dormitory, or conducting the Bach Choir, or in playing grandmother's footsteps with his grandchildren.

He was dependable and well organized. He wrote excellent letters to Boris Ord after his election to the organ scholarship, thanking him for explaining the duties of the choir, enquiring about sending his belongings to Cambridge, telling him of his musical progress. In each letter he would add a charming touch: he hoped that the choir treat they had been preparing for had been a success – he'd noticed the weather had been good that day.[178] On another occasion he told Ord that at a recent reunion of old boys of their school he had met a Fellow of King's whom Ord would doubtless know.[179]

The BBC had found it difficult to communicate at all with Ord. Willcocks always responded to them punctually and his letters were invariably clear, detailed, accommodating, considerate. On one occasion the BBC had generously allocated nine hours of rehearsal time in preparation for a broadcast from Worcester. But the orchestra concerned knew this work and might get stale with so much rehearsal. So Willcocks suggested the rehearsal be shortened. Could there be a slight reorganization of a rehearsal schedule so that the choristers need not hang about unnecessarily?[180] When fourteen of the sixteen boys were in bed with flu he wrote that he had planned a service for men's voices if the BBC would prefer that to holding a service elsewhere at this short notice or playing a recording.[181] Alec Vidler knew when he came to King's as Dean in 1956 that organists were said to be temperamental and difficult, but Willcocks could not have been 'more uniformly or consistently easy to work with'.[182]

By 1955 Boris Ord was beginning to be afflicted by what was described by a college historian as 'disseminated sclerosis',[183] and in 1957 Willcocks was requested by the College to return, to assist Ord as organist, and to succeed him when he retired. In the event, the symptoms of Ord's illness advanced rapidly and he was given leave of absence for the Lent and Easter Terms of 1958 and formally retired in May that year at the age of sixty. Willcocks played the organ in the Michaelmas Term 1957 – and so played for the Christmas Eve service that year – and was in overall charge of the music from January 1958.[184]

The number of services at King's had been reduced during the war. The two Sunday services were retained but otherwise Evensong was sung only on Tuesday, Thursday and Saturday. This arrangement was retained after the war until an additional Evensong sung by boys' voices alone was introduced in May 1946. Choral evensong was not resumed every day until the Michaelmas Term of 1950, when one was sung by men alone, one by boy's voices and one was unaccompanied. And so it remained until the Michaelmas Term of 1958, David Willcocks' third term in charge of the choir, when Evensong for boys alone was abolished, one Evening Prayer each week, usually on Monday, being said.

Willcocks said that he owed everything to his predecessor. In an obvious sense he did owe him a great deal: similarities between the recorded performances of the two directors are clearly evident. Just as striking, though, are the differences. They can be felt immediately when the home-made recording of Ord directing the song from *Schemellis Gesangbuch* in 1956 is contrasted with the commercial recording of it Willcocks made three years later, which is steadier and lighter and less emphatic.[185]

Boris Ord was passionate about opera. Opera performance must necessarily leave many details to chance; co-ordinating the singing and the movement of soloists, chorus and orchestra cannot be planned in advance in quite the same way as the antiphonal declamation of verses in the singing of psalms, or the precise timing of consonants on a beat's rest in an anthem. Boris Ord was insistent about accurate tuning and meticulous about details in the score and about ensemble. He wished nonetheless to give any performance sweep and intensity; he valued above all spontaneity and the illusion of improvisation. The precise directions Ord gave during a rehearsal might or might not be reproduced during the actual performance. Willcocks left nothing to chance and the hand movements he gave during a practice would be reproduced exactly in the service following. Boris Ord was not averse to giving the lay clerks free rein on occasion. Willcocks kept both choristers and choral scholars constantly on a very tight rein indeed.

The singing of King's under Boris Ord certainly conveyed a sense of calm and discipline and of timeless contemplation. But Willcocks' performances were characterized even more by their control; listeners intimately familiar with the singing style described them as less 'emotional' than Ord's.[186] There was even more precision, even closer attention to detail, to the timing of consonants, to the explosive attack on initial vowels. Willcocks would sometimes mutter the beat under his breath and emphasize the weak beats to keep the rhythm absolutely taut – 'one, TWO, three, FOUR' – and yet when he did this the result never felt lopsided or contrived. A phrase would be shaped with *crescendi* and *diminuendi* under Ord, which were almost completely missing under Willcocks.[187]

A chord under Willcocks' direction would be held at an absolutely level dynamic, with no attempt to inject into it some expressive nuance or shading. Ord's choir shaped the phrase 'I *sing* of a *mai*–den' in Patrick Hadley's setting; Willcocks' choir would sing the words with the very slightest lilt, with only the smallest emphasis on the stressed words.[188]

The Chapel is, in Willcocks own words, 'a wonderful acoustical environment'. A very quiet sound is audible throughout the building. This certainly enriches and colours the sounds but also muddies and blurs them. Willcocks thought that generally speaking the dynamic range should extend from *ppp* to *forte* rather than from *piano* to *fff*. Because the acoustic prolongs and exaggerates, clarity and precision must be a constant concern. It is possible, though, a composer for the choir noticed, for details of all kinds to emerge in King's Chapel that do not do so in some other large resonant spaces, perhaps because of its simple rectangular shape. Sometimes, Willcocks remembered, the choir could 'ride over the full organ'.[189]

Willcocks ran his choirs like an army battalion and his orders were obeyed without question, as he expected them to be. He was meticulous about tuning, obsessive some thought. He would stop and say: 'That note isn't actually flat, but it *might* be flat!'[190] One choral scholar said that it felt as though you ceased to be an individual person, a personality in your own right. You were a cog in a wheel, he said. It suited anyone in the 1960s coming from a boys' independent school. You never had any doubt as to what you had to do. Willcocks was always very clear and explicit. And you didn't forget it if you failed to meet his demands.[191]

To choral scholars Willcocks' barbs could be as cutting as those of his teacher at Clifton. He could make the legs of strapping undergraduates turn to jelly and their throats go dry. He once left the playing for Evensong to the organ scholar and simply observed the choir from the organ loft. He saw two first-year undergraduates not paying constant attention to the choral scholar who was indicating the rhythmic flow of the psalms on the other side of the stalls. After the service he strode into the choral scholars' vestry and addressed them all: 'If you do not watch, you are not worth a place in this great choir.' He let that hang in the air, then turned on his heel.[192] He once enquired kindly of a choral scholar how things were going:

'Fine, David, I'm just beginning to sing out.'

'Oh, yes . . . *Don't*'.

'There's a nasty noise coming from somewhere over here,' Willcocks might say, pointing steadily and precisely at a particular bass.[193] After he had been in charge of the choir for a year his organ scholar reported that, so far, he had not reduced any of the choral scholars to tears.[194]

Why then, in spite of such acid comments, did he inspire both awe and affection in most undergraduates? His musical gifts never ceased to amaze everybody: the accuracy of his ear, the speed with which he could identify slips, his party trick of playing the piano with his hands behind his back. In middle age he could still beat undergraduates hollow at squash. He was a wiry figure, alert, his head held high. He invariably walked quickly. His courage as a soldier was the stuff of legend. About his acts of bravery you knew little but there was no need to know. He spoke and moved and directed operations like a general. Yet to singers it did not feel as if he was giving instructions so much as making music with them, engaged in a common endeavour, listening minutely and reacting instantly, with a finger or an eye, to what he heard going on. And although he was so tough and demanding, although he could become furious if he ever thought standards were not being maintained, men and boys knew that he asked of nobody more than he asked of himself.

He had an unforgettable glint in his bright eyes and he retained a boyish sweetness of disposition. (He had proposed to his wife by a telegram on her birthday.) He was capable of spontaneous gestures that the choristers never forgot. If he arrived a few moments late – which he very rarely did – and the boys were still playing football he might join in. Of course he was wonderfully fast and skilful and strong. He seemed as good at football as he was at music.[195] There was a rule at Salisbury that a single yawn at early morning practice was acceptable. Two yawns, though, and you had to put your head under a tap of cold water. The rule applied to choirmaster and choristers alike.[196] So a yawn by Willcocks at early morning practice – and the prospect of his receiving a soaking – would invariably seize the attention of everyone, and suddenly, from head chorister to youngest probationer, the boys were all concentrating like mad. His choristers would have laid down their lives for him, an organ pupil of Willcocks concluded, watching him with the boys at Worcester.[197] He was '*magic*', one of them at King's said.[198] Every day, there in that extraordinary space at King's, this man would work with them to create such beauty as they had never imagined, let alone imagined possible from themselves.

The singing under Willcocks' direction was always felt to have tremendous authority: it was always 'immensely accomplished',[199] everything this choir did was 'characterised by technical and artistic assurance'.[200] The singers' 'good diction, intelligent phrasing [and] limpid tone' were always admired.[201] The sheer beauty of the singing was never denied, nor the radiance of the tone and the purity of the intonation.[202] The sweetness of the trebles' voices was frequently compared to the tone of boys in foreign choirs such as the famous Thomanerchor, which was found 'grating and harsh'.[203]

In the 1960s some thought that the choir's 'pure tone and quiet intensity seem perfectly suited' for the singing of Byrd's masses but that the 'sweet, flute-like boys' tone of English cathedral tradition' that King's exemplified was not appropriate for forthright eighteenth-century music like Handel's four Coronation Anthems.[204] One critic simply thought the tone-production of the King's boys 'monotonous'.[205] One reviewer of a King's disc of hymns was reminded of a line he had seen quoted recently in a newspaper article: 'Good Taste is not enough: we must have Communication'. These hymns were all beautifully sung and carefully accompanied, he agreed, but they lacked conviction.[206] A leading opera critic was irritated by the adulation of the King's trebles: 'there is nothing milder in the universe than the sound of a traditional Anglican choirboy, and when these cherubs sing phrases in Bach's St John Passion like "Away with him!" in rapid tempo, the hearer's mental vision is rather of Purcellian fairies than of a bloodthirsty rabble.'[207] One scholar and composer regretted that the choir sang consistently with an 'objective detachment', whether the sixteenth-century music was by English, Flemish, Italian or Spanish composers, or whether the text was reflective and tranquil – *Iustorum animae* – or an anguished plea for mercy – *Ave verum corpus*.[208]

Willcocks certainly thought that a choir had a vocal identity, like a singer, and that it would be 'fussy and pernickety' to expect a choir to vary the tone-quality it produced.[209] Nevertheless, even under his disciplined control, recordings confirm that the style evolved. When the choir recorded Byrd's motet *Ave verum corpus* in 1964, five years after Willcocks' first recording, there were slight but readily identifiable changes.[210] Long notes, instead of being held absolutely steady, now tended to intensify, and the dynamic range had increased a little. How could these changes be accounted for? No doubt Willcocks was determined to assert his full authority when he began at King's. After a little while he seems to have relaxed the tautness of his performing style, no doubt instinctively.

But there were other kinds of changes. The singing gradually began to develop a more incisive edge. When he was pressed to examine the tradition, to listen to the recordings – which he would not normally do – he had to admit that over a decade the singing style had indeed changed, though certainly that had not been his intention. It was likely to have happened, he suggested, through the frequent recording sessions with orchestras that the choir began to have from about 1960. His sensitive musicians had instinctively reacted to balance and rival the volume and attack of a full orchestra.[211]

And they inevitably carried these developments into their daily singing in Chapel. Even by 1963 one commentator was saying he had the impression that 'those silky-voiced and virtuosic choristers and choral scholars are encouraged by David Willcocks to sing out more than they previously did. No less beautiful than before, the tone has more body in it.' The commentator loved the way they sang *Personent hodie*, a magnificent tune that seemed, he thought, 'to have come stamping down the centuries, reeking of medieval Baltic forays and only press-ganged into devotional service'.[212]

For some English music-lovers, though, German choirs singing

Bach were 'infinitely preferable' to the exquisite but insipid sounds of King's. The 'expressive individuality' of a choir like the men and women of the Westfälische Kantorei seemed 'so much more spontaneous and penetrating'.[213] Some disliked what they took to be the habitual clipped 'exaggerated' consonants of King's[214] and some lamented the habitual weakness of the lower parts, 'the inevitable lack of sheer vocal maturity'.[215]

But many more loved and admired the utterly distinctive music-making of King's under Willcocks. They sang Croft's Burial Service on a disc released in 1962 'about as perfectly as one could imagine', one critic thought.[216] Another considered their recording of Fauré's Requiem made in 1967 'as near as can be to absolute perfection from start to finish'. He thought the use of treble voices added an 'unforgettable radiance and serenity to their part, impossible to sopranos, however good'.[217] Historically, King's under Willcocks was regarded by the choral conductor John Rutter as 'the embodiment of an ideal of perfection'. Such unfailing security of intonation and such blending of the voices had never been heard before.[218] Some thought the style mannered and noticed a 'faint preciosity of style'.[219] 'Preciousness' was not an infrequently made charge against the singing. If the critics meant that the style was affected, that it was artificially cultivated in some sense by Willcocks, they were wrong. The singing style was 'in the King's tradition'. It was also emphatically Willcocks' own style.

Even the sophisticated recording techniques of the 1960s could distort the intended effect of the singing. The first long-playing discs of King's were made by the record label Argo, founded in 1952 by a man who had learnt a little about electronics as a signals officer in the war. When he came home he joined his father's book publishing business and then decided to start a record company as a hobby. A few years earlier, before the revolution in tape recording and the reduction of the expense in making recordings, this would have been unimaginable. In 1951 Argo ceased being a hobby and became a full-time job for the founder and in 1952 was registered as a private limited company.

Their advertisements between 1955 and 1958 offered 'aural integrity': 'our records are as close to the original sound as we can achieve'. They boasted that the tape recorders they used, at 30 inches per second, were 'the latest in Europe', and that their microphones were 'the finest obtainable anywhere in the world'. In fact they could only afford one microphone, at least in the mid-1950s.[220] All Argo could do at King's was to attempt to catch from one location the extraordinary mix that the Chapel itself made of the sounds being created. Listeners thought that in this they succeeded exceedingly well.

But in 1957 the Argo record company was taken over by the large and powerful Decca, who could afford a great many microphones, which were used by highly imaginative producers and sound engineers to solve questions of clarity and balance in recording large forces, most famously of all in recording Britten's *War Requiem* and in the first complete recording of Wagner's *Ring* cycle.[221] Microphone-placing was becoming an art form, and its importance was being recognized by musicians, record producers and by many listeners, certainly by record producers. Sound engineers were acutely aware of the opportunities technology was offering them and they wished to experiment and to outdo their counterparts in other record companies in discovering new effects. The last thing they wished to do was to connect up their equipment, set up a microphone or just a small handful of microphones in the same position as for the last recording in this particular location and be seen to do nothing mysterious at all. But in an astonishing acoustic that might be all that was required. The temptation to be ingenious was not always resisted in King's. It was perhaps the desire to achieve a greater clarity than was ever possible while actually listening in the building itself that led to the creation of discs on which it is possible to hear individual voices of the lower parts very clearly indeed. Microphones took the choir to pieces but didn't put it together again as the stupendous acoustic did.[222]

An EMI engineer who recorded at King's in the later 1960s – for the College agreed in 1964 to sign contracts with EMI as well as Decca[223] – remembered competing with his rivals at Decca in multi-miking, and then suddenly being startled at hearing the naturalness and presence of earlier recordings made with much simpler micro-phone placings, and also by BBC broadcasts of music at that time which he knew were made with a pair of stereo microphones.[224] He himself made a number of recordings of the choir at King's in which the aim was clearly to capture the synthesizing effect heard in the building itself.[225]

The question remains, if the Argo engineers in the mid-1960s were failing to realize the sound ideals of the musicians, why didn't the musicians protest?

David Willcocks never listened to recordings. He didn't even listen to complete run-throughs of session playbacks, or listen attentively to test pressings.[226] This was partly a question of character and person-ality. He belonged to a generation to whom music-making was very important and who never acquired the habit of spending time listen-ing to records. He wasn't a practical man. He wasn't interested in gadgets. He wasn't interested in the way organs work, let alone tape recorders. He flourished as a war-time army officer and liked being part of a team and was able to delegate. He expected the engineers to do their job as he did his, once he was satisfied with their compe-tence. But that the record was another thing, not a reflection of a musical performance but a text to be preserved – that would not have occurred to him. At this time the record producer for Decca, John Culshaw, was saying that musicians realized that a record was more important than a performance, since they knew that a recording would outlive then.[227] This would have been unintelligible to Sir David Willcocks. Or at least he would have shrugged his shoulders. Not to him it wasn't.

If Willcocks' performances were considered unemotional, so did he too appear unemotional. He accepted the conventions into which he was born and the importance of moderation, formality, polite-ness and self-restraint, and his musical expressivity was of a piece with what this society took these defining virtues to be and the gestures in speech and in movement with which they were associated. In *Emma*, Jane Austen exemplified what she described as 'the true English style' in the way two gentlemen greeted each other with ' "How d'ye do, George?" and "John, how are you?" . . . burying under a calmness that seemed all but indifference, the real attachment which would have led either of them, if requisite, to do every thing for the good of the other'.[228] Willcocks understood what was meant by the 'dignity, simplicity, restraint' advocated by the compilers of the Anglican report on *Music in Worship* published in 1923.[229] He understood what Sir Henry Hadow meant when he spoke of Parry and his music being representative of 'sanity . . . strength and tenderness'.[230]

Noel Annan, the Provost of King's when Willcocks was director of music, considered that the ideal inculcated into children of his generation – 'the insufferable ideal', he called it, of the men who went to university between 1919 and 1951 – was that of the English gentleman: 'To strain to be original was a sign of side, conceit, vanity and showing off. To be determined to distinguish oneself from one's fellows was considered disagreeable.'[231] Above all else, the Provost thought, the public schools that educated this generation wished to instil in boys 'manliness and loyalty'.[232]

Willcocks seemed to accept without questioning or at least without close examination or anguished reflection the conventions of the world into which he had been pitched. He did not dismiss or look down on other ways of living, but this world and its values all made sense to him and he got on living his life wholeheartedly. He was not given at all to self-reflection.

Even with the calm and equable temperament with which David Willcocks seems to have been born, such control was preserved at a cost. He visited his six-year-old granddaughter every day when she was in hospital having her tonsils out, even though she was there with her mother, Sarah, Willcocks' daughter, all the time. Sarah suddenly realized the terrible pain he had endured, the fear of having been abandoned, left alone in hospital, when he was having the same operation as a chorister, far from home and without a single visit from his parents. It reminded her of the emotional independence and resilience and a kind of stoicism that were so characteristic of him. She had long known that he belonged to an epoch and a society in which you didn't pour your heart out. Willcocks certainly admired his own father for never mentioning the TB he had suffered from as a child and his resulting shortened leg and the 'iron hoof' he had to wear throughout his life. And he himself never mentioned the aches and pains of old age. Sarah remembered how startled she had been as a teenager to see tears in his eyes when he had visited the hill in Normandy on which the wartime battle had been fought in which he had won the Military Cross. Had she ever seen tears in his eyes before? she wondered.[233]

Willcocks played the organ at the funeral of his younger son, James, who died of cancer as a young man. His family knew that he was distraught. Yet he conducted a concert later the same day. Thereafter he was unable to talk about James or to take part in any conversation about him or indeed listen to others' recollections of him. The doctor who treated the angina attack he suffered a few weeks later described this as 'repressed grief'. It was David's way of experiencing his sorrow. It could be treated, he was sure, and he was indeed successfully operated on. And time would heal. Or at least make the ache liveable with.[234]

Some educationalists and cultural historians of more recent times might have considered that such an ethos provided 'a systematic denial of emotional life'.[235] Willcocks would not have seen it in those terms. He told his students at the Royal College of Music that they did not come 'merely to achieve proficiency as a performer or as a composer'. They came to develop 'mental and physical toughness', 'to learn how to be modest in success and resilient in the face of failure and disappointment'.[236]

In 1964 a young art student, Kaffe Fassett, came to London from San Francisco. There he had been dancing on the tables in the sunshine. In England he found cold and damp and he felt utterly miserable, incapable of connecting with the restrained English men and women he came across and their calculating, buttoned-up natures. And then suddenly there were some Christmas carols on the radio and the radiant singing of a choir from Cambridge. He realized that behind the frosty, deadpan exteriors there was a deep love of exquisite beauty and an English soul that he had begun to suspect did not exist. His fears and prejudices began to melt away. Later he heard these voices singing Allegri's *Miserere* and he fell in love with England and the English. He knew then that he wanted to make his home here and express himself as an artist among such sensibilities, strong, delicate, profound.[237]

5

The 1960s: Beyond King's

CHANGING VOICES AND CHORAL SCHOLARSHIPS

If it was true, as Provost Austen Leigh claimed in 1899, that the choir at King's was reckoned among the best in the Kingdom, and that this improvement had been achieved in part at least through the introduction of choral scholars,[1] why were greater efforts not made to create such scholarships at more of the colleges at Oxford and Cambridge?

The advertisements for the first choral scholars at King's stipulated that candidates must 'not be more than 25 years of age'. In 1914 St John's College, Cambridge, advertised their choral studentships as open to candidates who were under twenty-four at the time of examination'.[2] Should schoolboys between the ages of, say, fifteen and eighteen, be singing at all? Some nineteenth-century teachers did seem to have considered it treacherous for an adolescent boy to sing very much. Some thought that the voice could be used very gently. Some thought that every voice was different and the adolescent boy's voice had to be individually monitored.[3] In 1892 George Martin articulated the widely held view that the voice should never be used for singing as the treble voice was being lost. 'It is likely to injure the vocal tone for ever after. Many otherwise fair musicians have been deprived of vocal power by this reprehensible practice. A boy whose voice is changed or broken, ought no more to be allowed to sing than a man with a fractured limb ought to be permitted to walk or use it. There is no doubt that many valuable voices are lost through overstraining their powers at the period of the break.'[4]

After a lecture on English choristers that Sir Sydney Nicholson gave in 1944 a member of the audience said he was very pleased indeed to hear that this eminent church musician was sure that singing during the change of voice did no harm at all. The chorister, he said, was often at sea when he lost his voice and was forbidden to sing with the men, and permanently lost to music and the Church.[5] Another member of the audience reported that a great nineteenth-century laryngologist, Sir Morell Mackenzie, had always insisted that there was no evidence to show that singing during the change of voice caused damage. He would say that it was only like using your arms and legs when they're growing.

Nicholson himself wondered whether in fact the term 'break' – he himself preferred 'change' – had not been propagated by all those Italians who flooded into England in days gone by when it was assumed that anything good in music had to come from abroad. This must have been the reason, he thought, and no wonder that they thought boys' voices 'break', considering the strangulated kind of noises they forced their trebles to make.[6] During the earlier years of the School of English Church Music, Nicholson had concentrated on the trebles in parish church choirs. But in the later 1930s he made a special point of encouraging teenage boys to sing.[7] In 1940 he established an annual Festival Service in Gloucester Cathedral for schoolboys from all over the country, and then in 1942 was able to build on its success by arranging a fortnight's summer course for two groups of fifty boys, each group singing daily services in the cathedral for a week, all this while the cathedral choir was on holiday. The Dean was astonished at the results. Most of the boys, who were strangers to one another, were strangers to most of the music too. They sang their first Even-song on the day after their arrival. It was a little lacking, perhaps, the Dean thought, in leadership and confidence, but the tone the choir produced was very beautiful and rich 'and rendered in an impressive spirit of religious devotion'. The rapid improvement of the choir could be gauged, the Dean thought, by the singing of the most difficult music at Evensong, the psalms. Quite soon the choir were chanting 'with something of the precision of a trained cathedral choir'. They sang Matins and Choral Eucharist as well as daily Evensong. They sang the Litany in procession round the whole cathedral and pitch was maintained with absolute accuracy. There was one moment as the choir were processing under the screen back into the Choir when there was a 'slight discordance', as the Dean called it, between choir and cantors, but the singers had the confidence and presence of mind to enable them to make the swiftest of recoveries. The choir's nerve and resolve and musicianship were perhaps most fully demonstrated when they sang during another procession, at a Sunday Choral Eucharist. They processed round the cathedral singing the hymn 'Blessed city, heavenly Salem' to the adaptation of the closing alleluias of Henry Purcell's anthem O God, thou art my God. Singing in Gloucester in procession was notoriously difficult and co-ordination of choir and organ and congregation really impossible with the time lag and the acoustic. All these problems were solved at a stroke. The choir sang the hymn unaccompanied; this held no terrors for them. Between each verse the organist improvised. The voices remained together throughout in spite of the distance between the head and the end of the procession. The timing was immaculate; the choir arrived back in the stalls at exactly the right moment. Nothing, the Dean said, could have been more inspiring. During the fortnight there were admirable and confident soloists among the trebles. Certainly the chief weakness was the lack of sustaining power in the tenors and basses. But this was inevitable given that the oldest singers were only eighteen. And there were really good and pleasing voices here too, and for the most part the choir maintained a commendable balance.[8] These annual summer courses were one crucial factor that lay behind an increase in the number of candidates for choral scholarships.

Not everyone was convinced. In 1920 New College, Oxford, had reintroduced choral scholars, after the abortive attempt sixty years earlier, with just one or two singing alongside lay clerks between the wars.[9] But in 1944 the organist, H. K. Andrews, obtained permission to do away with them and appoint one lay clerk instead of two choral scholars, there now being six lay clerks in total.[10] This seems odd in view of the success of School of English Church Music summer courses, but perhaps Andrews was unaware of these. A BBC producer had asked Dr Andrews whether he had been listening to the broadcasts from the other place, from King's. He had caught just a few minutes of one or two of them, he said. And what did he think? Well, 'it seemed very nice singing but a trifle pansy'.[11] Perhaps he really did not want young voices. Perhaps he wished the men in the choir to have strong, fully developed voices, and the particular kind of blend and meticulous ensemble that was being demonstrated by King's did not compensate for the strength of older men.

But mostly organists were convinced of the advantages of young singers. In 1959, Christ Church, Oxford, began to offer exhibitions in choral singing and by the late 1960s there were four or five of these in addition to the six singing men it had had throughout the first half of the twentieth century.[12] At the same time the cathedral began to appoint recent graduates as lay clerks. They came from New College, Magdalen, King's College, Cambridge, and some of them were taking a postgraduate qualification in teacher training.

New College appointed a graduate as the first post-war academical clerk in 1954, a singer who had been a choral scholar at King's and was now reading for a degree in theology in two years before becoming ordained.[13] In the 1960s, like Christ Church, it began to appoint as lay clerks former choral scholars who were taking a postgraduate teacher-training qualification.[14] By 1980 both Christ Church and New College had six choral scholars and six lay clerks, most of them under thirty years old.[15] Some of the young graduates were freelance singers beginning their careers, some of them teachers, some of these hoping too for a career as a singer. David Willcocks thought highly of this arrangement at Christ Church, which would allow solos to be covered more effectively, he thought, and yet not necessarily destroy the blend.[16]

The men of nearly all the other cathedral choirs of the time were a mixture of young and old, and a mixture too of vocal talents and aptitude, and still – the complaint of centuries – with one or two voices or sometimes more worn out and of little use. In 1961 there were discussions between the organist at Durham and the Professor of Music at the university there about the introduction of undergraduate choral scholars into the choir and in 1962 Durham University gave formal approval for such a scheme. A number of student singers were tried to assess the feasibility of the idea. In 1962 two postgraduates were appointed, one taking a diploma in education course, the other training for the priesthood, and in November 1964 the University advertised for three choral scholars, one for each voice, to be appointed for three years. The three successful candidates began singing in October 1965.[17]

At York Minster a scheme of choral scholarships was established in 1964 drawing on the students at the new university founded there in

1963 and on the students at St John's College, a teacher-training college in the city. By 1977 there were four songmen and six choral scholars.[18] An organ scholarship with the new University of East Anglia was established at Norwich Cathedral in 1967 and in the late 1960s an informal scheme of choral scholarships that was eventually formalized in 1975. The statutes of 1966 provided for 'not fewer than twenty choristers, including probationers' and 'as many lay clerks as the administrative chapter consider suitable, after consultation with the organist'. By the 1990s this had become six lay clerks and six choral scholars.[19]

Two colleges decided to do away with their lay clerks altogether after decades of hesitation. As long ago as 1888 a Fellow of St John's College, Cambridge, had written to the Master offering funds from anonymous benefactors – of which he was one – to establish eight choral scholarships for undergraduates to replace eventually the four lay clerks.[20] The College agreed to establish four to sing alongside the lay clerks and so it remained more or less for many decades, with the choir singing twice on Sundays and Evensong on Saturdays and on occasional saints' days. In 1948 a tenor lay clerk retired after forty years' service and though the remaining two offered to continue sing-ing without payment,[21] it was decided in November 1949 to dispense with their services and to establish twelve choral scholarships.[22]

And then there was Magdalen College, Oxford, which had had choral scholars, or 'academical clerks' as it called them, for decades. But only in 1960 did it feel able to retire its last lay clerk and to rely on twelve students, usually undergraduate singers.

THE CHOIR OF MAGDALEN COLLEGE, OXFORD

When Magdalen appointed Haldane Campbell Stewart organist in 1919 it was appointing a university man, a professional man, to the post previously occupied by Varley Roberts, a journeyman church musician from a humble background. At first sight this succession appeared to complement the appointment of Boris Ord after A. H. Mann. Haldane Stewart was the son of a barrister, and a chorister at

Magdalen, to which he returned as an exhibitioner in classics. He was then a schoolmaster at Lancing, Wellington and Tonbridge before his appointment as Informator Choristarum at Magdalen.[23]

But Magdalen did not make Haldane Stewart a Fellow. He was modest and self-effacing and though he was richly gifted he spread his talents too widely, some thought, to achieve renown in any one sphere. He was an excellent choir-trainer and a much-admired composer, though his output was small; his Evening Canticles in C sharp minor, his carol *On this day, earth shall ring* and his motet *Veni sancte Spiritus* long retained their place in the services at Magdalen, though he also wrote a number of songs and hymns and some instrumental pieces, including a full-scale sonata for cello and piano – his wife was a cello teacher and his daughter, Jean Stewart, the viola player in the Menges String Quartet.[24] But he also played cricket for Kent for many years, played both soccer and rugby for Sussex, had a golf handicap of 2, and was a first-class player of lawn tennis, rackets and billiards, and quite a reasonable ice skater.

A cricketing magazine of his time carried large photographs of famous players in each issue and under the picture of Stewart there was a one-word caption, 'Elegance'.[25] And yet even with teachers who possessed such talents and such a kind and generous-minded nature as Stewart evidently did, it was still an uphill battle kindling enthusiasm for music at boys' schools. Essentially the situation remained as the music-master at Sherborne described it in his lecture in 1893. The parents of boys at these schools generally had no interest in or knowledge of music. If a master was able to persuade a boy to persist and practice a piece thoroughly throughout the term he was quite likely to hear that the headmaster had received 'an angry letter from a stern parent', questioning his abilities for employment as a music teacher. The son had come home able to play only a single piece, 'one piece and that a piece with no tune in it'. Neither was there much understanding of music among the other masters in these schools. Games were of supreme importance and consumed immense amounts of time. The music master had to adopt an attitude of 'watchful sinuousness', snatching moments whenever he could find them to try to rehearse, before breakfast, during a shower of rain while the boys were playing cricket, just before going to bed.

The most important aspect of such a master's work in a public school was the attempt to show boys that there were 'no terrors in the higher forms of music'. There were house singing competitions at most of these schools and school songs were indeed useful 'in fostering a patriotic love of the school and a healthy esprit de corps'. In some schools there were solo competitions for solo singing as well as competitions for the houses of the school. The master at Sherborne was against these. He was sure that it was 'better to keep the soloist's vanity out of the boy as long as possible'. It was certainly true that the best way to appreciate and love the great oratorios, the only way to gain an intimate knowledge of them, was by taking part and singing in them. But you were not training voices, you were training taste.

There were questions and comments at the end of the lecture. One member of the audience remembered that at Harrow it was considered something 'quite out of the ordinary way for a schoolboy to play an instrument – that was regarded as rather effeminate, with a suspicion of the improper'. Another remembered a fellow of King's College, Cambridge, remarking that music was 'a very nice amusement for a man who can't afford to hunt'.[26]

At any rate the result of the continuing suspicion of a musical boy meant that the number of good singers suitably qualified for choral scholarships remained very small. At King's in the 1930s a large number of schools provided one singer: Haileybury College, St Edmunds School, Canterbury, City of London School, King's School, Bruton, Clifton College, Stowe School, Windsor County Boys' School, Worksop College, King's School, Canterbury.[27] Gifted masters in some schools certainly managed to instil a love of music in certain boys. But there were no schools that could be identified as the training grounds of exceptional musical talent, providing a stream of successful candidates for choral scholarships. There were very few applications from state schools.

So when Magdalen College, Oxford, appointed Haldane Stewart to be the organist in 1919 it did not follow King's example and appoint choral scholars to replace all its lay clerks. From 1900 until the 1950s it continued to use six lay clerks and two or three academical clerks.[28]

In the first half of the twentieth century applicants for lay clerkships at Magdalen were typically aged between their late twenties and their mid-forties. They might have been educated at an elementary school

to the age of about fifteen, or at a grammar school and then at a
teacher-training college, or at a technical college. One had been a
chorister at Lichfield Cathedral and had then attended a commercial
college until the age of fifteen and a half. The applicants had had previous experience as lay clerks or supernumerary lay clerks at Norwich
Cathedral, King's College, Cambridge, Southwell Minster, Bristol and
Exeter and Rochester and Canterbury Cathedrals, York Minster,
Leeds Parish Church and Lancaster Priory.[29] The attractions of a lay
clerkship at Magdalen were obvious: the services at Magdalen had
long been renowned for their 'devotional fervour' and the 'refinement'
of the singing in 'that celebrated sanctuary',[30] and there was a better
pension scheme than at many of the other choral foundations.

The applicants had had previous additional employment as a mechanical engineer, a private music teacher, a clerk in a printer's office, a wages
and store clerk in an engineering factory, a part-time clerk with a gas
company, a 'despatch and order clerk in the music trade'.[31] One candidate applying in 1950, though, had quite different qualifications: he had
been a chorister at Magdalen, a choral scholar at St John's College, Cambridge, a postgraduate for a year at King's College, London, and he
already held a teaching post at Magdalen College School.[32]

When Magdalen advertised for a new organist in 1956 it informed
candidates that, on the recommendation of Sir William McKie, a
former college organist and currently organist at Westminster Abbey,
it had decided to replace lay clerks with academical clerks, that is,
with choral scholars, the reason given being that it was, 'at present . . .
extremely difficult to recruit Lay Clerks'.[33] Even now the advantages of
using choral scholars were not at all self-evident to the university authorities. At a meeting of the Chapel and Choir Committee on 5 March
1959, however, it was agreed that the remaining lay clerk, a bass called
Harold Boult, 'should be informed that his retirement from singing
duties with the Choir would date from the end of Trinity Term 1960'.[34]

Thus at the start of the Michaelmas Term in 1960 the back rows of the
choir stalls were filled with choral scholars alone for the first time.[35]
There were soon twelve of them, mostly undergraduates at Magdalen;
occasionally there would be a graduate student singing and sometimes
an undergraduate was recruited from another college.[36]

There were several reasons now why there were more young men who might aspire to sing in a college chapel choir. There were the summer vacation cathedral courses at the Royal School of Church Music, formerly the School of English Church Music. There was the establishment of the Bachelor of Arts degree in music at both Cambridge and Oxford after the war, an ordinary degree like any other which required three years' residence.[37] This was not intended as a vocational qualification; indeed many choral scholars read other subjects. But it indicated that music was now recognized by the universities as a subject worthy of academic study. An article in *The Times* in February 1964 drew attention to the enrichment of the nation's musical life by university-trained musicians. As an example of what universities were achieving, the writer described the scope and richness of music at Cambridge, the last three holders of the professorial chair there having been a scholar and translator, Edward Dent, a composer, Patrick Hadley, and a scholar and performer, Thurston Dart. The article did not neglect to mention 'the distinctive and highly influential style of choral singing developed by the Choir of King's College Chapel under Boris Ord and David Willcocks'.[38]

The abolition of the lay clerks at Magdalen was certainly welcomed by the man who was appointed Informator Choristarum in 1957. Bernard Rose had been a chorister with a most beautiful voice at Salisbury under Sir Walter Alcock, and then, after studying at the Royal College of Music, an organ scholar at St Catharine's College, Cambridge, and after that the organist at The Queen's College, Oxford. He was the first organist to be made a Fellow of Magdalen College on his appointment.[39]

The singing of Magdalen College Choir under Rose was characterized by the kind of immaculate blend and ensemble that King's had been demonstrating under Boris Ord, and by very clear articulation. 'No attempt is made to cheapen the music by exaggerated phrasing or tempi: everything is in its place and well controlled', was one contemporary critic's description of the choir singing Thomas Tomkins. 'A gentle serenity' informed the performances.[40]

The trebles who emerged from the tuition and encouragement that Rose provided were skilful and adroit with a straightforward and unmannered delivery.[41] They could be capable soloists if required but were not often called on to sing alone; Rose preferred to maintain an impersonal, unindividual tone quality by using two boys for a solo. For such duets he would pair a junior boy with a senior one, to give the younger one experience and confidence.

The academical clerks came mainly from the same kind of independent schools as the choral scholars at King's. In some years it was not always possible to elect singers to fill the vacancies; both the shortlisted tenors in 1961 failed to satisfy the College's admissions committee in their academic subjects. In 1962 it had been possible to shortlist nine for four vacancies, though three of these were conditional on A Level results. For the 1962 scholarships notices were circulated to the Royal College of Music and to thirty-six schools, of which Winchester was the only major public school. Several of them were schools that had from time to time sent boys to King's as choral scholars: Ardingly, Rossall, Uppingham, King's, Canterbury, King's School, Ely, Bloxam, Taunton and Stowe.[42]

The voices of the Magdalen academical clerks, like those of the choral scholars at King's, were small-scale, but all of them were distinguished by the accuracy of their singing and tuning and their stylistic confidence – they knew the style they were being required to cultivate. The lightness and the restraint of the singing of the academical clerks in 1963 is immediately apparent if it is compared with the rough-and-ready singing of York Minster in 1927 and the lay clerks of New College in 1949.[43] As long as older lay clerks with wide vibrato were retained – or even one lay clerk with such a voice – the characteristic blend of Magdalen and King's was impossible to achieve, at least in all dynamic ranges.

Although the chapel at Magdalen was small, the singing could convey a wonderful spaciousness – as if Rose were imagining himself back at Salisbury – as it does in the recording made in June 1963 of Stanford's Evening Canticles in C.[44] The tone was never harsh, though the choir could be assertive and passionate. There could be an improvisatory elan to the singing which close listeners to the long-playing discs contrasted with the tighter control of Willcocks at King's. After he had once listened to a recording of King's College Choir singing Byrd's Five-Part Mass, Bernard Rose said aloud in obvious exasperation: 'Why can't he just let them *sing*?'[45]

But the two choirs were clearly in the same mould and both moved and startled listeners with their discipline and the compelling inward intensity of their music-making, with the way in which every note was charged with meaning, even when they were singing quietly and performing the simplest music.

THE CLERKES OF OXENFORD

Willcocks recorded the three Byrd masses, Tye's Mass 'Euge bone' and Taverner's Mass 'Western Wind', together with a large number of Latin motets by Tallis, Byrd, Philips and Taverner, almost certainly more pre-Reformation polyphony than was being sung in any cathedral choir at that time. Much of this music had been introduced into the repertory by Boris Ord.

Willcocks' performances of this music had tremendous authority. But sixteenth-century polyphony was much more frequently heard sung by the secular, concert-giving choirs of men and women that were proliferating. In June 1936 the men and women of the Cambridge University Musical Society broadcast Taverner's 'Western Wind' Mass, and in January 1938 and again in August 1950 Tallis's forty-part motet *Spem in alium*. The latter work was broadcast in March 1948 from the Central Hall, Westminster, sung by the Morley College Choir conducted by Michael Tippett, and they then recorded it on two 78 rpm discs. This was essentially an amateur choir of devotees, 'musicians of sensibility, if not actually good singers', as one of the tenors remembered them. There was the composer and journalist Antony Hopkins, the composers Anthony Milner and Peter Racine Fricker, Michael Tillett, who prepared Tippett's scores for publication and did the piano reductions, and one or two excellent sopranos, some of them girlfriends of the musicians or else, one of the tenors thought, girls who were 'potty about the conductor'. And alongside them were some professional stiffeners from the Choir of St Paul's.[46]

The Renaissance Singers introduced many Londoners to Tallis's *Lamentations* in the late 1940s and they recorded it, together with the Four-Part Mass setting, on a disc released in 1958.[47] The choir had been formed by a young organist named Michael Howard in 1944 'to encourge the correct performance of music in accordance with the intentions of the Early Masters themselves, as revealed by contemporary evidence'. Initially contraltos were used; later these were replaced by countertenors, women's voices being retained only for the soprano lines, for which boys' voices had been employed for a few early recitals but soon abandoned as being impractical. The number of adults used to begin with was about twelve; later the choir was enlarged to twenty voices or a few more. There were professional musicians who were not professional singers; there were young and gifted singers who had just come down from the choral foundations in Oxbridge chapels – some of them singing in the choirs of Westminster Abbey and the Catholic Westminster Cathedral and Brompton Oratory. But the choir also included in 1951 a doctor, a schoolmaster, an accountant, a chemist, a civil servant and a solicitor.[48]

There were the Schola Polyphonica singers. On the evening of 14 December 1951, they sang the music of John Browne and Walter Lambe in the chapel of Eton College, the first time it had been heard there for almost four hundred years, as Frank Ll. Harrison noted in the preface to his Musica Britannica edition of the Eton Choirbook.[49] This was for broadcast later that month. This group was directed by Henry Washington, the organist at Brompton Oratory, and drew on the same pool of musicians as the Renaissance Singers. So did Pro Musica Sacra, founded by Bruno Turner, a businessman making sumptuous wallpaper. The amateurs in his choir gave back the fees they earned from making recordings; the professionals earned £2 a concert.[50]

There were also the Ambrosian Singers, frequently heard on the radio, which had been formed in 1952 by Denis Stevens, a young scholar working as a producer for the BBC Third Programme. This group used only professionals, whose average age was probably between twenty-seven and thirty. Its size varied between four for madrigals and forty for a work like the Monteverdi Vespers, and practical considerations meant that Stevens used contraltos or countertenors or sometimes a mixture of the two.

In 1964 Michael Howard was able to establish the Cantores in Ecclesia as a sixteen-voice professional ensemble. Cantores in Ecclesia regularly appeared at major European music festivals, including the Henry Wood Promenade Concerts, and their recordings won prizes, including the 1975 Gustave Charpentier Grand Prix du Disque.

Cantores in Ecclesia made a three-LP set of the complete 1575 Cantiones Sacrae issued in 1969,[51] and a disc of Tallis's Mass 'Salve intemerata' issued in 1974.[52]

So in the 1960s and '70s this pre-Reformation music was being recorded in 'the cathedral tradition' of King's, and by secular, more or less professional choirs. The men's voices of these choirs often displayed a richness and maturity beyond the abilities of choral scholars, though the characteristic seamless blend and ensemble of King's and the resulting sense of distance and impersonality were rarely achieved. Indeed the members of such choirs did not necessarily seek to emulate such qualities.

There were different views about the use of women's voices in this music. The traditional view was that only men and boys could produce the impersonal effect intended by the composer and 'the greater emotional appeal' of women's voices was not at all suitable.[53] When the Renaissance Singers made a recording in 1958 and substituted the choristers of Ely Cathedral for the women who usually took the top line, one critic thought this 'on the whole an improvement, particularly in the verse anthems by Amner and Byrd, where the cool impersonality of the boys' voices completely alters the character of the performance'.[54]

But then came the Clerkes of Oxenford.

In 1961 one of Bernard Rose's pupils, David Wulstan, an academical clerk at Magdalen, formed an ensemble of Oxford choral scholars. They called themselves the Clerkes of Oxenford after Chaucer's clerk in 'The Miller's Tale':

> And over all there lay a psaltery
> Whereon he made an evening's melody,
> Playing so sweetly that the chamber rang;
> And *Angelus ad virginem* he sang.

They would always include this famous carol that came to England in the thirteenth century, *Angelus ad Virginem*, in their Christmas concerts.

They sang mainly sixteenth-century polyphony, and they quickly developed loyal audiences in Oxford, delighted with the finesse of their performances, the blend and ensemble and marvellously accurate tuning, which skills they had acquired in the choirs at Magdalen and New College. The style had become second nature to them.[55]

Wulstan was beginning doctoral work on a sixteenth-century composer who had been Informator Choristarum at Magdalen, John Sheppard, and the Clerkes included works by this little-known composer in their programmes. There were several reasons why his music was unfamiliar, even here at Magdalen, where he had lived and worked. Much of his music is preserved in part-books with one part missing, and the reconstruction of such a missing part is by no means easy or straightforward. E. H. Fellowes had hoped to publish his music in folio volumes forming part of a sequel to the ten Carnegie Trust-financed volumes of *Tudor Church Music* published in the 1920s. This second series was to have been financed by a wealthy American, but the Wall Street Crash put paid to this.[56]

There was a further problem: it was not clear at what pitch Sheppard's music should be sung. If the bass part in the works for both men's and boys' voices was to be sung at a comfortable pitch for twentieth-century Magdalen choral scholars, the parts for the trebles would be stratospherically high. If the music was pitched so that the trebles at Magdalen might negotiate the composer's lines successfully, the basses could only ineffectively growl. For over a hundred years the importance had been recognized of a note in the copy formerly at St Michael's College, Tenbury, of the *pars organica* of Thomas Tomkins' *Musica deo sacra* published in 1668. This states that an organ pipe two and a half feet long will produce the note called tenor F. At modern pitch – A above middle C = 440 cps – such a pipe would produce a note which lies somewhere between G and A flat. The clear implication then is that music of the Jacobean period should be transposed upwards about a minor third. Ouseley drew attention to the note in his 1873 edition of Gibbons' anthems and accepted its implications. Ouseley in fact transposed the music upwards a tone whereas Fellowes regularly made a minor third adjustment in his own performing editions. As a result of this upward transposition a small number of pieces of the Jacobean period are found to have a top part with an exceptionally high tessitura. Peter le Huray came upon this phenomenon while preparing an edition – it appeared in 1962 – of the verse service by Thomas Weelkes that is entitled 'for trebles', presumably so designated precisely to draw attention to its special feature, a treble part in the full sections a fourth above the norm. But Wulstan considered there was sufficient evidence to indicate that the division of boys' voices into high treble and lower 'mean' had been a characteristic feature of English choirs not just during a short period in the Jacobean era but throughout the sixteenth century. Such a voice would indeed be required if the upward transposition implied by the *Musica deo sacra* note was applied to the music of the previous hundred years. Wulstan came to the conclusion that the evidence demonstrated that the adjustment should indeed be made to music going back to the Eton Choirbook compiled at the very beginning of the sixteenth century.[57]

Wulstan claimed that many records indicated that men of eighteen and even older were often still singing treble in Sheppard's time. The explanation for this was principally dietary. The older boys were bigger, stronger, with much greater chest size and so, he contended, could negotiate these terrifyingly high lines that younger twentieth-century boys could not contemplate.

Wulstan would explain it all in later programme notes about the Clerkes of Oxenford: 'women's voices were . . . incorporated into the ensemble . . . [and] . . . The change introduced a painful transition from what was by now the well-established excellence of the men, through an uncertain period when the women's voices threatened the homogeneity of the group, and in which their lack of apparent success met with insistent demands for a return to the earlier make-up of the ensemble. These tribulations came to an end, however, when persistence was finally vindicated and the high treble voice triumphantly reconstructed. It was not without irony that the agility and boyish clarity of the women's voices were by now perceived as typifying the tone quality of the Clerkes.'[58] Few of the larger-scale pre-Reformation works had been heard in performances by cathedral and collegiate choirs; mostly they had been heard sung by the BBC choirs. The differences with these new performances by the Clerkes were startling.

It is not clear whether David Wulstan used any pieces of historical evidence apart from the musical scores – images of singers, or textual descriptions – for the reconstruction of these high sixteenth-century treble lines. How did the singers learn to sing as he wanted them to? How did he indicate the historical style he was aiming at?

The women who sang the top lines in the Clerkes attended Evensong at Magdalen; they all knew very well the records of King's College,

Cambridge. The boys at both colleges produced very similar sounds. When they were asked to sing like a sixteenth-century chorister, about whom they knew nothing, the women instinctively sang like the best choristers they had heard.[59] When they did so they were congratulated and encouraged.

Wulstan gave quite explicit instructions to his singers, the soprano Sally Dunkley remembered. They were not to open their mouths wide. They were not to lift their heads high. Their vowels must be carefully differentiated and not modified to sing more powerfully and make the transition between registers more smooth, which advice went against what most singing teachers encouraged. Consonants had to be articulated much more clearly than the sopranos had ever been asked to do before. Wulstan prohibited any wobbling or bulging, as he called them; there was never to be the slightest hint of vibrato nor the swelling or intensification of a held note. The dynamic range between loud and soft was very moderate. One of the sopranos felt that Wulstan, who had been an alto academical clerk himself, always allowed the altos to sing louder than anyone else and so to colour the sound, which she described as having a 'cut-glass' quality, a glitter and a shine and a particular plangency. Certainly the altos and means and trebles gave the sound its unmistakable lightness and brightness.

In this and in all its essential features it came near to the sound and style of the choirs at King's and Magdalen at this time. Most of the repertoire that was sung by the Clerkes, however, had never been heard by members of their audiences. A few pieces had been sung by choirs such as the BBC Singers. But women had never sung like those in the Clerkes. It was the shock and the excitement of the new.[60]

Sally Dunkley sang sixteenth-century polyphony in choirs directed by Michael Howard as well as in the Clerkes. The starting point for Howard was the words, their meaning, drama and emotion. He recruited singers, explained the meaning of the text, and then drove them very hard with passionate intensity. The performance of a Byrd motet could be terrifying, emotional and theatrical. The description of the Clerkes as 'a miracle of the choir-trainer's art' was nothing less than the truth, she thought. It was often thought that these singers had never had singing lessons, that they were raw material that Wulstan simply had leaned on and gently moulded. This was not true.

The academical clerks at Magdalen had lessons as part of their scholarships. Almost all the sopranos had had or were having lessons. Wulstan explained that he had to un-educate them, to contradict what singing teachers were attempting to inculcate. This could be hard and frustrating and undoubtedly some singers resented it. But many were astonished by the results and willing, at any rate for a time, to suspend disbelief. Wulstan was in effect creating a new kind of soprano voice, a consort voice, that choral scholars at King's and, very recently, at Magdalen had learnt to cultivate. Professional singing teachers of the time were in effect creating voices of a recognized type to sing as soloists, whether in opera or oratorio, with power and distinctiveness, and twentieth-century taste had created expectations of vibrato. The essence of the singing of the Clerkes was the choir's understatement. This coolness the young singers of the 1960s considered very cool, or at least some of them did.[61] Wulstan directed with very small movements and if you sang correctly and things were going well, he used to beat with smaller and smaller movements until sometimes he seemed to be doing nothing. Sometimes there was just a smile left.

It was claimed to be an exercise in historical reconstruction. This music was best served, Wulstan wrote, when it was 'allowed to speak for itself'. 'Exaggerated dynamics, tempi and "expression", together with mannered pronunciation, or articulation, are . . . inimical to the composer's intentions.'[62] And yet it deliberately avoided sixteenth-century pronunciation; Wulstan thought this would be an 'irritation' to modern listeners. It avoided, too, any rhetorical engagement with the words. It strove for extreme metrical regularity.[63]

Nonetheless it was indeed often claimed or seemed to be being claimed that this music-making was based on very accurate data that had been accumulated painstakingly by scholars. 'After almost a hundred years of experimentation, we are at last beginning to understand what sort of vocal production is necessary to produce aesthetically pleasing results in the performance of 16th-century choral music,' explained one distinguished American musicologist in 1975. The lines had to be 'crystal clear'; balance and blend were of paramount importance and so voices had to be light, without vibrato, or with a very small amount and the sound produced 'well forward in the head'.

Because of these essential requirements it was not surprising that England, which had maintained its choral foundations and its countertenors and trebles, had the edge over other countries in being able to sing the choral music of the Renaissance 'marvellously well'.[64]

Wulstan's pitch theories were not universally accepted.[65] Wulstan insisted that the high treble voice fell into disuse during the course of the sixteenth century, the Cambridge scholar Roger Bowers that 'its first appearance can apparently be dated with some confidence to the 1570s'.[66] Wulstan saw his own researches as 'bringing the work of Ouseley, Fellowes, and others to its logical conclusion';[67] Bowers described Wulstan's theories as they relate to pre-Reformation choirs as 'unsustainable and invalid'[68] and as they relate to notation 'entirely imaginary'.[69] Bowers conceded that 'changing patterns of nutrition have made twentieth-century men and boys taller and heavier than their sixteenth-century ancestors', but denied that these factors 'have affected the prevailing pitches of their respective voices ... Neither physically nor vocally ... can the early Tudor chorister have differed very much from his present-day successor'.[70] Where two distinct timbres of boys' voices were cultivated before the Reformation, he maintained, the boy's part they termed 'mean' we should recognize as simply the boy alto, a voice that is widely used on the continent today and in England at Coventry and Westminster Cathedrals.[71] As for the countertenor voice, Andrew Parrott claimed that 'there is not a scrap of unequivocal evidence for any falsetto singing in England in the whole of the sixteenth century'.[72]

The theories continued to be contested, very bitterly, though very slowly, and with long periods of sour silence in between the musicological machine-gunning. But the long scholarly silences were filled with the energetic music-making of the Clerkes with women's voices from the late 1960s, and the emergence of other groups such as the Tallis Scholars in 1973 and The Sixteen in 1979 whose style owed much to the Clerkes.

The full disclosure of the musicological evidence was not made until David Wulstan's book in 1985, *Tudor Music*, and Roger Bowers' article 'The Vocal Scoring, Choral Balance and Performing Pitch of Latin Church Polyphony in England c. 1500–58', in 1986.

Whatever the truth or error contained in the musicological ideas behind the style, and much of the data concerning a performing style – and especially a singing style – is unverifiable, the Clerkes' singing certainly owed a great deal to the new style forged by King's in the previous thirty years.

NIGEL ROGERS AND JOHN POTTER

In the first half of the twentieth century very few choristers or choral scholars at King's went on to earn their living as singers. Few became lay clerks, though one sang in the choir at Winchester Cathedral from 1921 until 1960.[73] Most who did this in the 1950s and 1960s sang in cathedral choirs while holding a teaching appointment. In the second half of the century a few choral scholars became renowned soloists, the tenor Robert Tear, for example, and the bass-baritone Gerald Finley, who became so famous that he was put on postage stamps in his native Canada.[74] But a considerable number became professional singers who appeared as soloists and also worked as consort singers. Such singers demonstrated what constituted essentially a new kind of vocal exper-tise, which emerged partly because of the new audiences for early music.

Nigel Rogers went to King's as a tenor choral scholar in the Mich-aelmas Term of 1953. He had sung as a treble in the parish church of his home town of Wellington in Shropshire and was not like a King's treble at all, he himself thought. He was taught to sing by his mother, a piano teacher, and he imitated her vibrato. He thought the warm emotional expressivity of his treble voice also owed something to the famous male voice choirs he heard in the Welsh Marches. He used his light tenor voice with great confidence and self-assurance as a choral scholar,[75] and his ambition as an undergraduate reading mod-ern languages was to sing Verdi and Puccini.[76]

After graduating he studied for a year in Rome and then for another in Milan but was 'not entirely satisfied' with what his teachers there tried to do with his voice. Perhaps they wondered about the size and robustness of his small voice against a full orchestra in Verdi. Rogers found his way to Munich and was drawn into a group of musicians round the American Thomas Binkley, a lutenist, and player of record-ers, the shawm and other medieval instruments, who had first gone to Munich on a Fulbright scholarship from Illinois University. Rogers spent several years touring in Binkley's group, the Studio der frühen Musik. This consisted of two instrumentalists, Binkley and another Illinois graduate student, Sterling Jones, who played the vielle and the viola da gamba, and two singers, Rogers himself and Andrea von Ramm, a mezzo-soprano from Estonia who had arrived in Munich after studying in Freiburg and Milan, and who had planned to make a career in oratorio. As a student Binkley had played in the Collegium Musicum at Illinois, which in 1954 recorded the complete secular works of Guillaume de Machaut for the Westminster label. The four musicians were all intellectually curious and sought out historical sources to assist in developing performing styles. Rogers examined Conrad von Zabern's *De modo bene cantandi choralem cantum* of 1474 and Giovanni Camillo Maffei's *Discorso della voce* ('Discourse on the voice and the method of learning to sing ornamentation') of 1562 and Giulio Caccini's *Le nuove musiche* of 1602. Over such treatises and documentary evidence they argued energetically. But they all loved performing and spent hours rehearsing together day after day. Andrea von Ramm especially, with her tall figure and striking presence and insistence on examining the words and their precise meanings, demanded an original, individual response. She refused to fix every detail in advance but required spontaneity in each performance and wished the musicians to trust the moment. These mercurial musicians were alive to many influences and they later became famous and, in some circles, notorious for playing medieval music in 'the Arab style'. This was the result of a tour in north Africa, where they discovered numerous folk instruments which seemed to have remained the same for centuries. These they employed in performing medieval music from the Iberian peninsula and from southern France, and Binkley also borrowed characteristics of twentieth-century north African players whose musicianship so impressed him.

Studio der frühen Musik performed at a conference of musicians and musicologists in Delhi in 1964 entitled 'Tradition and Change in Indian and Western Music'. There were concerts by Yehudi and Hephzibah Menuhin, and the Drolc String Quartet from Berlin, and Ravi Shankar and Ali Akbar Khan, and a Bharatanatyam recital by Tanjore Balasaraswati, the legendary classical dancer from Madras. It was here that

Nigel Rogers first heard Indian musicians, the singers trained not for tonal beauty but first of all for astonishing agility. This was a revelation. He thought he saw here the technical means of obtaining the clarity and precision in the *fioriture*, the embellishments and runs, demanded by Italian composers, including Monteverdi. The technique for doing this he did not exactly learn from Indian singers but, having heard it done, he experimented and practised and assimilated it.[77]

Soon afterwards Rogers left Munich and returned home and built a career as a soloist. He was admired for a most mellifluous voice and his effortless delivery of the most technically demanding passages. He demonstrated that early music need not be quaint and polite and ideal for amateur recorder groups and folk-song singers but that some ancient airs demanded dazzling virtuosity. The expectations that many music-lovers had about the singing of Monteverdi derived from the much-loved pre-war recordings directed by Nadia Boulanger. Here were new interpretations and these were deemed historically accurate, 'authentic', the experts agreed.[78]

In June 2010 Andrew Parrott's 1984 recording of Monteverdi's Vespers was still the preferred choice of one distinguished critic, particularly for its virtuoso soloists, who included David Thomas, another King's choral scholar, as well as 'the peerless' Nigel Rogers, who had 'an airy precision and flexibility to give expressive meaning to even the most taxing passages'.[79] On the recording's original release one critic, a specialist in sixteenth-century Italian music of the Renaissance and Baroque periods – he also happened to be a Fellow in Music at King's – had described Rogers as 'surely the most accomplished and convincing singer of the early seventeenth-century Italian virtuoso repertoire to be found anywhere'.[80] Not only was he valued for his virtuosity, verve and intelligence, but he quickly earned a reputation as a soloist who was also one of the finest consort singers in Britain. No doubt he learnt much from his mother's informal lessons and from those Welsh choirs he heard in the Marches, and he certainly took what he needed from Indian classical singing traditions. But his musical persona was also crucially formed by those mercilessly supervised practices and the performances that took wing day after day in that astonishing acoustic in the Fens.[81]

Nigel Rogers and other former choral scholars from King's, including

Grayston Burgess, David Thomas, Martyn Hill and John Whitworth, all appeared in an early music group presenting medieval and Renaissance repertoires called Musica Reservata. This was formed in 1960 by Michael Morrow, who wished for a much harsher, brasher sound than was common among such groups, at least in England. He thought extant early instruments might provide some clue as to vocal timbre, and the oral traditions of folk singers in the Balkans too. A reviewer of one of their discs – one who didn't like the performances – thought the whole idea was to combat preciousness and the 'heigh-nonny-no school of dainty madrigal singers'.[82] Morrow himself had to admit that he did not wish his musicians to sound like the BBC Singers or a University Choral Society, or indeed anything at all to do with the English cathedral tradition.[83] That he had to draw on former King's choral scholars, from an effete tradition he rather despised, bore witness to their vocal and musical expertise and to their prominence among early music singers in London in the 1960s and 1970s. And perhaps their expressive range was a little wider than he had thought.[84]

For the very few choral scholars at King's who wished to become professional singers there were few opportunities for further training in the UK except to do a postgraduate course at a college of music, and this meant, for serious students, joining an opera class. This was not entirely satisfactory for ex-choral scholars like John Potter, a chorister at King's for the last year of Boris Ord's time and the first years of David Willcocks', and then a choral scholar for one year only at Caius College, who, as he put it, liked 'cleanness of line, smallness of scale, accurate intonation, countertenors'.[85]

For such singers, though, other work was suddenly becoming available. For the lightness and leanness and incisiveness of choral scholars matched very well contemporary ideas about early music and the use of old instruments. Early music was the new music for many who were uneasy or bewildered or scornful of the polemics that much contemporary music carried with it, or those who just didn't like the sound it made. What was changing everything for singers in early music was the long-playing disc and the dawning realization by the early 1970s that there was a limit to the canon of the greatest masterpieces that could continually feed the record industry. New repertory was needed.

Early music had been important ever since the long-playing disc had arrived and had been presented with encyclopaedic thoroughness by the German label DG Archiv. But now there were star performers. The early music movement seemed – to some of its practitioners at least – boldly anti-establishment, neither wrapped up in the impenetrable jargon of the avant-garde, nor suffused with the solemnity of chamber music, nor decked out with the social trappings of opera. At least not with the arrival of David Munrow and figures such as Michael Morrow and Andrew Parrott. Their music-making was not quaint or antiquarian and did not immediately bring to mind delicate recorder-playing and the candle-lit concerts of Arnold Dolmetsch, and summer schools of earnest amateur musicians who wore sandals and were sustained only by fresh pears and bowls of muesli.

John Potter sang on the three sets of discs of David Munrow released in the mid-1970s, *Music of the Gothic Era*, *Music of the Middle Ages* and *The Art of the Netherlands*. For many years he sang in the Hilliard Ensemble, an alto and two tenors and a bass, which called itself after the Elizabethan miniaturist Nicholas Hilliard, not only because he was contemporaneous with much of the late fifteenth- and sixteenth-century music at the core of its repertoire, but also because he is renowned for his exquisite detailing and refinement, qualities to which the singers aspired. Three of the founder members sang in the Choir of St Paul's, and two had been choral scholars at Magdalen College, Oxford.[86] With the Hilliard Ensemble Potter sang the works of Pérotin, who flourished around 1200, Guillaume de Machaut from the fourteenth century, music in the Old Hall Manuscript from the late fourteenth and early fifteenth centuries, Guillaume Dufay and Jean de Ockeghem from the fifteenth, a whole host of composers from the sixteenth, Cristóbal de Morales, Orlande de Lassus, Carlo Gesualdo, Palestrina, Tallis, Byrd. The Hilliard Ensemble sang Heinrich Schütz from the seventeenth century, J. S. Bach from the eighteenth. But they also sang contemporary music. Composers were drawn to the clean-edged sounds such voices produced and to the lack of 'expressive' gestures, composers like Gavin Bryars and Arvo Pärt. Potter also founded Red Byrd in 1989,[87] another small ensemble singing music old and new, by Gibbons, Tomkins, Monteverdi, John Blow and Scottish medieval music, but also new music by Ivan Moody, Nigel Osborne, John Surman, Gavin Bryars and Steve Reich. He also sang as a session musician, in which work the sight-reading abilities of choral scholars were particularly prized. He himself was to sing with a vocal backing group for Manfred Mann, Mike Oldfield and The Who, and to sing lute songs – songs not only by John Dowland and Thomas Campion but also by the Genesis keyboardist Tony Banks, the Led Zeppelin bassist John Paul Jones and Sting.

The starting point of the performance style of the Hilliard Ensemble and of Red Byrd was the understated and highly disciplined singing of King's under Willcocks and Magdalen under Rose. John Potter thought that he learnt more from David Willcocks than from any singing teacher and that most of the choristers who ended up singing for a living would feel the same.[88]

THE KING'S SINGERS

For as long as anybody could remember the choral scholars at King's had taken part in concerts and college feasts singing a mixture of sacred pieces, madrigals, and close harmony songs and arrangements of folk songs, popular songs and songs from musicals. Dr Mann remembered a quartet in the 1890s that used to go round Cambridge singing Christmas carols.[89]

In the 1950s there was a group that called themselves The Cam River Boys. In the mid-1960s a group of six of them arranged concerts in their old schools and sang at friends' parties and receptions, as 'Choral Scholars of King's College, Cambridge' or sometimes as the 'Schola Cantorum pro Musica Profana in Cantabridgiense'. And then this sextet was asked to sing in the newly opened Queen Elizabeth Hall on London's South Bank, their first appearance as the King's Singers. This was in a concert given on May Day in 1968 by the Academy of St Martin in the Fields, conducted by Neville Marriner whose son had been a chorister at King's, with Simon Preston, a former organ scholar, playing solos and a Handel organ concerto, and the singers performing a sequence of carols by a recent volunteer in the choir, Sebastian Forbes.[90]

Five of the original six singers were King's choral scholars, the two countertenors Nigel Perrin and Alastair Hume, the tenor Alastair Thompson, the baritone Simon Carrington and the bass Brian Kay.

The second baritone, Anthony Holt, was educated at Christ Church, Oxford. When they decided to attempt to make a living out of singing as such a group Willcocks was highly sceptical. They might be good enough choral scholars but they were not, in his usage of the term, 'really good singers'.[91] They began by singing madrigals, cover versions of pop songs, folk- and show-song arrangements that they had first sung at the Cambridge Footlights and on university Rag Days. They began to ask their friends to write them close-harmony arrangements and quite soon they began to commission works from composers such as Richard Rodney Bennett, Malcolm Williamson, Paul Patterson, and less obvious ones like Luciano Berio and Krzysztof Penderecki. Their reputation was sealed in 1972 when they were offered a tour of Australia and New Zealand with thirty-five concerts, and trips to South Africa, Canada and the United States soon followed. They filled TV guest slots in front of millions alongside Val Doonican, Twiggy, Lulu and Nana Mouskouri. Their self-deprecating English charm and generous humour could not hide their vocal virtuosity as they effortlessly crossed the boundaries of pop, classical, easy listening and western art music on album after album, *Folk Songs of the British Isles*, *A Tribute to the Comedian Harmonists*, Ligeti, Thomas Morley's *The Triumphs of Oriana* of 1601, *The Beatles Connection*, Carlo Gesualdo. The enunciation of 'Raindrops keep falling on my head' remained as precise as in the psalms for the day, their blend in Paul Simon's 'Bridge over troubled water' as immaculate as in Charles Villiers Stanford's *Beati quorum via*. Their style, they themselves thought, owed something to the American quartet of men's voices The Hi-Lo's, formed in the 1950s, something to a German sextet between the wars called The Comedian Harmonists, and something to a group of schoolmasters at Abingdon School in the 1960s, The Mastersingers. But they owed most to the training they had received from David Willcocks at King's.[92]

THE MONTEVERDI CHOIR

J. S. Bach's motet *Jesu, meine Freude* was sung at Boris Ord's memorial service on 23 January 1962 and one undergraduate at the College simply hated it. The blend and the sweetness of the choir's singing were too well mannered, 'precious, etiolated', and the English in which the motet was sung enunciated 'with effete and lip-wiping prissiness'.[93] He wanted to rebel against what he considered the outworn Victorian style of King's College Choir under David Willcocks, which, he thought, sang Palestrina as if it were Stanford and Bach as if it were Stainer.[94] He wanted to bring 'passion and expressivity' to the vocal music of the Baroque, and to use original languages, and to come close to the idiosyncratic personality of the composer whether it be Bach or Schütz or Purcell or Monteverdi. John Eliot Gardiner himself was not an outstanding executive musician – he had attempted to join the College Chapel Choir as a volunteer tenor, but was not taken[95] – and his harmony and counterpoint exercises were, according to the French pedagogue under whom he went on to study, Nadia Boulanger, 'a *tragédie* without name'.[96]

But he was very intelligent and intellectually curious, energetic, a good linguist, bold, self-assured and driven. He approached the Professor of Music, Thurston Dart, who helped him create his own edition of Monteverdi's *Vespro della Beata Vergine* of 1610, and then, as a twenty-year-old reading history, he arranged a performance of the work in the College Chapel. This being Cambridge, though, Gardiner had to enlist the support of choral scholars, from King's and other colleges, on whose expertise both he and the talented undergraduate sopranos could rely. Most of those who were there for the inaugural performance of Gardiner's Monteverdi Choir on 5 March 1964 have never forgotten the occasion. Why was it a revelation even to the King's choral scholars, who had thought they knew it all?[97]

Gardiner was after all drawing on these highly disciplined choral scholars – countertenors as well as tenors and basses – and the music-making was certainly characterized by voices with very little vibrato, steady tempos and immaculate tuning, all of them qualities which defined the singing of the Chapel Choir too. Most of what felt and sounded new was Gardiner's insistence on words and vocal colour and rhythmic pungency. The sopranos, clear and steady, were louder than the trebles. The work had never been performed in the Chapel and this particular music in this particular space was startling, the fabulous contrasts of grandeur and power and intimacy and delicacy. Gardiner himself felt that the Monteverdi Choir were blazing a new trail and doubtless many in his audience felt that too. To him it was an act of rebellion and this undoubtedly gave his efforts a psychological boost – he was in effect taking an existing tradition and adapting it, masterfully and with extraordinary imaginative energy. Its roots were in the singing style that had been developed at King's over the previous three decades by a collection of young musical amateurs whose art was now recognized and admired and loved worldwide – an art that the young sopranos singing in the choir could not quite banish from their minds, even if they wished they could. Gardiner himself would later say that he 'rounded up my own choir and taught them to sing in a multi-coloured, almost operatic way'.[98] Opera singers would probably not have agreed with this, but it was certainly quite new to hear an English chorus singing in concert with such lithe, disciplined buoyancy. An expert in this music recognized this when he listened to them singing the Vespers in Ely Cathedral in 1967: 'the sheer musicality of the performance,' he thought, 'was remarkable. The Monteverdi Choir has a bright, clear tone, and the rhythms were brought off quite splendidly, in contrast to certain performances heard in Italy this year, where *bel canto* has had a tendency to remove consonants and firm attack ... There were no romantic lingerings over cadences, no sudden and un-called-for changes of speed.'[99]

Gardiner demonstrated the way these very enthusiastic young English singers, under a different director, as young as themselves and equally enthusiastic, could find their way to developing and adapting the highly disciplined singing style into which they had been initiated. The exhilaration of the occasion must in part have derived from the sense of its newness; these young musicians were not attempting to acquire a skill, to get things right, as it felt when they sang in Chapel under David Willcocks' direction. For, as many of his singers testified, 'Willcocks knew exactly what he wanted'. Or at least he gave the impression that he knew exactly what he wanted. With Gardiner they were creating something, but they knew not quite what. Neither did the conductor, notwithstanding his confidence. The performance demonstrated that the expressive range of this English style was wider than most music-lovers, and even the singers themselves, thought it could be. Retrospectively it could be seen as an indicator that singers such as these might be able to progress and forge careers as new kinds of professional musicians singing in a new way. The performance in King's was enthusiastically received. It would be looked back on fifty years later as the moment when a twenty-year-old undergraduate 'put a rocket under the musical establishment', when he decisively rejected 'an approach to music-making that prioritised sonic beauty and technical perfection over meaning, directness, and intensity'.[100] In fact the singing of King's under Willcocks was not at all merely concerned with beauty of tone and technical discipline devoid of meaning and intensity – the calmness and control of the singing were highly expressive – but Gardiner's was a different kind of athletic expressivity.

For him and maybe some of the singers too the early performances of the Monteverdi Choir were acts of patricide, a shocking, gleeful rejection of all that their elders held dear. In truth this music-making declared its parentage unmistakably – by David Valentine Willcocks out of King's College, Cambridge, as the bookies might have described it – even though it was clearly ridden by John Eliot Gardiner.

In 2014 at a fiftieth-anniversary celebratory performance in King's of the Vespers, the music-making sounded to one listener 'often very beautiful, sometimes awe-inspiring, but maybe just a little too manicured and sumptuous'.[101] To another the performance was 'curiously English', 'a little chaste', with a lack of 'Italianate sensuality'. Anything further from earthy Italian vocalism would be hard to imagine.[102] To another the singing of the Monteverdi Choir in 2014 was 'more polished, more refined, more virtuosic . . . than ever'. For all his striking out on a different path, Gardiner remained 'a prisoner of his own King's College background' in his preference for 'small, pure-toned voices'.[103] Gardiner thought his own efforts with Monteverdi in 1964 might have been 'crude and exaggerated' but 'at least they did not sound half-baked or indistinguishable from Anglican pieties during a wet November Evensong'.[104] The singing on that first appearance of the Monteverdi Choir was certainly not crude, even though it might not have been as immaculate as later performances by these musicians habitually were. It certainly had startling vigour and energy; it must have felt as if the choral scholars had been let off the lead and were enjoying the experience enormously. But in fact it

owed much to the singing heard at Evensong in the Chapel on wet
November afternoons in the 1960s.

THE CHOIR OF WESTMINSTER
CATHEDRAL

In 1966 a choirmaster from Malvern spent his summer holidays at
the Three Choirs Festival. Guy Harland had been a chorister himself
before the war at a famous choral foundation, at St George's Chapel,
Windsor. He had sat down there in Worcester Cathedral that summer and listened to those singers from Gloucester, Hereford and
Worcester, and immediately realized something was horribly wrong.
Cutting through the fine English Cathedral tone and the sound of
true English trebles there was, from one of the choirs, a fantastic,
hideous, nasal, 'continental' tone quality. He wrote an agitated letter
of protest to *The Musical Times*, deploring 'this sinking of our standards, tastes and individuality by adoption of this hybrid, fashionable,
artificial gimmick'. He exhorted his readers to 'cherish certain cathedral choirs in this our land . . . whose tone, intonation, and blend are
still matchless . . . Is it too fanciful,' he had asked, 'to suggest that
those advocates of the kind of tone to be deplored are unconsciously
displaying one more sinister symptom of the disintegration of our
national individuality?'[105]
It seems clear from the memories of those who knew those three
choirs well in the 1960s that the boys to which Mr Harland took
exception were those at Worcester. That today the few recordings
made of the Worcester Choir in the mid-1960s do demonstrate the
trebles' confidence and forcefulness but do not startle us, even less
outrage us, perhaps only emphasizes Mr Harland's sensitivities. One
record reviewer at the time drew particular attention to the 'vibrant'
tone quality, the way a consistent tone was maintained throughout
the whole compass of the Worcester trebles, the clean enunciation,
and the way in which the boys' voices in Handel's *Let the bright sera-
phim* and the choirmaster's own Magnificat for trebles rang out with
dramatic effect.[106]
When a BBC producer responded to Harland's letter to *The*

Musical Times by explaining that 'the style of the boys' tone is no yardstick with which to judge artistic achievement',[107] he was right of course but, for Harland, it wasn't quite a question of artistic achievement. It was a question of tribal and generational loyalties and identity and the threat to identity. It was bewilderment at what seemed to him a rejection of social and moral and spiritual values.

> [And] life was never better than
> In nineteen sixty-three
> (Though just too late for me) –
> Between the end of the *Chatterley* ban
> And the Beatles' first LP.[108]

It was too late, not only for Philip Larkin, but for Guy Harland too, who was surely an enthusiast neither of *Lady Chatterley's Lover* nor of the Beatles. As a young man he had perhaps studied *The Progress of Music*, a book on music history by George Dyson that appeared in 1932, and read there about the fashionable masses of eighteenth-century France, Austria and Catholic Germany, which were often, he was told,

> of a shallowness and incongruity beyond belief. The dance-tunes, the orchestral ritornelli, the vocal flourishes, the pseudo-dramatic choruses, all were frankly transported from the theatre to the church, and every serious contemporary witness has testified to a growing degradation of taste ... Since the operatic movement arose in Italy in the seventeenth century, no liturgical work of supreme quality has been written within [the Catholic] Church ... what is the repute of all the conventional masses which [Mozart] and the two Haydns and Schubert wrote? They are less convincing works of their respective composers. Genius itself could do nothing with the style of church music prevailing in their day.[109]

And yet now, in the 1960s, these masses were being performed by Anglican choirs. In 1972 the Prime Minister was even to present a box of Haydn masses recorded by the choirs at two English choral foundations when he had an audience with the Pope.[110]

In 1922 when some choirs from Rome, including the choir from the Vatican, came to London and sang in the Albert Hall, an organist of Chichester Cathedral was aghast at the performing style and tone quality: 'gusty changes from *pp* to *ff*, sudden *pp*'s at points where neither text nor music seem to call for them, an almost entire absence of any degree of power between the extremes of soft and loud, and the trick of ending most works with a long-held whisper, do not appeal to us when applied to the Palestrina school'. He did not like the lack of balance between the voices, the way individual voices stood out, nor the shrillness of the boys when they rose above *mezzo forte*. If a London church choir had sung like this on Sunday morning the congregation would have said that 'the choirmaster should be sacked and the boys smacked'.[111] But in the 1960s, to Harland's bewilderment, here were English choirs adopting stylistic features which had so often been condemned in the recent past and producing 'hideous nasal notes'.

How had this style infiltrated the choral foundations, threatening to corrupt the English traditions, as Harland thought? Although he could not bring himself to mention it by name, he certainly knew that there had been a Roman Catholic choir in the nation's capital city that seemed to have assaulted the sensitive ears of the English and knocked all sense of propriety out of a new generation of choir-trainers with no sense of historical style whatsoever. This was the Choir of Westminster Cathedral, founded in 1902, which enjoyed a considerable reputation during its first two decades when Sir Richard Terry was its director, famous most of all for bringing pre-Reformation polyphony into the Catholic liturgies. It is not easy to conclude much about the effect of the choir's singing in Westminster Cathedral from the recordings made before the First World War, a few lay clerks singing Palestrina, a handful of boys with one man on each of the lower parts in Mozart's *Ave verum corpus* with a harmonium accompaniment.[112] But they at least confirm that the sound quality of Westminster Cathedral Choir was not at the time particularly distinctive, certainly not distinctively Catholic in any way. Terry was a Catholic convert and had been a choral scholar at King's College, Cambridge, under A. H. Mann. He himself considered the tone of the boys in continental choirs 'raucous and horrible'. 'There are many things we might learn from the Continent and America,' he thought, 'but choir-boy training is not one of them.'[113]

Because there was no tradition of training Catholic organists and choirmasters in England as there was for Anglican foundations, there were few obvious candidates for such a choirmaster's post. George Malcolm, in charge of Westminster Cathedral Choir from 1947, had been trained as a pianist at the Royal College of Music from the age of eight. He came back from the war and spent the money he was given on discharge from the army in buying a harpsichord. Because harpsichords were much less commonly found in the 1940s than now, and the early music revival was quickening its step and concert promoters needed harpsichords and harpsichord-players, they asked him for his instrument, and because it was assumed that if you had a harpsichord you could play it, he was asked along too. He was in fact a marvellously inventive and gifted keyboard player and very quickly gained a reputation as a brilliant harpsichordist.

In 1962, two years after he had left Westminster Cathedral, Malcolm wrote a famous article on boys' voices. He thought that the sound commonly made in England by boys was as if the voice had been castrated – the voice, not the boy himself – rendered harmless, as it were, so it couldn't crack a stained-glass window, pleasant, comforting, sentimental. The training that boys currently received in England left on one side the 'dangerous and troublesome elements' in a boy's voice. He himself wanted none of that tame cooing and 'pretty flutingsound'; 'an insult to boyhood' he considered it, an artificial and quite unnatural sound even though it was not at all uncommon and much admired and popularly known as 'Cathedral Tone'.[114] He didn't mention King's by name – he simply referred to the timbre 'cultivated in the "best" English church choirs' – but nobody would have been in any doubt. He wanted power and resonance, which he knew boys could produce, and no more emasculated angels on Christmas cards. A description he used that 'singing is a controlled form of shouting' would have been utterly rejected by John Stainer and George Martin and completely unintelligible also to David Willcocks.[115]

Whether Malcolm actually formulated a programme or a plan for creating a different and distinct timbre for the choir, especially for the boys, may perhaps be doubted, but one certainly evolved. He mentions the gramophone as having provided opportunities for music-lovers to experience other styles of singing. He himself may have heard the discs of Dijon Cathedral that were well known in England before he ever began training the boys at Westminster.[116]

George Malcolm had never trained a choir of boys and men before he was appointed; maybe his inexperience was an advantage in that it allowed him to think about training boys' voices from first principles. But he had learnt much from two famous choirmasters, Father John Driscoll SJ and Fernand Laloux. Driscoll was choirmaster at the Church of the Sacred Heart, which is affiliated to Wimbledon College, the Jesuit school next door, where Malcolm was educated. From 1928 Driscoll was also choirmaster at the Jesuit Church of the Immaculate Conception in Farm Street, Mayfair, where Malcolm was taken by his father on Sundays. Laloux was for fifty years singing teacher and then Director of Music at Wimbledon College and had been Driscoll's assistant at the Church of the Sacred Heart.[117]

John Driscoll was a singer himself and had studied singing with a very famous Spanish singing teacher, Manuel García, who spent the second half of his life in London, teaching at the Royal Academy of Music until 1895. García was born in 1805 and died at the age of 101. He had been taught by his father, also Manuel, who was educated at the choir school of Seville Cathedral. This Manuel García was a hot-blooded tenor who created a number of roles in Rossini's operas, including Count Almaviva in *The Barber of Seville* and the title role in his *Otello*.

The great English music critic Ernest Newman considered that in the 1920s Farm Street were the finest choir in Europe. Malcolm himself said that it was in sitting in on choral rehearsals taken by Laloux that he learnt 'far more than from any other source'.[118] But even if allowance is made for the taming of the impact of the sounds by the technology of the time, the recordings of Farm Street under Laloux[119] don't quite explain the timbre and style of the choir at Westminster Cathedral under Malcolm's direction.

The boys' choir school at Westminster had been disbanded during the war and George Malcolm was starting again from scratch. This too was perhaps another fortuitous advantage. Nobody had any preconceptions about the task in hand. The style forged by Malcolm at Westminster Cathedral in the 1950s was un-English and very distinctive indeed. It owed something no doubt to Farm Street before the war and the style of singing encouraged by Driscoll and Laloux. It owed something also to the styles of cathedral singing heard at

Montserrat in Spain and Dijon in France and perhaps at the Sistine Chapel and perhaps also to George Malcolm's regular appearances at the Aldeburgh Festival from its inauguration in 1948 and the intense, virtuosic playing of chamber music to which he contributed there. His brilliance as a pianist and harpsichordist brought him into contact with worlds far beyond the cathedral organ loft.

But the extraordinarily forceful sounds he created with his choir surely derived in part from his own idiosyncratic character. He had been director of the band of Bomber Command during the war. He was good at conducting light music. He was reserved and something of a loner but he was a daredevil too. As a student he had been an inveterate roof-climber as a student and almost killed himself in a fall. The intensity of his performances of the *Goldberg Variations* was legendary, but he also recorded Alec Templeton's *Bach goes to Town*, and, because the record producer needed something for the other side of the disc, Malcolm composed his own *Bach Before the Mast*. He distrusted – despised – musical 'correctness'. He refused ever again to sit on international juries of keyboard competitions after he had watched one competitor mesmerize an audience, a player he thought of compelling brilliance and subtlety who was not allowed to proceed beyond the first round. She had committed 'crimes against authenticity' in registrations and in ornamentation. Her mistakes, if they were indeed mistakes, were trivial in his opinion. Historical correctness meant almost nothing to him. We know jazz, we know Puccini, we know Stockhausen, and we can't unknow these experiences, he thought. As a young man he was regarded as a workaholic perfectionist. He had an impish sense of humour and was also subject to bouts of the deepest melancholy.[120]

English reviewers were astonished by a recording of the Westminster Cathedral Choir released in 1960 of Tomás Luis de Victoria's Tenebrae Responsories for Holy Week,[121] the drama and fervent emotion, the way George Malcolm changed speeds to reflect changes in the mood of the text. One doubted whether it would be possible 'to hear it sung as beautifully and as fittingly as this anywhere else in the world today'. They praised the admirable trebles with their 'slightly reedy quality of tone', as one reviewer described it, 'which is foreign to the Anglican cathedral tradition, but absolutely right for this music and, one could say, necessary to fill the large spaces of this particular building'.[122] *The Times*' critic described the tone of the boys at Westminster as 'brazen'[123] and the organist at Brompton Oratory said they sang 'with a searing range of tone and emotion, far removed from the blanched piety of many an Anglican choir-stall'.[124] In 1960 another critic described the choir as producing 'a full-blooded and unaffected style of singing which is almost unique in this country, and is certainly authentic'.[125] By 'authentic' the writer meant for the music of the Spaniard Victoria.

How did this performing style strike the musicians in Anglican foundations? Many undoubtedly liked and admired the Choir of Westminster Cathedral enormously. The Westminster Choir made no commercial recordings at all after the war until that Victoria disc, recorded after Malcolm had been there twelve years, and very few broadcasts. Just before he left, Malcolm gave the first performance of a work written for him by his friend Benjamin Britten, a Missa brevis for boys' voices and organ. It was recorded by the BBC and later issued as a commercial disc by Decca.[126] The cathedral clergy's unwillingness ever to give permission for recording was one of the sources of tension which eventually led to Malcolm resigning in 1959. Barry Rose, at Guildford, whose stylistic aspirations focused on King's, Cambridge, was nonetheless a great enthusiast and urged his singers to listen to the discs of Victoria and Britten. The sound of the choir might have had wider impact if there had been a series of records during the 1950s.

Bernard Rose, the organist at Magdalen, reviewed the score of Britten's Missa brevis for *Music & Letters*. He held the music in high regard. He noted the Mass had been written for George Malcolm and his choir at Westminster Cathedral and explained that 'continental voice production' was really an essential requirement for 'the full effectiveness of the music'.[127] This was immediately contested in the pages of *Music & Letters* by a correspondent in Canterbury who did not know what was meant by the phrase 'the full effectiveness of the music'; he had heard the Anglican-toned boys at Canterbury Cathedral recently give a very satisfactory and satisfying and enjoyable performance.[128] Perhaps what Bernard Rose was hinting at was that, while he clearly recognized the existence of a non-English singing style in England,

and however much he may have respected the accomplishment of Malcolm and his singers, theirs wasn't a style that he himself or any choir of his could ever entertain thoughts of imitating.

Certainly Guy Harland in Malvern would have accepted that King's under David Willcocks preserved 'the true English style', untainted by the extraordinary sounds of the Westminster Cathedral Choir. Thinking of another chapel, but naming no names, he nevertheless murmured with a shudder that, 'These fantastic phenomena are even evident in a Cambridge college choir.'[129]

THE CHOIR OF ST JOHN'S COLLEGE, CAMBRIDGE

In 1965 during recording sessions for a disc of music by Benjamin Britten, one of the trebles present put up his hand and asked the choirmaster: 'Do you want a touch of "continental tone" there, sir?'[130] Barely forty years earlier the organist at Chichester had been outraged at the 'painfully shrill' and emotional singing of some choirs from Rome. He had not wished deliberately to offend the sensibilities of these visiting musicians but he had had to state the unvarnished truth: that these boys had not been trained to sing by any knowledgeable authority. Whether such singing was heard in the Vatican or in a remote village church, this was simply 'bad singing'.[131]

How was it that the Choir of St John's College, Cambridge, was deliberately aping a style and technique that had so recently been condemned? Here was an Anglican foundation actually employing sounds made by foreigners.

David Willcocks at King's considered that the sound of a choir and its habitual singing style defined its character, the expressive personality of its members at any particular time, and that it was unrealistic and in some sense dishonest to try to adapt your style on particular occasions, as if you were changing a coat. It was part of your identity and character and personality – and not just your musical identity – and one choir had essentially one style.[132] George Guest at St John's, by contrast, thought it possible, indeed desirable, to encourage the singers in a choir to develop the ability to modify the singing style depending on the composer and period. Stanford should be sung mel-lifluously; Victoria should be sung more passionately with a touch of stridency at times. There were different interpretative possibilities, Guest conceded, but sixteenth-century polyphony need not sound ethereal and angelic. The texts of the Kyrie and the Agnus Dei of the Mass could not be more passionate; when singing such words to a set-ting by Victoria or Palestrina it was important to create a tone tinged with the emotional fervour that characterized the ethos of the Spanish and Italian civilizations out of which these works had sprung.[133]

He encouraged brilliant, trumpet-like tenor sounds in such Medi-terranean music and he himself liked Italianate tone, though he was not a purist over tone quality and he had never tried to develop an Italianate countertenor. But he did try to distinguish between Cath-olic music and music originally composed for the Anglican ritual. Catholic music – he was thinking particularly of Poulenc, Langlais, Vierne – arose from different attitudes and frames of mind. In the Agnus Dei, for example, there was this tremendous concept of 'tak-ing away the sins of the world'; to an Anglican sensibility this was most appropriately articulated in hushed tones, in a penitential mood. To a Catholic mind, these concepts might best be conceived as 'the shriek of a tortured soul'. He might feel admiration for well-balanced, poised, floating singing. He was startled at the disciplined beauty of the performances he heard at King's under Boris Ord when he first arrived in Cambridge, but he was not moved. He could admire the technique of the singers but would yearn for emotional engagement.[134] It was important, he thought, that no two notes in a melodic line were ever at the same dynamic level.[135]

George Guest was the undergraduate organ scholar at St John's between 1947 and 1951 and was appointed organist the year he grad-uated. He thought it was wrong to talk of 'a boy's voice'; you should talk of 'boys' voices'. So he gradually developed two 'stops' for the boys, like organ stops, a flute and an oboe. Most boys could create two kinds of sound, one for contrapuntal music, one for homophonic music like that of Stanford and Harris and Howells. The characteristic tone of the boys evolved, with the drier acoustic of the chapel at St John's requiring a livelier sound than the astonishing spaces of King's. He found that most boys could develop a much wider compass than was generally cultivated, and trained the boys to sing up to E, two octaves and a third above middle C, and down to the E flat below middle C. As well as developing the tone this gave a treble a feeling of safety. If he could sing a top E, the top Cs in Allegri's *Miserere* would hold no terrors for him. He encouraged them when singing top notes not to maintain a relaxed physique but 'to adopt something of the poise of an all-in wrestler'.[136]

It was all done by experiment. Guest appears to have had no pre-conceptions as to precisely what he was aiming for, nor precise ideas about how new sounds might be obtained, though, like Willcocks, to his singers he seemed able to convey a sure sense that he knew exactly what he wanted. After a year or two of his direction, the trebles at St John's showed no distinguishing tonal colouring.[137] He did let the boys listen to recordings of Spanish choirs and to the Copenhagen Boys' Choir, which he himself had heard when they came to the Alde-burgh Festival in 1952.[138] Some thought the change in timbre might have been sparked by one or two boys whose voices developed an edge to the sound; it would have been comparatively straightforward to encourage other boys to imitate them. But even choral scholars singing in the choir at the time of the transformation were quite mys-tified, when they looked back, as to how the phenomenon occurred.[139]

A brief historical account of the emergence of the new sound and style might easily give the impression of steady progress and an al-most inevitable resolution into the desired timbre,[140] but an internal BBC memo after a broadcast in February 1956 suggests that the out-come was not always so clear and certain. 'I listened to this broadcast,' wrote a BBC official, 'and was most disappointed with the singing of the boys. They produced strident tone and the intonation was far from satisfactory. Was this an off day?'[141]

By the 1960s St John's was recognized as a formidable choral estab-lishment, not so extreme in style and timbre as Westminster Cathedral under George Malcolm but utterly distinctive in Anglican circles. One critic compared the 'almost hard-edged quality' achieved by Guest, the 'punch' of the singing, with the 'unalloyed sweetness' of King's.[142] By others the sounds were often described as 'harsher' and 'edgier' than the sounds that distinguished the Anglican tradition as rep-resented by King's under David Willcocks.

College choirs with choral scholars being forever in a state of flux, it is not surprising that the recorded evidence of St John's indicates continually occurring shifts in timbre. From the recordings it is not quite possible to follow the distinctions Guest seems to have encouraged in timbre between singing the homophony of Victorian and Edwardian composers and singing sixteenth-century polyphony, say, or between a setting by a Catholic composer and an Anglican one. But as he himself always pointed out, such qualities can never be imposed, and particular singers at particular times will have their own special qualities. Critics of the time praised the robustness of the style, the trebles' 'edge' and 'throatiness'. A French critic who regretted the very tight rein kept on the singers of King's[143] saluted St John's in 1963 as the best such choir in England at that time. It would even bear comparison, he thought, with the men and boys at Montserrat. There were indeed male altos at St John's, he pointed out, but nothing of those colourless specimens that certain types of 'discofiles' listen to with such rapture, 'rien de ces voix détimbrées que certains écoutent avec ravissement'.[144] Certainly the trebles at St John's sounded much more French than English when singing Poulenc in 1971.[145]

Why should this change in musical style have happened at one college rather than another? It is by no means sufficient that the acoustics of the chapels are very different. Whenever Russian choirs or the Vienna Boys' Choir have sung in King's Chapel – or indeed when St John's College, Cambridge, have sung there – listeners have not pronounced as vociferously as might be imagined (given the strictures of choirmasters on the dictates of the building) on the obvious incongruity of certain singing styles in such a building. More persuasive than pronouncements on the stylistic characteristics appropriate for Anglican and Catholic liturgies, or the imagined differences between sixteenth-century English and Mediterranean voices, were the differences in character and temperament and education of David Willcocks and George Guest.

Willcocks, as we have seen, found no difficulty in embracing the values and gestures of the world of an English choir school in the 1920s and of an English public school and the army. Reticence was his hallmark. George Guest by contrast was very proud of his Welsh origins – 'a Welsh nationalist', as one of his obituarists described him[146] – and the bright burning sonorities of the male voice choirs of Wales. As far as church-going was concerned, though an Anglican, he felt at home, he said, almost anywhere, 'except when people go to church as a matter of form'. Willcocks was an unbeliever who did go to church just because it was a matter of social custom. St John's sounded different, Guest thought, because they were more concerned with the text, with the words, to make them expressive. He wished St John's primary focus to be on emotion rather than technique. The sound of St John's under Guest, one of his pupils and organ scholars thought, could not be described as 'a "cool sound"'. It was 'a very lively, passionate, and vibrant sound'.[147]

And then there was King's and its chapel. Surely Guest and his singers would not have developed their sound and style quite as they did had it not been for Willcocks and his singers and 'the quint-essence of the traditional English cathedral style' sounding quiet and clear not two minutes' walk away.

6

The Style Since the 1960s

THE CHOIR AT CHRIST CHURCH AND SIMON PRESTON

There were certainly some lay clerks who were still singing well in their sixties and who were highly valued by their choirmasters in the second half of the twentieth century. Maurice Bevan, born in 1921, was one, an academical clerk at Magdalen for a time during the war – he did not complete his degree[1] – who sang at St Paul's into his sixties and deputized there into his seventies, and was the bass of the Deller Consort for more than forty years. In the 1950s he might also often be heard on the radio – 'Twinkle, twinkle little star' on *Listen with Mother* in the afternoon and the service of Compline in the evening.[2] The life of the countertenor particularly was often thought to be a short one, though James Bowman, who became a Gentleman of the Chapel Royal in October 2000, at the age of nearly fifty-nine, was an exception.[3] But most cathedral choir-trainers in the later decades of the twentieth century preferred to work with younger lay clerks. 'Without a shadow of doubt vibrato comes with age, voices get looser, lose focus', as one of them put it in 1980.[4]

In the 1970s and 1980s, as we have seen, two choirs established a system using six young lay clerks together with six choral scholars, allowing solos to be taken by more mature voices and experienced singers without any sacrifice to the blend of the full choir.[5] These choirs were both in Oxford, Christ Church and New College. From 1970 the choir at Christ Church was directed by Simon Preston, who had been a chorister at King's under Boris Ord and then an organ scholar under David Willcocks. After a few years as assistant organist at Westminster Abbey and several months as acting organist at St

Albans and several more as a freelance organist – he was a virtuoso recitalist – he was appointed in 1970, at the age of thirty-two, organist and choirmaster at Christ Church.[6] From his experience at King's he had learnt about tuning and blend and an insistence on unsleeping attention to accuracy over the smallest details. His drive and nervous energy, and his uncanny ability himself never to play a wrong note, gave him tremendous authority. His movements directing the choir were forceful and animated. He quickly raised the standards at Christ Church and his choir, it was said by competent critics, showed the Anglican tradition at its finest.[7] Others considered that the strength and brightness and vigour of the singing constituted a development of the tradition, by which they meant in comparison with King's.[8] Others talked of the asperity of the singing, of the mettlesome quality of the voices, which Preston explained he cultivated because of the blandness of the cathedral's acoustic. The choir at King's, he thought, with its sublime acoustic, always had to work much harder when they sang elsewhere.[9]

Recordings were usually not made at Christ Church but in mellower and richer spaces, like the Chapels at Merton College and Keble.[10] The disciplined professionalism and dependability of the choir at Christ Church, both men and boys, astonished even hardnosed professional orchestral players who performed with them. By 1977 one expert considered that they were probably the best English cathedral choir, demonstrating the hallmark qualities of absolutely secure intonation, admirable blend, a wide range of vocal colour and the ability to perform a broad repertory idiomatically.[11]

Clearly the personality and temperament of the choirmaster, the building in which they habitually sang and the mature voices of some of the men all played a part in moulding the particular qualities of the singing. Inevitably, as this was a university town, the music-making at Christ Church had a decisive influence on young musicians. Their recording of Handel's *Messiah*, which appeared in 1980, changed for ever the way the work was performed and listened to. Here was a performance given by a small choir of men and boys, with women singing the soprano and alto solos, and with the Academy of Ancient Music playing on eighteenth-century instruments or modern copies, the same forces and kinds of instruments that Handel himself would have used. Tempos were brisk, textures light, ornamentation adhered to what the most up-to-date scholarship suggested, and the performance possessed astonishing energy and vitality.[12]

Stanley Sadie, the editor of *The New Grove*, considered that this recording took 'the crucial final steps towards re-creating the work in the terms in which Handel conceived it . . . although some of us [musicologists] have been pleading for it for years'. He found 'its impact very great', and as a musicologist intent on grasping the music's historical meaning he was delighted that this performance provoked him into considering again 'what kind of a work' *Messiah* was and 'what Handel was saying in it'.[13] For these singers had been performing just like this since the eighteenth century, had they not? This was the midsummer of 'authenticity' in music and the world would soon become less wide-eyed about historical verisimilitude.

That the tenor and bass soloists were both former choral scholars, the bass at King's, the tenor at Magdalen, singing in a style that clearly derived all its crucial features – especially its lack of vibrato – from the characteristics of the voices nurtured by David Willcocks and Bernard Rose, clearly inspired younger choral scholars as it moulded the taste of listeners. The voices of the three women soloists too were small-scale and they sang with little vibrato. One of the sopranos, Emma Kirkby, had sung with the Schola Cantorum at Oxford as an undergraduate and in many student concerts, and she seemed to belong to the same world as the men stylistically. She was to go on to become an early music voice par excellence, the perfect vocal complement to the delicate sounds of lutes and viols and fortepianos.[14]

Jeremy Summerly, a young choral scholar at New College who was also a violinist heard a friend enthusing about the recording soon after it came out. He was not thrilled. Did he really have to listen to another *Messiah*? He had played for several performances of this old warhorse for local choirs when he was at school. He reluctantly gave way and got hold of a copy of the discs. The performance transformed his life, he said, especially his ideas on speeds. It was not the thought that the performance might come close to eighteenth-century timbres and speeds. It was the newness and the vitality of the music-making that so fired him. He did not stop to consider the rationale behind the performing style. He just picked up his violin and attempted to copy the style. He copied it whatever he played. He copied the style when he practised Mendelssohn's Violin Concerto.[15]

Some thought the choir's style clearly appropriate for twentieth-century neoclassicism and for modernist scores too in its coolness and 'objective' expressivity. Some laughed when Preston began to record Stravinsky: what, with English male altos? Mostly, Stravinskians marvelled at the results, judging the performing style and the 'unearthly, white tone of the boys' singularly appropriate for the neo-classical *Symphony of Psalms* and also for the serial *Canticum sacrum*,[16] capturing what one critic felt as 'the quasi-medieval ideal of humility and anonymity' of these works.[17]

Christ Church under Preston – he remained there until 1981 – could sound more assertive than King's under Willcocks, just as meticulous in intonation and blend and ensemble, just as beautiful, but with an extraordinary boldness and vigour. Twenty years earlier at an international conference of musicologists there had been a recital of cathedral music for delegates in the cathedral. Some of the choir's singing lacked 'subtlety and precision, and was unworthy of its grand setting', in the estimation of one of the English delegates.[18] Under Preston, the Christ Church Choir could appear at an international music festival like the Henry Wood Promenade Concerts without any incongruity. They sang Vaughan Williams' Mass in G minor and Britten's *Rejoice in the Lamb* at St Augustine's, Kilburn, in the 1974 Proms and Handel's *Messiah* with the Academy of Ancient Music in the Royal Albert Hall in September 1979 – this a few months before the recording was issued.[19] The choir was now 'a virtuoso instrument' in the words of one critic, the best English cathedral choir in the opinion of some.[20]

THE CHOIR OF NEW COLLEGE AND EDWARD HIGGINBOTTOM

In the 1970s New College still had older lay clerks whose musicianship and reliability were greatly prized. But the wide vibrato of even one singer in a choir of this size meant that it was impossible to obtain the kind of blend at all dynamic levels that King's had been demon-strating for forty years.[21] From 1980, though, all the six lay clerks were young, most of them under thirty, and they sang with six choral scholars.[22]

There were sixteen boys on the foundation at New College until in 2006 they were increased to eighteen. Until the 1990s some boys boarded, while a smaller number were day boys. From 1994 all the choristers were day boys, though all of them still attended New College School.[23] In the middle of the twentieth century there would have been fifty boys at a voice trial at New College and most came to the audition from a parish church choir, some with two years' experi-ence behind them and a difficult solo in their satchel. In 1999 there might be twelve or fifteen. At the end of the century there was only one church choir in Oxford with a boys' top line, and most of the trebles coming for a voice trial had had no experience of singing. The College organized open days for boys and their parents to come and see what being a chorister entailed.[24]

Edward Higginbottom, who was Director of Music in the Chapel at New College between 1976 and 2014, consciously tried to move away from the traditional English sound with his trebles. Although others talked of a 'New College sound', he himself did not have an ideal that he strove to cultivate. He wanted each chorister to discover the quality and timbre of his own voice, not to conform to a partic-ular 'English' sound. He tried to enable a boy to 'release' himself as an individual, to feel in no way inhibited, and so to give a 'performance with impact'.[25] Blend was not quite so crucial for Higginbottom as it was for Willcocks. 'I go for resource, power and vigour, and only secondly for refinement. I concentrate a great deal on producing a vocal quality which is fairly chesty, open and loud, and take that as the basis on which I refine their sound. Their tone is steely, clear, forthright, the warmth derives from timbre and sonority rather than from vibrato.'[26] And the boys were singing with young lay clerks, with bigger and more mature voices than choral scholars, who under-stood the importance of blending but were not shy in employing the full power of their voices. This undeniably had an effect on the choral scholars and on the boys too. Among both lay clerks and choral scholars there would usually be a number, as at Christ Church, who were hoping to attempt a singing career. The tenor and the bass solo-ists on the choir's recording of *Messiah* made in January 2006 were former choral scholars at New College; both were appearing on the concert platform and opera stage as soloists, and the bass also sang in consorts and ensembles such as The Sixteen and Ex Cathedra and the Monteverdi Choir.

One of the singers who gave the choristers individual lessons in the 1990s explained that he tried to develop the head voice fully but not to neglect the use of the chest voice – the use of all the vocal cords or folds – and to move effortlessly between the two. This had allowed the boys at New College to develop characteristically strong voices, he thought, without the harshness that is often said to result from employment of the chest voice.[27]

The sound of the trebles at New College was described as 'reedy, plangent' and 'sharp-edged',[28] and Higginbottom certainly produced a succession of skilful trebles singing with admirable self-confidence.[29] A number of them demonstrated their technique and stylistic sophis-tication in the recordings of all Purcell's music recorded by the King's Consort. Unlike George Guest, Higginbottom did not modify the sound for different repertoire, he explained, but trained them to sing with a certain timbre and in a certain style because he believed it to be 'the right way to sing'.[30]

When Higginbottom began at New College in 1976 his job was to produce fine music for daily worship in the Chapel. Thirty years later, by which time he felt that the Church of England barely retained a foothold in college life, he felt he had a responsibility to keep the tradition alive as a cultural and educational phenomenon. In order to flourish in the twenty-first century it was crucial to seize the opportu-nities offered for international concert tours and for recording. The singers, both boys and men, must be given fresh opportunities and challenges – the choir had released many previously unrecorded works by Byrd and discovered Maltese Renaissance music. Higgin-bottom liked to marry scholarship and performance, and he put forward the recorded performances of music he had edited – a set of discs of Pergolesi alongside the editions he had produced – for the government's research assessment exercise, just as his musicolo-gist colleagues put forward the books they had written. It became important too during his four decades at New College to explore repertory beyond the works sung in chapel services, to perform Bach's St John Passion, for example, and to sing not just not for a congregation but to perform facing an audience.[31] In the 1990s New College sang at the Albert Hall, in several Proms, Bach's motet *Komm, Jesu, komm* and the *Magnificat* in D major, and the Proms premiere of Handel's *Deborah*.[32] Choirs at the English choral foundations had not sung regularly in the Albert Hall half a century earlier; neither had they sung in Handel's *Deborah*. Very few of them tackled Bach's motets. Choirs such as New College and Christ Church and King's were now ranked alongside fully professional adult ensembles.

By the 1980s a steady stream of recent choral scholars, adept at learning music fast, who could sing unfailingly in the middle of every note and with minimal vibrato if required, was feeding the growing appetite for medieval and Renaissance and Baroque music.

The sound and style of the admired choirs like King's and Christ Church in the 1960s and 1970s, and of the soloists who were beginning to sing with them, had evolved in the recent past. But there was an inclination to believe that because similar choirs of men and boys had first sung the music of Byrd and Gibbons and Purcell and Handel, the modern ones must have been coming close to the performing style that the composers themselves would have recognized. Surely the countertenor, the English alto, preserved from extinction, everyone said, in the stalls of cathedral choirs, surely that voice enshrined the sound and timbre and technique of an ancient performing style? But then the howling of the altos at Norwich in 1852 is remembered, that description of Lowell Mason of an entry by the altos being like a severe body blow.[33] And the singing styles of later twentieth-century examples don't seem to share many features with the earliest recorded examples of countertenors.[34]

Alfred Deller, born in 1912, and a lay clerk at Canterbury and then at St Paul's, was thought in the 1950s to have in some way rediscovered a lost art. This was at a time when Baroque and medieval and Renaissance music was attracting the attention of scholars in expanding university music departments, the imaginations of composers like

Britten and Tippett were captivated by the music of Purcell, and broadcasting and the LP were fuelling the appreciation of early music repertoires. No doubt choral scholars did listen over and over again to the earliest solo recordings of Alfred Deller released on 78 rpm discs between 1949 and 1954.[35] The precise, delicate singing of such countertenors as Roger Job at Magdalen and the unnamed one at St John's singing on a disc released in 1961 suggests this.[36] But the singing of James Bowman, a choral scholar at New College and then a lay clerk there and at Christ Church, had an even greater impact.

When in 1967 David Munrow was forming his Early Music Consort he intended it as an instrumental ensemble. But then he heard Bowman sing and instantly recruited him: 'here was the most fabulous "noise" I'd ever heard'.[37] Bowman found instant fame that year when he was discovered by Benjamin Britten and sang the part of Oberon in *A Midsummer Night's Dream*. He sang in Cavalli's *La Calisto* at Glyndebourne in 1970, in Handel's *Semele* for English National Opera in 1971 and in Peter Maxwell Davies's *Taverner* at Covent Garden in 1972. Such a voice was required to sing everything, from the music of the Crusades to highly dissonant new music in which the perception of exact pitching was essential. Crucially Bowman's was an exceptionally big voice for a countertenor. He himself did not eschew singing with vibrato on principle. But, having been brought up in the English cathedral tradition as a chorister at Ely, he could sing, magisterially, without it. This Christopher Hogwood required him to do, on more or less historical grounds, when he sang Vivaldi.[38] Whether Vivaldi would have recognized the singing as Italianate and idiomatic can hardly be guessed at; a choirmaster at one of the choral foundations in the later twentieth century would certainly have judged it English and idiomatic.

Neither Ord nor Willcocks nor Preston nor indeed Willcocks' successors, Philip Ledger and Stephen Cleobury, were authenticists: 'there can be no such thing as pure authenticity', was Cleobury's straightforward view on the matter; 'supposing you could prove what the sounds actually were . . . you've still got the audience listening with twentieth-century ears'.[39] The interpretive detail with which performers were often so concerned was, as one scholar pointed out, 'outside accumulated musicological knowledge', and was therefore 'either conveniently forgotten about (because we don't know) or deliberately disparaged (because certain people think they do)'.[40]

One critic marvelled at the impact of the Christ Church *Messiah*: 'The biting edge of the gut strings, the airy buoyancy of the total instrumental ensemble, the utter transparency of the choral singing, the sharply etched musical profile of every familiar member freed from any suggestion of a Romantic silky-rich vibrato.' The critic thought that the 'scholarly thoroughness' behind the performance was beyond dispute. He knew that this performance was like none other in the twentieth century. (The large number of recordings and accounts of performances of the work would corroborate this.)

But how was he sure that it was very similar to performances in the eighteenth century? What he also admired was 'the sheer joyous brilliance of the execution' and it was this quality and its startling newness that marked it out, not its correctness and faithfulness to eighteenth-century stylistic norms.[41]

If music-lovers and journalists and church musicians themselves early in the twenty-first century were asked about the best choirs in England singing cathedral music they would certainly mention King's and St John's, Cambridge, New College, Oxford, St Paul's and the Choir of Westminster Abbey, all of them choirs of men and boys at the choral foundations. But such lovers of the tradition would now also rank other choirs besides those of men and boys. They would include some provincial cathedral choirs with girls very highly, like Wells and Salisbury. And they would undoubtedly name the best of the Oxbridge choirs with men and women, Trinity and Clare and Caius at Cambridge, and Queen's and Merton at Oxford. And then there were choirs and consorts of professional singers, men and women, such as Stile Antico, the Tallis Scholars, the Cardinall's Musick, the Dunedin Consort, The Sixteen, Polyphony and the Monteverdi Choir.

In 2011 an American composer and conductor was asked what he considered the salient features of the singers in all such choirs, choirs belonging to what he termed 'the British choral tradition', for which he had a deep love and admiration. It was their impeccable tuning, he said, as a result of which the music seemed to shimmer. It was their excellent sight-reading abilities. It was their bright and clear tone with little vibrato. It was their awareness of style, the ability to be expressive without being sentimental. It was their intelligence – 'British choirs simply get it'.[42] These were the distinguishing qualities of King's under Boris Ord, made so familiar to the world in the particular style forged by David Willcocks. When Willcocks went back to King's in 1957 the cathedral and college choirs with girls and women and the professional concert-giving choirs and consort choirs did not exist. How were these choirs created and how had they attained international renown? What differences could be identified between the singing of boys and girls and boys and women, and between the singing of King's under Willcocks and all these choirs singing half a century later?

WOMEN IN CHAPEL CHOIRS

The opening of the Cambridge colleges to women, most of them in the 1970s, was soon followed by the establishment of three chapel choirs of about two dozen men and women which quickly attained very high standards, and they have remained among the best college choirs in England. The choir at Clare College was created as a mixed-voice group in 1971. Gonville and Caius' modern choir was constituted in 1979. Trinity College had long had a choir of men and local boys and a succession of distinguished organists, Sir Charles Stanford, Alan Gray and Hubert Middleton (a pupil of Walter Parratt), who had previously been organist of Truro and Ely Cathedrals. In 1946 Middleton was the first organist to be made a Fellow of the College; he played an important part in devising the syllabus for the Music Tripos instituted at Cambridge in 1945. After he resigned in 1957 the boys of the choir were done away with. Between 1958 and 1968 Raymond Leppard directed a choir just of undergraduate men's voices and a succession of organ scholars played for services.[43] The College first admitted women in 1978, and a choir of twenty-four choral students, men and women, first sang in the Michaelmas Term of 1982.[44]

These three choirs now number between two dozen and thirty singers each. Most of the singers are undergraduates of the college concerned, a few are postgraduates and a few are members of other colleges. At Clare College an undergraduate organ scholar had formerly directed the choir. Now all three colleges appointed professional directors of music, senior members of the university, or reappoint existing directors, on the formation of their new choirs. The singers now have singing lessons with eminent teachers who also teach at leading music colleges and conservatoires, often with experience in opera as well as lieder and oratorio, some with particular experience in choir and consort singing; some who have themselves sung in college choirs as undergraduates and continue to sing as soloists with choirs such as the Monteverdi Choir. Choral scholars or choral volunteers in these three choirs are expected today to attend about five hours of rehearsals each week. These three choirs sing fewer services, typically three each week, mostly Evensong but also the Eucharist, and sometimes Compline, occasionally Matins and other occasional services like carol services, and they sing at college feasts in hall.

Soon after their establishment all of these choirs began to give recitals and concerts, to record and broadcast and to make tours. At the heart of their repertories was the same Anglican repertory as at King's and their directors were all former organ or choral scholars at Oxford or Cambridge, some of them former choristers at choral foundations. Timothy Brown, who directed the choir at Clare between 1979 and 2010, had been a chorister at Westminster Abbey, a choral scholar at King's and a lay clerk at New College.[45] Richard Marlow, Director of Music at Trinity between 1968 and 2006, had been a choirboy at Southwark Cathedral and organ scholar at Selwyn College, Cambridge – he had turned down the organ scholarship at King's because he wanted to run a choir, not act only as an assistant.[46] His successor, Stephen Layton, was a chorister at Winchester and an organ scholar at King's, and Organist and Director of Music at the Temple Church before he came to Trinity.[47] Geoffrey Webber, Precentor and Director of Music at Caius, was a chorister at Salisbury, a music scholar at King's School, Worcester, and an organ scholar at New College, Oxford.[48]

Critics and commentators immediately found in the three choirs the familiar characteristics that had marked out King's in recent decades, the blending of the voices, the brightness of the tone quality, the way the sound gleamed, the 'whiteness' and 'cleanness' of the sound, the 'boyish purity' of the top lines, the impeccable intonation, and they marvelled at how beautiful performances were, how ethereal, how eloquent.

Attempting to write about their performances one American critic couldn't move his pen, he was 'frozen in place by the sheer otherworldly beauty of what I was hearing'.[49] The Englishness of both Trinity and King's – their smooth-running, their dependability, their stylish imperturbability – was likened to that of Rolls-Royce cars.[50]

In December 2012 the Choir of Trinity College, Cambridge, sang Bach's *Christmas Oratorio* at St John's, Smith Square, with the Orchestra of the Age of Enlightenment, and they sang it all from memory. In the summer of 2013 the Choir of Trinity toured with a varied programme of music ranging from Tallis to the Latvian composer Ēriks Ešenvalds (b. 1977), unaccompanied but for Britten's *Rejoice in the Lamb*. It was all sung from memory – this was not uncommon in the choir's concert appearances – and the first five works were given in the Chapel of Cheltenham College with members of the choir scattered singly throughout the Chapel and audience. It felt, one critic reported, as if you were hearing the music from the inside, with the polyphony 'being woven around you'.[51]

Stephen Layton himself saw his choir as being firmly in the Anglican tradition. Ten new members or so joined his choir at Trinity each September and it took him merely a matter of hours to lick them into shape. In part the reason for this, he was sure, was that many of them had been choristers in cathedral choirs 'which have inherited and maintained the great tradition of choral singing'.[52] He spoke of the 'tradition like none other', a tradition in England that had continued 'for five hundred years'.[53] As we have seen, that was not true. But to the musicians themselves and to many of those who listened to them, the style was so associated with ancient music and ancient buildings, and it was so strong and so distinctive and had seeped so deep into the subconscious, that its authority required no evolutionary analysis.

The voices of the boys in King's College under David Willcocks produced a lighter and more delicate sound than that of the modern college choirs with women, whose sound was more opulent and creamier. The difference in the sound of the alto line was usually even more telling. In a recording of music by Herbert Howells that Trinity made in 2014 there are ten altos – eight women and two men.[54] On a disc of Advent music made by Clare College in 2012 there are four altos, one of them a man;[55] on one disc of contemporary and medieval music recorded by Caius College in 2004 there are six altos, one of them a man.[56] Many of the women in the choirs made a similar sound to a male alto. But very few were indistinguishable from countertenors at all dynamic levels. The diamond-etched lines of four or six male altos singing with boys, the unearthly glitter, could not quite be reproduced with women, even when the voices were singing quietly.

The tone colours, though, that could be created from mixing in varying numbers male countertenors and female altos continued to surprise and encouraged experiment. In 2010 Peterborough Cathedral appointed a female alto lay clerk[57] and in 2011 Lincoln Cathedral appointed a female twenty-two-year-old graduate choral scholar.[58] In 2017 St Paul's, which had placed a female alto on its list of authorized deputy lay clerks in 2010,[59] appointed its first full-time female alto vicar choral, who had been a choral scholar at Caius College, Cambridge.[60]

Clearly the women in the college choirs in the twenty-first century had more experience at sight-reading and the ability to memorize long works, which most children do not quite have. A few would be hoping to become singers by profession and of those some would be hoping to sing as consort singers and a very few to sing principally as soloists. A director of a chapel choir like Graham Ross, appointed Director of Music at Clare College in 2010, who continued to work as a professional conductor of orchestras and in opera houses, was a new phenomenon. David Willcocks and Philip Ledger were members of the university music faculty with teaching duties, who took score-reading classes and gave occasional lectures; Stephen Cleobury never was. The duties of a college organist and choirmaster had become too onerous and too specialized. In the twenty-first century some college organists at Cambridge were designated 'affiliated lecturers' – these in 2017 included the organists of Caius and Sidney Sussex and St

Catharine's, who were also directors of studies at their colleges, super-vising the general progress of the music students – but not the organists at King's, Trinity or St John's.

Although rooted in a weekly round of liturgical duties the college choirs at Clare, Caius and Trinity performed to audiences on stages and platforms much more than did King's under Willcocks. These choirs did indeed include voices of great individuality and character, which also knew how to vary vibrato and to blend scrupulously.[61] And such was the vocal expertise of these twenty-first-century choral scholars that when they had to sing a work like John Tavener's *God is with us*, written for the Choir of Winchester Cathedral but stylis-tically in a Russian Orthodox manner, they could momentarily turn aside from their own stylistic inheritance with startling effect.[62]

GIRLS IN CATHEDRAL CHOIRS

In 1991 Salisbury Cathedral established a choir of girls alongside their boy choristers, to sing services with the lay clerks and, occasion-ally, on high days and holy days, to sing together with the boys.

A girls' choir had been established at St Edmundsbury Cathedral in 1960. They sang by themselves until in 1971 they joined the boys in singing the top line together with the lay clerks. The girls had been dropped on the insistence of a Provost appointed in 1981, which led to the resignation of the organist in 1984.[63] A girls' choir was formed at St David's in Wales in the early 1970s.[64] St Mary's Cathedral, Edin-burgh, admitted girls to sing alongside boys on the treble line in 1978,[65] and at Bradford Cathedral girls were introduced in about 1986 to form a mixed choir of girls and boys.[66] There had been a girls' choir of some kind at Leicester Cathedral, not usually singing with the boys, since 1974.[67]

The girls at St David's, Bradford and Leicester were recruited, orig-inally at least, because of the difficulty of finding boys. There was no such difficulty at Salisbury in 1991, which was the first ancient choral foundation with existing daily choral services to admit girls into the choir. This was clearly a radical departure from a tradition that had existed at the choral foundations for hundreds of years. Many feared that it was dangerous to tamper with a tradition that had lasted so long.[68]

Some thought girls were being introduced out of a sense of fairness and equality, out of a concern for social justice of which the establishment of the Equal Opportunities Commission in 1975 and recent legislation on equal pay, sex discrimination, race relations and disability provision were evidence.[69] Any sense of injustice was misplaced, many organists were sure. In respect of their singing voices boys and girls were indeed unequal. But the ordination of the first woman deacon in the Church of England in 1987 and the first woman priest in 1994 changed for ever perceptions of the role of women within the Church. The 1992 *Report of the Archbishops' Commission on Church Music* recommended that the choir schools should seek ways of providing 'the same musical and liturgical education for girls as that enjoyed by boys'.[70]

Although the Chapter and musicians at Salisbury remained confident and buoyant from the moment the scheme was hatched, there were formidable problems to be faced. Would it be possible for the Salisbury Chapter to carry out its intentions and sustain both sets of sixteen boys and sixteen girls? Some within the Church of England already questioned the cost of running cathedral choirs. How would they react to additional financial burdens? Would the choirmasters have the time to carry out the additional musical and administrative duties? If the work of the choristers were divided equally between boys and girls this would result in a smaller repertoire for each set of choristers than was formerly necessary for the boys alone to learn. This might potentially result in higher standards. But it might not. The singing of the psalms, for example, required constant effort to attain mastery. And the demands of unceasing public performance were surely in themselves a useful spur in developing alertness and confidence.[71]

Such concerns, though, did not quite explain the antagonism of some cathedral musicians and of many who loved the tradition, the 'stiff, sometimes venomous opposition' that Salisbury encountered, according to the Dean at the time.[72] Some saw the traditional constitution of the cathedral choir as 'a stupendous inheritance' and were sure that the introduction of the girl's voice would lead to 'a total transformation' of the sound and the style of singing in cathedrals, a style which had taken centuries to perfect, they were certain. The boy's voice was 'natural', 'pure', 'platonic'. It was not 'fleshly'. It was 'a unique spiritual resource', 'a crystalline cry to a world outside and beyond us . . . providing poignant comfort and spiritual insight'.[73]

A cathedral precentor was sure in the 1980s that most organists would throw up their hands in horror at the thought of girls in cathedral choirs. In 1968 when the choir at St Edmundsbury had lost some of its senior trebles and was struggling a little, the Provost gave permission for eight from the girls' choir to join the boys just for the installation of a new bishop, a service that was being televised. Some in the cathedral thought they would become a laughing stock because of this and steps were taken to ensure that the girls were hidden from view, or at least hidden from the television cameras. When girls were mixed with the boys in the 1970s the organist thought that some cathedral organists never forgave him.[74]

Most would have said that girls could not make 'the right sound'. No one, though, was quite sure why this was. There was 'a certain amount of talk about vocal cords', one precentor observed.[75] The sound of girls under thirteen singing was 'windy and awful', one cathedral organist explained. Another described the sound as 'vapid'.[76] Few knew, however, whether there were important physiological differences between pre-pubertal girls and boys or not. And how did anyone know how trained girls' voices would sound when there were so few examples of girls aged twelve or thirteen who had been trained to sing fourteen hours each week, thirty-five weeks of the year, from year four to year eight?[77]

Church musicians had consciously struggled for so long to rid their profession of the taint of effeminacy. They had worked to create a singing style which they at least recognized as masculine, without expressive nuances that might be felt or construed as feminine. This was music that had been written for and always sung previously by men and boys in a style that was, as they thought, self-evidently masculine. The whole ethos of the training of the boys reinforced the manliness of the enterprise. One headmaster of a choir school noticed that in a co-educational school boys and girls liked to divide and pursue single-sex activities. He doubted that the same kind of disciplined approach to rehearsing that boys experienced could be applied to boys and girls learning together.[78] The nature of such a disciplined approach might be inferred in one cathedral organist's explanation that the boys were not his friends but rather professional colleagues working constantly under pressure. He doubted that girls were tough enough to withstand being 'pushed around' as the singers in his choirs would have to be.[79] The boys had to be 'pushed around' because singing in a cathedral choir was what men did, and men pushed people around. The choirmaster who introduced girls at St Edmundsbury in 1960 conceded that boys liked to be regimented, to be given orders, and girls must be persuaded and encouraged. But every form teacher in a mixed school knew that, he was sure, and treated his charges accordingly.[80]

However dubious many choir-trainers might have been initially, seventeen new girls' choirs were created in the six years after Salisbury established the girls' choir there, followed by a steady stream of others up to the present day.[81] By the summer of 2016 only four Anglican cathedrals remained without any kind of girl choristers: Chichester, St Paul's, Christ Church in Oxford and Hereford.[82]

Salisbury had the same number of girls as boys, sixteen of each; they were of the same age, between eight to thirteen, and attended the same school, the cathedral school, as boarders or day pupils. Choristers did not have to be full-time boarders but had to board during the busiest times of the year such as Christmas and Easter. They shared the duties equally over a fortnight; there were nine choral services each week, the choristers singing with six lay clerks. The arrangements were similar at Wells and York with the duties equally divided, though there were eighteen boys and eighteen girls singing at Wells and twenty of each at York, and at both the choristers sang with twelve men on the lower parts. The choristers did not have to board at Wells and at York it was a day school. But there were a great variety of different arrangements. Most choir schools were privately run, but Bristol was a state school. Where there was no choir school both boys and girls attended a variety of schools, as they did at Southwark and Liverpool. At Rochester, Norwich and Winchester the boys

were educated at the cathedral's own independent school but the girls
came from different schools in the cities and beyond. At Rochester
they were aged between ten and sixteen, at Norwich between eleven
and eighteen, and at Winchester between twelve and seventeen. At
Truro the boys, aged between eight and thirteen, attended Polwhele
House Preparatory School and the girl choristers, aged between thirteen and eighteen, were educated at the independent Truro School.
The girls at Ely were aged from thirteen to eighteen and all of them
attended the cathedral's independent school, the King's School, as
boarders. They were funded and supported by the King's School, not
the cathedral, and they had their own director and assistant director,
not the organists of the cathedral. They were called the Cathedral
Girls' Choir; the men and boys constituted the Ely Cathedral Choir.
At most cathedrals the boys sang more than the girls. At Exeter the
girls sang at three services each week, the boys at four or five. At Ely
the girls sang Evensong twice a week and exercised full Sunday duties
about once a month. The girls at Norwich sang Evensong on Tuesdays and sang one Sunday Eucharist and Evensong each term. The
girls at Winchester sang one service every Sunday as well as at services and concerts at Christmas and Easter. It was at such festivals
that girls and boys sang together in many cathedrals. At Peterborough, though, there was a weekly choral evensong for high voices
with both girls and boys singing.[83]

With these fundamental changes in the English cathedral tradition,
what had happened to the singing style itself? How did these choirs
of girls sing? What effect had the introduction of girls had on the
singing of the boys? Had the sound and style of the English cathedral
tradition been transformed? Or had it been destroyed?

When the organist, Richard Seal, was preparing to welcome the first
girls at Salisbury Cathedral he was sure that they would make a
different sound from the boys, indeed he hoped that they would. He
didn't know what sort of sound it would be but he hoped he would
never tell them to make a sound 'like the boys'. He anticipated that it
would be 'a female sound' in that he thought it would be 'slightly
frailer, with less carrying power maybe'. He explained that just before

a boy's voice changed it could become very strong and focused. A girl's voice did not 'flower', he thought, until she was fifteen or sixteen. But if the girl's voice might be fragile he was sure that it could be 'just as musical' as a boy's.[84]

The views of those who studied the sound minutely did not always seem to be in agreement. At the choral foundations there seemed to be varied assessments and different aims and objectives. A precentor at Norwich considered it not possible for girls under eleven, say, to make the sound of boys of the same age, but he thought that older girls could be trained to sound 'like boys'. That is why the girls' choir at Norwich was established for girls between eleven and eighteen.[85] The girls' choir-trainer at Ely seemed to have different objectives, or at least the results struck one specialist listener as far removed from the characteristic sound of English choristers: to this historian of English cathedral choirs the sound of the girls was 'distinctly non-treble', the sound of a 'group of young women', 'not childlike'. About half of them 'have, or are developing, a natural vibrato'.[86] The organist at Liverpool, who in the 1990s created a Cathedral Girls' Choir while he was organist at Coventry, which consisted of fifty singers aged between the ages of eight and sixteen,[87] thought that the tone of his boys at Liverpool was 'quite a strident, well-focused sound'. They tended to sing loudly habitually, unless they lost interest and just sang along quietly making no impact. Usually it was hard to restrain them and their voices could fill that vast building. The girls sang habitually more quietly, generally in a middle dynamic range. He thought this reflected differences he saw in personality and character, that girls didn't like risking failure, didn't want to be challenged; boys were much more competitive and badly behaved. The girls could stay still and think if they were asked a question; the boys considered a moment's silence an opportunity to talk or mess about. He considered boys' voices and girls' voices to be of a different quality and timbre, like a diapason and a flute stop on the organ, both beautiful but different.[88]

The organist at Exeter, though, considered the sound of girls' and boys' voices 'very similar'. He thought regional accents and dialects could make a difference to the timbre of a child's voice. He believed the acoustic of a cathedral and the character and temperament of a director to be most significant of all. He was certain that there could be as much contrast in the voices of two boys or two girls as between a boy and a girl.[89]

Surely it was not surprising, an organist at Salisbury pointed out, that the boys and girls of the same age, singing the same repertory in the same acoustic and trained in the same way often by the same choirmaster, and performing with the same men, should sing in a similar way. He was not too concerned with attempting to quantify or qualify any differences. He made music by instinct.[90]

The reactions provoked seemed in part to depend on whether the sounds were being examined through a microscope or a telescope. Different listeners responded according to their own backgrounds and cultural expectations. Germans and Americans and Australians were more likely to hear the family resemblances of all these English choirs. Many writers and commentators did indeed seem to give particular authority to the distinctiveness of King's College Choir in the middle of the century. It was the style of Willcocks' choir and not just of King's that remained a touchstone. Earthly choirs may have sung of 'eternal changelessness' but their singing could not but change, from year to year, from day to day. And anyway musicians didn't wish to copy but to be different. They might have imitated a mannerism but if they wished to reproduce a style they would surely fail and the ways in which they failed might reveal the most distinctive strands of their own corporate personalities.

In 2002 a Professor of Education who had made a special study of children in English cathedral choirs considered that, at least with pre-pubertal girls and boys whose voices had been trained, there was 'considerable potential for female choristers to be confused as male'.[91] It could be difficult distinguishing between the singing of girls and boys. Lovers of the sound of boys' voices had often been mistaken; cathedral musicians had often been mistaken. The possibility of telling them apart depended on many factors: the number of singers – the singer of a solo would normally be easier to identify; the tessitura of a passage; the loudness of the singing; on whether the trebles or sopranos were singing alone in unison or as the top line of a four-part texture; on whether they were unaccompanied or accompanied by the organ; on the acoustic; on the familiarity of the listener with a particular acoustic; on the exact position in an acoustic of singers and listeners or of microphone placings.

The introduction of girls did not appear to have destroyed the tradition. In 2015 there were about 850 boys in all the cathedral choirs and Westminster Abbey (not counting the college choirs) and 690 girls.[92] And the characteristic features of King's in the middle of the twentieth century – which so distinguished that choir from the others at the English choral foundations at that time – were now usually displayed by most of these choirs. They were taken for granted. One of the new girl choristers at Canterbury in 2016 explained that immaculate ensemble was 'so important because if everyone's doing the same thing it can be so effective'. Which comment begged many questions and in so doing demonstrated the chorister's instinctive acceptance of the tradition.[93] The absence of vibrato that was so pronounced a characteristic of King's under Willcocks did not characterize quite all the choirs in the early years of the twenty-first century – but then it hadn't in the 1960s either.

In 2015 a historian reported that the organist of York Minster did not hold to 'the traditional notion of the Anglican choral sound, recognisable by a delicate straight tone. In York Minster Choir, a straight tone is used occasionally only for effect, such as in a *pianissimo* section, or to convey a certain mood of the text.'[94] The director of the choir encouraged 'a natural vibrato', according to the historian, one 'that blend[ed] well with the other voices in the large space'.[95] Treble and soprano voices in the choir in 2011 did indeed cultivate a wider vibrato than Willcocks would have wished for. In quieter passages the blend was very similar; in louder passages, though, the vibrato did tell more on sound and texture and the singing lost that particular distinctiveness that Ord and Willcocks created. King's at the beginning of the twenty-first century was certainly not such a dominating exemplar as it had been fifty years earlier. That the choirmaster at York and the historian both talked of the 'Anglican choral sound' and 'a delicate straight tone', though, did indicate that the style pioneered by King's in the mid-twentieth century still lingered in the minds of church musicians.

SACRED OR SECULAR?

The Clerkes of Oxenford were an amateur choir of young men and women that came close to the sound and style of King's and Magdalen in the 1960s. The Tallis Scholars too were a choir of amateurs, choral scholars and others, directed by an undergraduate, who gave their first concert in November 1973 in St Mary Magdalen's Church in Oxford.[96] There were very few professional singers at that time who sang with the tone quality and had the skill in blending and ensemble that were held to be so important to the style, at least by their director, Peter Phillips.

But this disciplined style that was nurtured by the college choirs, and particularly by King's and Magdalen, was now being developed by former choral scholars increasingly taking part in professional performances. Former choral scholars like James Bowman, Charles Brett and Martyn Hill appeared with David Munrow and his Early Music Consort of London in the early 1970s and inspired a generation.[97] A new kind of voice and a new kind of musician were being created, essentially from the ranks of choral scholars. But there were still comparatively few of them working as professional musicians. There were, however, some of them – lawyers, teachers, accountants – eager to continue singing, who were glad to be given the chance to sing alongside professional musicians, London lay clerks or young singers aspiring to sing as soloists in early music performances or opera or oratorio.

Of the solo quartet in the Tallis Scholars' famous 1980 recording of Allegri's *Miserere* only one, Michael Chance, was aspiring to a career as a professional musician.[98] But Equity, the singers' union, objected at this time – the later 1970s and early 1980s – to the mixing of amateurs and professionals, even though professional singers weren't being denied work. There were simply not enough of them possessing the required technique. Equity would allow groups like the Tallis Scholars to operate using either unpaid amateurs or professionals paid according to the union's going rates, but not to mix them. Peter Phillips was anxious to enter the professional world, for his choir's musicianship and the music they sang to be assessed by the highest professional standards, and for the singers to be presented and marketed with professional expertise. More and more of the best of the former choral scholars were contemplating a professional singing career, but would their dreams be realized? Would tastes be created and larger audiences be formed and markets created? Would there be enough work to sustain careers as choral singers? All this remained uncertain. For the time being each of the singers in the Tallis Scholars was paid the basic union rate, the amateurs as well as the professionals, in order not to infringe Equity rules.[99]

Their disc of two masses by Josquin des Prez, 'Pange lingua' and 'La sol fa re mi', which was released in 1987,[100] was judged the best record in the early music category of the *Gramophone* magazine awards that year and was then preferred above the winners in all the other categories – choral, orchestral, operatic, chamber, period performance, contemporary, instrumental and so on – and named as the Record of the Year. This led to general recognition of the choir's status as mainstream and thoroughly professional and to their appearances in international artists' series in major concert halls all over the world. It led to increased opportunities not just for the Tallis Scholars but for other choirs like them – The Sixteen, Polyphony, the Taverner Choir – and to increased work for this new kind of professional singer.[101]

A soprano in the Clerkes of Oxenford had probably sung in a school choir and then in one of the Oxbridge undergraduate choirs like the Schola Cantorum in Oxford, as well as in one of the men's college chapel choirs like Merton on Sunday evening and probably for a weekday Evensong as well. A woman joining one of the professional groups in the twenty-first century might have been a chorister in a cathedral choir, have won a choral scholarship to Trinity College or Clare College, Cambridge, and sung several days a week and broadcast and recorded – in other words she may now well have followed a similar path as the men in these choirs. She may then have trained at a music college before auditioning for one of the choirs, as well as beginning a career as a soloist singing with choral societies.

In the 1960s a young singer, whether a man or a women, would have trained at a conservatoire to sing in opera. Such singers at the start of their careers might, temporarily, have sung in choirs – including church choirs – to widen their experience and earn some money. But such activity was looked on askance, it being necessary in a church choir to 'hold back' your voice, to restrain that vocal individuality which you spent the rest of your time endeavouring to cultivate and develop. At the end of the century you could enrol in an 'early music' section of a department of singing. You could study consort singing. The particular kind of voice valued by those who directed early music consorts was now recognized as a valuable acquisition: it now had a market value and could sustain a career. A specialist teacher would now be sought to develop a technique 'appropriate for choral singing, especially Renaissance Polyphony and chant', as the website of one of the most expert sopranos teaching the style put it.[102]

A century earlier Henry Davey had written about fifteenth- and sixteenth-century music for his *History of English Music* – which was eventually published in 1895 – using secondary sources, which were largely unsympathetic. He then began to look at the actual manuscripts for himself and this caused him to reject everything he had already written on this music and spend three years in their study. He concluded his five-hundred-page survey with an encomium for the composers of the Renaissance: 'let us ever reverence these men; the English musicians of the fifteenth and sixteenth centuries have dowered the whole world with a glorious new art.'[103] A century later the vast quantities of polyphony from Europe as well as from England were being listened to with the greatest enthusiasm by audiences the world over.

But not quite by everybody. Roger Bowers taught medieval and Renaissance music at Cambridge University from 1978 and had spent a lifetime in the study and analysis of well over a thousand pieces of music of the period and of several thousand archival documents. We have seen that he considered Wulstan's high-pitch theory mistaken and so the choice of pitch and vocal scoring for many pieces inappropriate. In 1995 he also thought that female voices were 'unacceptable as a substitute for the unique sound of the voices of boys'. He also regarded the vocal sound and style of modern groups inappropriate for the music, the tone too large and resonant, since modern performances miss 'the sense of intimacy and introspection generated within a late medieval chancel or chapel by singers performing for themselves and for their deity alone, there being no congregation in attendance to edify or entertain'. His verdict on nearly all modern performances was that they were 'distorted, superficial and false'.[104]

The choirs continued to proliferate nonetheless. The Monteverdi Choir had been founded in the 1960s, the Tallis Scholars, the Taverner Choir and The Sixteen in the 1970s, Polyphony and the Cardinall's Musick in the '80s, the Dunedin Consort in the '90s, Alamire, Tenebrae, Voces8, Exaudi and Stile Antico all in the first decade of the new century. These were some of the most celebrated and successful. One singer in the Tallis Scholars in 2016 also worked as a chartered accountant for Deloitte LLP.[105] But more typically a singer would sing in a number of such ensembles: besides working for the Tallis Scholars one soprano in 2016 sang in Stile Antico, Tenebrae, the BBC Singers, the Monteverdi Choir, Polyphony, the Cardinall's Musick and the Dunedin Consort.[106] A bass in Stile Antico was Head of Academic Music and Director of Lower Chapel Music at Eton College and also worked as a composer, arranger and writer about music.[107] One tenor with Stile Antico worked as a conductor, vocal coach and répétiteur as well as a singer, and had worked at Glyndebourne, English National Opera and Chicago Opera Theater, and conducted for the Royal Opera, Welsh National Opera and Opera North.[108] One bass was the Director of Music at the Church of St Mary Magdalen, Oxford, conductor of the Frideswide Voices and the Orlando Chamber Choir, Chorus Master of Ludus Baroque, and he also sang with Stile Antico, Polyphony and the Eric Whitacre Singers.[109] One soprano sang in Polyphony, The Sixteen, Alamire, Tenebrae, the Retrospect Ensemble, Stile Antico and the Spanish group La Grande Chappelle. She had begun singing as a chorister at Salisbury Cathedral under Richard Seal. She had been a choral scholar at Trinity College, Cambridge, and as a soloist she had toured with the Monteverdi Choir. She had sung in Fauré's Requiem with the Liverpool Philharmonic Orchestra and Moscow Chamber Orchestra, in Monteverdi's Vespers in Winchester Cathedral, in Mozart's Requiem in St Martin-in-the-Fields, in Handel's *Messiah* at St John's Smith Square and Salisbury Cathedral. She also sang as the female soloist for the Irish show Riverdance in packed arenas across Europe and America. She had acted as a musical assistant on courses for the National Youth Choirs of Great Britain, the Ulster Youth Choir and the Royal School of

Church Music. She taught choir directors working with children in disadvantaged areas of Mumbai in India for the charity Songbound. She did a part-time degree in climate change. She enjoyed climbing rock faces.[110]

All such groups in England drew largely on the same pool of singers. The similarities between them were obvious to the ear. What were the differences? Some sang with one or two voices to a part. Voces8 were always eight voices; The Sixteen were not always exactly sixteen voices and could be thirty or so for big pieces by Bach and Handel. Polyphony often sang with about thirty voices. The Cardinall's Musick was a consort of solo voices, six singers or eight or ten perhaps depending on the scoring of a particular work. Exaudi usually sang with one voice to a part, and ranged from three to eighteen voices. There was Tenebrae, typically sixteen voices, and the Tenebrae Consort, which might sing with eight. Stile Antico consisted of twelve singers and were exceptional in working without a conductor.[111] The blending of the voices, however many, was often the most arresting quality for those not familiar with the style, without any vocal idiosyncrasies of this tenor or that soprano obtruding.

Most of these choirs and consorts regarded themselves as specialists in Renaissance music and particularly in the polyphony of the sixteenth century, both English – written for pre- and post-Reformation liturgies – and continental. The Tallis Scholars had sought, their site explained, 'to bring Renaissance works to a wider audience', but they also included in their repertory some contemporary music, including works by John Tavener, Arvo Pärt, Eric Whitacre, Nico Muhly and Gabriel Jackson.[112]

The Cardinall's Musick commissioned music from composers such as Judith Weir, Michael Finnissy, Simon Whalley and Matthew Martin besides singing the English Renaissance music for which they were best known;[113] and Stile Antico also sang works by a few contemporary composers, such as John McCabe, Huw Watkins and Nico Muhly.[114] Tenebrae performed Renaissance polyphony – Victoria and Tallis – but gave early music no special place in their repertory. They sang Berlioz's *L'enfance du Christ* and the Rachmaninov Vespers, Brahms and Bruckner and Parry, and Fauré's Requiem, and described themselves as 'a dedicated advocate for contemporary composers' such as Judith Bingham, Alexander Levine, Paweł Łukaszewski, Paul Mealor, Hilary Tann, John Tavener and Will Todd, Ola Gjeilo and Alexander L'Estrange.[115]

Exaudi were exceptional in being a contemporary music group first with a special affinity, as they explained, 'for the radical edges of contemporary music, at home equally with maximal complexity, microtonality and experimental aesthetics'. They sang music by Birtwistle, Ferneyhough, Xenakis, Skempton, Cardew, Eötvös, Sciarrino and many others, and also younger composers like Ignacio Agrimbau, Matthew Shlomowitz, Claudia Molitor, Chung Shih Hoh, Marcus Trunk and Joanna Bailie. Even Exaudi, though, occasionally sang early music – Obrecht, Schütz, Taverner, Byrd, Lassus, Josquin, Gibbons, Tomkins. For, as they explained, the group drew inspiration for their sound 'from that of early music ensembles, a strong but focused tone that is ideal for the performance of harmonically intricate contemporary music'.[116]

The Sixteen's linear descent from the Clerkes of Oxenford could not be clearer. Harry Christophers, the founder, who remains the chief conductor after nearly forty years, was an academical clerk at Magdalen under Bernard Rose and he had sung in the Clerkes under David Wulstan's direction. The Sixteen had their origins in the singing together of friends made at that time. John Sheppard, the music in the Eton Choirbook, Tallis and Byrd – those remained composers that the choir continued to explore. But they encompassed the music of all centuries: Palestrina, Victoria, Monteverdi, Buxtehude, Henry Purcell, the seventeenth-century Polish composer Bartłomiej Pękiel and Gutiérrez de Padilla (c. 1590–1664), a Spanish composer who worked in Mexico. They sang Bach and Handel, Mozart, Fauré's Requiem and Brahms' German Requiem in the composer's own arrangement for piano duet accompaniment; the piano used in their recording was a Bösendorfer from 1872. And from the twentieth century The Sixteen sang music by a whole host of composers: Frank Martin, Benjamin Britten, the Americans Barber, Bernstein, Reich, Fine, Copland and del Tredici, the French composers André Jolivet, Olivier Messiaen, Jean-Yves Daniel-Lesur, and contemporary composers like Tarik O'Regan, Ruth Byrchmore and Roderick Williams, Antonio

Teixeira, James MacMillan, Will Todd, Matthew Martin and Rox-anna Panufnik.[117]

Perhaps the most wide-ranging of all in terms of repertoire was the Monteverdi Choir. They sang Monteverdi, Tallis, Byrd, Victoria, Morales, Buxtehude, Rameau, Bach and Handel, Mozart, Beethoven, Brahms, Percy Grainger, Stravinsky. They sang unaccompanied, with early instruments, with modern symphony orchestras. Yet listeners constantly marvelled at the 'beautiful voices' of the choir, their 'precision and clarity', the 'unity and unanimity', 'an instantly recognisable "core" sound',[118] whose ancestry was not in doubt.

In 1983, when Brian Kay became the chorus master of one of the most famous large choirs in the north of England, the Huddersfield Choral Society, one of the singers described the way he strove to obtain the same precision of ensemble with over two hundred singers as he had experienced as one of the six voices of the King's Singers.[119] The real source of the style Kay was attempting to teach was the chapel choir at King's, and the discipline the King's Singers had adopted came from David Willcocks.

As many testified, even the same singers sounded different in slightly different combinations and under the influence of the different person-alities and temperaments of different conductors. For one thing there were pitch differences that could alter the colour and impact of the sounds in innumerable subtle ways. In the earlier years of these choirs David Wulstan's pitch theories still held weight among some of the directors, though they never appeared to be rigorously or formulaically applied by any of them. The pitch of a work seemed more likely to be chosen to fit the needs of particular singers on a particular occasion. In *Spem in alium*, Wulstan raised the pitch a minor third, Andrew Parrott raised it a semitone, and Phillips a whole tone. In the *Lamentations* Phillips transposed up a minor third, the Hilliard Ensemble raised the pitch a semitone, but Parrott – who considered evidence for the counter-tenor's existence in the sixteenth century to be unconvincing – transposed the work down a tone, employing a tenor on the top line.[120] Undoubt-edly the absence of the male alto voice in the Taverner Choir was a determining factor in its characteristic sonority: the sound is very full and bold and in the 1989 recording of Tallis's *O nata lux*, transposed up a semitone into a bright A flat, for example, it is wondrously forth-right and sure.[121]

And yet it was the similarities between these English choirs and consorts that struck many listeners. An expert commentator, one who was a scholar, a linguist, a musicologist and a singer who had herself sung as an undergraduate in the Chapel at Clare College, wrote in 1990 on performances of the Byrd Five-Part Mass by the Tallis Scholars and The Sixteen. She noticed differences in the shaping of lines and structure: The Sixteen's melodic arches were 'more rounded, less pointed – romanesque rather than gothic – so that the overall effect is smoother, the angles erased'. In the two ensembles' articulation of the movements' structure, The Sixteen made 'more of contrasted blocks of sound while the Tallis Scholars prefer to mesh the phrases, relying more on pointing the rhythms to give a sense of direction and impulse'. But even such an erudite, learned and musicianly writer had to admit that there was little to choose between the two in terms of blend and intonation, that they did sound 'curiously the same'. Not that this surprised her, for there was 'an inherent sound-quality' in such English choirs as these, with directors who were probably brought up 'in the chorister tradition' and those musicians' 'shared coolness of approach that enhances the abstract qualities of the music so that it is somehow as pure, as reserved, as untouchable as light filtered through stained glass'.[122]

In 1999 a distinguished musicologist listened to English choirs singing sixteenth-century polyphony and considered that, 'whatever else has happened in early music over the last quarter century, not much has changed in the performance of Tudor church music'. Joseph Kerman had been listening to performances of Tallis's Mass 'Puer natus est nobis' recorded by the Tallis Scholars, The Sixteen and Chapelle du Roi. In fact he was contemplating a period during which a new kind of voice had entered the ranks of professional singers. Some listeners did notice changes. In 1997 the voices in the Tallis Scholars were 'deafeningly loud', Peter Phillips told an interviewer, if you were standing next to them on stage. Ten singers then, in the 1990s, sang 'more powerfully, more excitingly, and with more varied dynamic control than the twenty amateur singers we used to have'. He encouraged new members of the group to sing out, never to hold back or sing half-voice, so that he could mould and shape the sound of the ensemble.[123] Kerman was right, however, to the extent that, as the voices had developed more power and technical control, the characteristic features of the singing style pioneered by the Clerkes and its offspring the Tallis Scholars and The Sixteen had remained the same. The description of a concert by the Clerkes in 1979 of music by John Sheppard in St John's, Smith Square, in London talked of the 'crystal-clear female trebles, accurate, clean-edged "means" . . . hard, firm countertenors (a little nasal?), bell-like tenors, and crisp, resonant basses'. There were 'no cotton-wool edges in any section, no overblown expressiveness'.[124] Another considered their recording of Tallis's Mass 'Puer natus est nobis', issued that year, in which every detail of the music was caught with 'control and tact . . . difficult changes of material and mood . . . are negotiated without fuss and with perfect discipline'.[125] That could have been a description of the singing of one of these choirs twenty years later.

For some music critics, though, who had been living with these performances for twenty years the music-making was not quite so alive and arresting as it had been in the 1970s. When The Sixteen gave a concert at the Proms in the Royal Albert Hall in July 1994 a leading London critic considered that their singing of Antonio Caldara's sixteen-part *Crucifixus* had been 'like a Grecian urn: elegant, flawless and bloodless'. Bach's Cantata 131, *Aus der Tiefe*, 'had scarcely touched perceptible emotion'. The expressive range of the singing, 'from *mezzo* this to *ma non troppo* that, had all the abandonment of a Swiss banker on tranquillisers'. The critic exhorted Harry Christophers 'to unbutton his personality'. He wondered whether the Oxford and Cambridge college chapels, which fed so many of the top choirs, were breeding 'too many urbane, polite girls and chaps. Somebody needs to put the grit in their oysters.'[126] The organist at Westminster Abbey may have expected little disagreement when he asserted in the 1920s that 'the unemotional, passionless style of boys' singing seems particularly suited to that austerity which is so characteristic of the best church music'.[127] When seeking to praise the singing of these professional choirs and consorts at the end of the century a critic did not immediately reach for epithets like 'unemotional', 'passionless' or 'austere' as words of praise.

There had to be a place in human life for warmth and colour and passion. Concepts of masculinity had changed by the end of the century. The fathers of Willcocks' generation had been discouraged from hugging their sons, for example, to ensure that the boys learnt to control their emotions, to behave in ways that would strike a parent of the twenty-first century as emotionally cold.[128] The education that David Willcocks and Boris Ord had received tended to encourage, it was now considered, a systematic denial of emotional life and the checking of impulse, imagination and self-indulgence. That is how it must have appeared to some.

Whether it was a deliberate response to journalistic criticism or arose spontaneously from the sensitive antennae of the musicians to changing tastes, perceptible differences in the style and sound of The Sixteen certainly did appear. In the twenty-first century there were voices in The Sixteen with greater vibrato and 'graininess' (as it was termed)[129] than when the injunctions of Bernard Rose and David Wulstan and the sound of the Clerkes of Oxenford were louder in the conductor's ears.[130] Indeed the choir became anxious to draw attention to these characteristics and on its website in 2016 quoted a critic who explained that 'Some choirs of high renown aim for a kind of robotic perfection in synch with the digital age. Christophers' troupe contains human beings colouring the lines with individual hues, yet still acting and breathing as one.'[131] The disciplined blend and tight ensemble the critic imagined to be in synch with the 'digital age', however, belonged in fact to the far-off days of the conductor's youth when listeners described them not as robotic but as angelic. Some choirs though, such as the Tallis Scholars, did indeed wish to preserve the immaculate blend characteristic of earlier times. Musicians will not be instructed by sharp-penned critics nor by the subtleties of the zeitgeist. Besides they all want to be different from one another.

What differences were there between the singing of the professional choirs and consorts like the Tallis Scholars, The Sixteen and Polyphony early in the twenty-first century – sometimes characterized as 'high-octane' choirs – and the singing of the choirs of men and boys which had constituted their original model? The recordings at the end of the twentieth century testified to the astonishingly high standards of some of the cathedral choirs, and performances were not infrequently compared with the secular choirs, not always to the secular choirs' advantage. In recorded performances of Tallis's *Gaude gloriosa*, the rich, mellow reading of Andrew Parrott and the Taverner Choir was 'extremely accomplished', a reviewer acknowledged in 1989, but the 'lean, eager sound' of the Tallis Scholars was 'even more enticing', and a performance by the Choir of New College 'transcends the secular world of the concert hall and, replete with soaring boys' voices, is transported back into the world of ritual and liturgy to which it properly belongs'.[132] 'In Taverner's *Dum transisset Sabbatum* the Worcester trebles are to my mind every bit as good as the ladies in Peter Phillips' highly expert Tallis Scholars and the Worcester basses blend a good deal better than do their counterparts,' wrote one reviewer in 1995.[133] Another, in 1997: 'Some may prefer the lush and homogenized textures of the Tallis Scholars, and others the star-studded and delectably finished Taverner Choir under Andrew Parrott. Each says a great deal about this wonderful music but St John's can join them in this colourful and exquisite corner of Tallis's oeuvre.'[134] The sheer energy of the Winchester Cathedral choirboys in the Mass 'Salve intemerata virgo' delighted yet another.[135]

That same year, though, Peter Phillips himself expressed his view that 'even by the lowest professional standards these boys' choirs do not sound very good', and that it was 'hardly surprising that on average these children find it difficult to blend and [sing in] tune, to overcome the natural breathiness in their voices, to interpret with maturity'.[136] Commenting on this, Edward Higginbottom thought that, as far as standards went, Phillips was generalizing from too little evidence. There was no endemic feebleness in boys' voices, he was sure, after a lifetime of working with them, and he thought it was downright insulting to claim that boys could rarely blend or sing in tune. He suggested that Phillips should perhaps hear New College choristers 'turn a *tremblement appuyé*, temper a major third, cross-accent the metre'. Perhaps most crucially of all he pointed out that the fact that the singers were children constituted an important part of the aesthetic force of the sound they made. We do not listen to sounds regardless of the human beings generating them; knowledge of the singers themselves – who they are, how old they are – helped the listener to create meanings out of the sound and the style. A nuance of tone or a particularity in phrasing, which might be judged a shortcoming in vocal technique in a thirty-year-old soprano, might generate quite a different response when articulated by an eleven-year-old boy.[137]

A choirmaster as long ago as 1894 tried to convey what he took to be the singular effect that a good chorister could produce, 'the modesty and simplicity and freshness in the characteristic delivery, the absence of self-consciousness . . . without any airs and graces, without any nods and becks and wreathed smiles'.[138] The age and gender of the performer were clearly always crucially important, as well as the age and gender of the listener.

The Clerkes of Oxenford in the 1970s certainly did convey an inward quality, mostly because the restraint was an intrinsic component of the musical style, but also because of the singers' youthful inexperience as performers. The professional groups of the twenty-first century were performers of the greatest expertise and not so unselfconsciously self-effacing. Compared to pop or jazz singers or to the singers on the operatic stage or even to lieder singers, the demeanour and physical gestures of a group like Voces8 were subdued and their movements slight. Nevertheless their extraordinarily virtuoso performances of, for example, Gibbons' *O clap your hands* without copies of the music[139] were not too far from their performances of Paul Simon's 'Feelin' groovy',[140] the flicker of a smile, the eyes closed for an expressive moment. The sounds themselves were not so far from those of the Clerkes in the 1970s, nor indeed from King's in the 1960s. The significance and meaning of that performance though was a world away from the liturgical unfolding of such music with men and boys not high on a platform facing an audience but half hidden in the choir stalls and lit only by candlelight.

A music critic visiting Cambridge for the fiftieth-anniversary performance of the Monteverdi Vespers by the Monteverdi Choir in 2014 was struck by the difference between performance and ritual: 'this Vespers,' he thought, 'remains a concert performance, with Gardiner at its centre, rather than a piece of religious music in a liturgical context. That is what English choral tradition gets so right – a point amply demonstrated by the St John's College Chapel Choir at evensong just a couple of hours before Vespers at King's.'[141]

But what had happened at King's itself? What had happened to that singing style whose matchless beauty had so startled the world on long-playing discs half a century earlier?

RETURN TO KING'S: PHILIP LEDGER AND STEPHEN CLEOBURY, 1974–

Willcocks left King's in December 1973 to become Director of the Royal College of Music and was succeeded by Philip Ledger. Ledger had not been a cathedral chorister nor an organ scholar like Willcocks but he knew about the singing tradition at King's very well – he had attempted and failed to obtain a choral scholarship there. He was awarded a place to read History but he changed to read Music and his abundant musical talents were quickly demonstrated. He was awarded a First in both parts of the Tripos and a distinction in the Mus.B. degree,[142] and while he was at Cambridge he passed the fellowship exam of the Royal College of Organists with the highest marks in the performance section.[143]

He left Cambridge and at the age of twenty-four was appointed organist at Chelmsford Cathedral, the youngest cathedral organist at that time. This was not an ancient foundation and the choir sang only Matins and Evensong on Sundays, a full Evensong on Saturdays and Evensong with boys' voices on Thursdays.[144] Although Ledger had never had responsibility for such a choir before, he quickly demonstrated that the confidence of those who had appointed him to the office was not misplaced.

His gifts as a choirmaster were clear and he was ambitious; before he left he had persuaded the Provost to create the post of assistant organist and to appoint to it John Jordan, a young musician who had been organ scholar at Emmanuel College, Cambridge, and, like Ledger himself, a prizewinner in the FRCO exams.

In 1965 Ledger was made Director of Music at the new University of East Anglia at Norwich; the post was given the title Director rather than Professor because a new kind of curriculum was envisaged, one that combined training in performance and composition with courses on the history of music, musical criticism and acoustics. His abilities as an organizer and administrator, crucial for a twentieth-century cathedral or college organist, which Willcocks possessed in abundance, were recognized early on in Ledger too: he was Dean of the School of Fine Arts and Music between 1968 and 1971.[145]

Ledger had been working with Britten at the Aldeburgh Festival since 1963 and in acting as a referee for the post at Norwich the composer described him as 'a first-rate musician of quite uncommon gifts ... a splendid musical scholar'.[146] It was indeed extremely uncommon for an organist and choir-trainer to be so effective in both roles as Ledger was proving himself to be. He gave broadcasts as an organ recitalist, but he was also an excellent pianist and harpsichordist. He was appearing regularly as a continuo player, in broadcasts of performances of Bach's Passions and cantatas and Brandenburg Concertos and the *Christmas Oratorio*, Haydn's *Creation*, Purcell's *Fairy Queen*. He was the organist in early broadcasts of Britten's church parables. He conducted his own choirs at Norwich in church music and part-songs and also took part in broadcasts as a conductor of Purcell's *King Arthur* at the Proms, and of Haydn's *Return of Tobias* and Rameau's *Castor et Pollux*. He played chamber music with members of the Melos Ensemble, piano trios by Haydn, Mozart's Quintet for Piano and Wind Instruments K452, Schumann's *Märchenerzählungen* op. 132. He played the harpsichord in performances of the songs of Purcell and of Handel's Italian cantatas. He acted as the piano accompanist in song recitals with such singers as Janet Baker and John Shirley-Quirk and also Robert Tear, who had been a contemporary when Tear was a choral scholar at King's.[147] Ledger and Tear were to go on and make recordings of songs by Britten, Schubert, Rachmaninov, Schumann and Philip Radcliffe, a tutor in music at King's who spent his whole life living in college.

So when he was appointed at King's, Philip Ledger brought with him experience of all kinds of music-making at the very highest level. Perhaps something of the invariable intensity and seriousness of Ledger's music-making derived from his work with Britten. A singer in a male voice choir directed in a BBC studio by Britten when he was

20. Boris Ord in the 1950s with one of the toys with which he used to welcome candidates for choristerships. When the trial began the boy was expected to turn his attention away from the toy and never turn back.

21. David Willcocks in 1951 when he was organist of Worcester Cathedral.

22. Bernard Rose in the early 1970s. As Organist and Informator Choristarum at Magdalen College, Oxford, in the 1960s and 1970s, Rose, like Willcocks at King's, directed a choir with undergraduates singing the lower parts. The singing was held by contemporaries to represent the very best of the 'traditional English style'.

23. The cover of the Christmas 1958 issue of *Radio Times*, Willcocks's first Christmas Eve as director of music at King's.

24. A break in the recording of a forty-five minute programme for BBC TV in 1964.

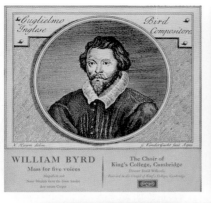

25–7. The LP made the sound and singing style of King's world-famous. The homespun company they began recording with, Argo, was taken over by Decca in 1957. King's ended their exclusive contract in 1964 when they began recording with both Decca and EMI. King's and David Willcocks – here in the choirstalls in 1965 – had become big names with the leading labels.

28–9. Benjamin Britten and George Malcolm with the choristers of Westminster Cathedral in 1959 at the time of the first performance of Britten's *Missa brevis*. The BBC's tape of the live broadcast of this was issued as a commercial disc by Decca. It quickly became famous for the 'continental' timbre of the voices.

30–31. George Guest outside the Chapel at St John's, Cambridge, in 1991. In the 1960s St John's, like King's, was recording for Argo. The two choirs were now competing in the market-place, affecting the repertoire and singing style of both.

32. The Choir of Christ Church Cathedral, Oxford, in 1972, recording its first disc, of music by William Walton, in the Chapel of Merton College, Oxford, under the direction of Simon Preston. There were six lay clerks, six choral scholars and two recent choral scholars brought in for the recording sessions. There was only one older lay clerk, the alto Arnold Reason (*far right*), who retired later that year.

33. Simon Preston was a chorister at King's under Ord, and was then Willcocks's first organ scholar. He was organist at Christ Church from 1970 to 1981 and then at Westminster Abbey from 1981 to 1987. His nervous energy never cooled, though he appeared to be nerveless himself.

34. Edward Higginbottom, director of the Choir at New College, Oxford, between 1976 and 2014. Higginbottom did not wish the voices to blend into 'the traditional English sound', but encouraged each voice to develop its individuality.

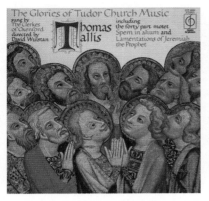

35–8. The amateur singers who had forged their styles from that of King's under Willcocks became professionals, and the style gradually became applied to expanding repertoires, from Tallis's *Spem in alium* to Tavener's *Ikon of Light*, from 'Morning has broken' and 'Strawberry Fields Forever' to Purcell's *Thou knowest, Lord, the secrets of all hearts*.

39–40. A style created for depersonalized liturgical use became the expressive medium of consummate performers. Sometimes these concert-giving choirs and consorts would sing pieces in the cathedral repertory from memory. Each became a brand and as carefully marketed as any other twenty-first century cultural product, as in these publicity shots for Tenebrae (*above*) and Voces8 (*below*).

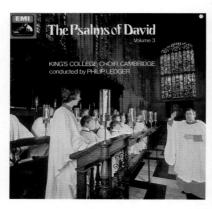

41–43. Philip Ledger (*above*) was in charge of the choir between 1974 and 1982, followed by Stephen Cleobury (*right and below*).

barely twenty-four recalled that the composer 'never swore at me but he frightened me out of myself'.[148] Certainly some of his singers at King's also found Ledger's demands 'terrifying'.[149]

When you worked for Britten it was never routine, an orchestral leader remembered, everything was always 'an occasion'.[150] Similarly, when one of the periodic discussions in the College Council at King's came up about the top hats and tails the choristers wear, and a feeling was expressed that perhaps these should not be worn every day but on Sundays and special occasions, Ledger pointed out that every choral service in King's College Chapel was special.[151]

He wanted his singers to surprise themselves by their music-making. And he succeeded: 'on a dull midwinter afternoon the psalms during Evensong would become filled with spine-tingling intensity', they would remember, 'while an anthem would be transformed from something polished and well-executed into an experience that was transcendental and overwhelming'.[152]

It was from David Willcocks himself, Ledger said, that he had learnt about the practicalities of doing the job at King's and the ways in which the problems of the Chapel's acoustics could be solved. He considered that he had inherited from Willcocks a choir 'at the peak of perfection'. His aim had been to maintain the high standards and to bring something of his own to the music-making, something of his own particular style.[153] He did not reveal whether he had identified particular qualities he consciously wished to develop. A reviewer of his first recording, though, thought that he detected a new incisiveness in rhythm and diction and a wider dynamic range. The works on this first recording could not have been chosen to demonstrate better these particular qualities, Britten's *Rejoice in the Lamb* and Leonard Bernstein's *Chichester Psalms*, each with dancing, angular, animated movements. Ledger seemed to accept the clipped consonants – which reflected the natural speech characteristics of both Ord and Will-cocks, though they were certainly old-fashioned by the 1960s – simply as an aspect of the performing style, and he emphasized them even more, not just for intelligibility but additionally for expressive effect and for intensity. They remained a defining characteristic of the singing under his direction.[154] Not everyone liked the explosive consonants, at least not in all the repertory. When the choir sang motets in German by Brahms, one reviewer thought, they sounded 'too spry and chirpy, especially for the darker sonorities of Luther's Bible'.[155]

Up to the end of his time at King's, Willcocks usually accompanied the psalms himself, having a choral scholar on each side as a 'beater', though for broadcasts he himself would direct the psalms, leaving his organ scholar to accompany.[156] From his first term Ledger was down in the choir stalls for the psalms much more often. For his first disc of psalm singing, recorded in December 1974, his organ scholar, Francis Grier, accompanied throughout.[157] A reviewer of this disc admired the smoothness, elegance and intelligence of the singing but wondered whether something had been lost. He remembered the effortless spontaneity of the singing when Willcocks was accompanying. Now the chanting was so meticulously and carefully done he felt he was witnessing a performance, not sharing a ritual as before.[158]

Like his predecessor, Ledger sought out singers who had a good ear, a fine sense of pitch and intelligence rather than voices necessarily of great force and individuality. Like Willcocks he wished for sixteen boys who could blend as one voice: 'we go . . . for the head voice rather than the chest voice. We like good *pianissimos*, perfect intonation and texture; not stabbing *staccatos* or long-sustained *fortissimos*.'[159] Nevertheless he encouraged individual vocal development and agility. He took the boys through exercises at the beginnings of practices, which Willcocks had almost never done. There were scales and arpeggios – including common chords up and dominant sevenths down – and chromatic scales up and down for expert tuning and control, which were expertly and memorably harmonized by Ledger.[160]

And, just occasionally, for fun, the choristers sang one verse of a hymn 'in the style of the Vienna Boys' Choir', very loud, even with the hint of a wobble, as they imagined prima donnas to sing.[161] It seems unlikely that Willcocks ever let his King's choristers, even for fun, imitate the boys of the Vienna Boys' Choir. At any rate Ledger did produce some very confident choristers with strong and very beautiful notes throughout their range and admirable breath control.[162]

Ledger was certainly fortunate to have a succession of excellent choral scholars, some of whom went on to become outstanding performers and chorus masters themselves, singers like Michael Chance, Simon Halsey, Matthew Best, Charles Daniels, Mark Padmore,

Christopher Purves and Gerald Finley. This was the moment when professional choirs and consorts like The Sixteen and the Tallis Scholars were beginning to emerge and more choral scholars were beginning to contemplate the possibility of careers as singers.

Perhaps because music was being taken very seriously now by candidates for university places, Ledger also had one outstanding organ scholar after another. Willcocks had appointed his first two: James Lancelot became organist of Durham Cathedral and Francis Grier, the first of a dozen organ scholars from Eton in the next half-century, became organist of Christ Church at the age of twenty-six. Two of Ledger's organ scholars became organists at Gloucester Cathedral, Adrian Partington and David Briggs, Briggs leaving to become a distinguished recitalist – as was another of Ledger's organ scholars, Thomas Trotter. John Butt, the organ scholar between 1979 and 1982, earned renown as a keyboard player, of the harpsichord and clavichord as well as the organ; as a conductor, the director of the Dunedin Consort, the leading Scottish Baroque ensemble; as well as a scholar, being appointed Gardiner Professor of Music at Glasgow University in 2001.[163]

Clearly Ledger wished to preserve the immaculate blend that had been such a startling characteristic of the choir under Ord and Willcocks and unmatched among English cathedral choirs. He pushed the voices a little more, though under Willcocks they undoubtedly grew more assertive than he had allowed in his earliest years. Ledger was certainly aware of the forceful singing of Christ Church under Simon Preston. Even in such an English community as King's reticence was becoming a less valued personal attribute than it had been in the 1930s when Willcocks arrived in the College.

In 1977 one music critic identified changes in the singing. He did not like 'those mannerisms which we associate with the "King's sound"', the impersonal, anonymous singing style which some English men and women associated with a kind of tame, self-conscious, timid Anglicanism that denied, they thought, all forms of spontaneity and life. Listening to their performance of Bach's *Christmas Oratorio* released in 1977 he concluded that Ledger favoured 'a more detached approach to choral singing . . . than his predecessors'. He found the timbre 'more natural' than before and therefore, to him, 'more pleasing'. He could even distinguish individual voices from time to time and this he applauded.[164] Maybe there were some strong and characterful voices at the moment these cantatas were recorded; maybe the microphone placing did not reproduce the sounds as they were habitually heard in the Chapel's acoustic. It does not seem to have been Ledger's intention to sacrifice the characteristic blend of the voices, and later recordings certainly accord with his expressed wish to create a unison line of boys or men sounding as a single voice.

What was described as the 'clear-toned sound' of the choir, the brightness and the lightness, remained little changed. After all, Ledger was working with exactly the same kind of young voices in the same extraordinarily rich acoustic. 'The chapel gives its blessing to you,' he explained, 'if you are singing properly'.[165] One commentator could still speak of the 'celestial purity' of the singing in Duruflé's Requiem. He had never heard the passage in the work speaking of souls passing from death into the life eternal 'more beautifully rendered, the music hushing to silence and halting to immobility'.[166]

But tautness of rhythm and clarity and dynamism of diction were the hallmark characteristics of the performing style Ledger nurtured, whether in pieces like Kenneth Leighton's *Let all the world*, or William Mathias's *A babe is born*, or in the cross rhythms of Palestrina's eight-part *Hodie Christus natus est*. The whole sweep and intensity and energy of the recording of the Procession with Carols upon Advent Sunday recorded in December 1979 represented quintessential Ledger and was more hard driven than Willcocks. There is some very beautiful quiet singing in *The Cherry Tree Carol*, for example, and in an arrangement by Ledger of a Japanese tune for *King Jesus has a garden full of wondrous flowers* and in the Old Basque carol *Gabriel's Message*. One choirmaster listened to 'this choir's sparkling tone, but . . . enjoyed most, perhaps, the harder sounds, as in the sheer drive of the hymns . . . splendidly four-square and the treatment completely metric, the verses rolling on without pause . . . That in itself is a thrill, but the additional belligerence of organ tone and the surprising aerial attacks by boys with descants provide further astonishment.'[167]

Ledger's years at King's coincided with the days when many musicians and scholars held the re-creation of the styles of performance and the timbres cultivated by the composers of the past to be a realistic ideal, indeed to be crucial for a proper understanding and appreciation of the music. Some listeners for a time heard choirs such as King's or Christ Church as exemplars of idiomatic performance of eighteenth-century choral music, of Handel's *Messiah*, of what they would call 'authentic' performance. English choirs of men and boys of roughly the same size had been singing this music since it was composed. These must be models worthy of imitation. Others disagreed. This style was of recent origin, evolved within the past century, and the ' "cushiony" effect of soft-focus breathiness typical of present-day boys' choirs . . . with vocal individuality at a discount' was too 'anaemic' for the music of, say, Henry Purcell. Purcell's church musicians were 'young, often rowdy', and the solo parts of his verse anthems required 'dramatic commitment . . . an outspoken, "actorly" quality'.[168] Those were the views of a musicologist, a specialist in seventeenth-century English music. Willcocks had always been reluctant to sing verse anthems at King's with young choral scholars whose voices had not reached maturity. But in full anthems he thought his choir could compete with anyone.[169] Not so, said the scholar. He thought the 'clinical correctness' of the choir in Purcell's Funeral Sentences, even with Ledger's more forthright singers, 'fails to mirror a human conviction: the accuracy is technically admirable but fatally cool.'[170] This at least demonstrates that even to such a close listener the differences in the performances under Willcocks and under Ledger were very small compared with the similarities.

In 2009 EMI released a two-CD album entitled *England, my England* containing new recordings as well as reissues of recordings directed by Stephen Cleobury, who succeeded Ledger in 1982, alongside much older ones directed by Philip Ledger and David Willcocks.[171] There was not felt to be any incongruity in this; all the recordings were recognizably of the same choir. The three tracks that do perhaps convey a slightly different impression are the three psalms recorded in the Chapel of Trinity College under Willcocks; the more intimate acoustic imparts a different character to the verbal stresses and the effect is more personal and less majestic.

In the popular imagination King's has remained among the very

best choirs at the English choral foundations and, some church musicians would still claim, exemplifies a style to which other such choirs
aspire.[172] At Christmastime in 2015 a leading music critic explained
'Why King's is still the best carol service in town'.[173]

The singing in the twenty-first century was still distinguished by its
discipline of blend and ensemble. In 2005 the singing of the Rachmaninov Vespers was said to be in 'the Anglican tradition' in which
'beauty and refinement are the keynotes . . . [with] precision of ensemble and subtlety of dynamic shading'.[174] Early twenty-first-century
performances that were particularly valued of, say, the Byrd masses
tended to be 'more dramatic and more ardent' than those of King's
under Willcocks, though the earlier ones were enduring 'classics' in
the opinion of critics and reviewers.[175]

In December 1983, at the end of Stephen Cleobury's first year as
director at King's, a critic detected 'a noticeable absence of any hint
of throaty, chesty production: this was the head voice, pure and simple'.[176] In other words, this new man was fostering the King's tradition.
Perhaps the critic had expected otherwise. Stephen Cleobury had after
all been a chorister at Worcester Cathedral under Douglas Guest, the
organ scholar at King's before David Willcocks, and later acted as
Guest's assistant at Westminster Abbey. But he had also sung as a
treble under Christopher Robinson, the same choirmaster who had
so offended Guy Harland from Malvern. And he had been an organ
scholar under George Guest at St John's and in charge of the music
at the Catholic Westminster Cathedral, working, then, with the two
choirs most frequently held up as exemplifying the 'continental' style
in England. One critic reckoned that the epithet 'continental' was not
based on any close analysis of the actual sound of foreign choirs and
that it would be better in England to speak of a King's tradition and a
'non-King's' tradition.[177] Of both traditions, however they might be
designated, Stephen Cleobury had had intimate experience.

In the 1990s some choral scholars thought that the sound of both
boys and choral scholars had become more 'focused' than in the
recordings of earlier years. They thought that the individual singing
lessons the boys were now given – individual singing lessons for the
boys had started soon after Cleobury arrived[178] – enabled them to
have better control over their breath and to 'support' the voice better.

They 'projected' their voices better. The sound was a little louder. The effect was more 'robust',[179] though production of the voice always relaxed, the head and body always held still. The boys were reminded that they should be able to see a top note in a hole in the ground. A film of the choristers without a soundtrack should not be able to indicate whether the boys were singing high notes or low notes.[180]

Like Ledger but unlike Willcocks,[181] Cleobury usually began practices with the boys stretching their arms above their heads and bringing them down to their sides while standing straight and still with feet a little apart. The boys sang a note as they glissandoed on a hiss. They regularly sang a series of arpeggios.[182]

Inevitably Willcocks cultivated certain sounds which reflected his own style of spoken English, perhaps more the received pronunciation of English he heard as a chorister at Westminster Abbey in the 1930s than that of the 1960s. So *alleluia* became 'e-lleluia'. 'I know thett my Redeemer liveth, ent thett he shell stent . . .' Consonants were distinct and clipped with military precision under Willcocks.[183] In 2015 Cleobury complained that, because of the 'sloppy way' the boys and men spoke – much lazier than in the recent past – he had to work harder to encourage the choir to articulate clearly.[184] But if they said 'twenny' instead of 'twen-ty' and 'law r'un order' instead of 'law and order', they were perhaps simply articulating a new received pronunciation. The clarity and energy of the consonants in a phrase like *Past three o'clock* were certainly distinctive under Willcocks.[185] Only if you were seated near the choir perhaps would you have been able to catch the words if you didn't know them. But the clipped enunciation was a component of the style and character of the singing.

In 1992 Cleobury thought that if the sound of the choir had changed – and he had not set out to change the style deliberately – it might be because he had encouraged the choir to sing 'with a bright forward tone' and that even when they were singing in English he encouraged them to try to use Italian vowel sounds wherever possible.[186] In 2008 he thought that he had allowed the cultivation of 'vibrancy' but not at the expense of discipline, articulation and ensemble.[187] So that in *Ding dong, merrily on high* he emphasized an open vowel on 'high', as *ah*, with the diphthong articulated swiftly right at the end of the vowel. Similarly with *sky*, which must be

'Sk-ah-j'. 'In heaven the bells are ringing': the singers were to elongate the vowels on *ringing*, the 'i's, and not dwell on the closed 'ng' sound. In *Gloria* the 'gl' was to be articulated as quickly as possible with the singer's concentration fixed on the 'aw' sound.[188] On the other hand, Cleobury was sure, the articulation of consonants must be clear and incisive. While it was very easy to over-emphasize 't's and 'd's in the Chapel's acoustic – which quickly began to sound pedantic and ridiculous – it was necessary to work very hard to ensure 'f's and 'p's emerged distinctly.[189]

Certainly the singers' attention in recent years was constantly directed on the words being sung. Willcocks' choir sang in English and Latin. Music by Bach and Brahms would usually be sung in English translation. In recent times music by these composers would nearly always, at least in the usual chapel services, be sung in German and there would be occasional performances too of the German Magnificat and Nunc Dimittis by Heinrich Schütz. In recent years there have been carols in German, French, Spanish, Latin, Swedish and Church Slavonic. But it was Latin, with its pure vowels, which has been sung much more in recent years than in Willcocks' day, with the regular Latin Masses and the settings of the evening canticles in Latin.

By the 1990s Stephen Cleobury saw it as a general trend among Anglican choirs to cultivate the best of both 'English' and 'continental' traditions, the immaculate blending of one and the brightness and colour and vibrancy of the other.[190] His own choral scholars at the time seemed to confirm his own impressions, at least as they were manifested in the choir at King's. The cultivation of Italianate vowels was certainly having an effect, they thought, but blend was still of paramount importance and they remained, quintessentially, an English choir; there was none of the harshness of, say, a German choir.[191]

King's too was in the same world as New College and some of the professional choirs. Cleobury encouraged the development of the individual timbre and character of a particular voice – it was he after all who had initiated individual singing lessons for each treble – and blend was not quite as astonishingly impersonal as it had been under Willcocks. This was what lay behind Willcocks' remark that he never had any good singers in his choirs at Salisbury, Worcester or

King's. He was referring specifically to the boys but he could have said the same about his lay clerks and his choral scholars. This was quite deliberate; he did not want any. During his career, a professional singer was essentially a solo singer with markedly individual characteristics and with a constant vibrato, since that was the fashion of the day. The new attitudes towards music – and Willcocks himself with his insistence on habitual attention to tuning and ensemble and the disciplined professional attitude to music-making that he instilled into not only choral scholars but choristers too – had been instrumental in developing a new kind of singer, a new kind of professional musician who possessed the techniques to specialize in consort singing of various kinds. Many such singers cultivated a very small vibrato and others were able to employ a more distinctive vibrato whenever they sang as soloists or performed in consort in a particular repertoire. Some of the choral scholars in recent decades were not sure whether they wished to specialize in consort singing, but they did not feel that they had to suppress their individuality in the twenty-first-century choir as they might have done under David Willcocks.

Under Willcocks the expressive lilt of *In dulci jubilo* was hardly enhanced at all, though it was by the phrasing of the choir forty years later.[192] The expressive shaping of phrases, the intensification of a note or series of notes (which Wulstan as well as Willcocks so disliked), seemed now to be applied instinctively – 'I *sing* of a **mai**-den' – and was not so restrained, more like Ord than Willcocks.[193]

What differences do expert musicians who have lived with the sound all their lives detect in the singing now from the style of performance under Willcocks? Two such musicians looking back over four decades characterized the singing under Willcocks as 'disembodied'. The singing was astonishingly unworldly, other-worldly. Then, one of them thought, it was the singing of angels; now it is of 'earthlings', though still of extraordinary beauty and refinement.[194]

Half a century after Willcocks the dynamic range of the choir seemed wider and the singing a little more assertive, partly because the singers concentrated on supporting the voice more than in his day. Expressive inflections were more common and the 'vibrancy' Cleobury said he strove to cultivate did not repudiate all trace of vibrato. Given the constant turnover of singers the sonic image of the

choir had a remarkable constancy. Given the youth and the intelligence of the singers the choir's approaches to different repertory
could display great suppleness and flexibility. It was able to shape the
style with great subtlety when it performed Giovanni Gabrieli in
2015 and sang with a straight, steady, forthright tone which matched
the cornets and sackbuts with telling effect.[195]

Repertory inevitably had an important effect on the singing style.
The duties of the choir and the repertory had not quite remained the
same over half a century. Until the 1980s the regular Sunday services
were Matins and Evensong with two Sunday Sung Eucharists a term
instead of Matins. From the mid-1980s there was a Sung Eucharist
every Sunday except for two Sundays a term when Matins would be
the morning service. From the Lent term of 1992 there was additionally a Sung Eucharist on Thursday evenings in place of Evensong, all
of which meant that a much greater number of communion services
were sung. Most of these were Latin Masses – now not just the three
Byrd masses and Palestrina's Missa 'Aeterna Christi munera' and
Vaughan Williams' Mass in G minor, which had figured in Boris
Ord's lists, but Palestrina's Missa brevis and his Missa 'Dum com-
plerentur', masses by Tye and Josquin and Victoria and Lassus,
masses by Mozart and Schubert, Dvořák's Mass in D, Rheinberger's
Cantus Missae op. 109, Widor's Mass in F sharp minor for two
choirs, Poulenc's Mass in G, Duruflé's Messe 'cum iubilo', the Missae
breves of Kodály and Berkeley and Walton, Frank Martin's Mass for
double choir, Stravinsky's Mass with double wind quintet, Robin
Holloway's Missa Caiensis and many others. Occasionally the boys
would sing a Eucharist by themselves, performing Britten's Missa
brevis or Fauré's Messe basse.

The canons of the Church of England have always allowed authorized forms of divine service to be said or sung in Latin in university
colleges, but it is only in recent decades that the canticles at Evening
Prayer at King's have been sung regularly in Latin, several times each
term. The Latin settings of the Magnificat used have been taken from
the great number written for Vespers and of the Nunc Dimittis from
the much smaller number written for Compline. Some of these
that have been sung at King's are by English composers and written
for pre-Reformation liturgies in England – settings by Fayrfax and

Dunstable, for example – but most of them were by the greatest continental composers, a few from the fifteenth century, like Dufay and Binchois, but most from the sixteenth, like Palestrina and Lassus and Victoria; and a few more were modern settings, such as Francis Grier's Magnificat and Gustav Holst's Nunc Dimittis. Occasionally settings of the evening canticles in German by Buxtehude and Schütz have been used.

Certain works took their place in the choir's repertory because of recording plans. This may have been the reason Britten's *Hymn to St Cecilia* and *Rejoice in the Lamb* became sung as anthems. Hitherto they were rarely if ever sung anywhere in a liturgical setting. Afterwards they were included as anthems in spite of their length and in the repertory of other choral foundations as well. When EMI invited King's in 1998 to record Rachmaninov's Vespers, Cleobury was able to include each of the fifteen short canticles for Russian Orthodox services as anthems or introits appropriate for the Church of England's seasonal liturgies. It was particularly fortunate that they had at that time a bass choral scholar who was half-Czech, conversant with East European languages and with Church Slavonic, was reading Russian for his degree, and had a vocal range of Russian proportions so that he could negotiate the bottom B flats of the Rachmaninov with consummate ease.[196]

A great many of the classic anthems of the English cathedral tradition still sung at King's were sung in Willcocks' day. Indeed a considerable number were included by Dr Mann in the volume of anthems sung at King's he published in 1882: Byrd's *Sing joyfully*, Gibbons' *O clap your hands* and *Hosanna to the Son of David*, Purcell's *Rejoice in the Lord alway* and *Remember not, Lord, our offences*, Maurice Greene's *Lord, let me know mine end*, Jonathan Battishill's *O Lord, look down*, Mendelssohn's *Hear my prayer*, and Wesley's *Wash me throughly*, *Cast me not away*, *Thou wilt keep him in perfect peace* and *The wilderness*.[197] Mann added many composed during his lifetime, which became classics and took their place at the centre of the cathedral repertory. Many were sung under Willcocks' direction and are sung still: Charles Wood's *Expectans expectavi*, Bairstow's *Save us, O Lord, waking*, Parry's *My soul, there is a country*, Elgar's *O hearken thou* and *The spirit of the Lord*,

Balfour Gardiner's *Evening Hymn*, E. W. Naylor's *Vox dicentis, Clama*.

Under Willcocks the choir sang little contemporary music, and what he did introduce came in for strong criticism even within the precincts of the College. A Fellow in Music in 1967 objected to the style of singing in the Chapel altogether; musically the services 'belonged to the fruity old Victorian tradition' that should have been swept aside years earlier. He disliked the carol service particularly with those 'elaborate and anachronistic arrangements'. The singing of the 'traditional' carols should have striven to capture the 'robust, secular flavour' of the originals and more medieval carols should have found their way into the service. And when new carols were introduced into the Christmas Eve service they should be by young composers and not by old-fashioned fuddy-duddies as they had been in recent years.[198]

David Willcocks introduced new descants and arrangements into the Christmas Eve service that were loved by many radio listeners and then taken up enthusiastically by a great many choirs when they appeared in the series *Carols for Choirs*, the first volume of which was published in 1961. Willcocks' arrangements were deftly written and extremely clever. The descant to the verse beginning 'Sing, choirs of angels', for example, in 'O come, all ye faithful' started off imitating the well-known refrain of *Ding dong, merrily on high*, a delightful conceit for all choristers. Willcocks' lines were always perfectly crafted and exploited the vocal and musical strengths of the singers, such as the lightness, grace and precise ensemble in *Tomorrow shall be my dancing day*. Boys and men loved to sing them and were able to convey their pleasure, the joyousness of carol singing. With the descants in the matchless acoustic of King's the trebles were able to ride over a full organ and vast congregation with thrilling effect. But the Fellow of King's was by no means alone in protesting against the arrangements by Willcocks and by other musicians that he used. 'Saccharine', 'anachronistic', 'archaic', were the kinds of words used against them, these 'fancy arrangements' with their 'jazzed up archaic sounding harmonies', snorted one Professor of Music listening in 1970.[199] The tunes were imprisoned in stolid arrangements for four voices, some thought, the textbook harmony conventional and pre-dictable, the 'quicksilver brilliance of a dance carol'[200] destroyed by four-part, four-square harmonies, or new carols drawing on the same kind of harmonies and clichéd syncopations of advertising jingles or radio comedy revues. It was as if at any moment a trombone slide might be introduced to raise a smile, or the last verse cranked up a semitone and the speed suddenly increased as the choral scholars reached for their straw boaters to add to the jollity.

Some carols and carol arrangements of this nature Willcocks' suc-cessors retained; they made up their own descants and carol settings. Cleobury also immediately began commissioning a new carol each year for the Christmas Eve service, often from a composer who had earned a reputation as a composer of orchestral works or pieces for other kinds of large instrumental groups or operas, and was not necessarily known at all, or not known exclusively, in the world of Anglican music: men and women such as Jonathan Harvey, Alex-ander Goehr, Peter Sculthorpe, Einojuhani Rautavaara, Judith Weir, Nicholas Maw, Tansy Davies and Harrison Birtwistle.

Although Cleobury pointed out that choristers did not have the inhibiting preconceptions that many adults do and that the demands in singing Byrd and Palestrina could be as challenging as contempor-ary music,[201] nevertheless the idioms of some of the modern carols would have been startlingly new even to the most experienced chor-isters. One treble in 1992 did 'actually quite like the two pieces' that Judith Weir had written for King's. 'But they're plain odd. I mean they're very discordant. But they're interesting to sing.'[202] Some of these carols were much more technically challenging than anything in the repertory ever sung under Ord or Willcocks or Philip Ledger (though Ledger had introduced difficult music by a handful of living composers, including Gordon Crosse, Graham Whettam and John McCabe). Cleobury's carol commissions were full of rhythmic and tuning obstacles of all kinds, with divided parts in several – trebles and tenors each divided into three parts in one – and extended vocal ranges in a number, a solo chorister with a top B in one, and difficult unaccompanied phrases for solo voices in another. Giles Swayne's *Winter Solstice Carol* for voices and solo flute was by no means the most difficult of the commissions, but even here there were passages with divided trebles and basses, tuning and pitching problems, difficult rhythms and half the boys having a top C.[203]

There were many reasons why the choir could perform such pieces with accuracy, authority and utter dependability at the first performance. Most of the singers had received or were receiving a fine musical education at their schools. There was the experience that the choral scholars had had in, for example, the National Youth Choir or on the Eton Choral Courses. There they had to sing formidable repertory and learn quickly alongside teenage girls, their equals in vocal skills and just as ambitious as they themselves were. There had also been an increased number of occasions on which the singers became performers. The principal duties of the choir in the 1930s – essentially its only duties – remained the singing of the daily services in the Chapel during the full university terms, continuing after the end of the Michaelmas Term until Christmas. A fortnight or so after the ending of the Easter Term in June, choral services resumed for about a month, lasting through most of the Long Vacation Term. The choir might give occasional concerts in the Chapel, of Tudor or Restoration church music, say, some of them with the chapel choirs of St John's and Trinity Colleges. And occasionally there were concerts of choral and organ music, or – while the organ was being rebuilt in 1932 – with the choral pieces interspersed with piano solos: Bach, Beethoven and Debussy played by Boris Ord, while the choir sang John Wilbye, Palestrina, Victor Kalinnikov, Charles Wood, Stanford and Haydn. Occasionally the choir would visit Eton College and give concerts in the Chapel there, singing both by themselves and with the Eton Chapel Choir. There would be occasional extra-liturgical performances of, for example, Charles Wood's *Passion according to St Mark*. There were also the carol services.

In Willcocks' day there would be the annual Evensong with St John's and occasional services with Eton and with New College, Oxford, and also choral evensong at a college living, perhaps to mark the installation of a new vicar. Founder's Day would be commemorated with a concert in which former choral scholars would join the choir and sing a large-scale work like Handel's *Messiah* or Haydn's

Creation with a scratch orchestra mainly of students. The choir also gave an increasing number of concerts, not only in Cambridge as they had occasionally done in the 1930s, but now in Westminster Abbey, at the parish church at Stratford-upon-Avon, in Lincoln Cathedral or St Edmundsbury Cathedral. They began to appear at the Aldeburgh Festival. In 1968 there was a televised performance of *Messiah* in the recently restored Chapel as well as the TV carol service and in 1970 a programme of Handel's Coronation Anthems. In 1970 as well the choir were invited to Windsor to sing carols to the Queen and her family.

Early in the twenty-first century the King's College Choir gave occasional concerts in Cambridge and they continued to make occasional visits to Eton. They also still sang Evensong at College livings, at Kingston Parish Church in Surrey, at Prescot in Lancashire. But now they frequently gave concerts in cathedrals – Norwich, Chester, Durham, Canterbury. In addition to the Evensong they had long sung with St John's in Cambridge, they now also sang with other choral foundations, with the Choir of St George's Chapel at Windsor Castle, and with the Choirs of Westminster and St Albans Abbeys during the International Organ Festival at St Albans.[204]

The choir also appeared in Symphony Hall in Birmingham and at Manchester's Bridgewater Hall, The Dome in Brighton, Sage Gateshead, and at London's Royal Albert Hall, Cadogan Hall and Kings Place. They sang at music festivals all over the country, at the Newbury Festival, the Spitalfields Festival in London, the York Early Music Festival. In 2005 Stephen Cleobury established a festival at Passiontide, 'Easter at King's', in which one of the Bach Passions and the services on Maundy Thursday, Good Friday and Easter Day sung by the choir were complemented by concerts of seasonal music, choral music, chamber music or organ recitals. The choir itself took part in some of these, in works like Handel's *Brockes Passion* (in 2016) and *Israel in Egypt* (2014), and James MacMillan's *Seven Last Words from the Cross* (2012). At the festival in 2009 two performances of Handel's *Messiah* were given, one of them shown live in cinemas in the European Union, and then, in a delayed relay, in the United States. It was made into an acclaimed DVD. In 2015 the choristers, singing alongside the choristers of New College and Magdalen College, Oxford, and with the choir Britten Sinfonia Voices, sang in James MacMillan's *St Luke Passion*. In 2009 the choral scholars sang with the sopranos of Jesus College in works by Haydn, his *Salve regina*, Te Deum and Grosse Orgelsolomesse.

The choir had for decades toured internationally. There was the tour to Scandinavia, Holland and Germany in 1936. In 1952 and 1955 the choir made ten-day tours singing in churches and concert halls in Switzerland, but from 1965 there were regular short tours to Western Europe.[205] In 1972 there was a tour to West Africa and in 1973 one to Canada. The choir sang in the United States in 1976, Japan in 1978 and Australia in 1980. But now there were international tours, long or short, in almost every vacation. In June 2007 the King's College Choir sang at the Istanbul Festival, in August in Estonia, Latvia, Lithuania and Finland. In September they gave concerts at the Benedictine Abbey of Notre-Dame d'Ambronay in the Rhône-Alpes region of eastern France and at the Beethovenfest in Bonn. In December they gave concerts in São Paulo, in April 2008 in New York, Chicago, St Louis, Baltimore, Dallas, Minneapolis–Saint Paul, Cincinnati, Westport in Connecticut and Ann Arbor in Michigan.[206]

The choral scholars also sang by themselves as they had always done, performing at college balls and on the river. But in 2008 they recorded a disc of motets by Giaches de Wert in an edition specially prepared by one of them, and in 2007 they sang in Peterborough and Ripon Cathedrals, at the Church of St Mary and All Saints, Fotheringhay, in Northamptonshire, and at Brocket Hall in Hertfordshire. In 2002 they had undertaken their own first American tour. In 2009 they appeared with Dizzee Rascal at the BBC Electric Proms.[207]

At the end of the century the Director reaffirmed that the Chapel services remained 'at the centre of the Choir's work'.[208] But it was these extra-liturgical activities, concerts and recording sessions, that constituted the most significant differences between the choir of the 1930s and the choir of recent decades – what it sang and how and where it was listened to.

How have these additional duties been fitted in? In the Michaelmas

Term of 1965 sung services continued as usual up to Christmas with Sung Eucharist and Evensong on Christmas Day itself.[209] In the next few years sung services during Advent were gradually reduced until in 1972 there were the usual services on the First Sunday in Advent, 3 December, and then no choral services until Christmas Eve with the Carol Service and the Midnight Mass sung by the men. That year a note in the service list explained: 'Choral Services will be suspended between Monday 4 December and Saturday 23 December inclusive. During this period the Choir will be recording *The Creation* (Haydn) in King's College Chapel, and filming *The Childhood of Christ* (Berlioz) and a programme of Christmas music for BBC Television in Lincoln Cathedral.'[210] This remained the usual pattern into the next century.

In the 1980s choral services in the Easter Term were reduced by about a week to eight weeks or just under, and services during the Long Vacation were cut from a month to about three weeks. It was these weeks in December and the summer particularly that could be filled with recording sessions and tours, and days in September too could also be used when school term had resumed but before the university term had begun.

All of which meant that during the academic year 2012–13 – and this was not at all exceptional – the choir appeared at festivals in Dubrovnik, Rotterdam and Ghent. They gave five concerts in America, including one in the National Cathedral in Washington and another at Princeton University. They also gave performances in Beijing, Hong Kong and Singapore. In their own Chapel they sang with the Vienna Boys' Choir and gave a concert of works by Bach with the countertenor Andreas Scholl. They gave a Christmas concert in the Royal Albert Hall and they sang *Messiah* in Symphony Hall in Birmingham. In Kings Place in London they sang Bach's St Matthew Passion, of which they also gave two performances during their own Easter at King's Festival. They appeared in a BBC television series on 'Music and Monarchy'; they sang at a reception given by the Prime Minister at 10 Downing Street. In October 2012 the College launched its own record label with a version of the Festival of Nine Lessons and Carols, containing in addition the most recent carols commissioned by King's. In January they recorded works by Britten, including *St Nicolas*, for the new label. At the end of the year three services of Evensong were placed on the internet, the first of what was intended to be regular placings online of actual services.[211]

Some were sure that this amount of time spent performing on a stage must inevitably have affected the singing of the choir in the stalls in King's, that the inward intensity into which a congregation was drawn half a century ago cannot have been preserved. The microphone and television camera have certainly played a part in fostering intimacy and encouraging singers – and readers as well – to play to the camera and microphone. As early as 1961 one reviewer of the disc of the Advent Carol Service recorded the year before considered that the readers were 'giving a bit too much of a performance, rather than sinking their individualities into a corporate liturgical observance'.[212] In the 1954 TV broadcast of the carol service the soloist in Peter Cornelius's *Three kings from Persian lands afar* remained standing in his stall.[213] In the twentieth-first century he would usually leave his place and stand between the stalls. On at least one occasion, in 2008, the baritone sang this solo from memory; he sang not into the vast space of the Chapel with a congregation listening, but engaging with a TV audience who could watch the expressive movements of head and eyebrows as well as catching the vocal nuances.[214]

The history of the singing of 'Once in royal David's city' illustrated a similar evolution from an other-worldly experience to one much more intimate. The words were written by Mrs Cecil Frances Alexander and first appeared in 1848 in her book entitled *Hymns for Little Children*. The famous tune was written the following year by Henry Gauntlett, soon to become the organist of the Union Chapel in Islington. The composer's own harmonization of the tune suggested a gentle two beats, not four, in a bar, and a manner of singing that was quiet and intimate. A. H. Mann's re-harmonization of it and the slow speed at which he undoubtedly took the hymn transformed its character in that vast space and famous acoustic. Willcocks took the hymn a little faster than Ord, though his own slow speed and later his famous descant preserved the majestic and solemn transformation. Ledger took the hymn slightly slower, almost at the speed Ord adopted; Cleobury took it faster, with a lilting two-in-a-bar.[215] In

1998 he reintroduced Gauntlett's two-in-a-bar simpler harmony for the first two lines of each verse, keeping Mann's for the repetition of these first two phrases of the tune.[216] Both microphone and camera up close to the solo treble in themselves dissolved the mystery and created an intimacy in both sound and image hitherto absent. Of the recording made in 1998 of the Christmas Eve service one commentator wrote that it was a 'fresher, less consciously beautiful style' and that it 'suit[ed] and reflect[ed] the performing preferences of our age'.[217] The tradition of the singing of the first verse by a solo boy goes back only seventy years or so; before the war it seems that all the boys sang the first, third and fourth verses, the choir sang verse two in harmony, and the full congregation sang only verses five and six.[218] In the recordings of 'Once in royal David's city' made in July 1949 and August 1954 the treble is accompanied by the organ in the first verse because Ord felt he could not rely on a solo boy keeping in tune on a sticky summer's day during the tensions of a recording session. It is difficult to imagine such a solution being employed by any of the directors since.

If the descriptions of 'Daddy' Mann's performing style and the evidence of the few recordings of his are taken into account, and then the tremendous changes that Ord brought about and the recordings of the three later directors of music, it is surely the similarities of the performing style over the past eighty years that seem most striking. That these were decades when recording made easily available to everyone the whole bewildering range of changing singing styles in pop and rock and world music makes this phenomenon even more noteworthy. The nature of the tradition is also emphasized when the turnover of the singers is remembered: every five years it is a completely new choir. Most of the choral scholars remain only for three years and there will usually be at least four or five new choral scholars each year. In the Michaelmas Term of 1998 there were nine new choral scholars as well as a new organ scholar.[219]

With hindsight Stephen Cleobury thought it took him a few years to free himself from the weight of tradition he inherited at King's. But he gradually realized that he must rely on his instinct, not simply make 'a pale copy of what had gone before'.[220] The continuity is there for all to listen to but so too is the vigour and intensity of the music-making as the generations pass. No doubt directors of music have been helped by the youthfulness of their singers. Eight-year-old probationers rely a lot on instinct and undergraduates are not completely set in their ways.

7

The Meaning of It All

ALL SORTS AND CONDITIONS

At the turn of the twenty-first century the distinctiveness of the singing of English cathedral and collegiate choirs was recognized and the style and the particular skills of the singers admired all over the world. The singing at King's had been brought about by changes in fundamental notions about music and musicians in English society; these changes had led to the creation of new kinds of singers and to new kinds of singing techniques, and perhaps too to new kinds of instrumental styles and sonorities. Several of the choirs at the English choral foundations had global reputations. These choirs made recordings that won prestigious awards, while their concerts and tours were handled by highly professional agents and marketing gurus and were usually sell-outs. At the same time the professional concert-giving English choirs whose repertoires overlapped with those of the cathedral choirs fed audience appetites for the same music and for styles of singing that were judged by the same yardsticks.

Some English men and women in the twentieth century heard in the Anglican choral tradition first of all the singing of upper-middle-class Englishmen, and one Dean considered cathedrals 'elitist organisations catering for a minority with highbrow tastes'.[1] A choral scholar at King's in the 1990s observed that while you didn't have to have been 'to a posh school in the south of England', many of the choral scholars had attended just such schools.[2]

But it was only in the second half of the twentieth century that the poshest schools in England were forced, largely because of parental pressure, to take music seriously. For most of the twentieth century most of the choral scholars at King's came from a narrow stratum of

society and most had indeed gone to private schools, though not the
most famous. Until the 1960s, though, even parents with sons at these
schools could be distinctly suspicious of music. A choral scholar from
1949 – he had been educated at Sherborne School – remembered
going home after Christmas and overhearing his parents' friends
talking at a party. 'Where is Christopher now? Isn't he at Cambridge?'
one of them asked. 'Yes, he's doing law at King's,' replied his father,
who was himself a lawyer. 'Oh, yes, King's! Yes, I heard that service
on the wireless. The carol service on Christmas Eve. Marvellous,
wasn't it?' 'Oh, yes.' His parents were too ashamed to confess that
their son was singing on the broadcast.[3]

Broadcasting brought the sound of the singing to huge audiences
on Christmas Eve. Why was it not tainted irredeemably with associations of privilege or class or milk-and-water Anglicanism but welcomed
by all sorts and conditions of men and women? King's certainly
had an awesome reputation, for the College's obvious antiquity and
beauty, for its intellectual authority, for its social exclusivity (though
the historic link with Eton was ended in 1861), as a bastion of
maleness – for had not Virginia Woolf been chased off its lawns and
barred from its library because she was a woman?[4]

It was compelling to those early listeners partly perhaps simply
because of the Christmas Eve broadcast itself: the College was throwing
its doors open to everyone. Because denominational ramparts were
lowered at Christmastime – one of the readers was a representative of
the Cambridge churches – at the first service he was 'a free church
minister'. Perhaps because of the sense of vulnerability conveyed by the
singing of children, or because you were suddenly asked to remember
'the poor and the helpless, the cold, the hungry and the oppressed;
the sick in body and in mind and them that mourn; the lonely and the
unloved; the aged and the little children'. Because the singing was so
extraordinarily beautiful.

Critics might complain of the men's voices at King's that they were
'immature' or 'too gentlemanly', or that in this singing style the singers were not encouraged to explore the extremes of their dynamic
range. One scholar and performer spoke of the 'unmatchable acoustic of King's College Chapel, Cambridge';[5] another scholar regarded
the acoustic as 'a musically unsavoury substance' since it didn't allow

every note of the texts he had painstakingly edited of Byrd and Taverner to emerge clearly enough.[6] Writing after the 1966 Christmas Eve service one reviewer noted that the musical style was 'open to criticism on many counts'. But, he added, the singing had a quality all its own, 'a studied perfection', which rendered criticism 'irrelevant'. 'For the ordinary listener,' he thought, the Christmas Eve service was 'unquestionably one of the great broadcasting events of the year.'[7] Half a century later an English journalist writing his Christmas column could still remind his readers that, on 24 December, 'Cambridge once again becomes the centre of the world'.[8]

THE DECLINE IN BELIEF

The primary function of the choirs at the choral foundations is to adorn and beautify the beliefs and the teachings of the Church of England. The chapters at the cathedrals have certainly been eager to celebrate the skill and the renown of their musicians in the earlier years of the twenty-first century. At Canterbury in 2016 the Cathedral took 'great pride in the music performed at its Services'.[9] The Chapter at St Paul's explained that silent cathedrals were 'at best awesome monuments; fill them with music and you have one of the most potent keys of man's devising for unlocking his earthbound spirit.'[10] The Dean of York welcomed visitors by telling them that the Minster was 'one of the world's most magnificent cathedrals, a masterpiece in stained-glass and stone . . . and its vast spaces are brought to life with the glory of worship and heavenly music'.[11] 'The sacred space of Winchester Cathedral,' the Chapter explained to visitors, 'has echoed to music every day for almost a thousand years, inspiring worshippers and visitors alike. Today, we continue this great choral tradition with daily services set to the music of great composers and sung in the unique English style.'[12] At Lincoln visitors could hear 'some of the most exquisite music to be heard anywhere in the world'.[13]

Yet the same decades which saw improvements in the singing and a growing love of this sacred music among congregations and audiences also saw a continuing decline in religious belief and in the membership of the Church of England. In the middle of the twentieth century half the population of England believed in a personal God. Half a century later a quarter did.[14] In 2015 less than half the population considered themselves Christian, and only half of the self-identified Christians believed in God.[15]

All the surveys suggested the same, that the number of men and women who practised their beliefs and declared them by regular attendance at Anglican services had been declining throughout the twentieth century and the decline had become steeper in the twenty-first. The 'establishment position', as one survey described it, was 'no religion'.[16] The 2014 British Social Attitudes Survey indicated that nearly 60 per cent of the population never attended a religious service. Of the 16 per cent who designated themselves as Anglicans half of these never attended services and only 10 per cent of those who identified with the Church of England attended a service weekly.[17]

And yet men and women who might not regularly attend their local parish church did continue to visit cathedrals. In his book on *England's Cathedrals* published in 2016, Simon Jenkins wrote that 'for the millions outside the church, including myself, cathedrals have an appeal that grows ever wider, despite falling church membership . . . a cathedral . . . is a place for all men and women'.[18] In March 2016 *The Daily Telegraph* reported increases in the number of students attending choral evensong in college chapels at Oxford and Cambridge. Christians, Muslims and atheists alike, the report ran, were seeking solace in the words of the 1662 Prayer Book and the music of the Anglican tradition. At New College a congregation of fewer than 150 was rare. At King's the busiest day of the week was Saturday when the Dean would expect between five and six hundred people. Many of them would certainly be tourists, though the chapel staff had begun to see more and more members of the University at Evensong.[19]

One survey in 2012 calculated that perhaps eleven million adults living in England had visited a cathedral in the previous year, leaving aside visitors from overseas. The survey was clear that the visitors included many who were from other denominations and other faiths and from the ranks of the non-religious too, and suggested that this provided cathedrals with 'mission opportunities'.[20] The survey considered that cathedrals could 'convey a sense of the spiritual and sacred even to those who are on the margins of Christian faith, or who stand some way beyond. In an age of amorphous, "emergent" spiritualities, this presents cathedrals with enormous potential.'[21] 'If the cathedrals are able to work with [the] duality of being both tourist destinations and places of pilgrimage, it opens up the possibility of encouraging a deepening of spiritual awareness and development.'[22] There was ambiguity here in the use of phrases like '"emergent" spiritualities', 'encouraging a deepening of spiritual awareness' and 'mission opportunities' when clearly so many visitors and students were not practising Christians and might have had no wish to join or return to a Church of England congregation. To many Anglican clergymen the word 'spirituality' itself was deeply suspect, and likely to be dismissed as New Age whimsy. But the popularity of choral evensong on the radio, Advent and Christmas carol services, music festivals in cathedrals, performances of the music by concert-giving choirs as well as cathedral and college choirs in the Royal Albert Hall in London at the Proms, all this provided evidence of higher standards of singing and the unflagging enthusiasm of congregations and audiences.

Why, if belief in God and membership of the Church of England were continuing to diminish, were so many people all over the world wishing to listen to the singing of English cathedral and college choirs? If the singing was not for the worship of God then what was it for?

The Church of England usually explained the continued fall in its membership with reference to secularization and multiculturalism. It certainly did seem likely that many attended church in Victorian England and in the first half of the twentieth century simply out of social convention. And then, later in the century, when so many others attended mosques or temples or football matches or went shopping on a Sunday, church attendance no longer seemed the social imperative it once did. Not many perhaps subjected their beliefs to critical examination, but some did, whether in the course of their general education or as a result of the stream of radio and television programmes and popular books by such writers as Don Cupitt, Karen Armstrong, Richard Dawkins, Christopher Hitchens and Richard Holloway. For many men and women a theistic view of the universe that implied a deity or some kind of beneficent force concerned with the destiny of human beings was not possible to reconcile with our twentieth-century knowledge of the world and of ourselves. The only distinctive and distinguishing and authentic marks of Christianity seemed to be its doctrines that those who gave up everything and followed Christ would be bodily resurrected and sit with Him for evermore. These could not be accepted by many who certainly accepted the prevalent moralities of mainstream Christianity in England, codes of behaviour which were not at all exclusively Christian.

By the first decade of the twenty-first century a former Archbishop of Canterbury considered that the Church of England was a generation away from extinction, and that it must evangelize and give cogent reasons for Christian belief to young people or it must die.[23] But cogent reasons for belief had been advanced by the Church of England for many decades and had continued to be rejected. At the Lambeth Conference in 1988 the Church had designated the 1990s a Decade of Evangelism. And yet, even then, however the work and influence of the Church of England were assessed in those years – whether by usual Sunday attendance, or Easter Day attendance, say, or attendance at Christmas services, or electoral roll membership, or the number of baptisms, or confirmations – the Church had continued to retreat.[24]

Belief had not been possible for Thomas Hardy in the nineteenth century who saw the congregation at a cathedral service and realized that from 'this bright believing band', as he took it to be, he was an outcast. Their beliefs had seemed to him 'fantasies', their 'Shining Land' just 'mirage-mists'. And yet he could not accept this loss of faith with equanimity; 'disquiet' clung about him, and his was 'a drear destiny'.[25] Many of the tourists – as many members of cathedral chapters would have regarded them – who visited cathedrals in more recent decades did so though not with disquiet but with enthusiasm and pleasure. A member of the Chapter at Lincoln in 1994 thought that 'Choral Evensong could hardly be less "contemporary" or populist, yet every year it seems to be received by more people as balm to their souls.'[26] It was not altogether clear whether he approved of this development or not. He called it 'folk-Christianity'. Certainly some members of cathedral chapters did not.

A one-time canon at St Paul's considered that in the last century and a half the English had devised a religion in which God had practically vanished. It was a religion of the 'nice country vicar' with polished shoes, who judged the marrows at the village fête, of hospital visiting and flower arranging, with a side offering of heritage conservation. It was a religion 'mired in nostalgia'. It was a religion of choral evensong. 'Safe in the knowledge that proceedings will be ordered, beautiful and modest, the English are happy enough to creep in at the back of the church and allow their spirits to take flight.' The country vicars and the frequenters of choral evensong were 'doctrinally inert'. Now though, in 2009, he thought, 'Belief is . . . back, often red in tooth and claw.' What was being imagined was 'a more energetic and vigorous church'. The difficulty, he was sure, was that society today cared more for old stones than for old people and religious people cared more for old stones than for God. The buildings of the Church of England were 'so loved by those who take no other interest in the church's proclamation' that the Church can't do away with parish churches with tiny congregations. 'The appropriate theological response to all this is called iconoclasm – creative destruction.' Cathedral music too was irrelevant to the Church of England's mission – 'only tourists go to choral evensong these days' – whose true concern should be the 're-evangelisation of England'.[27]

Such views were not new. Many churchmen had long seen the fabric of the Church and its cathedral music as the interest of aesthetes, not of believers, and many of the ancient buildings as 'obsolescent plant'.[28] An undergraduate who went to King's in 1923 objected to having to attend services in Chapel which he considered not really services at all but concerts.[29] Almost all the members of the College Council in 1966 thought that the Christmas Eve television broadcast could not have 'any religious significance whatsoever', either to those in the Chapel or to those watching at home.[30]

In 1992 a report on church music commissioned by the Archbishops of Canterbury and York concluded that 'we belong to a generation which has grown up knowing little of the language of religion, or of the basic doctrines and faith of Christianity. Our culture is fragmented and secular, and for most people Choral Evensong, for example, has little to offer except beautiful music.'[31]

What was 'beautiful music' though? The singing of cathedral choirs and the concert-giving choirs could certainly be listened to, and was not infrequently used, as muzak, to create the perfect ambience and to enhance customer experience in upmarket bookshops, for example. The sonic image of this music was also popular on certain radio stations, ideal tracks 'for the days when the rain just won't stop falling; for the days when the phone hasn't stopped ringing for a minute; for bad hair days and bad mood days', for 'Smooth Classics at 7'.[32]

CATHEDRAL MUSIC AND UNBELIEF

How would Hubert Parry have defined 'beautiful music'? Parry, whom Elgar saluted in 1905 as 'the head of our art in this country',[33] considered that men and women were impelled to reverence and aspiration, to thankfulness for the good things they enjoyed, impelled to wonder and exaltation, conscious of wrongdoing, conscious of tarnished self-respect, needing encouragement. And they could be helped to find what they needed, Parry thought, in the religious impulses enshrined in art of all kinds in which they found energy and vitality. Some were uplifted by the orderliness in art, some by subtle and perfect design, some inspired by expressions of tenderness and love they find. 'Some like a [musical] work for its complexity of line,' Parry thought, 'some for its colour, some for its sentiment, some for its force, some for its sensuousness, some for its austerity. A really great work of art has so many sides that it can provide spiritual food for people of most diverse temperament.'[34]

Parry wrote oratorios and canticles for the Church and anthems and hymn tunes. He wrote 'Jerusalem'; he set 'I was glad when they said unto me, Let us go into the courts of the Lord'. And yet Parry, who was the son of the man who painted the nave-roof at Ely Cathedral, thought that conventional church-going illustrated only the hypocrisy of purely ecclesiastical religion. He disdained theological subtleties which, he thought, merely distracted attention from the real needs of human beings. The sphere of religion, he believed, should be enlarged and include not just devotional exercises but art of all kinds.[35] And Vaughan Williams, who himself was a church organist, even though a ham-fisted one, and wrote great music for cathedral choirs, was a 'cheerful agnostic',[36] whose attitude was of a man who rejoiced in the natural and intense and spontaneous spirituality he recognized was possible for those who shared a common culture but not necessarily a particular religious creed or indeed any creed at all.

Parry and Vaughan Williams, whose agnostic attitudes were not in doubt, had an enormous influence on cathedral musicians, a moral and intellectual and spiritual influence, not just a musical one, particularly through their activities as teachers. One prominent cathedral musician, himself not at all an orthodox believer, came to the end of a rehearsal of Parry's *Lord, let me know mine end* and exclaimed: 'And yet that man says he has no religion.'[37] Walford Davies, the director of the music at the Temple Church and at St George's Chapel, Windsor, was the son of Nonconformist parents and a rarity among organists at the choral foundations, an evangelical Christian, and yet to him the unbelieving Parry was still a man 'after God's own heart'.[38]

Benjamin Britten – who set any number of sacred texts and wrote church operas and a Requiem, and composed anthems and settings of the Anglican canticles – was 'a convinced humanist rather than a believer'.[39] So was the best-known composer of cathedral music in the twentieth century an unbeliever, Herbert Howells. His daughter thought him 'an agnostic who veered toward belief'; he 'loved the tradition of the church, and the Bible as literature', she thought, but he was not 'deeply religious'.[40] A biographer described him as 'a deeply *spiritual* person'.[41] John Rutter described himself as a 'friend, fellow traveller, and agnostic supporter of the Christian faith'.[42] A conductor of one of the leading concert-giving consorts, which drew on men from cathedral choirs, was sure that lay clerks' 'main concern' in the stalls was to perform well in front of their professional colleagues and that some at least had 'little interest in religion'.[43] This was surely too sweeping. But where cathedrals had formerly stipulated that a prospective lay clerk should be a communicant member of the Church of England, such a requirement was usually missing in notices of vacancies in the twenty-first century. Now something much vaguer was desirable, that while lay clerks were 'not required to be practising Christians' they were expected 'to work and behave in sympathy with the worship, ministry and mission of the Cathedral', or some such formulation.[44]

In the early 1990s while making a documentary about King's the

BBC interviewed the choral scholars about their beliefs. One was a Jew who didn't take part in the spoken parts of the services – he never said the Creed – but was able to 'disconnect' himself from 'the religious side' of worship. Another had been baptized but no longer believed in God. About half the choral scholars received Communion.[45] David Willcocks said he didn't believe in God and his confirmation as a teenager had meant little to him. You accepted church-going, he said, but this did not mean that you believed in anything; it was part of a way of life into which he was born. He felt it his business as an organist and choir-trainer to make music as skilfully as possible in order to assist individual members of the congregation reach God, whatever they meant by that term.[46]

This was similar to Stephen Cleobury's stated aim; he hoped that those attending a service at King's would be enriched by the experience and he believed that traditional Christians, Buddhists, agnostics, atheists – men and women whatever their religious adherence – could be helped and inspired by the experience. At any rate that was the hope that sustained him. His paternal grandfather had been an Anglican priest and he had been devout as a teenager, 'a committed Christian', but later his religious feelings had 'cooled'. In middle age he discovered that his father, a psychiatrist who was an amateur church organist, was an unbeliever.[47]

A Cambridge anthropologist and historian was told by several heads of Cambridge colleges that they were not Christians and yet they attended Chapel because they could see how important it was. The Chapel was there and had always been there and stood for a spiritual dimension and coloured the minds of those who inhabited that place. There was dignity and reverence without dogma. It reminded him of Kyoto, the ancient capital of Japan, with its Buddhist temples and gardens and shrines, where he had found that religious beliefs were indistinct and that men and women were not happy if you pressed them on their beliefs.[48] Some cathedral musicians were orthodox Christians; some of them, like Harry Bramma at Southwark and Christopher Dearnley at St Paul's, had studied theology at university.[49] While some, like David Willcocks, did not consider themselves conventional 'believers' at all, all these cathedral musicians and composers writing for cathedral choirs pursued their vocation with unswerving seriousness of purpose and whole-heartedness.

William Temple (1881–1944) was one of the few English school-masters or clergymen of his time – and he was both, a headmaster and an archbishop – to grasp the potential power of music. 'There is no charm in the whole realm of art so subtle, so intangible, so eth-ereal as that of music,' he said to the boys at his school in 1911. 'It is the most spiritual and incalculable of all modes of expression.'[50] Eric Milner-White was overwhelmed with Howells' settings of the even-ing canticles for King's and for Gloucester. Their impact was 'of *spiritual* moment rather than liturgical. It is so much more than music-making; it is experiencing deep things in the only medium that can do it.'[51]

NEW SPIRITUALITIES

In his famous book published in 1902 William James described the religious experiences of many different people in many different kinds of society – their religious experiences, not the doctrine or dogma that might underpin their beliefs – as imparting 'a new zest which adds itself like a gift to life, and takes the form either of lyrical enchantment or of appeal to earnestness and heroism . . . an assurance of safety and a temper of peace, and, in relation to others, a preponderance of lov-ing affections'.[52] And he quoted the American psychologist J. H. Leuba: 'Not God, but life, more life, a larger, richer, more satisfying life, is, in the last analysis, the end of religion. The love of life, at any and every level of development, is the religious impulse.'[53]

In 1903 and 1904 a Fellow of King's gave a series of lectures en-titled 'Religion, a Criticism and a Forecast'. Lowes Dickinson wanted to distinguish between scientific knowledge, which he wished to be called truth, and a kind of faith which owed nothing to belief in God or to religious doctrine. He thought there was truth, which was scientific truth, and that to talk of religious truth as if there were certainties in this sphere was distorting. He wanted to designate a state of mind which he would like to call faith, though it owed noth-ing to religious dogma or doctrine. This kind of faith, he explained, was nearer to music or poetry than to science. It was an attitude marked by adventurousness and expectancy and optimism. It was the attitude of an explorer like Columbus, setting out with some ideas but no certainties.[54]

The Cambridge theologian Don Cupitt, whom Stephen Cleobury read and got to know and with whom he felt affinities, wished the Church to cultivate a contemplative wisdom, not looking for any future vindication of principles but looking for vindication in the present. This, he said, was nothing in the least esoteric. It was a state of mind, or a condition of existing, which was common to all kinds of artists and found in every mystical tradition. The world of the twentieth century showed him no timeless world of unseen realities, no hereafter, and this forced him into the present, to the eternity of the ephemeral. While this might sound rather Buddhist, being pushed towards 'a very cool ecstasis', as he put it, it was in fact all Christian; it could be illustrated from the tradition of Christian mysticism. Such ideas, he thought, should be embraced and not repudiated by the Church of England. He saw many people in Christian cultures already 'visiting their own churches and monasteries in a Hindu rather than an ecclesiastical spirit. The regular liturgical worship of the church presupposes a clearly defined and highly committed community. But most visitors to cathedrals are not nowadays members of such a community, nor do they wish to be. They prefer to be freelance pilgrims and holy tourists . . . the tourist may well be a person who loves Christian culture and is appropriating something of it in her own way, in order to build it into the myth, the morality and the project of her own life.'[55]

Karen Armstrong, the distinguished writer of many books on the place of religion in the modern world, stresses that religion has been regarded in many societies over many centuries as a practice, a way of life, not as a body of doctrine requiring the assent of its disciples. This was a modern aberration, a misunderstanding, in her analysis, which originated with the success and prestige of Newtonian physics in the seventeenth and eighteenth centuries. A whole structure of laws and generalizations susceptible of demonstration or verification was being built in the material world. It was only a matter of time, the Enlightenment thought, before such a rational analysis could be made of metaphysical and theological matters. But the task of religion, at least as formerly understood, 'closely allied to that of art, was to help us to live creatively, peacefully and even joyously with realities for which there were no easy explanations and problems that we could not solve: mortality, pain, grief, despair, and outrage at the injustice and cruelty of life.' Religion was 'a practical discipline, and its insights are not derived from abstract speculation but from spiritual exercises and a dedicated lifestyle'.[56]

Deans of King's themselves often seemed to stress the importance of psychological attitudes rather than doctrine or dogma. In 1987 John Drury chose a passage from a seventeenth-century Provost of the College as a preface in the service booklet on Christmas Eve:

> For, this you must understand; that Religion is not satisfied in Notions; but doth indeed, and in reality, come to nothing, unless it be in us not only Matter of Knowledge and Speculation; but doth establish in us a Frame and Temper of Mind, and is productive of a holy and virtuous Life. Therefore, let these things take effect in us; in our Spirituality and Heavenly-mindedness; in our Conformity to the Divine Nature, and Nativity from above. For, whosoever professes that he believes the Truth of these things; and wants the Operation of them upon his Spirit, and Life; he doth, in fact, make void, and frustrate what he doth declare as his Belief: and so he doth receive the Grace of God in vain; unless this Principle, and Belief doth descend into his Heart, and establish a good Frame and Temper of Mind; and govern in all the Actions of his Life and Conversation.[57]

If listening to and also singing in these choirs could be said to constitute spiritual exercises, what might be the nature of the experience to those who seek out music in sacred places, in Anglican cathedrals, and yet cannot accept the words of the Thirty-nine Articles of Faith or the Book of Common Prayer, those for whom 'God' was 'a term of poetry and eloquence' and the language of the Bible 'fluid, passing, and literary, not rigid, fixed and scientific'?[58] For such words as these of Matthew Arnold had sunk deep into the psyche of generations of English people.

'The cool and ancient order of the services', as King's described theirs for their visitors, 'gives a space and a frame, as well as cues, for

reflections on our regrets and hopes and gratitudes'.[59] The unbelieving Philip Larkin felt 'a hunger in himself to be more serious' and
would gravitate to a church:

> A serious house on serious earth it is,
> In whose blent air all our compulsions meet,
> Are recognized, and robed as destinies.[60]

To pray, according to W. H. Auden, was to fix one's attention on something or someone other than oneself. He quoted Ludwig Wittgenstein
with approval: 'To pray is to think about the meaning of life.'[61] As to
what to pray about, a great many men and women raised as Anglicans in the twentieth century had countless passages of the Authorized
Version of the Bible ingrained in their consciousness: 'Finally, breth-
ren, whatsoever things are true, whatsoever things are honest,
whatsoever things are just, whatsoever things are pure, whatsoever
things are lovely, whatsoever things are of good report; if there
be any virtue, and if there be any praise, think on these things.'[62]
Religious belief offered certainties and clarity, whereas spirituality
required continuous questioning and examination of first principles,
for which reason it was sometimes seen as a dangerous threat by
conventional religious organizations.[63]

 The thinking that accompanied the contemplation of art or music
was not likely to be linear or rational but inchoate and repetitive.
Fragments or flashes of insight were more probable, like the metaphors that tumbled from George Herbert in the seventeenth century
when he attempted to convey the quality of prayerfulness:

> . . . A kind of tune, which all things hear and fear;
> Softness, and peace, and joy, and love, and bliss,
> Exalted manna, gladness of the best,
> Heaven in ordinary, man well drest,
> The milky way, the bird of Paradise,
> Church-bells beyond the stars heard, the soul's blood,
> The land of spices; something understood.[64]

If cathedral music – or music in cathedrals – could assist personal
reflection and prayer, it could also sway or reinforce communal
feelings. When Beethoven's Violin Concerto was played in Hereford

Cathedral in 1952 the author of the note in the programme book prepared the audience with reference to Wordsworth. The qualities we might find in music, he explained, were the qualities Wordsworth hoped would be found in his own poetry:

> Truth, beauty, grandeur, love and hope . . .
> Blessed consolation in distress . . .
> And joy in widest commonalty spread.[65]

These qualities would be sought as part of a community. They would be sought in buildings of great architectural splendour which themselves cut you down to size. But you were not left in isolation. At choral evensong you were not witnessing a performance; the singers were not standing there before you, looking you in the eye and presenting the music to you. You were drawn in to a shared ritual.

Music could also assist in producing altered states of consciousness, as had been recognized for centuries in a great many civilizations. It might be an ordinary, everyday Evensong but there, in such settings, there was always the expectation of life-changing moments, 'heaven in ordinary'. The astonishing acoustics of many cathedrals and college chapels worked their effect on the voices: one listener heard the 'irresistible glamour' of a plainsong hymn sung in procession, and the simple chant in unison that took on 'a remote, magical, and disembodied quality – a grave ecstasy, radiant yet austere, impassioned yet serene – and glow as with a secret, inward fire'. The voices themselves seemed 'to undergo a curious transmutation and become impersonal, sexless, superhuman almost, giving expression to the inarticulate yearnings and aspirations, not only of the living, but also of the countless generations of the dead and the unborn'.[66]

In the twentieth century, music was listened to with subconsciously inherited nineteenth-century notions of profundity, of unembraceability, with the tacit realization that however deeply the listener plumbed the music's depths, any verbal description of the experience would have to end in three dots. Such notions were not altogether modern ones. William Byrd reminded his listeners that a piece of music – at least a piece that is 'well and artificially made' – must be listened to again and again: 'the oftener you shall hear it, the better cause of liking it you will discover, and commonly that song is best esteemed with which our ears are best acquainted'.[67] His compatriot, Richard Hooker, described music as:

> a thing which delighteth all ages and beseemeth all states; a thing as seasonable in grief as in joy ... The reason hereof is an admirable facility which music hath to express and represent to the mind, more inwardly than any other sensible mean, the very standing, rising, and falling, the very steps and inflections every way, the turns and varieties of all passions whereunto the mind is subject ... There is [one kind] that draweth to a marvellous grave and sober mediocrity; there is also [one] that carrieth as it were into ecstasies, filling the mind with an heavenly joy, and for the time in a manner severing it from the body.[68]

A King's chorister in 1960 – who at the time reckoned himself 'a hardened pro' at this singing business – never forgot the transcendent experience he had during Patrick Hadley's *I sing of a maiden* at the Advent Carol Service. Two quiet notes held on the distant organ, with no indication of a pulse, just poised there, and so quiet and so still and everyone being drawn in, and the gentleness as the music eased into the triple metre, 'He came all so still', and at the climax 'Mother and maiden was never none but she' – the boys hadn't seen their own mothers for weeks but it would soon be Christmas and home and their mothers there for them – and the close, 'God's mother be', *pianississimo*, the organ singing serenely above the boys in its own time, and the thirty-six beats on the last note, held there, on and on and on, and the peace enveloping them.[69]

One of the choral scholars at King's in the early 1990s remembered how he would be singing magnificent Tudor polyphony standing up near the high altar and looking down the length of the Chapel with the vaulting lit up and a congregation sitting in rapt attention, or he would be processing out after a service well sung and the organ would be blazing away and the west doors would be flung open. And he could only describe such experiences with reference to 'God'.[70]

In the early days of the choir at Guildford Cathedral, one of the tenors thought, it was first in the psalms that the new choir moved from competence, as he put it, to daily beauty. And then, just occasionally, there would be those rare moments, when 'the music assumed a life of its own and carried the performers into what can only be blunderingly described as total shared consciousness in which individual identity vanished'. It was such experiences that sustained him as a singer, and it was in the expectation of such moments that he was prepared to devote himself to the daily round of services.[71] Another lay clerk remembered a moment when Guildford were singing Evensong as a visiting choir at King's. In the anthem they had reached the words *illi autem sunt in pace*, 'but [the souls of the righteous] are in peace', and the words – the syllables – and the sounds and the stone and the light were all there interfused and the music went on and on. It was, he said, 'a rare and sublime moment'.[72]

Such experiences clearly gave the singers a sense of mastery; they lost themselves, body and mind, in a difficult, worthwhile corporate activity and this, psychologists tell us, brings human beings as near to what is usually meant by happiness as we can conceive.[73] Such experiences seemed not only to console and inspire both singers and listeners, but also to reconcile them to the unfathomable mysteries of existence, to assist them in feeding their minds in Wordsworth's 'wise passiveness'.[74] About such experiences the French philosopher André Comte-Sponville uses words like 'eternity' – that is, time suspended – 'plenitude' – when nothing seemed to be missing – 'serenity', 'acceptance'.[75] It seemed to be an acceptance of unanswered and perhaps unanswerable questions, when, as John Keats put it, 'man is capable of being in uncertainties, mysteries, doubts, without any irritable reaching after fact and reason'.[76]

The contemplation of profound moral truths and the practising of spiritual exercises chosen to suit individual temperaments and personalities dethroned the individual, removed him from the centre of the stage, Karen Armstrong suggested. And such moments could inspire selflessness.[77] 'One particular *meaning* of God' was passing away, Don Cupitt was sure, 'in the hands not of its enemies but of its own best proponents'.[78] But religious worship in the twentieth century could still convey 'a feeling of awe, sometimes tinged with a sense of unworthiness, that one may experience before sublimity or grandeur in Nature or art . . . [a] universal loving attitude'.[79]

The musicologist Frank Ll. Harrison pointed out that Nicholas Pevsner's description of the late perpendicular style of buildings of Eton and King's College, Cambridge, as 'a union of practical, matter of fact spirit, with a sense of mystery, and an almost Oriental effusion of ornament' was 'uncannily apt also to the best of the music of the Eton Choirbook', the famous collection of sacred polyphony assembled in the 1500s.[80]

The mysterious stillness of Japanese and Chinese traditional music, its 'magic sense of uneventfulness', in the words of the Cambridge-based composer Roberto Gerhard,[81] was a quality that fascinated a great number of post-war composers working in the Western European tradition. Like Pierre Boulez, the English composer Jonathan Harvey sought 'balanced universes of sound', he said, 'poised without any rootedness, and this to my ear tends to come close to the objective musics of our own distant past and of the East-objective in that they're more concerned with collective and spiritual existence'.[82] The music which was truly contemporary, according to Harvey, related directly to European music before 1600, before the evolution of the passionate dynamism of tonality. Harvey was a chorister at St Michael's College, Tenbury, and the strongest influence on him then was the sixteenth-century music he was singing. Besides an opera, many works for orchestra and chamber ensemble and many employing electronics, he composed several anthems, a setting of the evening canticles, a Missa brevis, a carol for King's, *The Angels*, as well as a number of organ works. He always felt he was making music for the glory of God, he said, because as a chorister at remote St Michael's, Tenbury, there was nobody to listen to the singing of the choir 'except God'.[83]

In adult life he practised Buddhism and was drawn to both Christian and Eastern mystical traditions. He agreed with Stockhausen that music could be regarded as 'entertainment, even a way of killing time' or, as he hoped his own music could be regarded, as 'an education, a school for life in which one's feelings are refined and one's philosophy and spirituality are led on to greater things'.[84] One distinguished music critic was stirred by both composers and the effect their music had on him was similar: he considered the music of both Harvey and Stockhausen 'ecstatic, inspired, filled now with contemplative rapture, then suddenly with exuberant, joyful dance, and always beautiful'. The music of them both, he said, quoting Milton, could 'with sweetness, through mine ear, Dissolve me into ecstasies, And bring all Heaven before mine eyes'.[85] Or as another mystical English composer, Gustav Holst, had once said, 'Music – being identical with heaven – isn't a thing of momentary thrills or even hourly ones. It's a condition of eternity'.[86]

That choral evensong was 'doctrinally inert' would not have concerned Alec Vidler, the Dean of King's when David Willcocks was appointed organist. The Dean suggested that for modern-day men and women – post-Darwinian, post-Freudian men and women – traditional religious symbols and mythologies and dogmas and doctrines had lost the power they once had to fire the imagination. Twenty years later in Cambridge, Don Cupitt was explaining that 'religious beliefs . . . are not universal truths but community-truths . . . rules of life . . . giving symbolic expression to our commitment to a particular community, its values, its sense of the shape and direction a human life should have – in a word, its spirituality'. 'All meaning and truth and value are man-made and could not be otherwise . . . We must choose what to be, what to value, and what world to constitute about ourselves . . .'[87]

Vidler thought it was not necessary for men and women to be required to be received into any Church or denomination or sect with its own peculiar systems and school of thought and doctrines and officials and regulations. The words and the life of Christ alone had the power to free human beings from fear and frustration and self-centredness towards the life of the Spirit, of which the fruit was 'love, joy, peace, patience, kindness, goodness, faithfulness, gentleness, self-control'.[88] It was impossible to foresee how we would come to terms with new knowledge of ourselves and of the world, new ways of thinking, new social habits, and what would replace the religious elements in historic Christianity. Some might survive chiefly as 'venerable archaisms or as fairy stories for children'. But in the search for 'religionless Christianity' – the phrase was Dietrich Bonhoeffer's – all that it was possible to hope for was that the Church of England might continue to allow great latitude in the interpretation of its formularies and the adaptations of its customs, and that all sorts and conditions of men and women including non-religious Christians, semi-detached believers and semi-attached agnostics too were made welcome.[89]

Jonathan Harvey envied cultures of the Middle Ages and of some

Eastern civilizations where music found a natural home in society's rituals. In the twentieth century, in the West, he valued the experience of listening to singers not standing up on a platform – striving to impress an audience, not able quite to banish thoughts of the box office, plagued by apprehension of career failure – but half hidden in the choir stalls, attempting to voice the thoughts and hopes and aspirations and sorrows of a community, some of whose members stood round and listened and lost themselves and maybe sometimes found themselves in the music:

> And countless congregations as the generations pass
> Join choir and great crowned organ case, in centuries of song
> To praise Eternity contained in Time and coloured glass.[90]

And as he wrote his evening canticles he was fired with a vision, he said, 'of our great cathedrals as once again the spearhead of all that is adventurous, imaginative and sacred in our torn culture'.[91]

In 1843 an earnest Tractarian in Cambridge watched 'a few miserable and effete singers running about from choir to choir, and performing, to a crashing and bellowing of organs, the most meagre and washy musick; how could Church men learn anything, under such a system,' he asked, 'of the depth and majesty and sternness and devotion of true church musick?'[92]

John Jebb and Sir Frederick Ouseley would surely have been surprised at the way cathedral music was transformed in the twentieth century, surprised too that it was to be a Cambridge college which provided the dynamism and focus of the transformation. They might not have been astonished that the Church itself did so little to effect the improvement in the singing at its choral foundations nor that it took so long for what were normally deemed educated Englishmen to grasp the potential value and importance of music in the lives of nearly everyone. But would anyone at the end of the nineteenth century have thought that music would become the most potent art form of the twentieth?

The composer Peter Maxwell Davies, who was Master of the Queen's Music between 2004 and 2014, said his attitudes towards religion were 'very open indeed'; in the music of any composer worth their salt, he felt there was something that was 'absolutely transcendental'.[93] He perceived a luminous spiritualty in the natural world all round him and hoped some such quality was conveyed in his own music. He regarded Judaism, Christianity and Islam all part of his inheritance as a European.[94] The singing at King's he considered 'a crowning glory of our civilisation'.[95]

It was certainly of a piece with Western European civilization. For it was the flowering of ideas that arose through those stupendous changes in historical consciousness we call Romanticism; through shifts in the attitudes of the English – especially the middle classes – to music and musicians, which owed not a small amount, some thought, to the enlightened ideas of a Queen's consort, a musical Prince of German origin.[96] This singing style emerged because of Wordsworth and the Oxford Movement; because of changing attitudes towards education and boyhood; because of a need for men and boys to display their particularly English kind of masculinity; because the sound had to be a Protestant one and not a Catholic one, and an Anglican one and not a Nonconformist one; because of particular men's temperaments and personalities and powers of leadership; because of developments in technology; because of convictions about moral and social values and ways of living; because of the vast acoustic of one of Europe's great buildings.

That's why they sang as they did.

A Note on Recordings

A great many recordings of King's and of the choirs at the other English choral foundations are now available on Spotify and iTunes. Many of these choirs are also making webcasts of their services available. The audio sources cited in this book, though, are mainly of commercial recordings on discs, acoustic and electrical 78 rpm records, LPs and CDs. There are also a few DVDs and a few audio and audio-visual recordings on YouTube.

Recordings of King's, especially those made under Sir David Willcocks's direction, have been reissued – and parts of original single discs reissued – many times with different catalogue numbers each time. (There is no full and comprehensive discography of King's.) The numbers given in the notes are of the discs actually used in the research, not the original numbers and not the latest numbers necessarily. Accompanying liner notes quoted may have only been issued with the particular release cited.

Most of the recordings cited were in the author's own private collection. But three public collections were also consulted. Besides commercial discs, the British Library's recordings include BBC broadcasts and the privately made recordings in the Brian Head King's College, Cambridge, Collection. This includes more than fifty hours of recordings made in the Chapel at King's between 1956 and 1959. The King's Sound Archive at King's College, London, includes 150,000 78 rpm discs, mostly UK issues, released from about 1900 to 1960 (https://www.kcl.ac.uk/artshums/depts/music/research/proj/ksa/index.aspx; accessed 10 February 2018); 5,000 sound files from the contents of this collection are available online (http://www.charm.kcl.ac.uk/sound/sound.html; accessed 10 February 2018). The

Archive of Recorded Church Music at Great Malvern in Worcester-shire holds recordings made from 1902 until the present day, commercial recordings, private recordings and test pressings, and also radio and television transmissions, as well as more than 6,000 photographic images concerned with the history of English church music (http://www.recordedchurchmusic.org; accessed 10 February 2018).

A number of anthologies of commercial recordings document the singing style at the English choral foundations up to the Willcocks years at King's, all on CDs except the first:

An *Anthology of English Church Music* on 78 rpm discs issued between 1950 and 1954 on the Columbia label consisting of thirty-nine 12-inch and eight 10-inch discs. The full contents are listed in Edward Sackville-West and Desmond Shawe-Taylor, *The Record Guide* (revised edn, London, 1955), pp. 889–95.

The Treasury of English Church Music 1100–1965 (originally issued on five 12-inch long-playing vinyl discs in 1965), EMI CLASSICS 0 84620 2 (5 CDs, issued 2011).

The Complete Argo Recordings of the Choir of King's College, Cambridge, Directed by David Willcocks, DECCA set 478 8918 (29 CDs, issued 2015).

The Complete Argo Recordings of the Choir of St John's College, Cambridge, Directed by George Guest, DECCA set 483 1252 (42 CDs, issued 2017).

Boris Ord, Choir of King's College, Cambridge: English Church Music, Favourite Christmas Carols, TESTAMENT SBT 1121 (issued 1997).

Salisbury Cathedral Choir & Organ Archive Recordings 1927–1965, SCS 276501 (issued 2000); *Salisbury Cathedral Choir & Organ Archive Recordings, Volume 2*, SCS 276502 (issued 2002); *Salisbury Cathedral Choir & Organ Archive Recordings, Volume 3*, SCS 276503 (issued 2004).

New College Choir: Archive Recordings 1927–1951, CHASS 971 (1997).

The Choir of Magdalen College, Oxford: Archive Recordings 1906–60, OXRECS DIGITAL OXCD 116 (issued 2012); *The Choir of Magdalen College, Oxford: More Archive Recordings 1960–76*, OXRECS DIGITAL OXCD 130 (issued 2012).

Choral Music from the 1937 Coronation and the Choir of St. George's Chapel, Windsor, Recorded 1926–1933, AMPHION PHI CD 183 (issued 2003).

Edward C. Bairstow, Organist, Composer, Conductor, Recorded 1926–1945, AMPHION PHI CD 138 (issued 1996); *The Choir of York Minster, Directed by Francis Jackson, Live & Session Recordings 1950–1976*, AMPHION PHI CD 184 (2 CDs, issued 2004); *Edward C. Bairstow, Choral Music: The Choir of York Minster, Directed by Francis Jackson, Live & Session Recordings 1956–1974*, AMPHION PHI CD 185 (issued 2004).

The Better Land: Great Boy Sopranos, six CDs issued between 1999 and 2007 on the Amphion label of discs of English trebles originally recorded between 1912 and 1970 (AMPHION PHI CDs 158, 159, 167, 168, 189, 220).

Master Ernest Lough and the Choir of the Temple Church, London, 1927–1938, NAXOS 8.120832 (issued 2005).

List of Abbreviations

BBC WAC	BBC Written Archives' Centre
BL	British Library
Bloxam I, II	John Rouse Bloxam, *A Register of the Presidents, Fellows, Demies, Instructors in Grammar and in Music, Chaplains, Clerks, Choristers, and other Members of Saint Mary Magdalen College in the University of Oxford, from the Foundation of the College to the Present Time*: vol. I, *The Choristers* (Oxford, 1853); vol. II, *The Chaplains, Clerkes, and Organists* (Oxford, 1857)
DNB	*Oxford Dictionary of National Biography*
ECM	*English Church Music*
EM	*Early Music*
Gr	*The Gramophone*; *Gramophone*
HCA	Hereford Cathedral Archives
KCA	King's College, Cambridge, Archive Centre
KCA BO	King's College, Cambridge, papers of Bernhard ('Boris') Ord
KCA EJD	King's College, Cambridge, papers of Edward Joseph Dent
KCA EMW	King's College, Cambridge, papers of Eric Milner-White
KCA JEN	King's College, Cambridge, papers of John Edwin Nixon
KCAR	King's College, Cambridge, Administrative Records
KCC	King's College, Cambridge
KCGB	King's College, Cambridge, Governing Body records
KCHR	King's College, Cambridge, Historical Reference
KCPH	King's College, Cambridge, photographs
M&L	*Music & Letters*

MCA	Magdalen College, Oxford, Archives
MT	*The Musical Times and Singing-Class Circular* (1844–1903); *The Musical Times* (1904–)
NCA	New College, Oxford, Archives
P.P. 1854	Parliamentary Papers: Session 1854, volume xxv: First Report of Her Majesty's commissioners, appointed November 10, A.D. 1852, to inquire into the state and condition of the cathedral and collegiate churches in England and Wales.
P.P. 1854–55	Parliamentary Papers: Session 1854–55, volume xv: Second Report of Her Majesty's commissioners, appointed November 10, A.D. 1852, to inquire into the state and condition of the cathedral and collegiate churches in England and Wales.
P.P. 1883	Parliamentary Papers: Session 1883, volume xxi: Cathedral Commission. Second Report of Her Majesty's commissioners for inquiring into the condition of cathedral churches in England and Wales.
P.P. 1884–85	Parliamentary Papers: Session 1884–85, volume xxi: Cathedral Commission. Report of Her Majesty's commissioners for inquiring into the condition of cathedral churches in England and Wales upon the cathedral church of Lincoln.
SJCA	St John's College, Cambridge, Archives

Notes

PREFACE

1. David Ffrangcon-Davies, *The Singing of the Future* (London, 1905), p. 69.
2. Emily Brontë, *Wuthering Heights*, 2 vols. (London, 1847), vol. 1, chapter IX.

I. AN ANCIENT ENGLISH TRADITION

1. Bernard Johnson, 'Organ Accompaniments and the "Cathedral Tradition"', *MT* 58/893 (July 1917), p. 305.
2. Peter Phillips, 'The Golden Age Regained [1]', *EM* 8/1 (January 1980), p. 3.
3. George Dyson, 'Of Organs and Organists', *MT* 93/1317 (November 1952), p. 492.
4. Barry Rose, presenter, 'The Choristers of Worcester Cathedral', 1987, http://www.youtube.com/watch?v=_Re5B4yjVnc&feature=related, accessed 12 February 2015.
5. George Malcolm, 'Boys' Voices', in *English Church Music 1967: A Collection of Essays* (Croydon, 1967), pp. 24–5. (This article originally appeared in the 1962 Aldeburgh Festival Programme Book.)
6. J. A. Rodgers, 'An Analysis of Choral Tone', *MT* 53/833 (July 1912), p. 440.
7. Percy Colson, 'Where England is Supreme: Some Beautiful Choir Records', *Gr* 12/133 (June 1934), p. 6.
8. *ECM* VII/1 (January 1937), pp. 4–5.
9. Ibid.
10. Internal memo dated 11 December 1942 from Mr Taylor, Religious Broadcasting Dept., Bedford, to Mr House, BBC WAC R27/50/1 File I, 4/200.
11. Richard Miller, *National Schools of Singing: English, French, German, and Italian Techniques of Singing Revisited* (Lanham, MD, and London, 1997), pp. 77, 192–3.
12. *The Times*, 8 June 1906.
13. An Address delivered in the Chapel at King's on Sunday, 24 November 1929 and reprinted in the College memoir *Arthur Henry Mann 16 May 1850–19 November 1929* (Cambridge, 1930), p. 7.

14. KCAR/8/2/1/C, CSV/75. For full details of this Evensong, see Nicholas Marston, '"As England knows it": "Daddy" Mann and King's College Choir, 1876–1929', in Jean Michel Massing and Nicolette Zeeman (eds.), *King's College Chapel 1515–2015: Art, Music and Religion in Cambridge* (London and Turnhout, 2014), p. 316.
15. *The Radio Times*, 18 December 1931, pp. 957–8.
16. KCA, Annual Report (1935), p. 19.
17. KCA, Annual Report (1937), p. 22.
18. KCA, Annual Report (1939), p. 19.
19. *The Manchester Guardian*, 27 December 1932, BBC WAC P134/3.
20. *The Birmingham Daily Mail*, 28 December 1932, BBC WAC P134/3.
21. *The Daily Telegraph*, 24 December 1938, BBC WAC P345/2.
22. *The Manchester Guardian*, 27 December 1938, BBC WAC P345/2.
23. Internal memo from Outside Broadcasts manager to Director-General BBC dated 22 October 1957, BBC WAC File R30/233/6.
24. KCA, Annual Report (1935), p. 19.
25. 'British Music Abroad: The King's College Choir in Scandinavia', *The Times*, 2 May 1936.
26. J. T. Sheppard, Provost of King's College, Cambridge, 'Carols from King's College', *The Radio Times*, 19–25 December 1948, p. 4.
27. https://www.youtube.com/watch?v=aGK5EsGzKIg, accessed 10 September 2013.
28. Vote of College Council, 11 May 1946, KCAR/8/3/29; letters between G. R. Barnes, Controller, BBC Third Programme, and Rev. A. R. Graham Campbell, Dean of King's, BBC WAC R30/233/3; KCA, Annual Report (1946), p. 26.
29. 'From Minerva House: Of Criteria and Values', *Musical Opinion* 921 (June 1954), p. 517.
30. 'English Collegiate Music', *The Times*, 28 December 1956.
31. Letter from Richard Heppel, HM Consul-General, Stuttgart, 20 November 1965, KCAR/8/3/9/2.
32. *The Monthly Letter*, May 1956, p. 16.
33. *The Monthly Letter*, July 1960, p. 12.
34. For example: Handel's *Messiah* recorded in 1957, Regensburg Cathedral Choir, UK PRODUCTIONS RD 40022 (mono CD, released 1997); soloists of the Regensburg Cathedral Choir 1933–1958, UK PRODUCTIONS RD 40023 (mono CD, released 2002); soloists of the Regensburg Cathedral Choir 1958–1963, UK PRODUCTIONS RD 40024 (stereo CD, released 1997); the Choir of the Sistine Chapel in 1957 on TRADITION TCD 1059 (mono CD, released 1997).
35. The fourth Christmas Eve carol service, or an abbreviated version of it, was released in 1978, HMV ASD 3778 (12" 33⅓ rpm stereo disc); the

fifth recording, released in 1999, was the first complete one, EMI CLAS-
SICS 5 73693 2 (two digital stereo CDs); the sixth was released in 2009,
EMI CLASSICS 6 86082 2 (two digital stereo CDs); and the seventh in
2012, THE CHOIR OF KING'S COLLEGE CAMBRIDGE KGS0001
KGS 0001 (two digital stereo CDs).

36. Simon Carpenter, *The Beat is Irrelevant* (Guildford, 1996), pp. 78, 86.

37. Stephen Cleobury and Nicolette Zeeman, 'Epilogue: The Sound of the Chapel',
in Massing and Zeeman (eds.), *King's College Chapel 1515–2015*, pp. 364–7.

38. Edward Higginbottom in Graham Topping, 'The Sound of Life', *Oxford
Today*, Michaelmas Issue 2006, p. 21.

39. James Fenton, 'Angelic Upstarts', *Independent on Sunday*, 20 December
1992.

40. http://www.singers.com/group/Choir-of-Kings-College-Cambridge, accessed
7 December 2016.

41. Matthew Parris, *The Times*, 23 May 2008.

42. Denis Stevens, *Gr* 38/445 (June 1960), p. 28.

43. Ibid.

44. Sylvia Plath, in Aurelia Schober Plath (ed.), *Letters Home* (New York,
1975), p. 200.

45. Campaign for the Traditional Cathedral Choir, *Newsletter* no. 13, November 2003, quoting a letter to the *Church Times*, http://www.ctcc.org.uk/
nl112003.htm, accessed 17 November 2011.

46. Joanna Trollope, *The Choir* (London, 1988), pp. 176, 175.

47. Tess Knighton, 'Vocal Heroes: Going Out on a Natural High, "High and
sweet and strong". Tess Knighton on what England Expects of her Cathedral Choirboys', *Independent*, 22 March 1993.

48. Bernarr Rainbow et al., 'Cathedral Choirs – New Directions: A Position
Paper by Dr Bernarr Rainbow and Others', originally in *Organists' Review*
(August 1997), http://www.ctcc.org.uk/position.htm, accessed 8 June 2016.

49. Undated 2009 press release written by Simon Lindley, President of the
Campaign for the Traditional Cathedral Choir, http://www.ctcc.org.uk/
news.htm, accessed 13 August 2015.

50. Editorial on 'The Cathedral Tradition', *ECM* IV/4 (October 1934), p. 97.

51. Percy A. Scholes, 'Cathedral Music', *The Oxford Companion to Music*, 3rd
edn (London, 1941), p. 146, referring to Lowell Mason, *Musical Letters
from Abroad: Including Detailed Accounts of the Birmingham, Norwich
and Dusseldorf Musical Festivals of 1852* (Boston, 1853).

52. Samuel Parr, quoted in Vivian H. H. Green, 'Routh, Martin Joseph (1755–
1854)', *DNB*.

53. Bloxam II, pp. ccviii–ccx.

54. 'Unisex Singing in the Choir: Arguments against Girl Choristers are Just
an Old Male Fetish', *The Times*, 17 July 1993.

55. Quoted from J. B. Mozley, *Letters*, in Jan Morris (ed.), *The Oxford Book of Oxford* (London, 1978), p. 236.

56. J. E. Millard, *The Island Choir; or, The Children of the Child Jesus* (London, 1847), p. 22.

57. William Shakespeare, *Twelfth Night*, Act I, Scene 4.

58. Thomas Hughes, *Tom Brown at Oxford* (London, 1861), chapter XVIII, 'Englebourn Village'.

59. Mason, *Musical Letters from Abroad*, pp. 12–13.

60. Ibid., pp. 14–15.

61. Ibid., p. 168.

62. Ibid., pp. 309–10.

63. Ibid., pp. 160–61.

64. Ibid., pp. 81–3.

65. Ibid., pp. 105–8, 112–15.

66. Ibid., pp. 129–30.

67. Ibid., p. 252.

68. Ibid., p. 262.

69. Ibid., pp. 309–10.

70. John Jebb, *The Choral Service of the United Church of England and Ireland: Being an Enquiry into the Liturgical System of the Cathedral and Collegiate Foundations of the Anglican Communion* (London, 1843), p. 229.

71. Ibid., pp. 391–2.

72. Ibid., p. 139.

73. Ibid., p. 140.

74. Ibid., p. 244.

75. Ibid., p. 250.

76. Ibid., p. 338.

77. Ibid., p. 456.

78. J. E. Millard, *Historical Notices of the Office of Choristers* (London, 1848), pp. 2, 5.

79. S. S. Wesley, *A Few Words on Cathedral Music and the Musical System of the Church, with a Plan of Reform* (London, 1849), pp. 7–10.

80. Ibid., p. 33.

81. Millard, *Historical Notices*, pp. 7–13.

82. P.P. 1854, p. 694.

83. Ibid., p. 706.

84. Ibid., p. 705.

85. Ibid., pp. 683–4.

86. Ibid., p. 685.

87. S. S. Wesley, *Reply to the Inquiries of the Cathedral Commissioners, Relative to Improvement in the Music of Divine Worship in Cathedrals* (London, 1854), p. 13.

88. P.P. 1854, p. 747.

89. Ibid., p. 701.

90. Ibid., p. xxxiv.

91. Ibid., p. 744.

92. Ibid., p. xxxiv.

93. Ibid., p. 5.

94. Ibid., p. 163.

95. Ibid., p. 722.

96. Ibid., p. 727.

97. Ibid., p. xxxiii.

98. Ibid., p. 695.

99. Jebb, *The Choral Service*, p. 109.

100. P.P. 1854, p. 708.

101. Ibid., p. 700.

102. Ibid., p. 708.

103. Ibid., p. 166.

104. Ibid., p. 682.

105. Ibid., p. 773.

106. The Magdalen statutes quoted in Bloxam I, p. 1.

107. See Bloxam I, *passim*.

108. 'A Former Chorister' [L. S. Tuckwell], *Old Magdalen Days, 1847–1877* (Oxford, 1913), p. 17.

109. F. M. Millard, 'Notes and Appendix', in ibid., p. iii.

110. Report of the Committee for proposing to the University Commissioners measures for the improvements of the Choir at Magdalen College, dated 29 June 1856, MCA PR31/2/MS2/12.

111. 'A Former Chorister', *Old Magdalen Days*, pp. 18–19.

112. Bloxam I, p. 223.

113. Minutes of College meeting of 24 July 1863, MCA PR/2/2, p. 350.

114. Bloxam II, p. ccviii.

115. R. D. Middleton, *Magdalen Studies* (London, 1936), p. 50; 'A Former Chorister', *Old Magdalen Days*, p. 5.

116. Jeremy Dibble, *John Stainer: A Life in Music* (Woodbridge, 2007), p. 74; Henry Cotton, *Indian & Home Memories* (London, 1911), p. 18.

117. http://www.magd.ox.ac.uk/libraries-and-archives/archives/online-catalogues/tuckwell, accessed 3 October 2015.

118. F. M. Millard, 'Notes and Appendix', in 'A Former Chorister', *Old Magdalen Days*, pp. iii–iv.

119. R. S. Stanier, *Magdalen School: A History of Magdalen College School, Oxford*, 2nd edn (Oxford, 1958), pp. 138–40.

120. Sydney Smith in a letter to William Hawes in 1844 in A. Bell, 'The Letters of Sydney Smith', *Bulletin of the John Rylands Library* 59/1 (1976), p. 37.

121. Jebb, *The Choral Service*, pp. 108, 15.

122. Owen Chadwick, *The Victorian Church: Part Two 1860–1901*, 2nd edn (Oxford, 1972), p. 385.

123. Charles Dickens, *The Mystery of Edwin Drood* (London, 1870), chapter I.

124. Jebb, *The Choral Service*, pp. 138, 244, 252.

125. F. A. Gore Ouseley, 'The Education of Choristers in Cathedrals', in J. S. Howson (ed.), *Essays on Cathedrals by Various Writers* (London, 1872), pp. 228–9.

126. Jebb, *The Choral Service*, pp. 374–5.

127. Ouseley, 'The Education of Choristers', p. 222.

128. Ibid., pp. 228–9.

129. Roger Ascham, *Toxophilus; the School of Shooting* (1545) (London, 1866), pp. 26–7.

130. John Locke, *Some Thoughts Concerning Education* (London, 1693), §§ 184–5.

131. R. Campbell, *The London Tradesman. Being a Compendious View of All the Trades, Professions, Arts, both Liberal and Mechanic, now practised in the Cities of London and Westminster. Calculated for the Information of Parents, and Instruction of Youth in their Choice of Business* (London, 1747), p. 89.

132. John Dennis, 'An Essay on the Operas after the *Italian* Manner' (1706), in *The Select Works of Mr. John Dennis*, 2 vols. (London, 1718) vol. 1, p. 467.

133. Ibid., p. 462.

134. Campbell, *The London Tradesman*, p. 93.

135. Ibid., pp. 89–93.

136. Daniel Defoe, *Augusta Triumphans: or, The Way to Make London the Most Flourishing City in the Universe* (London, 1728), p. 17.

137. Ibid., pp. 18–21.

138. H. Byerley Thomson, *The Choice of a Profession. A Concise Account and Comparative Review of the English Professions* (London, 1857), pp. 1–2.

139. Ibid., pp. 308–9.

140. F. A. Wendeborn, translated from the German by the author himself, *A View of England towards the Close of the Eighteenth Century*, 2 vols. (London, 1791), vol. 2, pp. 234–5.

141. *A Selection of Favourite Catches, Glees, &c. as Sung at the Bath Harmonic Society, with The Rules of the Society, and a List of the Members*, 2nd edn (Bath and London, 1799), pp. 9, iii–iv, 5.

142. 'Change in Vocal Art', *Quarterly Musical Magazine and Review* 1 (1818), p. 102.

143. Mason, *Musical Letters from Abroad*, p. 15.

144. George Hogarth, *Musical History, Biography and Criticism: Being a General Survey of music, from the Earliest Period to the Present Time* (London, 1835), pp. 303, 304.

145. Alvaro Ribeiro, SJ (ed.), *The Letters of Dr Charles Burney*, volume 1: *1751-1784* (Oxford, 1991), p. 96.
146. H. Watkins Shaw, 'Fellowes, Edmund Horace (1870-1951)', *DNB*.
147. E. H. Fellowes, *English Cathedral Music* (London, 1941; new edition revised by J. A. Westrup, 1969), pp. 9-10.
148. Mason, *Musical Letters from Abroad*, p. 18.
149. Wesley, *A Few Words on Cathedral Music*, p. 37.
150. Letter to the Editor from John Mason in *MT* 34/608 (October 1893), p. 618.
151. Campbell, *The London Tradesman*, p. 89.
152. Defoe, *Augusta Triumphans*, p. 16.
153. Gerard Manley Hopkins, 'Henry Purcell', in *Poems of Gerard Manley Hopkins, now first published. Edited with notes by Robert Bridges, Poet Laureate* (London, 1918), p. 42.
154. George Herbert, 'Easter' (1633).
155. Robert Browning, 'Abt Vogler' (1864).
156. A. M. Wakefield (ed.), *Ruskin on Music* (London, 1894), pp. 15-21.
157. Wesley, *A Few Words on Cathedral Music*, p. 52.
158. Ibid., pp. 54.
159. Ibid., p. 8.
160. Peter Maurice, Chaplain of New College and All Souls' College, Oxford, *What shall we do with Music? A Letter to the Rt. H. the Earl Derby, Chancellor of the University of Oxford* (London, 1856), p. 12.
161. Jebb, *The Choral Service*, p. 1.
162. See Owen Chadwick, 'The Mind of the Oxford Movement', in his *The Spirit of the Oxford Movement* (Cambridge, 1990), pp. 1-53.
163. This passage from Bishop Taylor's Preface to his *Apology for Authorized and Set Forms of Liturgy* (1649) is quoted in Jebb, *The Choral Service*, opposite p. 1.
164. Kenneth Clark, *The Gothic Revival: An Essay in the History of Taste* (London, 1962), p. 134.
165. *Parish Choir*, 2/31 (July 1848), p. 77; see Dale Adelmann, *The Contribution of Cambridge Ecclesiologists to the Revival of Anglican Choral Worship 1839-62* (Aldershot, 1997), p. 58.
166. Dale L. Adelmann, 'Music in The Chapel of St John's College, Cambridge, 1833-97', essay in ms, p. 33, SJCA ARCH 3.15.
167. Wesley, *A Few Words on Cathedral Music*, p. 49.
168. G. A. Macfarren, 'The Music of the English Church', *MT* 13/294 (August 1867), p. 117.
169. Letter written in 1858 to a friend by Bishop Samuel Wilberforce quoted in Owen Chadwick, *The Founding of Cuddesdon* (Oxford, 1954), p. 92.
170. Letters and Memoranda Concerning Discipline: 1860-1871, pp. 11-12, NCA 8561.
171. Hughes, *Tom Brown at Oxford*, vol. 1, chapter IX, 'A Brown Bait'.

172. *Oxford University Calendar*, 1860, pp. 376–7.

173. *Oxford University Calendars*, 1862 to 1868.

174. Hereford B. George, *New College 1856–1906* (Oxford, 1906), p. 86.

175. Annual *Oxford University Calendars*; Joseph Foster, *Alumni Oxonienses: The Members of the University of Oxford, 1715–1886: Their Parentage, Birthplace, and Year of Birth, with a Record of Their Degrees . . .*, 4 vols. (London, 1888).

176. George, *New College 1856–1906*, pp. 86–7.

177. Owen Chadwick, *The Victorian Church: Part One 1829–1859* (London, 1966), pp. 140–41.

178. 'On the Present State of Church Music in England', *Quarterly Musical Magazine and Review* 24 (1824), pp. 459–60.

179. *Hereford Journal*, 31 August 1836, under 'Friday's London Post' (reprinted from the *Bristol Journal*).

180. Chadwick, *The Victorian Church: Part One*, p. 130.

181. P.P. 1854, pp. xviii–xxi.

182. Wesley, *A Few Words on Cathedral Music*, p. 58, footnote.

183. P.P. 1854, p. 688.

184. Ibid., p. 682.

185. Ibid., p. xix.

186. P.P. 1854–55, p. xx.

187. Ibid., pp. xvii–xviii.

188. Ibid., p. xvii.

189. Ibid.

190. Jebb, *The Choral Service*, p. 250, footnote.

191. Wesley, *A Few Words on Cathedral Music*, p. 34.

192. P.P. 1854, p. 669.

193. C. T. Heartley, *Our Cathedrals and their Mission* (London, 1855), pp. 8–16, 31–2.

194. See E. H. Plumptre, Dean of Wells, 'Cathedral Singers in Times Past and Present', *MT* 24/490 (December 1883), pp. 665–6, and Edward A. Freeman, in P.P. 1883, pp. 22–3.

195. 'Dotted Crotchet' [F. G. Edwards], 'Worcester Cathedral', *MT* 46/753 (November 1905), pp. 708–10.

196. See Alan Mould, *The English Chorister: A History* (London, 2007), pp. 229–43.

197. P.P. 1884–85, pp. 11–12.

198. *Gloucester Citizen*, Tuesday, 9 October 1900.

199. A. Herbert Brewer, *Memories of Choirs and Cloisters* (London, 1931), p. 86.

200. For details of these vicars choral, see 'Biographical Memoirs of the Custos and Vicars admitted into the College at Hereford from 1660 to 1823 – Collected from public records and private researches by a former member of that Society'.

By the Rev. William Cooke, Vicar of Bromyard, Rector of Ullingswick and a magistrate of Herefordshire, died 18 October 1854, HCA 7003/4/4.

201. From a document that the Dean laid before the Chapter and stated that he had placed it in the hands of the Secretary of State for the Home Department and of the Ecclesiastical Commissioners. Chapter Acts, 26 June 1848, pp. 136–41, HCA 7031/20. The document was leaked and printed in the *Hereford Journal*, 1 August 1849.

202. Jebb, *The Choral Service*, p. 112.

203. Hereford Cathedral Chapter Acts, 14 November 1850, pp. 209–10, HCA 7031/20.

204. Hereford Cathedral Injunctions or Statutes dated 10 November 1870, HCA 449.

205. Hereford Cathedral Vicars Choral Acts, pp. 208–11, 13 and 25 November 1907, HCA 7003/1/7.

2. REFORM

1. Letters from F. A. Gore Ouseley to Wayland Joyce dated 21 and 28 October 1851, quoted in F. W. Joyce, *The Life of the Rev. Sir F. A. G. Ouseley* (London, 1896), pp. 76–8.

2. Hereford Cathedral Vicars Choral Act Book. Letter to the Chapter on the choristers by the Precentor to the Dean and Chapter dated 21 July 1857, HCA 7003/1/6.

3. M. C. F. Morris, *Yorkshire Reminiscences* (London, 1922), p. 87.

4. See John Stainer, 'The Character and Influence of the Late Sir Frederick Ouseley', *Proceedings of the Musical Association*, Sixteenth Session (1889–90), p. 36.

5. G. W. Kitchin, later to be Dean of Durham, quoted in Joyce, *Life of the Rev. Sir F. A. G. Ouseley*, p. 45.

6. E. H. Fellowes, *Memoirs of an Amateur Musician* (London, 1946), p. 9.

7. 'The Martyrdom of St. Polycarp. A Sacred Oratorio by F. A. Gore Ouseley', a review, *MT* 26/510 (August 1885), p. 487.

8. David Bland, *Ouseley and his Angels: The Life of St. Michael's College, Tenbury and its Founder* (Eton, Berkshire, 2000), pp. 51–65.

9. *Berrow's Worcester Journal*, Saturday, 2 October 1875, p. 4.

10. *The Cambridge Chronicle and Journal*, Saturday, 31 March 1860.

11. See Bland, *Ouseley and his Angels*, and M. F. Alderson and H. C. Colles (eds.), *History of St. Michael's College, Tenbury* (London, 1943); Charles Plummer (1851–1927) was the historian, an authority on Bede and Alfred, and the editor of an influential book by the fifteenth-century lawyer Sir John Fortescue, *The Governance of England* (Oxford, 1885).

12. *The Hereford Journal*, Wednesday, 9 October 1861.

13. *The Morning Post*, Saturday, 5 October 1872.

14. Joan Williams, 'The Library', in G. Aylmer and John Tiller (eds.), *Hereford Cathedral: A History* (London, 2000), p. 525.

15. Manuscript letter from the Reverend Francis T. Havergal to Maria Hackett dated 20 May 1873, inserted in the front cover of a copy of Joyce, *Life of Sir F. A. G. Ouseley*, in Hereford Cathedral Library, D 863/101.

16. *The Morning Post*, Saturday, 5 October 1872.

17. *The Hereford Journal*, Wednesday, 9 October 1861.

18. Ibid.

19. Alderson and Colles (eds.), *History of St. Michael's College, Tenbury*, p. 35.

20. F. G. E. [F. G. Edwards], 'A Visit to Tenbury', *MT* 41/693 (November 1900), p. 713.

21. Joyce, *Life of Sir F. A. G. Ouseley*, pp. 45, 82–3.

22. Frederic Hodgson, *Choirs and Cloisters: Sixty Years of Music in Church, College, Cathedral and Chapels Royal* (London, 1988), pp. 22–3.

23. E. H. Fellowes, 'The Music Library', in Alderson and Colles (eds.), *History of St. Michael's College, Tenbury*, pp. 78–101.

24. Stainer, 'Character and Influence of the Late Sir Frederick Ouseley', pp. 33–4.

25. F. G. E. [F. G. Edwards], 'John Stainer', *MT* 42/699 (May 1901), p. 297.

26. Arthur Whitley quoted in ibid., p. 298.

27. Jeremy Dibble, *John Stainer: A Life in Music* (London, 2007), pp. 30, 33.

28. Ibid., p. 141.

29. http://www.pennantpublishing.co.uk/sirjohn.htm, accessed 13 March 2016.

30. According to Frederick Bulley in E. Vine Hall, 'The Magdalen Vagabonds: A History of their Doings', unpub. Magdalen College Archives (MCA F33/1/ MS6/1 and MCA P293/MS1/1). Vine Hall was later ordained and became Precentor of Worcester Cathedral; see *MT* 50/798 (August 1909), p. 521.

31. MCA MS 444.

32. Alan Oscar [W. B. Whall], *School and Sea Days* (London, 1901), p. 9.

33. Dibble, *John Stainer*, p. 42. See also letter to Sir F. Ouseley in 're Mr Stainer, Candidate for the Organist's Place dated 26 December 1859', President's Note Book from 31 July 1857 to 10 October 1860, p. 187, MCA PR/2/1.

34. Note dated 18 May 1860, 'Stainer's conditions', President's Note Book from 31 July 1857 to 10 October 1860, p. 232, MCA PR/2/1.

35. Bloxam II, p. cciv.

36. Bloxam I, p. xvi.

37. R. S. Stanier, *Magdalen School: A History of Magdalen College School, Oxford*, 2nd edn (Oxford, 1958), pp. 151–2.

38. Ibid., p. 168.

39. Ibid., p. 171.

40. Ibid., pp. 171–2.

41. Report of the Committee for proposing to the University Commissioners measures for the improvements of the Choir at Magdalen College, dated 29 June 1856, MCA PR31/2/MS2/12.

42. Advertisement for a tenor academical clerk on 22 December 1898. The academical clerks received a stipend of £95 p.a. each. MCA PR/2/13, between pp. 107 and 108.

43. President's Note Book, undated entry but clearly December 1892 and entry for 18 December 1892, MCA PR/2/10, pp. 410, 436; John Murray (ed.), *The Magdalen College Record* (London, 1922), p. 126. Harry Köblich changed his surname by deed poll to Kingsley in 1915.

44. President's Note Book, entry for 15 December 1874, MCA PR/2/5, p. 244.

45. Ibid., entry for 16 November 1892, MCA PR/2/10, p. 401.

46. Ibid., entry for 7 June 1872, MCA PR/2/4, p. 500.

47. Ibid., entry for 25 March 1873, MCA PR/2/5, p. 54.

48. Ibid., entry for 25 March 1873, MCA PR/2/5, p. 54.

49. Ibid., entry for 3 June 1888, MCA PR/2/8, p. 337.

50. Ibid., entry for 1 October 1888, MCA PR/2/9, p. 21.

51. Notes by A. H. Mann giving short biographical summaries of choristers and choral scholars, possibly relating to the photograph collection listed in KCPH, KCAR/8/3/3.

52. Typed letter from President Warren to the Dean of Divinity dated 13 May 1924, MCA File DD/27/4.

53. 'Johnson, Basil', in Murray (ed.), *The Magdalen College Record*, p. 120.

54. The President's Note Book, entry for 6 February 1883, MCA PR/2/7, p. 70.

55. Ibid., entry for 14 October 1880, MCA PR/2/6, p. 351.

56. Ibid., entry for 25 October 1881, MCA PR/2/6, p. 473.

57. Ibid., entry for 22 May 1900, Choir Committee meeting, MCA PR/2/13, p. 361.

58. E. Vine Hall, 'The History of the Vagabonds', MCA F33/1/MS6/1; *MT* 29/543 (May 1888), p. 277; 'Music in Birmingham', *MT* 34/600 (February 1893), p. 92; 'Brief Summary of Country News', *MT* 34/609 (November 1893), p. 683.

59. President's Note Book, entry for 9 October 1877, MCA PR/2/6, p. 2; ibid., entry for 25 March 1879, MCA PR/2/6, p. 181.

60. Ibid., entry for 28 March 1899, MCA PR/2/13, p. 149; ibid., entry for 18 July 1899, MCA PR/2/13, between pp. 207 and 208.

61. Ibid., entry for 28 November 1865, MCA PR/2/13, p. 163.

62. W. A. Frost, Vicar Choral of St Paul's Cathedral, 'The Choir Benevolent Fund', *The Cathedral Quarterly*, 1/3 (July 1913), pp. 27–32.

63. J. B., obituary of 'William Alexander Barrett', *MT* 32/585 (November 1891), pp. 659–60; James D. Brown and Stephen S. Stratton, *British Musical*

Biography: A Dictionary of Musical Artists, Authors and Composers, Born in Britain and its Colonies (Birmingham, 1897), p. 31.

64. *MT* 25/494 (April 1884), p. 231.

65. *MT* 18/408 (February 1877), p. 85.

66. *MT* 17/388 (June 1875), p. 121.

67. *MT* 18/409 (March 1877), p. 138.

68. *MT* 22/455 (January 1881), p. 43.

69. *MT* 21/449 (July 1880), p. 322.

70. Chapel Service (Clerkes) Copy of Order, President's Note Book, entry for 1 April 1864, MCA PR/2/2, p. 434.

71. P.P. 1854, p. 685.

72. President's Note Book, entry for 24 May 1858, MCA PR/2/1, p. 28.

73. Dibble, *John Stainer*, p. 73.

74. F. G. E., 'John Stainer', p. 303.

75. 'The Stainer Memorial in St. Paul's Cathedral', *MT* 45/731 (January 1904), p. 27.

76. *Guardian* (weekly Anglican newspaper), 2 April 1901, quoted in Dibble, *John Stainer*, p. 78.

77. W. H. Hutton (ed.), *Robert Gregory, 1819–1911: Being the Autobiography of Robert Gregory, D.D., Dean of St. Paul's* (London, 1912), p. 158.

78. William Russell, *St Paul's under Dean Church and his Associates* (London, 1922), pp. 23–4.

79. Dean Mansel to Canon Gregory, November 1869, in Hutton (ed.), *Robert Gregory*, p. 168, quoted in Timothy Charles Storey, 'The Music of St Paul's Cathedral 1872–1972: The Origins and Development of the Modern Cathedral Choir', University of Durham MMus thesis, 1998, p. 29.

80. St Paul's Cathedral Library, Chapter Minutes, 30 November 1871, quoted in Dibble, *John Stainer*, p. 141.

81. Letter from Stainer to J. S. Egerton, 12 March [1872], in private hands, quoted in Dibble, *John Stainer*, p. 143.

82. 'Sir George Clement Martin, 1844–1916: Organist of St Paul's Cathedral, 1888–1916', *MT* 57/878 (April 1916), p. 189.

83. *The Musical Standard*, 14 January 1871, pp. 16–17, quoted in Storey, 'The Music of St Paul's Cathedral 1872–1972', pp. 2–3.

84. 'The Choir School of St. Paul's Cathedral', *MT* 41/687 (May 1900), p. 306.

85. Alan Mould, *The English Chorister: A History* (London, 2007), p. 201.

86. 'The Choir School of St. Paul's Cathedral', p. 306.

87. Letter to Dr Bright from Liddon, Christ Church, Oxford, 9 May 1878, in J. O. Johnston, *Life and Letters of Henry Parry Liddon ...* (London, 1904), p. 142.

88. Mould, *The English Chorister*, p. 201.

89. Liddon, quoted in Dibble, *John Stainer*, p. 161.

90. Letter to Dr Bright from Liddon, Christ Church, Oxford, 9 May 1878, in Johnston, *Life and Letters of Henry Parry Liddon*, pp. 142–3.

91. Dibble, *John Stainer*, p. 160.

92. Storey, 'The Music of St Paul's Cathedral 1872–1972', p. 31.

93. G. L. Prestige, *St Paul's in its Glory* (London, 1955), p. 99.

94. P.P., 1883, pp. 10–12.

95. Ibid., pp. 4–5.

96. Owen Chadwick, *The Victorian Church: Part Two 1860–1901*, 2nd edn (London, 1972), p. 386.

97. Ibid., p. 387.

98. George C. Martin, *The Art of Training Choir Boys* (London, 1892), p. 17.

99. Sir John Stainer in the discussion following Waldo Selden Pratt, 'The Isolation of Music', a paper given on 16 July 1895, *Proceedings of the Musical Association*, Twenty-First Session (1894–5), pp. 167–8.

100. Dibble, *John Stainer*, p. 260.

101. Ibid., p. 263.

102. Ibid., p. 199.

103. Ibid., pp. 230–31, 306.

104. Ibid., pp. 298–9.

105. 'The Sir John Stainer Dinner', *Musical World* (4 August 1888), p. 612.

106. Donald Tovey and Geoffrey Parratt, *Walter Parratt: Master of the Music* (London, 1941), p. 145.

107. Ibid., p. 149.

108. Obituary, 'Henry Lister Parratt', *MT* 45/733 (March 1904), p. 172.

109. Watkins Shaw, *The Succession of Organists of the Chapel Royal and the Cathedrals of England and Wales from c. 1538* (Oxford, 1991), p. 350.

110. 'Sir Walter Parratt's Inaugural Lecture as Professor of Music at Oxford', *MT* 50/791 (January 1909), p. 30.

111. The Evans Gambit in chess is an aggressive variant of the Giuoco Piano, first employed by the Welsh sea captain William Davies Evans, in London in 1827. P. C. Buck, 'Sir Walter Parratt', *ECM* V/3 (July 1935), p. 71.

112. Obituary, 'Walter Parratt, February 10, 1841–March 27, 1924 . . .', *MT* 65/975 (May 1924), p. 401.

113. Shaw, *The Succession of Organists*, p. 350.

114. H. C. Colles, review of *Walter Parratt: Master of Music* by Donald F. Tovey and Geoffrey Parratt, *M&L* 23/3 (July 1942), p. 257.

115. Buck, 'Sir Walter Parratt', p. 70.

116. Ibid., pp. 69–70.

117. Sir Hugh Allen, Director's address to the students, 5 May 1924, *Royal College of Music Magazine* 20/2 (1924), p. 30.

118. Tovey and Parratt, *Walter Parratt*, pp. 142–3; obituary of Parratt by Sir Walford Davies, *Royal College of Music Magazine* 20/2 (1924), pp. 38–42.

119. Buck, 'Sir Walter Parratt', p. 71.

120. Tovey and Parratt, *Walter Parratt*, p. 141.

121. Ibid., p. 67.

122. Obituary of Parratt by Davies, *Royal College of Music Magazine*, pp. 38–42.

123. Obituary of Parratt by Harold Darke, *Royal College of Music Magazine* 20/2 (1924), pp. 52–4.

124. S. S. Wesley, *A Few Words on Cathedral Music and the Musical System of the Church, with a Plan of Reform* (London, 1849), p. 72.

125. 1 Corinthians 14:34.

126. *ECM* X/1 (January 1940), p. 4.

127. Letter from 'Concerned', in ibid., p. 31.

128. Sydney H. Nicholson, *Boys' Choirs* (Glasgow, 1922), p. 3.

129. T. F. Smith, *The Devout Chorister* (London, 1848), p. 4.

130. Neville Wridgway, *The Choristers of St George's Chapel* (Windsor, 1980), p. 85.

131. James Walter Brown, 'Chorister Life in the Early Sixties', *MT* 50/796 (June 1909), p. 377.

132. P.P. 1854, p. 693.

133. Martin, *The Art of Training Choir Boys*, pp. 8–9, 16.

134. Ibid., p. 9.

135. J. Spencer Curwen, *Studies in Worship-Music, Chiefly as Regards Congregational Singing* (London, 1880), pp. 148–50.

136. J. Varley Roberts, *A Treatise on a Practical Method of Training Choristers*, 3rd edn (London, 1905; 1st edn 1898), pp. 3–4.

137. Walter S. Vale, *The Training of Boys' Voices* (London, 1932), pp. 73–4.

138. Martin, *The Art of Training Choir Boys*, p. 29.

139. Charles H. Moody, *The Choir-Boy in the Making*, 2nd edn (London, 1939), p. 9.

140. Roberts, *A Treatise on a Practical Method of Training Choristers*, p. 6.

141. Martin, *The Art of Training Choir Boys*, p. 29.

142. Ibid., p. 9.

143. Roberts, *A Treatise on a Practical Method of Training Choristers*, p. 5.

144. Ibid.

145. Martin, *The Art of Training Choir Boys*, p. 19.

146. Moody, *The Choir-Boy in the Making*, p. 8.

147. Ibid., p. 12.

148. Vale, *The Training of Boys' Voices*, p. 75.

149. Martin, *The Art of Training Choir Boys*, p. 12.

150. Ibid., p. 20.

151. Ibid., pp. 22–3.

152. Ibid., pp. 11–13.

153. Ibid., p. 13.

154. Ibid., p. 14.
155. Ibid.
156. Ibid., pp. 14–15.
157. A. Madeley Richardson, *Church Music* (London, 1904), p. 73.
158. Martin, *The Art of Training Choir Boys*, pp. 21–2.
159. Ibid., pp. 17–18.
160. Ibid., p. 18.
161. Richardson, *Church Music*, p. 65.
162. Ibid., p. 70.
163. Ibid., p. 61.
164. Moody, *The Choir-Boy in the Making*, p. 27.
165. James Fenton, 'Angelic Upstarts', *The Independent on Sunday*, 20 December 1992.
166. Vale, *The Training of Boys' Voices*, p. 72.
167. 'Sir John Stainer', *MT* 29/546 (August 1888), p. 474.
168. Francis Jackson, *Blessed City: The Life and Works of Edward C. Bairstow* (York, 1996), p. 87.
169. Ibid., pp. 98–100.
170. Cyril Bailey, *Hugh Percy Allen* (London, 1948), p. 35.
171. Sir William Harris, in a Presidential Address to the Royal College of Organists in July 1947, quoted in Hodgson, *Choirs and Cloisters*, p. 69.
172. Ibid., p. 68.
173. Ibid., pp. 68–9.
174. A cutting from the *Musical News* of 14 September 1895 of an article entitled 'English Music and American Visitors', between pp. 449 and 450 of President's Note Book, MCA PR/2/11.
175. Odeon catalogue, October 1906. British Library.
176. OXRECS DIGITAL OXCD 116 (mono CD, released 2012).
177. Undated entry but apparently in March 1890, President's Note Book, MCA PR/2/9, p. 346; entry for 11 February 1893, President's Note Book, MCA PR/2/11, p. 24.
178. There is a 1906 recording of John Lomas singing 'Vulcan's Song' from Gounod's opera *Philémon et Baucis* on OXRECS DIGITAL OXCD 116 (mono CD, released 2012).
179. E. M. Venables, *Sweet Tones Remembered: Magdalen Choir in the Days of Varley Roberts* (Oxford, 1947), p. 18.
180. Meeting of the Choir Committee, 12 June 1925; the minutes recorded that 'the question of the date of retirement of Mr J Lomas the Organist would wish for the present to leave entirely open', MCA CCM/1/1.
181. Venables, *Sweet Tones Remembered*, p. 18.
182. *MT* 38/655 (September 1897), p. 628.
183. *MT* 51/809 (July 1910), p. 462.

184. *MT* 30/561 (November 1889), p. 677.

185. *MT* 35/615 (May 1894), p. 344.

186. *MT* 48/772 (June 1907), p. 403.

187. Venables, *Sweet Tones Remembered*, p. 18.

188. John Lomas, 1901 Census, http://www.1901censusonline.com/results.asp?
wci=person_results&searchwci=ei_search_with_locale, accessed 13 May 2011.

189. Henry Wood, *My Life of Music* (London, 1938), p. 180.

190. Whole-page advertisement with 'press opinions' for the Meister Glee Singers, *MT* 34/601 (March 1893), p. 132. They sing 'Old Daddy Long-Legs wouldn't say his prayers' on a recording released in 1908, ZONOPHONE 12805 (7″ single-sided acoustic 78 rpm disc).

191. *MT* 41/689 (July 1900), p. 464; see also a cutting from the *Musical Courier* of 10 November 1900, quoting a piece written by Miles Farrow in the *Baltimore Sun*, the cutting inserted between pp. 251 and 252 in President's Notebook, MCA PR/2/13.

192. Richardson, *Church Music*, pp. 41–2.

193. *MT* 41/689 (July 1900), p. 464; see also the cutting from the *Musical Courier* of 10 November 1900, inserted between pp. 251 and 252 in President's Note Book, MCA PR/2/13.

194. *MT* 41/689 (July 1900), p. 464; MCA PR/2/13.

3. A NEW CHOIR AT KING'S

1. Alan Mould, *The English Chorister: A History* (London, 2007), pp. 190–91.

2. W. Austen Leigh, *Augustus Austen Leigh, Provost of King's College, Cambridge: A Record of College Reform* (London, 1906), p. 114; see also Thomas H. Case, *Memoirs of a King's College Chorister* (Cambridge, 1899), p. 11.

3. A handwritten letter dated 6 November 1912 to Dr Mann from Thomas Moore, a chorister from 1847 until 1855, KCAR/8/3/1.

4. Case, *Memoirs of a King's College Chorister*, unnumbered fourth page of the Preface.

5. Thomas H. Case, handwritten letter dated 25 April 1911 to Mr Clarke, King's College, KCAR/8/3/1.

6. A handwritten letter dated 24 June 1912 to Dr Mann from Thomas Moore, KCAR/8/3/1.

7. List of the occupations of choristers in the 1860s, manuscript, 'A Register of the Choir in the Kings [*sic*] College of Blessed Mary and Saint Nicholas in Cambridge 1860', KCAR/8/3/1.

8. An Address delivered by the Provost in King's College Chapel on Sunday, 24 November 1929, in *Arthur Henry Mann 16 May 1850–19 November 1929* (Cambridge, 1930), p. 5.

9. 'A Register of the Choir in the Kings [*sic*] College of Blessed Mary and Saint Nicholas in Cambridge 1860', KCAR/8/3/1.

10. Ibid.

11. e.g. Thomas Machin, 1861 census, https://www.ukcensusonline.com/image_viewer/?imagego=2BJWRLHPVJA0DBszwo_YXN8r-A7hXcU4_8Uu-_CH cgsnoJVoAQ--iWMaAdkNqHnk2UDzrspaDylo_Yju4HpSAQ, accessed 13 May 2011.

12. Case, *Memoirs of a King's College Chorister*, p. 18.

13. Handwritten document in formal handwriting, undated; on reverse of the sheet in another hand, 'Singing Men Dec 09' (i.e. 1809), KCAR/8/5/1/5.

14. 'Memorial of 1858 of lay clerks demanding a rise in stipend', dated 22 March 1858, KCAR/8/5/1/5.

15. Meeting of Congregation, 26 March 1858, KCGB/4/1/1/6.

16. Letter to the Provost and Fellows from the lay clerks dated 3 April 1858, KCAR/8/5/1/5.

17. Case, *Memoirs of a King's College Chorister*, p. 24.

18. Ibid., fourth and fifth pages of the unnumbered Preface.

19. Ibid., pp. 40–41.

20. Leigh, *Augustus Austen Leigh*, p. 115.

21. Case, *Memoirs of a King's College Chorister*, fourth and fifth pages of the unnumbered Preface.

22. 'A Register of the Choir in the Kings [*sic*] College of Blessed Mary and Saint Nicholas in Cambridge 1860', KCAR/8/3/1.

23. Christopher Morris, *King's College: A Short History* (Cambridge, 1989), p. 45.

24. Ibid., pp. 46–7.

25. A handwritten report, 'Service in Chapel', dated 11 June 1862, KCAR/8/3/1.

26. A. Austen Leigh, *King's College [A History]* (London, 1899), p. 290.

27. Report of the Committee appointed by Vote of a General Congregation, 9 February 1869, 'to consider what changes are necessary to ensure a satisfactory Choral Service in Chapel', dated 15 May 1869, KCGB/4/1/1/7.

28. Vote of Congregation, dated 21 February 1871, KCGB/4/1/1/7.

29. Votes of Congregation, dated 11 March 1871 and 15 June 1872, KCGB/4/1/1/7.

30. Vote of Congregation, dated 11 March 1871, KCGB/4/1/1/7.

31. Letter from A. A. Leigh to the Provost, dated 22 March 1871, KCAR/8/5/1.

32. For further details on the state of the choir in these years see Nicholas Marston, '"As England knows it": "Daddy" Mann and King's College Choir, 1976–1929', in Jean Michel Massing and Nicolette Zeeman (eds.), *King's College Chapel 1515–2015: Art, Music and Religion in Cambridge* (London and Turnhout, 2014), p. 305.

33. Handwritten letter to Dr Mann dated 6 November 1912 from Thomas Moore, KCAR/8/3/1.

34. Thomas Mace, *Musick's Monument; or, A Remembrancer of the Best Practical Musick, Both Divine, and Civil, that has ever been known, to have been in the whole World* (London, 1676), The First Part, Chapter XII, pp. 26–7.
35. Leigh, *Augustus Austen Leigh*, p. 115.
36. Handwritten lists in 'A Register of the Choir in the Kings [*sic*] College of Blessed Mary and Saint Nicholas in Cambridge 1860', KCAR/8/3/1.
37. By a vote at a General Congregation on 30 November 1875; R. J. Henderson, *A History of King's College Choir School, Cambridge* (Cambridge, 1981), p. 22.
38. Marston, ' "As England knows it" ', p. 307.
39. Henderson, *A History of King's College Choir School, Cambridge*, pp. 22, 25.
40. Ibid., pp. 25, 27.
41. Austen Leigh, *King's College [A History]*, pp. 290–91.
42. Henderson, *A History of King's College Choir School, Cambridge*, p. 31.
43. Ibid., p. 40.
44. Ibid., pp. 31–2, 40.
45. Ibid., p. 84.
46. Ibid., p. 59.
47. Ibid., p. 70.
48. Seiriol Evans, 'A Victorian Choir Master', typewritten manuscript of a talk given to the Church Music Society in May 1965, p. 3, KCAR/8/4/2; Patrick Magee, typed manuscript, 'A Journal: The Days of Patrick Connor Magee', p. 8, KCHR/8/9.
49. Henderson, *A History of King's College Choir School, Cambridge*, p. 104.
50. Draft letters of June 1872 from W. R. Churton and A. Austen Leigh to lay clerks, KCAR/8/3/44.
51. Minutes of the General Congregation adjourned from 3 June to 14 June 1873, KCGB/4/1/1/7.
52. Unattributed manuscript, KCAR/8/3/40.
53. Oscar Browning in a letter to *The Athenaeum* dated 12 January 1920, quoted in Percy A. Scholes, *Music, the Child and the Masterpiece* (London, 1935), p. 21.
54. Jane Austen, *Pride and Prejudice*, 3 vols. (London, 1813), vol. 1, chapter XVIII.
55. L. P. Wilkinson, *Kingsmen of a Century 1873–1972* (Cambridge, 1981), p. 68.
56. Austen Leigh, *King's College [A History]*, p. 291.
57. Minutes of the General Congregation of 1 March 1881, KCGB/4/1/1/8.
58. Obituary of William Austen Leigh, KCA, Annual Review (1922), pp. 1–2; donations recorded in Votes of Council, KCGB/5/2/1/1 (to 1904), KCGB/5/2/1/2 (1904–23).
59. Marston, ' "As England knows it" ', p. 308.
60. *MT* 22/456 (February 1881), p. 57.
61. J. J. Withers (ed.), *A Register of Admissions to King's College, Cambridge, 1797–1925* (London, 1929), p. 163.

62. Council minutes for 17 March 1883, p. 47, KCGB/5/1/4/1.

63. Editorial, 'Manliness in Music', *MT* 30/558 (August 1889), pp. 460–61.

64. Thomas Hughes, *Tom Brown's School Days* (Cambridge, 1857), part 2, chapter I, 'How the Tide Turned'.

65. Figures as given in the KCA, Annual Reports.

66. Andrew Parker, 'Mann, Arthur Henry, 1850–1929', *DNB*.

67. Watkins Shaw, *The Succession of Organists of the Chapel Royal and the Cathedrals of England and Wales from c. 1538* (Oxford, 1991), p. 179.

68. Frank Bates, 'Norwich Cathedral', *The Cathedral Quarterly* 2/5 (Easter 1914), p. 5.

69. Frederic G. Kitton, *Zechariah Buck Mus. D., A Centenary Memoir* (London, 1899), pp. 6, 65 (the port was taken 'after the second lesson').

70. *The Norwich Chronicle*, 16 January 1864.

71. *The Norwich Mercury*, 23 January 1864.

72. Tom Roast, *Zechariah Buck: Organist of Norwich Cathedral, 1819–1877: A Bicentenary Memoir* (Norwich, 1998), p. 10.

73. Ibid., p. 5.

74. Ibid.

75. Parker, 'Mann, Arthur Henry, 1850–1929'.

76. An Address delivered by the Provost in King's College Chapel on Sunday, 24 November 1929, in *Arthur Henry Mann 16 May 1850–19 November 1929*, p. 12.

77. Cyril Bradley Rootham, 'Arthur Henry Mann', *MT* 71/1043 (January 1930), pp. 30–31.

78. KCAR/3/2/3/8, p. 38, signed and end-dated 17 July 1882.

79. Marston, '"As England knows it"', p. 305.

80. 'The Three Choirs Festival', *The Gloucester Citizen*, 12 September 1888, p. 4.

81. 'Death of Dr Langdon Colborne', *The Gloucester Citizen*, 17 September 1889.

82. Handwritten note; on reverse: 'The Revd the Provost, King's College Lodge'; in another hand: 'With many thanks, G.W.'; on one corner – 'Organist to Lay Clerks June 1877', KCAR/8/3/40.

83. Letter in Mann's hand dated 3 July 1877; draft letter from the Provost to Dr Mann dated 5 July 1877, KCAR/8/5/1/3.

84. Marston, '"As England knows it"', p. 310.

85. Ibid., pp. 305–8.

86. Wilkinson, *Kingsmen of a Century, 1873–1972*, pp. 4–5.

87. Roast, *Zechariah Buck*, p. 7.

88. Evans, 'A Victorian Choir Master', p. 6.

89. KCAR/8/2/6.

90. Henderson, *A History of King's College Choir School, Cambridge*, p. 29.

91. Evans, 'A Victorian Choir Master', p. 6.

92. Ibid., pp. 6–7.

93. Edward J. Dent, 'Arthur Henry Mann 1850–1929', *The Monthly Musical Record* 60 (January 1930), p. 3.

94. KCA, OB/1/1052/A, 29 June 1882.

95. Marston, ' "As England knows it" ', p. 398, fn 32.

96. Draft letters between the Provost and Vice-Provost, December 1885, KCAR/8/5/1/4.

97. Spoken reminiscences of John Crowder in 1987 transcribed by Andrew Parker, KCAR 8/3/24.

98. An Address delivered by the Provost in King's College Chapel on Sunday, 24 November 1929, in *Arthur Henry Mann 16 May 1850–19 November 1929*, p. 10.

99. Thomas Freebairn-Smith, notes for a lecture, KCAR/8/3/25.

100. Magee, 'A Journal', p. 9.

101. A. H. Mann: notes on choristers, possibly relating to the photograph collection listed in KCPH, KCAR/8/3/3.

102. Magee, 'A Journal', p. 9.

103. Rootham, 'Arthur Henry Mann', pp. 30–31.

104. Reprinted from *The Cambridge Review*, 29 November 1929, in *Arthur Henry Mann 16 May 1850–19 November 1929*, p. 27.

105. L. P. Wilkinson, *A Century of King's, 1873–1972* (Cambridge, 1980), p. 95.

106. Parker, 'Mann, Arthur Henry, 1850–1929'.

107. An Address delivered by the Provost in King's College Chapel on Sunday 24 November 1929, in *Arthur Henry Mann 16 May 1850–19 November 1929*, p. 7.

108. Wilkinson, *Kingsmen of a Century, 1873–1972*, pp. 69–70.

109. Major public schools as they were sometimes designated after the Clarendon Commission, namely Charterhouse, Eton, Harrow, Rugby, Shrewsbury, Westminster and Winchester, St Paul's and Merchant Taylors'.

110. Hughes, *Tom Brown's School Days*, part 1, chapter VI, 'After the Match'.

111. Thomas Hughes, *Tom Brown at Oxford* (London, 1861), chapter XVI, 'The Storm Rages'.

112. Louis N. Parker, 'Music in our Public Schools', *Proceedings of the Musical Association*, Twentieth Session (1893–4), pp. 99–101.

113. Comment by Mr Sedley Taylor at the end of the talk by Louis N. Parker in ibid., p. 109.

114. Percy C. Buck, *M&L* 3/2 (April 1922), pp. 183–4.

115. Paul Victor Mendelssohn Benecke (1868–1944), undated essay on 'Church Music', MCA MS 290.

116. Austen Leigh, *King's College [A History]*, p. 291.

117. 'Dotted Crotchet' [F. G. Edwards], 'St. John's College, Cambridge', *MT* 45/742 (December 1904), p. 778.

118. Dale L. Adelmann, 'Music in The Chapel of St John's College, Cambridge, 1833–97', essay in ms, pp. 46–7, SJCA ARCH 3.15.

119. *Oxford University Calendars*.

120. *Musical Courier*, 10 November 1900, pp. 252–3; newspaper cutting reprinting what Mr Miles Farrow, organist and choirmaster of Old St Paul's Church, Baltimore, wrote in the *Baltimore Sun*, President's Note Book, MCA PR/2/13, between pp. 251 and 252.

121. C. R. Quinton, quoted in Kitton, *Zechariah Buck*, p. 89.

122. Mr Levien, in the discussion following a paper given on 27 April 1944 by Sir Sydney Nicholson, 'The Choirboy and his Place in English Music', *Proceedings of the Musical Association*, Seventieth Session (1943–4), p. 74.

123. Percy M. Young, 'Elgar and Cambridge', *The Elgar Society Journal* 11/5 (July 2000), pp. 270–71.

124. Evans, 'A Victorian Choir Master', pp. 3–5.

125. 'An Old Magdalen Chaplain Writes', *The Times*, 26 November 1929.

126. E. J. Dent, manuscript diary entry for Sunday, 14 March 1897 KCA EJD/3/1/1.

127. Dent, diary entry for Sunday, 17 June 1896, KCA EJD/3/1/1.

128. Dent, diary entry for Sunday, 14 June 1896, KCA EJD/3/1/1.

129. Ibid.

130. Dent, diary entry for Sunday, 24 January 1897, KCA EJD/3/1/1.

131. Dent, diary entry for Sunday, 28 February 1897, KCA EJD/3/1/1.

132. Brian Trowell, 'Elgar's Use of Literature', in *Edward Elgar: Music and Literature*, ed. Raymond Monk (Aldershot, 1993), p. 286.

133. Magee, 'A Journal', p. 9.

134. Ibid.

135. F. G. E. [F. G. Edwards], 'King's College Chapel, Cambridge', *MT* 43/710 (April 1902), p. 230.

136. From the notice which appeared in *The Times* on Wednesday, 20 November 1929, in *Arthur Henry Mann 16 May 1850–19 November 1929*, pp. 18–19.

137. '"The Messiah" at Cambridge', *MT* 35/617 (July 1894), p. 464. See also A. H. Mann, Letter to the Editor, *MT* 44/719 (January 1903), p. 28.

138. Arnold Dolmetsch (1858–1940).

139. Edward Elgar, letter dated 14 November 1900 to A. J. Jaeger, in Jerrold Northrop Moore (ed.), *Elgar and his Publishers: Letters of a Creative Life* (Oxford, 1987), p. 256.

140. Wilkinson, *A Century of King's, 1873–1972*, pp. 95–6.

141. KCA, Annual Review (1921), p. 8.

142. Eric Milner-White, letter to Herbert Howells, 3 February 1920, in Christopher Palmer, *Herbert Howells: A Centenary Celebration* (London, 1992), pp. 167–8.

143. Eric Milner-White, a ten-page memorandum presented to the King's College Council in 1918 after his election as Dean, p. 8, KCA EMW/2/4.

144. KCA, Annual Review (1921), p. 8.

145. W. R. Sorley, in C. H. Sorley, *Marlborough and Other Poems*, 4th edn (Cambridge, 1919), pp. vi–vii.

146. See Patrick Wilkinson, *Eric Milner-White, 1884–1963: A Memoir* (Cambridge, 1963); Philip Pare and Donald Harris, *Eric Milner-White, 1884–1963: A Memoir* (London, 1965); R. T. Holtby (ed.), *Eric Milner-White: A Memorial* (Chichester, 1991).

147. Nicholas Nash, '"A Right Prelude to Christmas": A History of *A Festival of Nine Lessons and Carols*', in Massing and Zeeman (eds.), *King's College Chapel 1515–2015*, pp. 332–3.

148. Eric Milner-White, 1918 memo, KCA EMW/2/4.

149. Christmas Eve Orders, KCA CSV/103.

150. See Erik Routley, *The English Carol* (London, 1958), pp. 228–32.

151. Christmas Eve Orders, KCA CSV/103.

152. The service sheet kept in 'A Register of the Choir in the Kings [*sic*] College of Blessed Mary and Saint Nicholas in Cambridge 1860', KCAR/8/3/1.

153. Ibid.

4. ORD AND WILLCOCKS AT KING'S, 1929–1973

1. E. J. Dent on the 1933 Congress in Cambridge in a letter to Clive Carey, quoted in Hugh Carey, *Duet for Two Voices: An Informal Biography of Edward Dent Compiled from his Letters to Clive Carey* (Cambridge, 1979), p. 143.

2. Jeffrey Pulver, 'Society for Musical Research', *Musical Opinion* 56/672 (September 1933), p. 1,019.

3. Ibid.

4. Paul-Marie Masson, 'Le Congrès International de Cambridge', *Revue de musicologie* 14/48 (November 1933), p. 217.

5. A. F. S. [A. H. Fox Strangways], 'Festival of English Music', *Observer*, 6 August 1933.

6. Eric Blom, Richard Capell et al., 'A. H. Fox Strangways', *M&L* 29/3 (July 1948), pp. 229–37.

7. Bach's 'God liveth still' ('Gott lebet noch' BWV 461, from *Schemellis Gesangbuch*) recorded on 19 July 1929 under Mann's direction (HMV B 3707, 10" 78 rpm disc, released 1931), and on 27 November 1956 under Ord's direction, BL shelfmark 1CDR0025639 (Brian Head King's College, Cambridge, Collection).

8. H. M-g., *Svenska Dagbladet*, 28 March 1936; E. M. S., *Social-Demokraten*, 29 March 1936; H. A-r., *Stockholms-Tidningen*, 29 March 1936; N. S-g., *Aftonbladet*, 29 March 1936; C. K., *Svenska Dagbladet*, 29 March 1936:

newspaper cuttings in KCAR/8/3/2; Maurice Willey, 'A Holiday with a Little Singing', *Choir Schools Today*, December 1986, pp. 31–2.

9. Philip Radcliffe, *Bernhard (Boris) Ord 1897–1961* (Cambridge, 1962), pp. 4, 7.

10. KCA, Annual Report (1926), p. 5.

11. http://admin.concertprogrammes.org.uk/html/search/verb/GetRecord/8135, accessed 26 January 2016.

12. Radcliffe, *Bernhard (Boris) Ord 1897–1961*, p. 5.

13. Clive Carey sings four English folk songs on COLUMBIA DB 335 (10″ double-sided electrical 78 rpm disc).

14. Steuart Wilson, 'The English Singers', *Recorded Sound* 20 (October 1965), pp. 375–9.

15. 'Discus', *MT* 64/966 (August 1923), p. 562; *Gr* 1/3 (August 1923), p. 43.

16. E. H. Fellowes, *Memoirs of an Amateur Musician* (London, 1946), pp. 126–7. The Magnificat of Byrd's Short Service was recorded on HMV E291 (10″ acoustic 78 rpm disc, released 1923).

17. Watkins Shaw, 'Edmund H. Fellowes, 1870–1951', *MT* 111/1533 (November 1970), pp. 1104–5. The editor of *The Musical Times* listed his criticisms of Fellowes' editorial methods in *The English Madrigal School* in the issue for September 1925, 66/991, pp. 803–6; Fellowes responded in the next issue, October 1925, 66/992, pp. 927–8. For a view of his methods in 1950, see Joseph Kerman's review of Fellowes' edition of *The Collected Works of Byrd*, vols. X–XVII (London, 1948), *Journal of the American Musicological Society* 111/3 (Fall 1950), pp. 273–7.

18. Orlando Gibbons, *Hosanna to the Son of David*, in *Novello's Collection of Anthems*, vol. VI (London, 1876), no. 129. The copy inspected was withdrawn from King's College Library and is in the private collection of Michael Guest. Orlando Gibbons, *Hosanna to the Son of David* ed. E. H. Fellowes, (London, 1924).

19. Printed programme of a concert given in King's Chapel on Sunday, 20 June 1926, KCAR/8/2/1/25/17; KCA, Annual Report (1926), p. 11. The English Singers recorded Byrd's *Ave verum corpus* on 29 January 1923, HMV E305 (10″ double-sided electrical 81 rpm disc, released 1923); their 1928 recording of Weelkes' *Hosanna to the Son of David* was reissued on M. C. PRODUCTIONS CD269N (mono CD, released 2013).

20. Deems Taylor in *McCall's Magazine*, quoted in an undated publicity brochure for the English Singers produced by the Atlanta Printing Co., NY, British Library Norman Stone Collection shelfmark MS Mus. 1838.

21. Otto Wend, *La Tribune de Genève*, 29 March 1934, British Library Norman Stone Collection shelfmark MS Mus. 1838.

22. Wilson, 'The English Singers', p. 379.

23. Eric Milner-White, 'The Establishment of the Choir (Men's Voices)', dated 27 February 1926, KCAR/3/1/2/4/9, pp. 2–4.

24. Eric Milner-White, Report on Chapel Expenditure, 16 February 1926, p. 7, KCAR/3/1/2/4/9.

25. A paper on 'Choral Scholarships' written for the College Council by Milner-White, dated 14 February 1931, KCGB/5/1/4/11.

26. Council Minutes, meeting of 21 February 1931, KCGB/5/1/4/11; confirmed by a vote of Congregation on 7 March 1931.

27. Vote I of Council, 29 October 1938, KCGB/5/2/1/3. Just occasionally since 1928, in exceptional circumstances, a singer has been designated a 'lay clerk'. In 1943 a tenor was offered a choral scholarship provided that he pass the required elementary Latin paper before admission to the College. Before matriculation, though, he was allowed to sing in the choir and was designated a 'lay clerk' (Vote XI of Council, 9 October 1943, KCGB/5/2/1/3.)

28. There seems to be no College regulation that was passed on practices. But P. M. Heywood, who had been a chorister, after he had been a choral scholar for one year, 1930–31, migrated to Trinity Hall to become organ scholar, as he had found that singing in the choir at King's meant that he did not have the time he wanted for cricket (KCA, Annual Report (1975), p. 32). This might suggest an additional, unexpected commitment had been introduced.

29. Andrew Parker, 'Mann, Arthur Henry, 1850–1929', *DNB*.

30. Printed register of services, KCAR/8/2/1/6A.

31. Ibid.

32. KCA, Annual Report (1931), p. 14.

33. Letter from E. H. Fellowes, dated 24 July 1933, to Milner-White, KCA BO/1/1. See also letters between Ord and Fellowes in 1937 and 1939, KCA BO/1/1.

34. KCA, Annual Report (1931), p. 14.

35. Ibid.

36. KCA, Annual Report (1930), pp. 13–14; KCA, Annual Report (1937), p. 23.

37. Fellowes, *Memoirs of an Amateur Musician*, pp. 125–6.

38. The four choral scholars were Arden Constant, Leo William Rolf Covey-Crump, Noel Henry Kemp-Welch and Geoffrey Thomas Berwick. The details here recorded are taken from Votes in Council, and the registers of members: John Venn and J. A. Venn (eds.), *Alumni Cantabrigienses: A Biographical List of All Known Students, Graduates and Holders of Office at the University of Cambridge, from the Earliest Times to 1900*, vol. 2, part 3: GABB–JUSTAMOND (first published 1947; published digitally New York, 2011).

39. H. Byerley Thomson, *The Choice of a Profession: A Concise Account and Comparative Review of the English Professions* (London, 1857), pp. 38–41.

40. R. J. Henderson, *A History of King's College Choir School, Cambridge* (Cambridge, 1981), pp. 56–7.

41. Ibid., p. 84.

42. Ibid., p. 70.

43. Ibid., p. 58.

44. Ibid., p. 97.

45. Ibid., p. 67.

46. Ibid., p. 84.

47. Ibid., p. 67.

48. Ibid., p. 47.

49. Anon. [A. V. Baillie], *The Making of a Man: Letters from an Old Parson to his Sons* (London, 1934), p. 46.

50. Charles Wesley, 'Forth in thy name, O Lord, I go'.

51. George Herbert, 'The Elixir', 'Teach me, my God and King'.

52. Henderson, *A History of King's College Choir School, Cambridge*, p. 76.

53. KCA, Annual Review (1916), p. 8.

54. http://www.kings.cam.ac.uk/news/2012/choral-scholar-varsity-match.html, accessed 23 May 2013.

55. Henderson, *A History of King's College Choir School, Cambridge*, p. 92.

56. Owen Chadwick, interviewed by Alan Macfarlane on 29 February 2008, Department of Social Anthropology, Cambridge, http://www.dspace.cam. ac.uk/handle/1810/198014, accessed 3 October 2011.

57. Patrick Wilkinson, *Eric Milner-White, 1884–1963, Fellow, Chaplain and Dean, Dean of York: A Memoir Prepared at the Direction of the Council of King's College, Cambridge* (Cambridge, 1963), pp. 4–6.

58. Anon. *The Making of a Man*, p. 46.

59. Henderson, *A History of King's College Choir School, Cambridge*, p. 62.

60. Owen Chadwick, *Michael Ramsey: A Life* (Oxford and New York, 1991), p. 8.

61. Of Douglas Lane Evans, KCA, Annual Review (1916), p. 10.

62. Of Owen Macaulay Eike, in ibid., p. 10.

63. Of Hugh Edmund Elliot Howson, KCA, Annual Report (1933), p. 4.

64. Of Digton Nicolas Pollock, KCA, Annual Report (1927), p. 5.

65. Eric Milner-White, *My God, My Glory* (London, first published in 1954, 3rd edn 1994), p. 29.

66. Ibid., p. 36.

67. Archbishop Cosmo Lang and H. Scott Holland, in the Preface to Charles Macpherson, Edward C. Bairstow and Percy C. Buck (eds.), *The English Psalter* (London, 1925), pp. xv–xvi.

68. C. Hubert H. Parry, *Johann Sebastian Bach: The Story of the Development of a Great Personality* (London, 1909), p. 1.

69. Charles L. Graves, *Hubert Parry: His Life and Works*, 2 vols. (London, 1926), vol. 2, pp. 176–7.

70. Walford Davies, quoted in ibid., p. 153.

71. Parry, *Johann Sebastian Bach*, p. 1.

72. Wilfrid Ward, *William George Ward and the Catholic Revival* (London, 1893), p. 66.

73. Edward Kershaw Francis (trans.), *Keble's Lectures on Poetry, 1832–1841*, 2 vols. (Oxford, 1912), vol. 1, p. 36.

74. Ibid., vol. 2, pp. 481–2. The last sentence is in Owen Chadwick's translation in *The Mind of the Oxford Movement* (London, 1963), pp. 70–71.

75. Isaac Williams, *On Reserve in Communicating Religious Knowledge* (Tracts for the Times, no. 80) (London, 1838), p. 53.

76. A. Madeley Richardson, *Choir Training based on Voice Production* (London, 1900), p. 8.

77. Christopher Palmer, *Herbert Howells: A Centenary Celebration* (London, 1992), p. 170.

78. W. H. Auden, 'Walter de la Mare', in *Forewords and Afterwords* (London, 1973), pp. 393, 394.

79. John Steane, *Gr* 76/909 (December 1998), pp. 67–8.

80. George Guest, *A Guest at Cambridge* (Orleans, MA, 1994), p. 16.

81. Sir David Willcocks, interviewed by Timothy Day at Sir David's home in Cambridge on 15 October 2003, BL shelfmark 1CDR0032918–20.

82. For a film of Ord conducting see *A Festival of Lessons and Carols 1954*, BBC OPUS ARTE OA 0815 D (DVD, released 2001); this can also be found on YouTube at https://www.youtube.com/watch?v=ofGxXwA8i7c &t=901s; accessed 19 November 2017.

83. David Willcocks, quoted in William Owen (ed.), *A Life in Music: Conversations with Sir David Willcocks and Friends* (Oxford and New York, 2008), p. 41.

84. Basil Douglas for the Music Organiser, BBC Internal Circulating Memo dated 7 March 1939, BBC WAC File R/30/233/1.

85. Internal memo for Music Booking Manager dated 6 February 1950, 'Duplicate Contracts for Boris Ord', BBC WAC Boris Ord, Artists, 1950–1953, File 1c.

86. Letter from Lord Caldecote, Second Bursar, dated 6 May 1953, to O. B. Manager, Outside Broadcasts – Sound. Cambridge: King's College, File 5 1950–1953, BBC WAC File R30/233/5.

87. Radcliffe, *Bernhard (Boris) Ord*, p. 7.

88. Patrick Magee, 'A Journal: The Days of Patrick Connor Magee', typed manuscript, KCHR/8/9, p. 7.

89. L. P. Wilkinson, *Kingsmen of a Century, 1873–1972* (Cambridge, 1981), p. 77.

90. Ibid., pp. 67–8.

91. Magee, 'A Journal', p. 22.

92. KCA, Annual Report (1964), pp. 25, 26.

93. L. P. Wilkinson, 'Ord, Bernhard [Boris] (1897–1961)', *DNB*.

94. John Pardoe, in *What Sweeter Music*, BBC R3, 24 December 1988, Archive of Recorded Church Music shelfmark 896.

95. Sir David Willcocks, interviewed by Timothy Day at Sir David's home in Cambridge on 15 October 2004 (interview 3), BL shelfmark 1CDR0032922–26.

96. Simon Goldhill, *A Very Queer Family Indeed: Sex, Religion, and the Bensons in Victorian Britain* (Chicago, IL, and London, 2016), p. 297.

97. Sir David Willcocks, interviewed by Timothy Day at Sir David's home in Cambridge on 15 October 2004 (interview 3), BL shelfmark 1CDR0032922–26.

98. E. M. Forster, 'Notes on the English Character', in his *Abinger Harvest* (London, 1936), https://www.scribd.com/doc/14248355/Notes-on-the-English-Character-by-E-M-Forster, accessed 27 March 2018.

99. Andrew Hodges, 'Turing, Alan Mathison (1912–1954)', *DNB*.

100. Cuttings from *The Daily Telegraph*, 24 December 1938, and *The Manchester Guardian*, 27 December 1938, BBC WAC P345/2.

101. BBC WAC R30/233/1.

102. Vote IX of Council, meeting of 4 October 1941, KCGB/5/2/1/3.

103. Vote XIV of Council, meeting of 25 April 1942, KCGB/5/2/1/3.

104. Vote XII of Council, meeting of 9 December 1944, KCGB/5/2/1/3.

105. Letter dated 16 April 1946 from G. R. Barnes, BBC Third Programme, to the Rev A. Graham Campbell at King's, BBC WAC R30/233/3; Vote XII of College Council, meeting of 11 May 1946, KCGB/5/2/1/3.

106. BBC Genome Project, http://genome.ch.bbc.co.uk, accessed 19 November 2016.

107. Walford Davies, 'About Church Music', *MT* 73/1072 (June 1932), p. 505.

108. Francis Jackson, *Blessed City: The Life and Works of Edward C. Bairstow* (York, 1996), pp. 187–8.

109. Minutes of the executive committee of the Church Music Society, dated 14 July 1937, in the Library of the Royal College of Organists.

110. *The Times*, 1 February 1938.

111. Martin Rowling, Worcester chorister 1952–56, in Richard Newsholme (ed.), *Memories of Worcester Cathedral Choir* (Worcester, 1997), p. 32.

112. Roy Massey, in Owen (ed.), *A Life in Music*, p. 129; Roy Massey, personal information.

113. Humphrey Clucas, *Taking Stock: The First Sixty Years* (Sutton, 2005), p. 35.

114. Seiriol Evans, 'A Victorian Choir Master', talk given to the Church Music Society in May 1965, typewritten script, p. 5, KCAR/8/4/2.

115. Internal memorandum from Music Programme Organiser to Home Service Music Organiser on 'British Cathedral Choirs', dated 11 November 1955, Church Music File 3, 1955–, BBC WAC R27/928/1.

116. Alan Mould, *The English Chorister: A History* (London, 2007), pp. 190–91; *The Cathedral Quarterly* 1/1 (January 1913), pp. 27–35. Some of the cathedrals may not have distinguished between 'choristers' and 'probationers'.

King's created probationers by Vote II of Council at the meeting of 16 March 1923: '(a) To authorize the Deans to call up boys on the list of choristers-elect so that there will always be two probationers in residence in addition to the sixteen', KCGB/5/2/1/2.

117. Chorister details 1934–50, KCAR/8/3/9/20.

118. E. H. M., 'Three Choirs Festival', *ECM* V/1 (January 1935), p. 18.

119. Geoffrey Bush, in the booklet accompanying *Salisbury Cathedral Choir & Organ Archive Recordings 1927–1965*, SCS 276501 (mono/stereo CD, released 2000), p. 8.

120. Frederic Hodgson, *Choirs and Cloisters: Sixty Years of Music in Church, College, Cathedral and Chapels Royal* (London, 1988), p. 45.

121. Paul Iles, 'Music and Liturgy since 1600', in G. Aylmer and John Tiller (eds.), *Hereford Cathedral: A History* (London, 2000), p. 434.

122. Quoted by Alan Gibbs in a letter to the editor, *MT* 96/1354 (December 1955), p. 654.

123. Hodgson, *Choirs and Cloisters*, pp. 70–71.

124. Henry Sandon, *Living with the Past* (London, 1997), pp. 58–9.

125. Clive R. Jenkinson, in the booklet accompanying *Salisbury Cathedral Choir & Organ Archive Recordings 1927–1965*, pp. 6–7.

126. Magdalen College applications for lay clerkships, MCA DD/7/4/2; DD/27/5.

127. 'Cathedral Singing a Part-Time Job', *The Times*, 20 February 1956.

128. Brian Crosby, personal communication.

129. Mould, *The English Chorister*, p. 225.

130. KCAR/8/2/1.

131. Jenkinson, in the booklet accompanying *Salisbury Cathedral Choir & Organ Archive Recordings 1927–1965*, p. 7.

132. 'Scaling Barriers', 'Robert Ashfield, now 87, Talks to Barry Ferguson', *Choir and Organ* 7/2 (March/April 1999), p. 17.

133. Editorial, 'Inflation in the Choir', *The Times*, 3 March 1956.

134. A. C. Benson, *The Trefoil: Wellington College, Lincoln, and Truro* (London, 1923), pp. 144–5.

135. Cyril T. H. Dams, letter to the editor of *The Daily Telegraph*, 24 August 1954.

136. John Roden, *The Minster School, York: A Centenary History 1903–2004* (York, 2005), p. 144.

137. Boris Ord, in a letter dated 16 April 1952, BBC WAC Boris Ord, Artists File, 1950–1953, File 1c. Richard Podger's solo voice can be heard on a recording of Stanford's Magnificat in G on 4 December 1951 and singing the first verse of 'Once in royal David's city' in the broadcast of the Christmas Eve carol service that year, BL shelfmark 1CDR0025693 (Brian Head Collection).

138. TESTAMENT SBT 1121 (mono CD, released 1997); CD 26 in DECCA set 478 8918 (29 mono and stereo CDs, released 2015).

139. Richard White, personal communication.

140. CD 28 in DECCA set 478 8918 (29 mono and stereo CDs, released 2015).

141. In *Ernest Lough, the First Famous Choirboy*, film made for Channel 4 in 1992, https://www.youtube.com/watch?v=zf9kmNl3lyg, accessed 16 July 2016.

142. Richard White, personal communication.

143. http://www.theguardian.com/news/2000/feb/24/guardianobituaries, accessed 24 March 2016; https://www.boysoloist.com/artist.asp?VID=360, accessed 24 March 2016. See *Master Ernest Lough and the Choir of the Temple Church, London, 1927–1938*, NAXOS 8.120832 (mono CD, released 2005).

144. Compton Mackenzie, *Gr* 5/2 (July 1927), p. 43.

145. C. M. Crabtree, *Gr* 5/2 (July 1927), pp. 59–60. See *Ernest Lough, the First Famous Choirboy*. Lough in that film said he was '14, 14½' when he was in fact 15 and 5 months (disc made 5 April 1927), and 16 and 4 months (30 March 1928); *Master Ernest Lough: Wings of a Dove. Original 1927–1938 Recordings*, NAXOS 8.120832 (mono CD, released 2005).

146. 'Discus', 'Gramophone Notes', *MT* 69/1028 (October 1928), p. 910.

147. 'Discus', 'Gramophone Notes', *MT* 69/1024 (June 1928), p. 517.

148. Sir Sydney Nicholson, 'The Choirboy and his Place in English Music', paper given on 27 April 1944, *Proceedings of the Musical Association*, Seventieth Session (1943–4), pp. 68–9.

149. *Gr* 11/122 (July 1933), p. 61. Two tracks by Leslie Day are included in AMPHION PHI CD 158 (mono CD, released 1999).

150. *Gr* 11/123 (August 1933), p. 101.

151. Jackson, *Blessed City*, p. 115. Elsie Suddaby recorded the song accompanied by Gerald Moore on 12 April 1928 (AMPHION PHI CD 134, mono CD, released 1995) and Ernest Lough, 'with piano', on 30 November 1927 (NAXOS 8.120832, mono CD, released 2005).

152. AMPHION PHI CD 138 (mono CD, released 1996). In live performances the forcefulness of the boys would be more apparent than it is on the recordings since the technology of the time favoured the lower voices, though digital restoration and the removal of disc surface noise make differences easier to appreciate.

153. Jackson, *Blessed City*, pp. 195–6.

154. Ibid., p. 222.

155. Donald Webster in a review of Jackson, *Blessed City*, in *M&L* 78/3 (August 1997), p. 459.

156. Jackson, *Blessed City*, pp. 10–13.

157. Ibid., p. 45.

158. As, for example, in Stanford's *A song of peace* with Francis Jackson accompanying in 1954, AMPHION PHI CD 189 (mono CD, released 2003).

159. AMPHION PHI CD 184 (2 mono CDs, released 2004).

160. See *Ernest Lough, the First Famous Choirboy*.

161. Choir of the Temple Church, Michael Ginn (treble), George Thalben-Ball (organ), recorded in the Temple Church, London, in 1982, GRIFFIN GCCD 4040 (stereo CD, released 2010).

162. Anne Stevenson, 'Carols in King's', in her *Astonishment* (Tarset, Northumberland, 2012). The phrase is from Shelley's *Adonais* and used by Stevenson as an epigraph to her own poem.

163. Owen (ed.), *A Life in Music*, pp. 5–6.

164. Ibid., p. 9.

165. Ibid., p. 21.

166. Ibid., p. 24.

167. Ibid., pp. 11–14.

168. Sir David Willcocks, interviewed by Timothy Day at Sir David's home in Cambridge on 15 October 2003, BL shelfmark 1CDR0032918–20.

169. Owen (ed.), *A Life in Music*, p. 15.

170. Ibid., p. 32.

171. Ibid., 26–32.

172. Willcocks/Macfarlane interview, 11 December 2008, https://www.youtube.com/watch?v=8WVqA3451Gw, accessed 3 September 2014.

173. Owen (ed.), *A Life in Music*, p. 32.

174. Ibid., pp. 36–7.

175. Ibid., p. 75.

176. Ibid., p. 165.

177. Willcocks 'struck a deal with the Vice-Chancellor who let him sit the Bachelor of Music exam, provided he told no one', in Karl Sabbagh (ed.), *A Book of King's* (London, 2011), p. 141.

178. Letter from David Willcocks to Boris Ord, dated 4 August 1937, KCA BO/1/2.

179. Letter from David Willcocks to Boris Ord, dated 31 May 1939, KCA BO/1/2.

180. Letter to David Cox, Yalding House, dated 19 February 1955, BBC WAC Willcocks, David V File I 1939–60.

181. Willcocks to Frank Anderson, dated 15 February 1959, Outside Broadcasts–Sound. Cambridge: King's College File 8, BBC WAC File R30/233/8.

182. Alec R. Vidler, *Scenes from a Clerical Life* (London, 1977), p. 159.

183. Radcliffe, *Bernhard (Boris) Ord*, p. 17; Wilkinson, *A Century of King's 1873–1972*, p. 128. A footnote to Willcocks's use of this term in Owen (ed.), *A Life in Music*, states, 'Now known as multiple sclerosis' (pp. 135–6). Willcocks describes the physical and mental changes in Ord in this passage. The writer of the obituary of Sir David Willcocks in *The Daily Telegraph* described it as 'a degenerative illness' (*The Daily Telegraph*, 17 September 2015).

184. By Council Vote III of 26 April 1957 Boris Ord, having filled the statutory post of College Organist, was given the new title of Director of Music from the beginning of the Michaelmas Term 1957, with David Willcocks being designated Organist, both appointments being for five years. Willcocks was given a fellowship and also a university lectureship and made University Organist. Ord was given leave of absence for the Lent and Easter Terms 1958 by Council Vote VI of 8 November 1957 and his resignation was formally accepted by Council Vote I of 16 May 1958. When Willcocks arrived as Organist for the Michaelmas Term 1957 there was no organ scholar. An organ scholar had ceased his duties early in 1956 through ill-health, and Hugh McLean, the previous organ scholar, had acted as assistant organist for a time. (See Council Vote VIII of 25 May 1956: 'To invite Mr Hugh Mclean to act as Assistant Organist during the Easter term and period of Long Vacation residence 1956 and to make him a payment of £75.') Eric Fletcher, the organ scholar at Selwyn, had also played for services and he accompanied the choir on the recording of 'An Easter Mattins' made in 1957, CD 29 in DECCA set 478 8918 (29 mono and stereo CDs, released 2015).

When it became clear that Willcocks was going to take sole command of the music, he indicated to the College that he would need an organ scholar and Simon Preston, who had been a chorister, was duly elected to the organ studentship by Council Vote I of 20 December 1957. Preston would normally have taken up his duties from the beginning of Michaelmas Term 1958 but, in the absence of an organ scholar, he came up immediately after Christmas and spent two terms playing the organ before he came formally into residence to read for a degree. He stayed on after completing his music degree and took the Mus.B. examination, acting as senior organ scholar to John Langdon, who began his duties in the Michaelmas Term of 1961. So Preston was in effect an organ scholar at King's for fourteen terms. Council votes in KCGB/5/2/1/4; Owen (ed.), *A Life in Music*, pp. 135–6, 139; Sir David Willcocks, interviewed by Alan Macfarlane on 11 December 2008, https://www.youtube.com/watch?v=8WVqA3451Gw, accessed 3 September 2014; Sir David Willcocks, interviewed by Alan Macfarlane on 15 December 2008, https://www.youtube.com/watch?v=ve4GY_oP_OM, accessed 3 September 2014.

185. The recording of Ord's performance of Bach's 'God liveth still' ('Gott lebet noch' BWV 461, from *Schemellis Gesangbuch*) was made on 27 November 1956, BL shelfmark 1CDR0025639 (Brian Head Collection); Willcocks' performance was recorded in July 1959, CD 4 in DECCA set 478 8918 (29 mono and stereo CDs, released 2015).

186. Christopher Bishop, in Owen (ed.), *A Life in Music*, p. 174.

187. For example in the opening phrase of Byrd's *Ave verum corpus* (*Gradualia* 1605) sung under Ord's direction on 19 July 1950, TESTAMENT SBT

1121 (mono CD, released 1997), and under Willcocks in 1959, CD 3 in DECCA set 478 8918 (29 mono and stereo CDs, released 2015).

188. The recordings of the performances of Hadley's *I sing of a maiden* are under Ord's direction with the organist Richard Popplewell on 2 December 1956, BL shelfmark 1CDR0025637 (Brian Head Collection), and under Willcocks' direction with the organist Simon Preston in December 1960, CD 5 in DECCA set 478 8918 (29 mono and stereo CDs, released 2015).

189. Owen (ed.), *A Life in Music*, p. 41; Stephen Cleobury and Nicolette Zeeman, 'Epilogue: The Sound of the Chapel', in Jean Michel Massing and Nicolette Zeeman (eds.), *King's College Chapel 1515-2015: Art, Music and Religion in Cambridge* (London and Turnhout, 2014), pp. 364-7.

190. Simon Carrington, in Owen (ed.), *A Life in Music*, p. 266.

191. Tim Brown, in ibid., pp. 183-4.

192. Brian Kay, in Owen (ed.), *A Life in Music*, p. 187.

193. Clucas, *Taking Stock*, p. 35.

194. William Palmer, 'Pen Portrait: David Willcocks', *MT* 100/1400 (October, 1959), p. 548.

195. Owen (ed.), *A Life in Music*, p. 98.

196. Rachel Willcocks, in ibid., p. 159.

197. Roy Massey, in ibid., p. 129.

198. Roy Goodman, in ibid., p. 168.

199. Jeremy Noble, *Gr* 39/462 (November 1961), p. 263.

200. Trevor Harvey, *Gr* 50/595 (December 1972), p. 1,182.

201. G. J. Cuming, *Gr* 40/470 (July 1962), p. 60.

202. Jeremy Noble, *Gr* 43/508 (September 1965), p. 160.

203. Denis Stevens, *Gr* 38/445 (June 1960), p. 27.

204. Desmond Shawe-Taylor, *Gr* 41/488 (January 1964), p. 320.

205. Brian Trowell, *Gr* 45/537 (February 1968), p. 441.

206. G. J. Cuming, *Gr* 40/470 (July 1962), p. 60.

207. Desmond Shawe-Taylor, *Gr* 38/455 (April 1961), p. 523.

208. Peter Aston, *MT* 106/1472 (October 1965), p. 778.

209. Peter Phillips, 'The Golden Age Regained 2', *EM* 8/2 (April 1980), p. 183.

210. CD 3 in DECCA set 478 8918 (29 mono and stereo CDs, released 2015); EMI CLASSICS FOR PLEASURE 5 86048 2.

211. For example, in the chorus 'Though an host of men' from *The Lord is my light* HWV 255, recorded in 1967 (CD 21 in DECCA set 478 8918 (29 mono and stereo CDs, released 2015)).

212. Christopher Grier, *The Listener*, 2 January 1964, pp. 36, 38; *Personent hodie* recorded in August 1962 (CD 10 in DECCA set 478 8918 (29 mono and stereo CDs, released 2015)).

213. *The Monthly Letter*, July 1960, p. 12.

214. Stanley Sadie, *Gr* 44/524 (January 1967), p. 380.

215. Jeremy Noble, *Gr* 36/431 (April 1959), p. 527.

216. G. J. Cuming, *Gr* 40/471 (August 1962), p. 105.

217. Alec Robertson, *Gr* 45/538 (March 1968), p. 495.

218. John Rutter, in the booklet accompanying *The Complete Argo Recordings of the Choir of King's College, Cambridge, Directed by David Willcocks*, DECCA set 478 8918 (29 CDs, issued 2015), p. 62.

219. Stanley Sadie, *Gr* 44/524 (January 1967), p. 380.

220. Harley Usill, 'A History of Argo: Problems of a Specialist Record Company', *Recorded Sound* 78 (July 1980), pp. 31–5.

221. See Timothy Day, *A Century of Recorded Music* (London, 2000), pp. 29–32.

222. For example in Tallis's *In manus tuas* on CD 16 of DECCA set 478 8918 (29 mono and stereo CDs, released 2015).

223. Council Vote XII of 15 May 1964, KCGB/5/2/1/5.

224. Christopher Parker, recorded in February 1984, British Library's Oral History of Recorded Sound C90/28, BL shelfmark 1CDR0023064. For an example of such a broadcast see BL shelfmark 1CDR0027100, a programme of music by Tallis sung by the Choir of Magdalen College, Oxford, directed by Bernard Rose, recorded on 17 November 1967 and broadcast on BBC Radio 3, 17 September 1968.

225. For example, on a disc of anthems recorded in July 1973, HMV CSD 3752 (12″ 33⅓ rpm stereo disc, released 1974).

226. Owen (ed.), *A Life in Music*, pp. 147–8, 173–4.

227. John Culshaw, *Putting the Record Straight* (London, 1982), p. 143.

228. Jane Austen, *Emma*, 3 vols. (London, 1815), vol. I, chapter XII.

229. *Music in Worship: Report of the Archbishops' Committee Appointed in May 1922* (London, 1923), p. 7.

230. Sir Henry Hadow, address delivered at the Musical Association on 17 June 1919, quoted in Graves, *Hubert Parry*, vol. 2, p. 165.

231. Noel Annan, *Our Age* (London, 1990), p. 30.

232. Ibid., p. 58.

233. Owen (ed.), *A Life in Music*, pp. 69, 209.

234. Ibid., pp. 209–10.

235. Anthony Fletcher, *Growing Up in England: The Experience of Childhood 1600–1914* (New Haven, CT, and London, 2008), pp. 21–2.

236. Sir David Willcocks, 'The Director's Address to the Royal College of Music, 21 September 1981', *The Magazine of the Royal College of Music* (1982), p. 77.

237. Kaffe Fassett, 'Allegri's *Miserere*', in the series *Soul Music*, BBC Radio 4, Tuesday, 1 September 2009, http://www.bbc.co.uk/programmes/boombkk4, accessed 18 September 2014.

5. THE 1960S: BEYOND KING'S

1. A. Austen Leigh, *King's College [A History]* (London, 1899), p. 291.

2. SJCA SBF 50/Chapel/General.

3. Mr Levien, in the discussion following Sir Sydney H. Nicholson, 'The Choirboy and his Place in English Music', paper given on 27 April 1944, *Proceedings of the Musical Association*, Seventieth Session (1943–4), p. 74.

4. George C. Martin, *The Art of Training Choir Boys* (London, 1892), p. 21.

5. Canon Galpin, in the discussion following Nicholson, 'The Choirboy and his place in English Music', p. 74.

6. Nicholson, 'The Choirboy and his place in English Music', pp. 63–4.

7. Letter from Sir Sydney Nicholson to C. V. Taylor, dated 21 February 1944, BBC WAC R27/5/2.

8. The Dean of Gloucester Cathedral [Harold Costley-White], *ECM* XII/4 (October 1942), pp. 25–7.

9. *Oxford University Calendar*, 1920, p. 393.

10. New College Stated General Meeting Report Book: report of a meeting of the Choir Committee, 10 January 1944, NCA MIN/Rep 3.

11. Letter from H. K. Andrews to C. V. Taylor, dated 20 January 1943, BBC WAC R 30/2.

12. See *Oxford University Calendar*, 1959, p. 134; *Oxford University Calendar*, 1964, p. 136. From 1959 the choral scholarships at Christ Church came under the heading of Smith Exhibitions, of which there were five 'awarded in Natural Science and Choral Singing . . . whose emoluments are charged to the benefaction of the late Mr R. C. Smith. The value of these exhibitions is £50 a year without inquiry into means and each Smith Exhibitioner is excused the payment of the usual Entrance Fee' (*Oxford University Calendar*, 1959, p. 134). Exceptionally Christ Church may have recruited an undergraduate singer, as they did in 1945 to replace a lay clerk on leave during the war (Peter Phillips, 'The Golden Age Regained [1]', *EM* 8/1 (January 1980), p. 5.)

13. Reverend Paul Burbridge, private communication.

14. The countertenor James Bowman sang as a choral scholar at New College from 1960 to 1964 and from then as a lay clerk until 1968, though singing for the final few months only sporadically. Between September 1964 and March 1967 he also sang as a lay clerk at Christ Church, singing Evensong twice each day, though on Sundays, when the services clashed, he provided a deputy from The Queen's College (James Bowman, private communication).

15. Phillips, 'The Golden Age Regained [1]', p. 9.

16. Ibid.

17. Brian Crosby, private communication.

18. Peter Aston, 'Music since the Reformation', in G. E. Aylmer and Reginald Cant (eds.), *A History of York Minster* (Oxford, 1977), p. 428.

19. Peter Aston and Tom Roast, 'Music in the Cathedral', in Ian Atherton, Eric Fernie, Christopher Harper-Bill and Hassell Smith (eds.), *Norwich Cathedral: Church, City and Diocese, 1096–1996* (London and Rio Grande, OH, 1996), p. 702.

20. SJCA, D103.184–6.

21. Ibid.

22. SJCA CM1921/4, 11 November 1949; SJCA SBF50; *Third Ear: Conversation between George Guest and Bernard Keefe*, BBC R3, 12 December 1991, BL shelfmark B8899.

23. H. Watkins Shaw, *The Succession of Organists of the Chapel Royal and the Cathedrals of England and Wales from c. 1538* (Oxford, 1991), p. 385.

24. http://www.hcstewart.com, accessed 22 April 2016.

25. http://www.hcstewart.com/biography–obituaries.html, accessed 22 April 2015.

26. Louis N. Parker, 'Music in our Public Schools', *Proceedings of the Musical Association*, Twentieth Session (1893–4), pp. 97–113.

27. See the annual *Cambridge University Calendar* for names of choral scholars; further details from R. H. Bulmer and L. P. Wilkinson (eds.), *A Register of Admissions to King's College, Cambridge, 1919–1958* (London, 1963).

28. Annual editions of the *Oxford University Calendar*.

29. Applications for lay clerkships in 1926, 1930 and 1950, MCA DD/7/4/2, DD/7/4/3, DD/27/5.

30. 'Magdalen College Chapel, Oxford', *MT* 41/688 (June 1900), pp. 386–7.

31. Applications for lay clerkships in 1930 and in 1950, MCA DD/27/5, DD/7/4/3.

32. Applications for a lay clerkship in 1950, MCA DD/7/4/3.

33. Report of the Magdalen Chapel and Choir Committee, dated 10 October 1956, with the text carrying the amendments decided at the meeting on 17 October 1956, MCA CMM/2/17.

34. Meeting of the Magdalen Chapel and Choir Committee, 5 March 1959, CCM/1/3.

35. *Oxford University Calendar*, 1960, p. 109.

36. Meeting of the Magdalen Chapel and Choir Committee on 4 November 1958; R. Lawrence of Worcester College, MCA CCM/1/3.

37. For an examination of the thinking that lay behind the creation of the Music Tripos at Cambridge see Hubert S. Middleton, 'Music Studies', *Proceedings of the Royal Musical Association*, Seventy-First Session (1944–5), pp. 49–68.

38. 'The Universities and Music', *The Times*, 21 February 1964.

39. http://www.magd.ox.ac.uk/libraries-and-archives/archives/online-catalogues/bernard-rose-papers, accessed 3 June 2016.

40. David Fallows, *Gr* 56/672 (May 1979), p. 1,926.

41. Such as Colin Wilson singing music by John Stainer, ARGO ZRG 811 (12″ 33⅓ rpm stereo disc, released 1975).

42. MCA DD/53.

43. Compare, for example, the performances of Gibbons' *O clap your hands* by the Choir of York Minster recorded in April 1927, AMPHION PHI CD 138 (mono CD, released 1996), with that of the Choir of Magdalen College, Oxford, recorded in the antechapel of Magdalen College, probably in June 1963, OXRECS DIGITAL OXCD 5287 (stereo CD, released 2000), or the performances of Stanford's *Beati quorum via* by the Choir of New College, Oxford, recorded on 22 March 1949, CHASS 971 (mono CD, released 1997), with that of the Choir of Magdalen College, Oxford, recorded in June 1963, OXRECS DIGITAL OXCD 5368 (stereo CD, released 2000).

44. OXRECS DIGITAL OXCD 5368 (stereo CD, released 2000).

45. Gordon Pullin, private communication.

46. John Amis, at http://www.kings-music.co.uk/spem_with_tippett.htm, accessed 20 July 2005.

47. ARGO RG 91 (12″ 33⅓ rpm mono disc).

48. Roy Bridge, 'The Renaissance Society', *MT* 92/1300 (June 1951), pp.253-4.

49. Frank Ll. Harrison (ed.), *The Eton Choirbook: I*, Musica Britannica X (London, 1956, rev. edn London, 1967), p. viii.

50. Peter Phillips, 'Scholarship & Performance: Peter Phillips interviews Bruno Turner', *EM* 6/2 (April 1978), pp. 199-201, 203.

51. L'OISEAU-LYRE SOL 311-3 (3 12″ 33⅓ rpm stereo discs).

52. L'OISEAU-LYRE SOL 337 (12″ 33⅓ rpm stereo disc).

53. Sydney Nicholson, 'Of women's *versus* boys' voices', in *Cathedral Music Today and Tomorrow: The Report of a Sub-Committee Appointed by the Cathedral Organists' Association and the Church-Music Society* (London/Oxford, 1941), p. 46.

54. Jeremy Noble, *Gr* 36/426 (November 1958), p. 255

55. The Clerkes as a group of men alone released one LP in 1966, ABBEY 603/S603 (12″ 33⅓ rpm mono/stereo disc), and one 7″ extended-play disc in 1968, ABBEY E 7638 (7″ 45 rpm mono/stereo disc), which were released together in 2017 as Griffin GCCD 4083 (stereo CD).

56. E. H. Fellowes, *Memoirs of an Amateur Musician* (London, 1946), p. 128.

57. David Wulstan, *Tudor Music* (London, 1985), pp. 192-249.

58. From the programme leaflet for a concert of music by Sheppard sung by the Clerkes at St John's, Smith Square, London, on 7 December 1986.

59. Sally Dunkley, interviewed by Timothy Day at the British Library on 26 August 2005, BL shelfmark 1CDR0028454.

60. Compare the Clerkes' singing of Tallis's *Gaude gloriosa Dei Mater* in the Chapel of Merton College, Oxford, in April 1973, EMI CLASSICS FOR PLEASURE 5 68062 2 (stereo CD, released 1993), with that of the BBC Chorus conducted by Alan Melville in a recording released in 1968, PYE VIRTUOSO TPLS 13019 (12″ 33⅓ rpm stereo disc).

61. Sally Dunkley, interviewed by Timothy Day at the British Library on 26 August 2005, BL shelfmark 1CDR0028454.

62. Wulstan, *Tudor Music*, p. 179.

63. See John Milsom, '*What We Really Do* by Peter Phillips' (review), *EM* 32/3 (August 2004), pp. 466–8.

64. Howard Mayer Brown, 'Performing Early Music on Record – 2: Continental Sacred Music of the 16th century', *EM* 3/4 (October 1975), pp. 373, 375.

65. See Roger Bowers, 'The Vocal Scoring, Choral Balance and Performing Pitch of Latin Church Polyphony in England *c.*1500–58', *Journal of the Royal Musical Association* 112/1 (1986), pp. 38–76.

66. Roger Bowers, 'The Performing Pitch of English 15th-Century Church Polyphony', *EM* 8/1 (January 1980), pp. 21–8, p. 25.

67. Wulstan, *Tudor Music*, p. 193.

68. Bowers, 'The Vocal Scoring, Choral Balance and Performing Pitch of Latin Church Polyphony in England *c.*1500–58', p. 46, n. 20.

69. Ibid., p. 53, n. 36.

70. Ibid., p. 48, n. 23.

71. Ibid., p. 67.

72. Sleeve note to Taverner's Mass 'Gloria tibi Trinitas', 'as sung in the context of High Mass for Trinity Sunday during the composer's time at Cardinal College, Oxford', EMI REFLEXE EL 749103-1 (12″ 33⅓ rpm digital stereo disc, released 1988). See also Andrew Parrott, 'Falsetto Beliefs: The "Countertenor" Cross-Examined', *EM* 43/1 (February 2015), pp. 79–110.

73. KCA, Annual Report (1969), p. 47.

74. 'Gerald Finley on Canada Post Stamp Collection', *Canada Post*, Sunday, 5 February 2017, http://www.geraldfinley.com/index.php, accessed 13 February 2018.

75. Rogers is heard as a choral scholar soloist in the extract from Bach's *Christmas Oratorio* used in the recording of an abbreviated Festival of Lessons and Carols made in 1954, CD26 in DECCA set 478 8918 (29 mono and stereo CDs, released 2015).

76. Nigel Rogers, 'The Re-creation of Baroque Singing Styles', British Library, 2 December 2003, BL shelfmark 1CDR0012257-8.

77. In his British Library lecture, as an example of the singing he heard in India, Rogers played Bhimsen Joshi on HMV 7EPE 1234 (7″45 rpm stereo disc, released *c.* 1964).

78. Compare, for example, the performances of Monteverdi's 'Zefiro torna' (*Scherzi musicali*, 1632) in the 1930s with Nigel Rogers's in the 1970s: Paul Derenne (tenor), Hugues Cuénod (tenor), Nadia Boulanger (piano), recorded in February 1937, EMI CDH 7 61025 2 (stereo CD, released 1988), and Nigel Rogers (tenor), Ian Partridge (tenor), with an instrumental ensemble under the direction of Jürgen Jürgens recorded in 1972, ARCHIV 437 075-2 (stereo CD, released 1992).

79. Lindsay Kemp, 'Music Sent from the Heavens', *Gr* 88/1058 (June 2010), pp. 46–51; Edward Greenfield, Robert Layton and Ivan March (eds.), *The New Penguin Guide to Compact Discs and Cassettes* (London, 1988), p. 667.

80. Iain Fenlon, *Gr* 62/744 (May 1985), pp. 1,369–70.

81. Timothy Robson, a report on 'The Second Symposium on Early Vocal Practices, Case Western Reserve University, 29–31 October, 1982', *The Journal of Musicology* 2/1 (Winter 1983), p. 99; Kirsten Yri, 'Thomas Binkley and the Studio der frühen Musik: Challenging "the Myth of Westernness"', *EM* 38/2 (May 2010), p. 273; David Fallows, 'Andrea von Ramm (1928–99)', *EM* 28/2 (May 2000), p. 325; David Lasocki, 'The Several Lives of Thomas Binkley', *Early Music America* (Fall 1995), p. 19; David Fallows, 'Performing Early Music on Record – 1: A Retrospective and Prospective Survey of the Music of the Italian Trecento', *EM* 3/3 (July 1975), p. 253.

82. Denis Arnold, *Gr* 46/550 (March 1969), p. 1,316.

83. See Timothy Day, *A Century of Recorded Music: Listening to Musical History* (London, 2000), pp. 250–52.

84. See, for example, a recital of songs by Josquin des Prez, ARGO ZRG 793 (12″ 33⅓ rpm stereo disc, released 1975).

85. John Potter, 'Past Perfect and Future Fictions', *Basler Jahrbuch für historische Musikpraxis* XXVI (2002), p. 14.

86. David James, 'The Hilliard Ensemble: Saxes, Crump-Tenors and Arvo Pärt', *The Guardian*, Friday, 14 March 2014.

87. https://www.allmusic.com/artist/red-byrd-mn0002285660/biography, accessed 23 November 2017

88. http://www.john-potter.co.uk/blog/category/david-willcocks, accessed 30 March 2016; there is a discography of the Hilliard Ensemble at http://www.medieval.org/emfaq/performers/hilliard.html, accessed 15 February 2018.

89. 'Notes by A. H. Mann giving short biographical summaries of choristers and choral scholars, possibly relating to photograph collection listed in KCPH, KCAR/8/3/3.

90. London Diary for May, *MT* 109/1502 (April 1968), p. 388.

91. William Owen (ed.), *A Life in Music: Conversations with Sir David Willcocks and Friends* (Oxford and New York, 2008), pp. 156–7.

92. See https://www.kingssingers.com/about-us, accessed 30 March 2016; 'The Story of Hi-Lo's', http://www.singers.com/jazz/Hi-Loshistory.html, accessed

30 March 2016; King's Singers, *A Tribute to the Comedian Harmonists*, EMI CDC 7 47677 2 (stereo CD, released 1985); 'The Definitive Story of the Mastersingers, the Weather Forecast, and the Highway Code', http://www. batesline.com/archives/2007/05/the-definitive.html, accessed 30 March 2016; Brian Kay, 'Pies to Penderecki: The King's Singers', *The Guardian*, 25 April 2008. For the early history of the group see Brian Kay, notes in the booklet to the CD *The King's Singers: Original Debut Recording with The Gordon Langford Trio*, recorded in London in 1970, CHANDOS CHAN 6562 (stereo CD, released 2005).

93. John Eliot Gardiner, *Music in the Castle of Heaven: A Portrait of Johann Sebastian Bach* (London, 2013), p. 5.

94. John Eliot Gardiner, in an interview with Richard Morrison, 'Prized for Period Perfection', *The Times*, 19 November 1991.

95. Humphrey Clucas, *Taking Stock: The First Sixty Years* (Sulton, 2005), pp. 39–40.

96. Gardiner, *Music in the Castle of Heaven*, p. 7.

97. Brian Kay, tribute to the Monteverdi Choir, http://www.monteverdi. co.uk/50/tributes, accessed 4 April 2016.

98. John Eliot Gardiner, 'Sir John Eliot Gardiner on Bach, Cambridge and the Prince of Wales', *The Daily Telegraph*, 19 September 2014.

99. Denis Arnold, on a performance of the Vespers in Ely Cathedral, *MT* 108/1497 (November 1967), p. 1,025.

100. Tom Service, '50 Years Ago – How John Eliot Gardiner Changed Music', *The Guardian*, 4 March 2014.

101. Andrew Clements, *The Guardian*, 6 March 2014.

102. John Allison, *The Daily Telegraph*, 6 March 2014.

103. Andrew Clark, *The Financial Times*, 6 March 2014.

104. Gardiner, *Music in the Castle of Heaven*, pp. 5–6.

105. Guy Aufrère Harland, *MT* 107/1485 (November 1966), p. 969.

106. Basil Ramsey, reviewing *Music from Worcester Cathedral*, ABBEY 611 (12″ 33⅓ rpm disc in mono and stereo versions), *MT* 108/1498 (December 1967), p. 1,126.

107. Sebastian Forbes, *MT* 108/1487 (January 1967), p. 71.

108. Philip Larkin, 'Annus Mirabilis', in his *High Windows* (London, 1974), p. 34.

109. George Dyson, *The Progress of Music* (London, 1932), pp. 35–6.

110. www.sjcchoir.co.uk/listen/releases/six-great-masses-haydn, accessed 21 June 2017.

111. Harvey Grace, *MT* 63/952 (June 1922), p. 419. There is a recording of the Sistine Choir 'under the direction of Monsignor Perosi, conducted by Monsignor Antonio Rella' recorded in June 1931 singing Palestrina's *Sicut cervus* 4vv, PRISTINE AUDIO PACO 016 (mono CD, released 2006).

112. GRAMOPHONE D 337 (12" double-sided acoustic 78 rpm disc, released 1911).

113. R. R. Terry, 'Why is Church Music so Bad?', in his *A Forgotten Psalter and Other Essays* (London, 1929), p. 105.

114. George Malcolm, 'Boys' Voices', in *English Church Music 1967: A Collection of Essays* (Croydon, 1967), pp. 24–7.

115. David Hill, in an interview with Katherine Dienes, *Choir and Organ* 3/6 (December 1995), p. 29.

116. Such as the Choir of Dijon Cathedral's recording of Palestrina's Missa 'Assumpta est Maria' released in 1933, PRISTINE AUDIO PACO 016 (mono CD, released 2006); see Compton Mackenzie, *Gr* 11/127 (December 1933), pp. 262–3; Edward Sackville-West and Desmond Shawe-Taylor, *The Record Guide* (London, 1951), pp. 319–20, 431.

117. www.sacredheartmusic.co.uk/choirs; www.farmstreet.org.uk/history_of_music.php, accessed 12 July 2017.

118. Richard Henwood and Nicholas Kenyon, 'George Malcolm, 1917–97', *EM* 26/1 (February 1998), p. 186.

119. For example, in their singing of the eucharistic hymn 'Sweet sacrament divine', released in 1932 on HMV B 4055 (10" double-sided electrical 78 rpm disc).

120. Patrick Russill, *The Tablet*, 25 October 1997, p. 28.

121. DECCA 433 914-2 (mono and stereo CD, released 1992).

122. Alec Robertson, *Gr* 37/444 (May 1960), p. 590; see the Argo advertisement, advert 33, in *Gr* 38/454 (March 1961), opposite p. 492.

123. *The Times*, 28 February 1967.

124. Russill, *The Tablet*, p. 28.

125. *The Monthly Letter* (April 1960), p. 16.

126. DECCA CEP.654 (7" 45 rpm extended play disc, released 1960).

127. B. W. G. R. [Bernard Rose], *M&L* 41/4 (October 1960), pp. 396–7.

128. Leslie Green, *M&L* 42/1 (January 1961), pp. 99–100.

129. Harland, *MT* 107/1485, p. 969.

130. Edward Greenfield, *Gr* 43/508 (September 1965), pp. 157–8.

131. Harvey Grace, *MT* 63/952 (June 1922), p. 419.

132. Peter Phillips, 'The Golden Age Regained 2', *EM* 8/2 (April 1980), pp. 182–3.

133. Stanley Webb, 'The Sound of St John's', *Gr* 47/563 (April 1970), p. 38; George Guest talking to Bernard Keefe, 'Third Ear', BBC Radio 3, 12 December 1991, BL shelfmark B8899.

134. Guest talking to Keefe, BBC Radio 3, 12 December 1991, BL shelfmark B8899; Hill, in interview with Dienes, *Choir and Organ* 3/6, p. 29.

135. Phillips, 'The Golden Age Regained 2', p. 181.

136. Ibid.

137. A collection of hymns exists recorded by the BBC Transcription Service on 78 rpm discs in 1952 (Archive of Recorded Church Music, shelfmarks S154

and S155) and a short service devised for the BBC recorded on 5 May 1953, BL shelfmark 1CDR0003620.

138. Recordings of the Choirs of Montserrat Abbey directed by Ireneu Segarra were released in about 1954, EDITION STUDIO SM 33-17 (12″ 33⅓ rpm mono disc), and in 1953 a recording of the Copenhagen Boys' Choir with Enid Simon (harp) conducted by Benjamin Britten, DECCA 436 394-2 (mono CD, released 1993).

139. Gordon Pullin, private communication, October 2011.

140. The first commercial recording of St John's was made in October 1958, CD 1 in DECCA set 483 1252 (42 CDs, issued 2017).

141. Memo dated 27 February 1956 from Harold Noble to Head of Religious Broadcasting, BBC Outside Broadcasts – Sound. Cambridge: St John's College 1935–1959, BBC WAC R30/234.

142. Tess Knighton, 'Vocal Heroes: Going Out on a Natural High, "High and sweet and strong". Tess Knighton on What England Expects of her Cathedral Choirboys', *Independent*, 22 March 1993.

143. Carl de Nys, *Diapason* 85 (March 1964), p. 26.

144. Carl de Nys, *Diapason* 76 (April 1963), p. 27.

145. Poulenc's *Litanies à la Vierge noire*, recorded in December 1969, CD 21 in DECCA set 483 1252 (42 CDs, issued 2017).

146. John Gummer, 'George Howell Guest, Choirmaster and Organist, born 9 February 1924; died 20 November 2002', *The Guardian*, 4 December 2002.

147. John Scott, BBC Radio 4, *Sunday*, 25 August 1991, BL shelfmark B8582.

6. THE STYLE SINCE THE 1960S

1. Magdalen Choir Committee 1920–1944, MCA CCM/1/1.

2. Obituary of Maurice Bevan, *The Daily Telegraph*, 21 July 2006.

3. https://holstsingers.com/about-us/president, accessed 10 June 2017.

4. Richard Seal, in Peter Phillips, 'The Golden Age Regained [1]', *EM* 8/1 (January 1980), pp. 5–6.

5. Phillips, 'The Golden Age Regained [1]', p. 9.

6. Mark Buxton, 'Simon Preston at 50', *MT* 129/1748 (October 1988), pp. 555–7.

7. Robert Anderson, *MT* 116/1586 (April 1975), p. 346.

8. David Fallows, *MT* 118/1608 (February 1977), pp. 133–4.

9. Phillips, 'The Golden Age Regained [1]', p. 182.

10. Recordings were made, for example, in Merton College Chapel (Walton, choral works, ARGO ZRG 725 (12″ 33⅓ rpm stereo disc, released in 1972)); in All Saints' Church, Tooting, in December 1974 (Stravinsky: *Symphony of Psalms*; *Canticum sacrum*, ARGO ZRG 799 (12″ 33⅓ rpm

stereo disc, released in 1975)); in Keble College Chapel (*Romantic Choral Classics*, Elgar, Rachmaninov, Bruckner, Verdi, Fauré, Kalinnikov, Brahms, ARGO ZRG 871 (12″ 33⅓ rpm stereo disc, released in 1977)).

11. Hugh Keyte, *Gr* 54/647 (April 1977), p. 1,582.

12. L'OISEAU-LYRE 430 488-2 (2 stereo CDs, released 1991).

13. Stanley Sadie, *Gr* 57/683 (April 1980), pp. 1,575–6.

14. Kate Bolton, 'Singing as She Speaks', *Gramophone Early Music Quarterly* 1 (Summer 1999), pp. 16–21.

15. Jeremy Summerly, BBC Radio 3, 19 January 1997, *Spirit of the Age*, BL shelfmark H8354/2.

16. Paul Griffiths, *MT* 117/1602 (August 1976), p. 663. Stravinsky's *Symphony of Psalms* and the *Canticum sacrum* together with Christ Church's recording of his Mass were released on DECCA 430 346-2 (stereo CD, released 1991).

17. Stephen Walsh, *Stravinsky: A Creative Spring: Russia and France, 1882–1934* (London, 1999), p. 499.

18. A. Hyatt King, 'The International Society for Musicology', *MT* 96/1351 (September 1955), p. 487.

19. http://www.bbc.co.uk/programmes/articles/3SsklRvCSPvfHr13wgz6HCJ/proms-performance-archive, accessed 10 October 2016.

20. Keyte, *Gr* 54/647, p. 1,582.

21. The sort of vibrato that was demonstrated by, for example, the bass soloist Frank Green, in the recording released in 1972 of the Nunc Dimittis of Stanford's Evening Canticles in G, singing with the Choir of New College, Oxford, with Jonathan Rees-Williams the organist, directed by David Lumsden, ABBEY LPB 716 (12″ 33⅓ rpm stereo disc).

22. Phillips, 'The Golden Age Regained [1]', p. 9.

23. Matthew Jenkinson, *New College School, Oxford: A History* (Oxford, 2013), p. 65.

24. Andrew Stewart, 'In with the New', *Classical Music* (25 April 1998), p. 27; Edward Higginbottom, a review of the CDs entitled *The Better Land*, reprinted from the April 2000 issue of *Church Music Quarterly*, http://www.thebetterland.org/bland020.html, accessed 19 February 2009.

25. Edward Higginbottom, in Graham Topping, 'The Sound of Life', *Oxford Today*, Michaelmas Issue (2006), p. 21.

26. Phillips, 'The Golden Age Regained [1]', p. 181. The kind of singing style and timbre characteristic of Higginbottom's boys is well demonstrated in their 2012 recording of Britten's *Ceremony of Carols*, NOVUM NCR 1386 (2 digital stereo CDs, released 2012), which may be compared to the singing style of the same choir's trebles in this work in a recording released in 1962, ALPHA ADV 002 (12″ 33⅓ rpm mono disc).

27. Colin Baldy, a review of the CDs entitled *The Better Land*, reprinted from the April 2000 issue of *Church Music Quarterly*, http://www.thebetter land.org/bland020.html, accessed 19 February 2009.

28. Fabrice Fitch, *Gr* 81/972 (November 2003), p. 101; David Fallows, *Gr* 65/770 (July 1987), p. 208.

29. For example, the treble soloists in anthems by William Croft recorded in August 1992, CRD 3491 (digital stereo CD, released 1994), or in the *Messiah* recorded in January 2006, NAXOS 8570131-32 (2 digital stereo CDs, released 2006).

30. Phillips, 'The Golden Age Regained [1]', pp. 182–3.

31. Higginbottom, in Topping, 'The Sound of Life', p. 21.

32. http://www.bbc.co.uk/programmes/articles/3SsklRvCSPvfHr13wgz6HCJ/ proms-performance-archive, accessed 11 October 2016.

33. Lowell Mason, *Musical Letters from Abroad: Including Detailed Accounts of the Birmingham, Norwich and Dusseldorf Musical Festivals of 1852* (Boston, 1853), p. 262.

34. Singers such as Charles Hawkins and Hatherley Clarke, OPAL CD 9848 (mono CD, released 1991).

35. Richard Wigmore, 'Alfred Deller', *Gr* 90/1092 (January 2013), p. 16.

36. Roger Job sings Tomkins' *My shepherd is the living God* in 1961 on ARGO ZRG 5249 (12″ 33⅓ rpm stereo disc, issued, 1961); an unnamed solo alto at St John's sings Weelkes' *Give ear, O Lord* in 1960 (CD 2 in DECCA set 483 1252; 42 CDs, issued 2017).

37. 'David Munrow Talks to Alan Blyth', *Gr* 51/612 (May 1974), p. 2,009.

38. L'OISEAU-LYRE 414 329-2 (stereo CD, released 2008). See 'Where do countertenors come from?', a discussion between James Bowman and Timothy Day, British Library Saul Seminar, 18 February 2003, BL shelfmark 1CDR0012221; a CD of the musical extracts used during the discussion is on BL shelfmark 1CDR0012222, which includes recordings of Bowman singing as a soloist in Purcell, Handel, Ockeghem and Vivaldi.

39. Stephen Cleobury, quoted in Paul Fisher, 'Questions of Belief', *Classic CD* (June 1991), p. 41.

40. Tess Knighton, *Gr* 68/811 (December 1990), p. 1,243.

41. John Rockwell, on Christ Church's 1980 recording of *Messiah*, http:// www.npr.org/blogs/deceptivecadence/2014/09/24/351193303/remembering- christopher-hogwood-an-evangelist-for-early-music?utm_medium=RSS& utm_campaign=storiesfromnpr, accessed 24 September 2015; see Richard Taruskin, 'The Pastness of the Present and the Presence of the Past', in his *Text and Act: Essays on Music and Performance* (New York and Oxford, 1995), pp. 90–154.

42. Eric Whitacre, 'The 20 Greatest Choirs', *Gr* 88/1066 (January 2011), p. 33.

43. Watkins Shaw, *The Succession of Organists of the Chapel Royal and the Cathedrals of England and Wales from c. 1538* (Oxford, 1991), pp. 370–72.

44. Several other colleges have instituted ambitious schemes in order to maintain very high standards with their chapel choirs; choral scholarships for most of the men and women were established at The Queen's College, Oxford, in 1997, at Sidney Sussex College, Cambridge, in 2005 and at Merton College, Oxford, in 2008, private communications, Owen Rees, The Queen's College and David Skinner, Sidney Sussex College. See Peter Phillips, 'Brains and Voice', *The Spectator*, 11 November 2006, pp. 70–71. Jesus College, Cambridge, has had a choir of men and boys since 1849, the boys still being from local schools in the city of Cambridge and not boarders at a choir school. Since 1982 there has also been a mixed choir of undergraduates, called the College Choir, and from 1999 this has had a professional director of music, http://www.jesuscollegechoir.com/site/the_choirs, accessed 15 August 2017.

45. 'Profile: Emma Disley Interviews Timothy Brown', *Mastersinger online* (Winter 2010), https://www.abcd.org.uk/storage/Tim_Brown_article.pdf, accessed 10 October 2016.

46. 'Adapted from the obituary by Dr A. V. Jones, published in the Selwyn College Calendar, 2012–2013, and reproduced with AVJ's kind permission. Acknowledgement is also made to David Harrison, Roger Williams, David Hindley, Catherine King, Oliver Hunt and Elizabeth Stratton', http://www.trin.cam.ac.uk/tcca/richard-marlow, accessed 3 April 2016.

47. http://trinitycollegechapel.com/whos-who/stephen-layton, accessed 15 August 2017; http://www.stephenlayton.com/about, accessed 15 August 2017.

48. http://www.mus.cam.ac.uk/directory/geoffrey-webber, accessed 10 October 2016.

49. From a review of *Choral Music by Paweł Łukaszewski*, HYPERION CDA67639 (digital stereo CD, released 2008), by Ronald E. Grames, *Fanfare* 32/3 (January/February 2009), trinitycollegechoir.com/recordings/review/fanfare-usa-01092008, accessed 12 June 2017.

50. Of Trinity: Maxim Boon, 'Review: The Choir of Trinity College, Cambridge (Musica Viva)' of a concert in the Melbourne Recital Centre on 19 July 2016, *Limelight* (20 July 2016), www.limelightmagazine.com.au/live-reviews/review-choir-trinity-college-cambridge-musica-viva, accessed 12 June 2017. Of King's: Barry Millington, *Evening Standard*, 10 May 2007, http://www.kings.cam.ac.uk/chapel/choir, accessed 11 August 2009.

51. John Quinn, 'Virtuoso Display by Choir of Trinity College Cambridge', *Seen and Heard International* (15 July 2013), http://seenandheard-international.com/2013/07/virtuoso-display-by-choir-of-trinity-college-cambridge, accessed 22 August 2016.

52. Michael Henderson, 'Chorus of Approval', *The Spectator*, 15 December 2012.

53. Documentary about Stephen Layton on Dutch TV in November 2012: http://trinitycollegechoir.com/youtube/dutch-tv-documentary, accessed 22 August 2016.

54. HYPERION CDA68105 (Choir of Trinity College; digital stereo CD, released 2016).

55. HARMONIA MUNDI USA HMU 907579 (Choir of Clare College; digital stereo CD, released 2013).

56. SIGNUM CLASSICS SIGCD 070 (Choir of Gonville and Caius College; digital stereo CD, released 2006).

57. Selwyn Calendar 2010–11, p. 59, https://issuu.com/sel-alum/docs/selwyn calendar2010-2011/59, accessed 12 July 2017.

58. *Mail Online*, 22 September 2011, www.dailymail.co.uk/news/article-2040040/Lincoln-Cathedral-Choir-takes-woman-time-900-years.html, accessed 12 July 2017.

59. Peter Phillips, 'Rare Voices', *The Spectator*, 13 November 2010.

60. *The Daily Telegraph*, 28 February 2017; https://www.cai.cam.ac.uk/news/caian-singer-makes-history-st-pauls, accessed 12 July 2017.

61. For example, the solo voices of Gonville and Caius College Choir heard in the five-part descant *Alma Redemptoris Mater*, SIGNUM CLASSICS SIGCD 070 (digital stereo CD, released 2006) or the solo soprano in Clare College Choir heard in Roderick Williams' *O Adonai, et Dux domus Israel*, HARMONIA MUNDI USA HMU 907579 (digital stereo CD, released 2013).

62. For example, the bass Nicholas Mogg, in the Choir of Clare College, Cambridge, in 2012 singing the intonation in the plainchant Advent Antiphon III *O Radix Jesse* and then as the bass soloist in John Tavener's *God is with us*, HARMONIA MUNDI USA HMU 907579 (digital stereo CD, released 2013).

63. Obituary of Harrison Oxley, *The Times*, 29 April 2009; Phillips, 'The Golden Age Regained [1]', pp. 191, 193.

64. Graham F. Welch, 'Culture and Gender in a Cathedral Music Context: An Activity Theory Exploration', in Margaret S. Barrett (ed.), *A Cultural Psychology of Music Education* (Oxford and New York, 2011), p. 234.

65. http://www.cathedral.net/music/choir/, accessed 14 September 2016.

66. Welch, 'Culture and Gender in a Cathedral Music Context', pp. 230–31.

67. Ibid., p. 231.

68. Bernard Rose and Lionel Dakers, quoted in Phillips, 'The Golden Age Regained [1]', p. 197.

69. Welch, 'Culture and Gender in a Cathedral Music Context', pp. 231–3.

70. *In Tune with Heaven: The Report of the Archbishops' Commission on Church Music* (London, 1992), p. 256.

71. Bernarr Rainbow et al., 'Cathedral Choirs – New Direction: A Position Paper by Dr Bernarr Rainbow and Others', originally in *Organists' Review* (August 1997), http://www.ctcc.org.uk/position.htm, accessed 8 June 2016.

72. From an unpublished manuscript of the Dean of Salisbury's sermon at a service celebrating the tenth anniversary of the formation of the girls' choir, p. 1, quoted in Welch, 'Culture and Gender in a Cathedral Music Context', p. 235.

73. Rainbow et al., 'Cathedral Choirs – New Directions'.

74. Phillips, 'The Golden Age Regained [1]', pp. 191, 193.

75. Duncan Thomson, quoted in ibid., p. 195.

76. Roy Massey and John Birch, quoted in Phillips, 'The Golden Age Regained [1]', p. 195.

77. Margaret S. Barrett, 'On Being and Becoming a Cathedral Chorister: A Cultural Psychology Account of the Acquisition of Early Musical Expertise', in Barrett (ed.), *A Cultural Psychology of Music Education*, p. 280.

78. Alan Quilter, quoted in Phillips, 'The Golden Age Regained [1]', pp. 195, 197.

79. Barry Rose, quoted in Phillips, 'The Golden Age Regained [1]', p. 197.

80. Phillips, 'The Golden Age Regained [1]', pp. 191, 193.

81. Welch, 'Culture and Gender in a Cathedral Music Context', p. 228.

82. Sarah MacDonald, director of Ely Cathedral Girls' Choir, 'Something to Sing About: The Rise of the Cathedral Girls' Choir', *The Daily Telegraph*, 8 June 2016.

83. Amanda Mackey, 'New Voice: The Patterns and Provisions for Girl Choristers in English Cathedral Choirs', PhD dissertation, Bangor University, 2015, p. 99, http://e.bangor.ac.uk/4774/2/New_Voice_BINDING%20FINAL; pdf; http://www.wellscathedral.org.uk; https://yorkminster.org/home.html; http://www.winchester-cathedral.org.uk; http://www.lichfield-cathedral.org/; http://www.trurocathedral.org.uk; http://www.elycathedral.org/; http://www.rochestercathedral.org; http://www.cathedral.org.uk/; http://www.exeter-cathedral.org.uk; http://www.peterborough-cathedral.org.uk/, all accessed 12 October 2016.

84. 'The Girls in Green', Richard Seal in discussion with Alan Mould about the introduction of girl choristers from September 1991, *Cathedral Music: Thirty-Fourth Annual Report of the Friends of Cathedral Music*, November 1991, p. 26.

85. Mackey, 'New Voice', pp. 195–6.

86. Ibid., p. 124.

87. http://davidpoulter.co.uk, accessed 19 October 2016.

88. David Poulter, in Mackey, 'New Voice', pp. 139–40.

89. Mackey, 'New Voice', p. 155.

90. Ibid., p. 182.

91. Graham F. Welch and David M. Howard, 'Gendered Voice in the Cathedral Choir', *Psychology of Music* 30/1 (April 2002), p. 102.

92. Church of England Research and Statistics, *Cathedral Statistics 2015* (London, 2016), p. 11.

93. Unnamed member of Canterbury Cathedral's Girls' Choir speaking while recording a CD of Purcell's music, which was released in March 2016, in

'The Girls' Choir and Lay Clerks of Canterbury Cathedral record Henry Purcell: Sacred Music', https://www.youtube.com/watch?v=66SM-8gytWk, accessed 20 July 2016.

94. Mackey, 'New Voice', p. 82.

95. REGENT REGCD 368 (digital stereo CD, released 2011), recorded in January 2011, demonstrates all these qualities and characteristics. The track listing does not distinguish between the choir singing with girls or with boys just as the York Minster service scheme at this time did not, https://yorkminster.org/worship-and-choir/choir-and-music.html, accessed 16 March 2018.

96. Peter Phillips, *What We Really Do* (London, 2003), p. 19.

97. e.g. in the 3-LP set *The Art of Courtly Love*, EMI SLS 863 (3 12″ 33⅓ rpm stereo discs, released 1973).

98. Phillips, *What We Really Do*, p. 79.

99. Ibid., p. 31.

100. GIMELL CDGIM 009 (digital stereo CD, released in 1987).

101. Phillips, *What We Really Do*, pp. 37–8.

102. Ghislaine Morgan, http://www.oiss.org.uk/tutors.html; website of the 2005 Tallis Scholars Summer Schools, accessed 15 July 2005.

103. Henry Davey, *History of English Music* (London, 1895), p. 499.

104. Roger Bowers, *Gr* 72/861 (February 1995), p. 6.

105. Amy Haworth, http://www.thetallisscholars.co.uk/amy-haworth, accessed 30 November 2016.

106. Katie Schofield, http://www.stileantico.co.uk/about/singers#katie-schofield, accessed 30 November 2016.

107. Matthew O'Donovan, http://www.stileantico.co.uk/about/singers#matthew-odonovan, accessed 30 November 2016.

108. Andrew Griffiths, http://www.stileantico.co.uk/about/singers#andrew-griffiths, accessed 30 November 2016.

109. Will Dawes, http://www.stileantico.co.uk/about/singers#will-dawes, accessed 30 November 2016.

110. Alison Hill, http://www.alamire.co.uk/people/alison-hill, accessed 30 November 2016.

111. http://www.stileantico.co.uk/about, accessed 6 December 2016.

112. http://www.thetallisscholars.co.uk/about, accessed 13 March 2016.

113. http://www.cardinallsmusick.com/about-us, accessed 30 November 2016.

114. https://www.stileantico.co.uk/about, accessed 30 November 2016.

115. https://www.tenebrae-choir.com/about/tenebrae, accessed 30 November 2016.

116. http://www.exaudi.org.uk/, accessed 6 December 2016.

117. http://thesixteen.com/, accessed 20 November 2016.

118. Quoted on the Choir's website, http://www.monteverdi.co.uk/50/tributes, accessed 4 April 2016; Jonathan Freeman-Atwood, *Gr* 88/1066 (January

2011), pp. 42–3, reprinted on http://www.monteverdi.co.uk/news-reviews/
concert-reviews/136-the-20-greatest-choirs-gramophone-magazine,
accessed 1 April 2016.

119. R. A. Edwards, *And the Glory: A History in Commemoration of the 150th Anniversary of the Huddersfield Choral Society* (Leeds, 1985), pp. 144–5.

120. Recordings of Tallis's *Lamentations* by: The Tallis Scholars/Phillips, GIMELL CDGIM 025 (digital stereo CD, released 1992); Hilliard Ensemble, ECM NEW SERIES ECM 1341 (digital stereo CD, released 1987); Taverner Consort/Parrott, EMI REFLEXE CDC7 49563-2 (digital stereo CD, released 1989).

121. Tallis's *O nata lux* by the Taverner Consort/Parrott, EMI REFLEXE CDC7 49563-2 (digital stereo CD, released 1989).

122. Tess Knighton, reviewing a recording of two eight-part motets by Byrd, *Ad Dominum cum tribularer* and *Diliges Dominum*, and the Mass for Five Voices sung by The Sixteen directed by Harry Christophers, Virgin Classics VC 7 90802-2 (digital stereo CD, released 1989) in *Gr* 68/808 (September 1990), p. 586.

123. Peter Phillips, in Bernard D. Sherman, *Inside Early Music: Conversations with Performers* (New York/Oxford, 1997), p. 124.

124. Nicholas Kenyon, review of a concert in St John's, Smith Square, given by The Clerkes of Oxenford, *The Financial Times*, 26 February 1979.

125. David Fallows, *Gr* 56/669 (February 1979), p. 1,454.

126. Richard Morrison, *The Times*, Friday, 29 July 1994.

127. Sydney H. Nicholson, *Boys' Choirs* (London, 1922), p. 21.

128. See, for example, John B. Watson, *Psychological Care of the Infant and Child* (London, 1928).

129. Sherman, *Inside Early Music*, p. 113.

130. Listen, for example, to The Sixteen directed by Harry Christophers in, the performances of Bairstow's *Blessed City* and Stainer's *I saw the Lord*), recorded in October 2008 in St Peter's Italian Church, Clerkenwell, London, UNIVERSAL CLASSICS 179 5732 (digital stereo CD, released 2009).

131. *The Daily Telegraph*, used for publicity on The Sixteen's website, http://thesixteen.com/about-us, accessed 27 September 2016.

132. John Milsom, *Gr* 66/792 (May 1989), p. 1,764.

133. John Steane, *Gr* 72/861 (February 1995), p. 99.

134. Jonathan Freeman-Attwood, *Gr* 75/891 (August 1997), pp. 86, 88.

135. David Fallows, *Gr* 79/941 (June 2001), p. 89.

136. Peter Phillips, 'Let the Women Sing', *The Spectator*, 12 July 1997.

137. Edward Higginbottom, 'Laudate pueri', *MT* 138/1858 (December 1997), pp. 3–4.

138. Louis N. Parker, 'Music in our Public Schools', *Proceedings of the Musical Association*, Twentieth Session (1893–4), p. 104.

139. https://www.youtube.com/watch?v=50smWzHMfwQ, accessed 1 December 2016.

140. https://www.youtube.com/watch?v=C2tYw_40RHo, accessed 1 December 2016.

141. Andrew Clark, 'Monteverdi Choir 50th Anniversary Concert, King's College Chapel, Cambridge: Five Decades After He Redefined Monteverdi's Significance, John Eliot Gardiner Still Exudes Musical Exhilaration', *The Financial Times*, 6 March 2014.

142. L. P. Wilkinson, *Kingsmen of a Century, 1873–1972* (Cambridge, 1981), pp. 76–7; http://www.guardian.co.uk/music/2012/nov/20/sir-philip-ledger, accessed 16 June 2013.

143. https://www.rco.org.uk/news_displaystory.php?newsid=178, accessed 12 August 2017.

144. David Forbes, personal communication.

145. http://www.sirphilipledger.com, accessed 1 March 2018.

146. Michael Sanderson, *The History of the University of East Anglia, Norwich* (Hambledon and London, 2002), p. 95.

147. http://genome.ch.bbc.co.uk, accessed 23 February 2018.

148. Humphrey Carpenter, *Benjamin Britten: A Biography* (London, 1992), p. 250.

149. Obituary of Sir Philip Ledger, *The Daily Telegraph*, 19 November 2012.

150. Carpenter, *Benjamin Britten*, p. 250.

151. Christopher Cook, 'Servicing Tradition', *Gr* 77/922 (December 1999), p. 10.

152. Obituary of Sir Philip Ledger, *The Daily Telegraph*, 19 November 2012.

153. Philip Ledger, in Stanley Webb, 'Master of King's', *Gr* 59/702 (November 1981), p. 671.

154. Ledger speaks about enunciating consonants in the film *The Story of King's College Choir: 'The Boast of King's'*, REGIS RDVD 101 (DVD, released in 1982) at 13:13 and at 14:32.

155. Eric Sams, reviewing the recording of Brahms' motets, *MT* 117/1596 (February 1976), p. 143.

156. James Lancelot, personal communication. In his very last term, though, Willcocks had a slipped disc and accompanied less often than he would otherwise have done.

157. EMI CLASSICS 5 85641 2 (2 stereo CDs, released 2003).

158. Stanley Webb, *Gr* 53/636 (May 1976), p. 1,795.

159. Philip Ledger, in Webb, 'Master of King's', p. 671.

160. James Lancelot and John Butt, personal communications.

161. Philip Ledger, in Webb, 'Master of King's', p. 671.

162. Listen, for example, to the treble in the first verse of 'Once in royal David's city', *Christmas Carols from Cambridge*, BBC TV, 24 December 1978, https://www.youtube.com/watch?v=REy_bS1j2vY, accessed 1 March 2018.

163. https://www.dunedin-consort.org.uk/artist/john-butt, accessed 28 February 2018.

164. Nicholas Anderson, *Gr* 55/653 (October 1977), p. 671.

165. Philip Ledger, in Webb, 'Master of King's', p. 671.

166. Michael Oliver, *Gr* 59/704 (January 1982), p. 1,038.

167. Gordon Reynolds, *Gr* 59/702 (November 1981), p. 748, reviewing HMV ASD 3907 (12" 33⅓ rpm digital stereo disc).

168. Eric van Tassel, 'English Church Music *c.* 1660–1700 – 1', *EM* 6/4 (October 1978), pp. 572, 577.

169. Phillips, 'The Golden Age Regained [1]', p. 15.

170. Eric van Tassel, 'English Church Music *c.* 1660–1700 – 2', *EM* 7/1 (January 1979)', p. 85.

171. *England, my England*, EMI 2 28944 0 (2 digital stereo CDs, released 2009).

172. Tess Knighton, 'Vocal Heroes: Going Out on a Natural High: "High and sweet and strong". Tess Knighton on What England Expects of her Cathedral Choirboys', *Independent*, 22 March 1993; review of performances of Rachmaninov's *Vespers* op. 37 in Ivan March, Edward Greenfield and Robert Layton (eds.), *The Penguin Guide to Compact Discs & DVDs* (London, 2005), p. 1,028.

173. Richard Morrison, 'Sing in Exultation! Why King's is Still the Best Carol Service in Town', *The Times*, 2 December 2015.

174. March, Greenfield and Layton (eds.), *The Penguin Guide to Compact Discs & DVDs*, p. 1,028.

175. Ibid., p. 326.

176. Nicholas Kenyon, reviewing a concert in the Queen Elizabeth Hall, *The Times*, 19 December 1983.

177. Knighton, 'Vocal Heroes'.

178. Stephen Cleobury, personal communication.

179. Robert Rice, in *Omnibus: King's College Choir*, BBC 1, 15 December 1992, transcripts of interviews 1, pp. 70–71, KCAR/8/3/20.

180. 'Barry Rose Interviews Stephen Cleobury on Choir Training', dated 'from 1987', https://www.youtube.com/watch?v=WdrmqoqyG_g, accessed 6 January 2015.

181. John Potter, personal communication.

182. *60 Years of Carols from King's*, BBC 2, 25 December 2014. https://www.youtube.com/watch?v=nKlnLmjLhsc, accessed 12 March 2016. The Christmas Eve programme as broadcast on BBC 2 was released together with this documentary programme on KGS0013 (DVD, released 2015).

183. John Rutter, in William Owen (ed.), *A Life in Music: Conversations with David Willcocks and Friends* (Oxford and New York, 2008), pp. 273–4; *60 Years of Carols from King's*, KGS0013 (DVD, released 2015).

184. Morrison, 'Sing in Exultation!'

185. *Past three o'clock*, recorded in December 1960, CD 5 in DECCA set 478 8918 (29 mono and stereo CDs, released 2015).
186. Stephen Cleobury, in *Omnibus: King's College Choir*, BBC 1, 15 December 1992, script of programme-as-broadcast, p. 33, KCAR/8/3/20.
187. Stephen Cleobury, in Toby Chadd, 'Fit for King's', *Varsity*, 18 January 2008.
188. As demonstrated in *Omnibus: King's College Choir*, BBC 1, 15 December 1992.
189. Stephen Cleobury, in *Omnibus: King's College Choir*, BBC 1, 15 December 1992, transcripts of interviews 1, p. 9. KCAR/8/3/20.
190. Cleobury, in ibid., p. 2.
191. Robert Rice, in ibid., pp. 73, 75, 77.
192. Anon., arranged by R. L. Pearsall, *In dulci jubilo*. There is a version by David Willcocks made in December 1958, CD 2 in DECCA set 478 8918 (29 mono and stereo CDs, released 2015), and one by Stephen Cleobury released in 1999, EMI 5 73693 2 (2 digital stereo CDs, released in 1999).
193. Patrick Hadley's *I sing of a maiden* was sung under Willcocks' direction in December 1960, CD 5 in DECCA set 478 8918 (29 mono and stereo CDs, released 2015), and Cleobury's in March 2004, EMI CLASSICS 5 57896 2 (digital stereo CD, released 2004).
194. Knighton, 'Vocal Heroes'; John Rutter, in Owen (ed.), *A Life in Music*, p. 272.
195. KGS0012 (SACD, released in 2015).
196. Brian Robins, 'From Rutter to Rachmaninov', *Fanfare* (November/December 1998), pp. 137–8.
197. E. C. Perry and A. H. Mann, *A Collection of Anthems for Use in King's College Chapel* (Cambridge, 1882).
198. From a paper by the Provost 'for the use of members of the Council', dated [23] January 1967, including a copy of the letter he wrote to the Clerical Dean-elect, 'Chapel Television Services', attempting to clarify matters before a discussion on this subject on 27 January 1967. The Fellow in Music he quoted was Philip Brett, KCGB/5/1/4/23, pp. 1–2.
199. Denis Arnold, *The Listener*, 31 December 1970, p. 926.
200. Elizabeth Poston (ed.), *The Penguin Book of Christmas Carols* (Harmondsworth, 1965), pp. 15–16.
201. Christopher Brodersen, 'An Interview with Stephen Cleobury', 10 June 2013, http://www.fanfaremag.com/content/view/51976/10261, accessed 17 June 2013.
202. Michael, chorister, in *Omnibus: King's College Choir*, BBC 1, 15 December 1992, transcripts of interviews 1, p. 233, KCAR/8/3/20.
203. The carol by Giles Swayne was recorded in *On Christmas Day: New Carols from King's*, the first twenty-one commissioned carols for Christmas

Eve together with the carol by Bob Chilcott, *The Shepherd's Carol*, commissioned for BBC TV's *Carols from King's* in 2000, EMI 5 58070 2 (2 digital stereo CDs, released 2005); the next six commissioned carols and a carol commissioned for the disc, John Rutter's *All bells in paradise*, were on a recording of the 2010 *Nine Lessons and Carols*, THE CHOIR OF KING'S COLLEGE, CAMBRIDGE KGS0001 (2 digital stereo CDs, released 2012).

204. KCA, Annual Report (2011), p. 46; KCA, Annual Report (2010), p.39; KCA, Annual Report (2008), p. 41; KCA, Annual Report (2009), p. 42.

205. KCA, Annual Report (1952), p. 33; KCA, Annual Report (1955), pp. 28–9.

206. KCA, Annual Report (2007), p. 41.

207. KCA, Annual Report (2008), p. 42; liner notes for SIGNUM CLASSICS SIGCD 131; KCA, Annual Report (2007), p. 42; KCA, Annual Report (2003), p. 36; KCA, Annual Report (2008), p. 42.

208. KCA, Annual Report (1999), p. 25.

209. KCAR/8/2/1/6A/29.

210. Printed register of services 1972–3, KCAR/8/2/1/6A/36.

211. KCA, Annual Report (2013), pp. 49–50. Online version: http://www.kings.cam.ac.uk/files/about/annual-report-2013.pdf

212. Jeremy Noble, *Gr* 39/462 (November 1961), p. 263.

213. https://www.youtube.com/watch?v=ofGxXwA8i7c, accessed 13 April 2015.

214. https://www.youtube.com/watch?v=GwBRLJt432U, accessed 27 September 2016.

215. The metronome marks of the following recordings represent the speed of the crotchet pulse when it has more or less settled down; the date is the year the recording was made: Ord 1949: 50 (last verse 46); Ord 1951 (the live Christmas Eve performance): 55; Ord 1954: 52; Willcocks 1958: 58/60; Willcocks 1964: 58/60; Ledger 1978: 54; Cleobury 1998: 66; Cleobury 2008: 68/70; Cleobury 2010: 66/68.

216. BL shelfmark 1CDR0025778, the live broadcast on Christmas Eve 1998; EMI 5 73693 2 (2 digital stereo CDs, released 1999), this hymn recorded in December 1998.

217. Richard Osborne, *Gr* 77/922 (December 1999), p. 61.

218. Nicholas Nash, '"A Right Prelude to Christmas": A History of *A Festival of Nine Lessons and Carols*', in Jean Michel Massing and Nicolette Zeeman (eds.), *King's College Chapel 1515–2015: Art, Music and Religion in Cambridge* (London and Turnhout, 2014), p. 340.

219. KCA, Annual Report (1999), p. 25.

220. Stephen Cleobury, interviewed by Alan Macfarlane on 4 July 2008, www.alanmacfarlane.com/DO/filmshow/cleoburytx.htm, accessed 12 May 2016;

Stephen Cleobury, quoted in Andrew Green, 'You Must Renew the Tradition', *Classical Music* (23 May 1987), p. 15.

7. THE MEANING OF IT ALL

1. Martin Thomas, *English Cathedral Music and Liturgy in the Twentieth Century* (Farnham, Surrey, 2015), p. 231.
2. James Crookes, in *Omnibus: King's College Choir*, BBC 1, 15 December 1992, transcripts of interviews 1, pp. 86–7, KCAR/8/3/20.
3. Christopher Zealley, private communication.
4. Virginia Woolf, *A Room of One's Own* (first published London, 1929; Penguin edition, Harmondsworth, 1970), pp. 7–10.
5. Denis Stevens, *Gr* 38/445 (June 1960), p. 28.
6. Philip Brett, 'Facing the Music', *EM* 10/3 (July 1982), p. 349.
7. Stephen Walsh, *The Listener*, 5 January 1967, p. 37.
8. Michael Henderson, 'Chorus of Approval', *The Spectator*, 15 December 2012.
9. http://www.canterbury-cathedral.org/worship, accessed 27 June 2016.
10. https://www.stpauls.co.uk/worship-music/music, accessed 27 June 2016.
11. https://yorkminster.org/about-us/governance/chapter-of-york/dean-of-york.html, accessed 16 August 2016.
12. http://www.winchester-cathedral.org.uk/worship-and-music/music-choir, accessed 27 June 2016.
13. https://lincolncathedral.com/worship-music, accessed 27 June 2016.
14. http://www.brin.ac.uk/figures/belief-in-britain-1939-2009/conventional-belief/belief-in-god-divinity-of-christ-and-the-resurrection, accessed 3 July 2016.
15. https://yougov.co.uk/news/2015/02/12/third-british-adults-dont-believe-higher-power, accessed 28 June 2016.
16. file:///C:/Users/User/Desktop/Downloads/WFD-No-Religion%20(1).pdf; Westminster Faith Debates: http://faithdebates.org.uk, accessed 11 June 2016.
17. https://humanism.org.uk/campaigns/religion-and-belief-some-surveys-and-statistics, accessed 26 June 2016.
18. Simon Jenkins, *England's Cathedrals* (London, 2016), p. ix.
19. John Bingham, 'Looking for Britain's Future Leaders? Try Evensong', *The Daily Telegraph*, 1 March 2016.
20. Report by the Christian think tank Theos, *Spiritual Capital: The Present and the Future of English Cathedrals* (London, 2012), intro., para. 2.
21. Ibid., intro., para. 8.1.

22. Ibid., ch. 1, para. 44.

23. George Carey in a lecture at the Shropshire Light Conference on 16 November 2013, http://www.glcarey.co.uk/Speeches/2013/ShropshireLight.html, accessed 16 June 2016.

24. See Leslie J. Francis and Carol Roberts, 'Growth or Decline in the Church of England during the Decade of Evangelism: Did the Churchmanship of the Bishop Matter?', *Journal of Contemporary Religion* 24/1 (2009), pp. 67–81; Leslie J. Francis, Patrick Laycock and Andrew Village, 'Statistics for Evidence-Based Policy in the Church of England: Predicting Diocesan Performance', *Review of Religious Research* 52/2 (December 2010), pp. 207–20.

25. Thomas Hardy, 'The Impercipient (at a Cathedral Service)', first published in *Wessex Poems and Other Verses* (London and New York, 1898).

26. Canon J. S. Nurser, 'Foreword', in Dorothy Owen (ed.), *A History of Lincoln Minster* (Cambridge, 1994), p. xv.

27. Giles Fraser, 'Resurgent Religion Has Done Away with the Country Vicar', *The Guardian*, 13 April 2006; Giles Fraser, 'We must do to our churches what Beeching did to the railways: high-morale, better-resourced bundles of energy could become local campaign headquarters for the re-evangelisation of England', *The Guardian*, 15 October 2015.

28. Alec Clifton-Taylor, *English Parish Churches as Works of Art*, 2nd edn (Oxford, 1986), p. 14.

29. Tribute to Hugh Spottiswoode, KCA, Annual Report (1961), p. 60.

30. Paper by Edmund Leach, 'For the Use of Members of the Council', dated [23] January 1967, attempting to clarify matters before a discussion on the televising of Chapel services on 27 January 1967. KCGB/5/1/4/23, pp. 1–2.

31. *In Tune with Heaven: The Report of the Archbishops' Commission on Church Music* (London, 1992), para. 640, p. 216.

32. In the liner notes for *Smooth Classics for Rough Days*, released by Classic FM in 2002, and quoted in the disc's publicity, http://www.amazon.co.uk/Smooth-Classics-London-Symphony-Orchestra/dp/B00006JOAJ, accessed 23 April 2014; these words were frequently used in broadcast trailers at this time for Classic FM's programme *Smooth Classics at 7*.

33. Percy M. Young (ed.), *Edward Elgar: A Future for English Music and Other Lectures* (London, 1968), p. 49.

34. Charles L. Graves, *Hubert Parry: His Life and Works*, 2 vols. (London, 1926), vol. 2, p. 334.

35. Ibid., pp. 316–17.

36. Ursula Vaughan Williams, *RVW: A Biography of Ralph Vaughan Williams*, 2nd edn (Oxford and New York, 1988), p. 29.

37. Cyril Bailey, *Hugh Percy Allen* (London, 1948), p. 139.

38. Walford Davies, quoted in Graves, *Hubert Parry*, vol. 2, p. 153.

39. Donald Mitchell, 'Britten, Benjamin (1913–1976)', *DNB*.

40. Michael White, 'The Sorrow that Sounds like Heaven: When Herbert Howells Lost a Son, the Church Gained Some Immortal Music', *The Independent*, Saturday, 10 October 1992.

41. Christopher Palmer, *Herbert Howells: A Centenary Celebration* (London, 1992), p. 197.

42. John Rutter, interviewed by Alan Macfarlane on 28 January 2009, http://www.alanmacfarlane.com/DO/filmshow/ruttertx1.htm, accessed 22 June 2016.

43. Peter Phillips, 'Brains and Voice', *The Spectator*, 11 November 2006, pp. 70–71.

44. Appointment of Lay Clerks, Peterborough Cathedral, www.peterborough-cathedral.org.uk/userfiles/bass-lay-clerk17.pdf, accessed 9 May 2017.

45. Choral scholars, in *Omnibus: King's College Choir*, BBC 1, 15 December 1992, transcripts of interviews 1, pp. 87, 114, 120–22, KCAR/8/3/20.

46. Sir David Willcocks, interviewed by Alan Macfarlane on 11 December 2008, https://www.youtube.com/watch?v=8WVqA3451Gw, accessed 18 June 2016; Sir David Willcocks, interviewed by Timothy Day at Sir David's home in Cambridge on 16 November 2004, BL shelfmark 1CDR0032927–30.

47. Stephen Cleobury, interviewed by Alan Macfarlane, 4 July 2008, www.alanmacfarlane.com/DO/filmshow/cleoburytx.htm, accessed 12 May 2016.

48. Owen Chadwick, interviewed by Alan Macfarlane, 29 February 2008, Department of Social Anthropology, Cambridge, http://www.dspace.cam.ac.uk/handle/1810/198014, accessed 12 October 2011.

49. Watkins Shaw, *The Succession of Organists of the Chapel Royal and the Cathedrals of England and Wales from c. 1538* (Oxford, 1991), pp. 272–3.

50. William Temple, 'Scientific Ideas among the Ancient Greeks', 1911, a paper read to the Repton School Scientific Society by the Headmaster, in A. E. Baker (selected and arranged), *William Temple and his Message* (Harmondsworth, 1945), pp. 56–7.

51. Palmer, *Herbert Howells*, p. 168.

52. William James, *The Varieties of Religious Experience* (New York, 1902), pp. 485–6.

53. Ibid., p. 507.

54. G. Lowes Dickinson, *Religion: A Criticism and a Forecast* (London, 1905), pp. 80–94.

55. Don Cupitt, 'We Are Grateful to Art', in his *Radicals and the Future of the Church* (London, 1989), pp. 101, 76–7.

56. Karen Armstrong, *The Case for God* (London, 2009), p. 306.

57. Benjamin Whichcote, Provost of King's College, Cambridge, between 1644 and 1660; part of a text used as a preface in the booklet for *A Festival of Nine Lessons and Carols, Christmas Eve 1987*, King's College, Cambridge, p. 5.

58. Matthew Arnold, *Literature and Dogma* (London, 1873), p. 152.

59. Introductory Note, *King's College Chapel: Services* (Cambridge, 1989), p. 3.

60. Philip Larkin, 'Church Going', *The Less Deceived* (Hull, 1955), pp. 28-9.

61. W. H. Auden, *A Certain World: A Commonplace Book* (London, 1971), p. 306.

62. The Epistle of Paul and Timothy to the Philippians, chapter 4, verse 8.

63. Yuval Noah Harari, *Homo Deus* (London, 2017), pp. 214-19. For an examination of contemporary uses of the word 'spirituality' see Philip Sheldrake, *Spirituality: A Very Short Introduction* (Oxford, 2012).

64. George Herbert, 'Prayer (I)'.

65. William Wordsworth, *The Recluse*, Part First, Book First, ll. 767, 769, 771, quoted in the booklet for *The Three Choirs Festival 1952: Hereford Music Meeting*, concert on 10 September 1952, in the cathedral.

66. Cecil Gray, *The History of Music* (London, 1928, 2nd edn 1931), p. 24.

67. William Byrd, *Psalmes, Songs and Sonnets* of 1611, 'To all true lovers of musicke, William Byrd wisheth all true happiness both temporal and eternal'.

68. Richard Hooker, *Of the Laws of Ecclesiastical Polity* (1593), http://www.cityofgodblog.com/2014/03/richard-hooker-on-usic/#sthash.3NAc1gfm.dpbs, accessed 21 July 2014.

69. John Potter, personal communication.

70. Richard Kaye, in *Omnibus: King's College Choir*, BBC 1, 15 December 1992, transcripts of interviews 1, p. 180, KCAR/8/3/20.

71. David Gibbs, quoted in Simon Carpenter, *The Beat is Irrelevant* (Guildford, 1996), p. 32.

72. Michael Barry, quoted in ibid., p. 87.

73. Mihaly Csikszentmihalyi, *Flow* (London, 1992 rev. edn 2002), pp. 3-4.

74. Used by Wordsworth in 'Expostulation and Reply', l. 24.

75. See André Comte-Sponville, *The Book of Atheist Spirituality* (English translation, London, 2007), pp. 164-81.

76. H. E. Rollins (ed.), *The Letters of John Keats*, 2 vols (Cambridge, 1958), vol. 1, p. 193.

77. Armstrong, *The Case for God*, pp. 271-2, 315-16.

78. Don Cupitt, *The Sea of Faith* (London, 1984), p. 17.

79. Don Cupitt, *Mysticism after Modernity* (Oxford, 1998), p. 141.

80. Frank Ll. Harrison, in sleeve note to ARGO ZRG 557 (12″ 33⅓ rpm stereo disc, released 1968).

81. Roberto Gerhard in a note in the score of his *Concerto for Orchestra* (London, 1965).

82. Jonathan Harvey, in *New Sounds, New Personalities: British Composers of the 1980s*, in conversation with Paul Griffiths (London, 1985), p. 52.

83. Jonathan Harvey, obituary, *The Daily Telegraph*, 6 December 2012.

84. Jonathan Harvey, 'Sounding Out the Inner Self', *MT* 133/1798 (December 1992), pp. 613–14.

85. Andrew Porter, *The Times Literary Supplement*, 19 November 1999.

86. Gustav Holst, in Michael Short (ed.), *Gustav Holst: Letters to W. G. Whittaker* (Glasgow, 1974), p. 25.

87. Cupitt, *The Sea of Faith*, pp. 19–20.

88. A. R. Vidler, 'Religion and the National Church', in A. R. Vidler (ed.), *Soundings: Essays Concerning Christian Understanding* (Cambridge, 1962), pp. 249, 254.

89. Ibid., pp. 254, 259–60.

90. John Betjeman, 'Sunday Morning, King's Cambridge', in *A Few Late Chrysanthemums* (London, 1954).

91. Jonathan Harvey, in the *Southern Cathedrals Festival Programme 1978*, p. 43, quoted in Thomas, *English Cathedral Music and Liturgy in the Twentieth Century*, p. 150.

92. *The Ecclesiologist* 3/25 (September 1843), p. 2, quoted in Dale Adelmann, *The Contribution of Cambridge Ecclesiologists to the Revival of Anglican Choral Worship 1839–62* (Aldershot, 1997), p. 34.

93. Tom Service, 'Peter Maxwell Davies at 80: "The music knows things I don't"', *The Guardian*, 19 August 2014.

94. Peter Maxwell Davies, in his answer to the question 'What is your attitude towards religion?', http://www.maxopus.com/resources_detail.aspx?key=33, accessed 5 May 2017.

95. https://www.stephencleobury.com/work-at-kings.html; accessed 12 December 2017.

96. Francis Hueffer, *Half a Century of Music in England, 1837–1887: Essays towards a History* (London, 1889), pp. 1–3.

Acknowledgements

The foundations for the book were laid in 2007 through the generosity of a Leverhulme Research Fellowship which was awarded to undertake research on the performing style of English cathedral choirs.

At the end of that year I had to lay the work aside and was only able to continue it in fits and starts until 2014. But the groundwork had been covered. At King's in 2007, Iain Fenlon, the Rowe Music Librarian, gave me invaluable guidance on the internal administration of the College, the function of the College Council and the Governing Body, and the nature and organization of the records. I profited enormously that year from the expertise of the College Archivist, Patricia McGuire, and have been benefiting ever since from her own unflagging assistance and from the support of her successive assistants, Elizabeth Ennion-Smith and Peter Monteith. In another eyrie looking out over another chapel, Robin Darwall-Smith performed a similar task at Magdalen College, Oxford, with endless patience and helpfulness. Other archivists have also given invaluable help and guidance: Malcolm Underwood at St John's College, Cambridge and Jennifer Thorp at New College, Oxford and more recently Rosemary Firman, the Librarian at Hereford Cathedral, and Rosemary Caird and Bethany Hamblen, the Archivists there, and Colin Brownlee at the Archive of Recorded Church Music at Malvern in Worcestershire. I am grateful for the care and consideration always shown me by the staff of the Bodleian Library, the BBC Written Archives' Centre and the Royal College of Music Library.

While I was working as a music curator in the sound archive of the British Library I was able to oversee in 2005 the acquisition of a unique collection which included more than fifty hours of recordings made of services in the College Chapel between 1956 and 1959. This was when the owner of the collection, Brian Head, was himself a choral scholar. Brian answered my enquiries about all kinds of details with care and relish over many years and I am saddened that he did not live to see the publication of this book.

I had already spent four days in 2003 and 2004 recording long conversations with Sir David Willcocks for the British Library and I am very grateful for the generous hospitality that both he and Lady Willcocks extended to me. We tried not to talk about professional matters over lunch when the microphone was turned off, but it was difficult to keep choristers and choral scholars and clergymen and lay clerks out entirely. On several occasions Lady Willcocks provided important glosses on Sir David's recollections, an amplification here, a slightly different perspective there, a raised eyebrow. I took note of them all.

I was also very fortunate in persuading Sally Dunkley to record an interview for the British Library in 2005 about her experiences as a consort singer who emerged out of the Clerkes of Oxenford to spend her life singing with groups like the Tallis Scholars and The Sixteen.

At King's College, London, where I was a Senior Visiting Research Fellow in the Music Department between 2006 and 2011, Daniel Leech-Wilkinson was the staunchest and most sympathetic of colleagues and friends. I had thought-provoking conversations too with the late lamented David Trendell, the College Organist and Director of the Chapel Choir.

John Potter and I talked endlessly when he held a visiting Edison Fellowship at the British Library and he and James Bowman kindly supplied information during the writing of the book and always provided enthusiastic support. I'm grateful also for particular details to Paul Burbridge, David Forbes, Andrew Giles, Francis Grier, Michael Guest, Francis Knights, James Lancelot, Richard Podger, Gordon Pullin, Graham Rose, Alan Rowland, Richard White and Christopher Zealley.

I have benefited from having been able to present different aspects of my findings at different stages to very varied audiences, to scholars and to music-lovers, at postgraduate seminars and at all kinds of conferences, of the Centre for the History and Analysis of Recorded

Music, the British Institute of Organ Studies, the Royal Musical Association, the Royal College of Organists, to members of the Friends of Cathedral Music and to a Three Choirs Festival audience. My friends at Hereford Cathedral have not ceased their encouragement. Andrew Piper, the Precentor at Hereford, invited me to speak to a conference of English precentors, and Geraint Bowen, the organist, to address the Cathedral Organists' Association.

I owe a great debt to John Butt, who read the complete manuscript and responded with detailed and astute comments. All of them stimulated my thinking and many of the additions and modifications he suggested I have incorporated into the final text.

I should like to thank John Murray for permission to quote lines from John Betjeman's 'Sunday Morning, King's Cambridge' in *A Few Late Chrysanthemums* (London, 1954) and Faber & Faber and Farrar, Straus & Giroux to quote from Philip Larkin's 'Annus Mirabilis' in *High Windows* (London, 1974) and 'Church Going' in *The Less Deceived* (Hull, 1955).

Finally, it was the greatest kindness of my friend Duncan Campbell-Smith to introduce me to Stuart Proffitt at Allen Lane. Stuart, who was unaware of this book until the manuscript was almost finished, welcomed it with enthusiasm and worked tirelessly helping me improve it. My heartfelt thanks to him and his team, Ben Sinyor, Pen Vogler, Olivia Anderson, Richard Mason, Dave Cradduck and Richard Duguid, and also to my imaginative picture researcher Cecilia Mackay.

Though I had all this help I sometimes felt lost. It was my partner Sue Gee who always enabled me to find my way again.

Index

Wesley, S. S. 15–16, 17, 31, 33, 34,
  37, 42, 43, 80, 155, 265
  and boys' voices 17, 77, 78
Wesley Chapel choir, Lincoln 66
Westfälische Kantorei 174
Westminster Abbey 240, 269
  choir 6, 11, 23, 91, 137, 191, 249
  Cleobury at 260
  organ playing 30
  Willcocks at 164–5
Westminster Cathedral Choir 123,
  191, 210–15
  and Cleobury 260
Whalley, Simon 245
Whettam, Graham 267
Whitacre, Eric 245
White, Richard 159
Whitworth, John 201
The Who 203
Widor, Charles-Marie: Mass in F
  sharp minor for two choirs 264
Wilberforce, Samuel 54, 56
Wilbye, John 268
Willcocks, James 178
Willcocks, Sir David 153–4,
  163–74, 183, 211, 215, 227,
  232, 250, 257, 262–3
  Cambridge organ scholarship
    exam 166
  as a Cambridge student 166–7
  Carols for Choirs 266–7
  character and temperament
    176–8
  at Clifton College 165
  and emotional control 169,
    176–8, 250
  and Guest 218–19
  King's Choir under 6, 168–74,
    188, 190, 203, 204–5, 206,
    207, 215, 222, 223, 229,

231–2, 239, 240, 247, 256, 257,
  259, 260, 261, 262, 263,
  265–6, 268–9, 272; broadcasts
  256, 269, 271; and Carols for
  Choirs 266–7; concerts
  outside Cambridge 268–9;
  recordings 6, 169, 172, 173,
  174–6, 189, 190, 259, 271;
  singing style 6, 169–70,
  172–4, 188, 189, 229, 231–2,
  239, 240, 261, 263, 266; tone
  quality/timbre 172, 173–4
  and the King's Singers 204
  and Ledger 255
  and Ord 148, 150, 166, 167–8
  as organist 167, 168
  and Potter 203
  as RCM director 167, 178, 253
  religious unbelief 284
  at Salisbury 167, 172
  at School of English Church
    Music 166
  and the scouts 165–6
  Second World War service 167
  at Westminster Abbey 164–5
  at Worcester 153–4, 167, 168, 172
Willcocks family 163, 164, 177–8
William of Waynflete 19
Williams, Roderick 246
Williamson, Malcolm 204
Wilson, Steuart 113, 132–3
Winchester Cathedral 277
  choir 233, 236–7, 251
Winchester College 14, 189
Windsor, St George's Chapel
  30, 74–7
Withers, Charlotte 32–3
Witley Court, Worcestershire 74–5
Wittgenstein, Ludwig 288
women's ordination 234

ALLEN LANE
an imprint of
PENGUIN BOOKS

Also Published

Donald Sassoon, *The Anxious Triumph: A Global History of Capitalism, 1860-1914*

Elliot Ackerman, *Places and Names: On War, Revolution and Returning*

Johny Pits, *Afropean: Notes from Black Europe*

Jonathan Aldred, *Licence to be Bad: How Economics Corrupted Us*

Walt Odets, *Out of the Shadows: Reimagining Gay Men's Lives*

Jonathan Rée, *Witcraft: The Invention of Philosophy in English*

Jared Diamond, *Upheaval: How Nations Cope with Crisis and Change*

Emma Dabiri, *Don't Touch My Hair*

Srecko Horvat, *Poetry from the Future: Why a Global Liberation Movement Is Our Civilisation's Last Chance*

Paul Mason, *Clear Bright Future: A Radical Defence of the Human Being*

Remo H. Largo, *The Right Life: Human Individuality and its role in our development, health and happiness*

Joseph Stiglitz, *People, Power and Profits: Progressive Capitalism for an Age of Discontent*

David Brooks, *The Second Mountain*

Roberto Calasso, *The Unnamable Present*

Lee Smolin, *Einstein's Unfinished Revolution: The Search for What Lies Beyond the Quantum*

Clare Carlisle, *Philosopher of the Heart: The Restless Life of Søren Kierkegaard*

Nicci Gerrard, *What Dementia Teaches Us About Love*

Edward O. Wilson, *Genesis: On the Deep Origin of Societies*

John Barton, *A History of the Bible: The Book and its Faiths*

Carolyn Forché, *What You Have Heard is True: A Memoir of Witness and Resistance*

Elizabeth-Jane Burnett, *The Grassling*

Kate Brown, *Manual for Survival: A Chernobyl Guide to the Future*

Roderick Beaton, *Greece: Biography of a Modern Nation*

Matt Parker, *Humble Pi: A Comedy of Maths Errors*

Ruchir Sharma, *Democracy on the Road*

David Wallace-Wells, *The Uninhabitable Earth: A Story of the Future*

Randolph M. Nesse, *Good Reasons for Bad Feelings: Insights from the Frontier of Evolutionary Psychiatry*

Anand Giridharadas, *Winners Take All: The Elite Charade of Changing the World*

Richard Bassett, *Last Days in Old Europe: Triste '79, Vienna '85, Prague '89*

Paul Davies, *The Demon in the Machine: How Hidden Webs of Information Are Finally Solving the Mystery of Life*

Toby Green, *A Fistful of Shells: West Africa from the Rise of the Slave Trade to the Age of Revolution*

Paul Dolan, *Happy Ever After: Escaping the Myth of The Perfect Life*

Sunil Amrith, *Unruly Waters: How Mountain Rivers and Monsoons Have Shaped South Asia's History*

Christopher Harding, *Japan Story: In Search of a Nation, 1850 to the Present*

Timothy Day, *I Saw Eternity the Other Night: King's College, Cambridge, and an English Singing Style*

Richard Abels, *Aethelred the Unready: The Failed King*

Eric Kaufmann, *Whiteshift: Populism, Immigration and the Future of White Majorities*

Alan Greenspan and Adrian Wooldridge, *Capitalism in America: A History*

Philip Hensher, *The Penguin Book of the Contemporary British Short Story*

Paul Collier, *The Future of Capitalism: Facing the New Anxieties*

Andrew Roberts, *Churchill: Walking With Destiny*

Tim Flannery, *Europe: A Natural History*

T. M. Devine, *The Scottish Clearances: A History of the Dispossessed, 1600-1900*

Robert Plomin, *Blueprint: How DNA Makes Us Who We Are*

Michael Lewis, *The Fifth Risk: Undoing Democracy*

Diarmaid MacCulloch, *Thomas Cromwell: A Life*

Ramachandra Guha, *Gandhi: 1914-1948*

Slavoj Žižek, *Like a Thief in Broad Daylight: Power in the Era of Post-Humanity*

Neil MacGregor, *Living with the Gods: On Beliefs and Peoples*

Peter Biskind, *The Sky is Falling: How Vampires, Zombies, Androids and Superheroes Made America Great for Extremism*

Robert Skidelsky, *Money and Government: A Challenge to Mainstream Economics*

Helen Parr, *Our Boys: The Story of a Paratrooper*

David Gilmour, *The British in India: Three Centuries of Ambition and Experience*

Jonathan Haidt and Greg Lukianoff, *The Coddling of the American Mind: How Good Intentions and Bad Ideas are Setting up a Generation for Failure*

Ian Kershaw, *Roller-Coaster: Europe, 1950-2017*

Adam Tooze, *Crashed: How a Decade of Financial Crises Changed the World*

Edmund King, *Henry I: The Father of His People*

Lilia M. Schwarcz and Heloisa M. Starling, *Brazil: A Biography*

Jesse Norman, *Adam Smith: What He Thought, and Why it Matters*

Philip Augur, *The Bank that Lived a Little: Barclays in the Age of the Very Free Market*

Christopher Andrew, *The Secret World: A History of Intelligence*

David Edgerton, *The Rise and Fall of the British Nation: A Twentieth-Century History*

Julian Jackson, *A Certain Idea of France: The Life of Charles de Gaulle*

Owen Hatherley, *Trans-Europe Express*

Richard Wilkinson and Kate Pickett, *The Inner Level: How More Equal Societies Reduce Stress, Restore Sanity and Improve Everyone's Wellbeing*

Paul Kildea, *Chopin's Piano: A Journey Through Romanticism*

Seymour M. Hersh, *Reporter: A Memoir*

Michael Pollan, *How to Change Your Mind: The New Science of Psychedelics*

David Christian, *Origin Story: A Big History of Everything*

Judea Pearl and Dana Mackenzie, *The Book of Why: The New Science of Cause and Effect*

David Graeber, *Bullshit Jobs: A Theory*

Serhii Plokhy, *Chernobyl: History of a Tragedy*

Michael McFaul, *From Cold War to Hot Peace: The Inside Story of Russia and America*

Paul Broks, *The Darker the Night, the Brighter the Stars: A Neuropsychologist's Odyssey*

Lawrence Wright, *God Save Texas: A Journey into the Future of America*

John Gray, *Seven Types of Atheism*

Carlo Rovelli, *The Order of Time*

Mariana Mazzucato, *The Value of Everything: Making and Taking in the Global Economy*

Richard Vinen, *The Long '68: Radical Protest and Its Enemies*

Kishore Mahbubani, *Has the West Lost It?: A Provocation*

John Lewis Gaddis, *On Grand Strategy*